New Forces,
Old Forces,
and the Future
of World Politics

New Forces, Old Forces, and the Future of World Politics

Seyom Brown

Brandeis University

Scott, Foresman/Little, Brown College Division
Scott, Foresman and Company
Glenview, Illinois   Boston   London

Library of Congress Cataloging-in-Publication Data

Brown, Seyom.
  New forces, old forces, and the future of world politics.

  Includes bibliographies and index.
  1. World politics—1945-   . 2.   United States—
Foreign relations—1945-   . I.   Title.
D842.B7   1988   909.82   87-16956
ISBN 0-673-39709-2

2 3 4 5 6 7 8 9 10 — PAT — 93 92 91 90 89 88

Printed in the United States of America

This work's precursor was *New Forces in World Politics* (The Brookings
Institution, 1974).

Acknowledgments

Chapters 1 and 9: Portions of these chapters are adapted from Seyom Brown,
"The World Polity and the Nation-State System: An Updated Analysis,"
International Journal 39, no. 3 (Summer 1984), pp. 509–528. © 1984 by the
Canadian Institute of International Affairs. By permission of the publisher.   *Chapter 15:* Adapted from Seyom Brown, "New Forces Revisited: Lessons
of a Turbulent Decade," *World Policy Journal* 1, no. 2 (Winter 1984), pp.
397–418. Copyright 1984, World Policy Institute. By permission of the publisher.

For the descendants
of Benjamin Brown,
pioneer builder of communities

Preface

Political leaders and social scientists alike want to know which patterns of politics are highly resistant to change and which are rather easily transformed. And they want to know precisely what forces have the most impact on established norms and institutions.

Success or failure in political life often depends crucially on assessments of what it takes to protect, reform, manipulate, or do away with prevailing institutions and regimes—on correctly anticipating who will win out in confrontations between the new forces and old forces. Similarly, the social scientist's power of analysis depends on an ability to distinguish the "constants" from the "variables" in a particular field of human behavior and to describe and explain the paths of change—that is, how and why alterations in one variable do or do not affect the other variables. But whereas policymakers frequently think they know (or feel compelled to act as if they know) which are the new forces and which are the old forces and who will be the winners and losers in the contests between them, social scientists characteristically resist coming to such conclusions "until all the evidence is in."

Policymakers were the main audience for this book's precursor, *New Forces in World Politics*, written while I was a senior fellow at The Brookings Institution in Washington, DC. Brookings is preeminently in the business of offering policy advice, as indeed I had been in my professional career up to then, and the Brookings study, published in 1974, reflected this emphasis. Although trained as a social scientist, I considered it to be my calling to "speak truth to power" in a way that would be relevant to the power holders. The book therefore went out on a limb, identifying the new forces and guessing who would be the winners and losers—before all the evidence was in. It also prescribed certain foreign policies for taking advantage of the presumably ascendant new forces.

If I may be allowed an immodest reflection on my own past work—looking back with the advantage of more than a decade's experience—it is now clear that a number of particular assessments were mistaken or premature; but the central prognoses of the fragmentation of the cold war coalitions and the rise of subnational and transnational challenges to the nation-state system have been validated by events. The fact that many of the policy recommendations have not been followed by statesmen is perhaps as much an indication of the inability of particular leaders to constructively adapt to the main currents of change in world society as it is an indication that the proposed policies were untimely.

However, it is not my purpose here to restate or defend judgments made more than a dozen years ago. Rather, it is to make a fresh attempt, informed by continuing observations in the "laboratory" of actual events, at understanding why the world works as it does and its potential for transformation. The compass of the inquiry is the same, but the nature of the probes is somewhat different, and the results also are somewhat different in form and substance.

Many of the observations presented in these pages were undertaken from a different vantage point than those reflected in the earlier *New Forces* book. My current writing is the product of having resided more in the academic community than in the policy community in recent years—though I still straddle both worlds.

The theoretical apparatus is a bit more elaborate than in the Brookings study but once again purposefully kept from dominating the exposition. The analysis delves back into history more, but the historical forays still are constrained by the purpose of gaining insight into what is more or less durable or changeable in the contemporary world. The spectrum of alternative futures is wider and more differentiated, but this is balanced by a greater effort to assess their plausibility and likelihood. In the spirit of academic detachment, the analysis is less ethnocentric and oriented toward the needs of *US* policymakers; yet I have retained a final chapter on the implications of the analysis for US interests, and again offer suggestions for a foreign policy responsive to these implications.

In short, despite the valuable insights about international relations and world politics I have gained from my fellow academics, my writing here still is less about how scholars think about the subject than about what is going on in the world "out there." I intend in the near future to write a book about theory, theory-building, and methods of analysis in this field (graduate students in my seminar on international relations theory know that I have strong views on these matters); readers should be alerted, however, that the present work—by design—is not yet that. The writing, rather, is more directly about the challenges facing contemporary statesmen and stateswomen, in particular the need to reduce today's unprecedented threats to the survival of the human species.

Being less determined to make an original contribution to a particular academic "discipline" than to contribute relevent knowledge to the imperatives of constructive statecraft, I have borrowed liberally from the ideas of others—I hope with sufficient acknowledgment (in the endnotes) of the writings that have influenced my analysis. I could not even begin to give sufficient acknowledgment to all the insights I have absorbed in addition in seminar and corridor dialogs with colleagues in the policy community as well as academia.

I would, however, like to give special thanks to those scholars who generously reviewed and commented on the manuscripts, in particular: Steven Burg, Brandeis University; James E. Harf, Ohio State University; Alex Roberts Hybel, University of Southern California; Charles Kegley, Jr., University of South Carolina; Robert Paalberg, Wellesley College; Randolph Siverson, University of California at Davis; Herbert Tillema, University of Missouri–Columbia; and Paul Watanabe, University of Massachusetts–Boston.

I am also grateful for the guidance and support, even through the down times, provided by John Covell of Little, Brown, and for the expert manuscript editing of Cat Skintik. Pierce McClesky deserves special recognition for the care with which he prepared the useful index.

S. B.

Contents

New Forces,
Old Forces,
and the Future
of World Politics

Introduction

Taken as a whole, this book is not only a set of analyses but a sustained argument. The presentation of material within each chapter and the sequencing of chapters are designed to present a coherent thesis about the historical and future evolution of world politics.

Part One, *The Inherited Foundations* (Chapters 1 and 2), shows how the contemporary configuration of the nation-state system is the evolved product of centuries of struggles between "old forces" and "new forces."

Part Two, *The Existing System in Crisis* (Chapters 3 through 10), argues that the struggles between old and new forces now taking place are not only destabilizing the post-World War II international order, but are undermining the most basic of the evolved structures of world politics: the nation-state system itself.

Part Three, *The Emergence of New Patterns of World Politics* (Chapters 11 through 13), examines the range of plausible outcomes of the contemporary struggles and concludes that the most likely outcome is a "polyarchic" configuration—in which there is no clear global pattern of dominance and subordination; political and economic power is widely diffused; international coalitions have overlapping and cross-cutting memberships; and national, subnational, and transnational groups compete for the loyalty of individuals.

The emerging global polyarchy, it is argued, could evolve into a dangerous variant threatening the survival of the human species or, alternatively, given enlightened statecraft, could evolve into a new form of world politics with structures and processes of effective conflict management and intergroup accountability.

Part Four, *Practical Applications* (Chapters 14 and 15), outlines the essential features of the enlightened statecraft required to assure that the emerging polyarchy evolves into a constructive variant, and it shows how the country in which the author lives, the United States, could assume some responsibility for assisting the constructive evolutionary process.

PART ONE

The Inherited Foundations

Will the human species destroy itself with its continually growing capacity to transform the natural world, or will it adapt positively to the terrible physical power it has created? The answers depend crucially on how inventive the species can become in the fields of government and politics.

As yet, the most highly developed structure of governance is the so-called *nation-state system*. Comprising some 165 countries of widely varying size and power, this world of nation-states has evolved over the course of human history into its present configuration. How the nation-state system reacts to forces very different from those that brought it into existence will determine whether or not the human species will survive or become extinct in the century ahead.

The nation-state system's persistence up to now is often credited to the international *power-balancing process*: Each nation, in order to sustain an independent existence as a self-governing state, will attempt to acquire sufficient strength, usually in the form of military power, to prevent rival countries from subduing it. The required national power is obtained either unilaterally or in alliance with other countries. Through this power-balancing process, generated almost naturally by the desire of nation-states to retain their independence, a would-be world conqueror presumably will be stopped in time from amassing sufficient power to establish a world empire or single world state.

The dominant contemporary expression of the international power-balancing process has been the global rivalry between the United States and the Soviet Union for coalition partners. Each side has justified its accumulation of allies on the grounds that the other is engaged in an "imperialistic" drive to rule the world and that therefore one's own protective embrace is needed and sought by the smaller countries.

In addition to international coalitions formed explicitly to counter the power of presumably hostile countries, *regimes of limited international cooperation* have emerged from time to time, usually confined to particular regions of the globe or particular fields of economic interaction. Even members of rival political–military coalitions have cooperated with one another in such regimes. Characteristically, however, these cooperative arrangements or institutions have been expressions of the nation-state system and prevailing power balances rather than attempts to restructure the system or transform the existing pattern of international alignments.

An appreciation of the durability of the dominant characteristics of the world's political order up to now—the nation-state system and the international power-balancing process—is therefore a necessary starting point for analyzing the prospects for a continuing evolution of the human species...or the quite plausible alternative: the violent destruction of the world.

Chapter 1 briefly capsulizes the inherited structure and norms of the contemporary nation-state system, highlighting the basic functions it performs for human society.

Chapter 2 provides a summary overview of the evolution of the nation-state system up through the bipolar pattern of the cold war. The purpose of the historical retrospective is twofold: One, it offers insight into how the structures and processes of international relations at the political level (hierarchies of power, balances of power, and regimes of limited international cooperation) have been determined by basic material and social forces; and two, it explores how the material and social forces have been shaped and channeled by the prevailing structures and the processes of international statecraft.

Part One thus lays the groundwork for the assessment in Parts Two and Three of the ability of the inherited structures and processes of international politics to deal adequately with today's "new forces."

CHAPTER ONE

The Nation-State System:
Basic Structure and Fundamental Norms[1]

The world's human population is divided into territorially demarcated "countries," and each person, normally, is assumed to belong to one of them. In the late 1980s there were some 165 countries, ranging in area from the sprawling Union of Soviet Socialist Republics (encompassing 8.6 million square miles) to the tiny kingdom of Monaco (only one-tenth as large as Washington, DC), and varying in numbers of inhabitants from China's greater than a billion to Tuvala's fewer than 10,000.

Every country claims to be a self-governing community—a *state*—and generally is recognized by the other countries as possessing full legal authority, or "sovereignty," over what happens in its territory. The institutional apparatus of the state, its official organizations for formulating and enforcing the laws of the country, and those who run these organizations are commonly referred to as the government.

The ability to sustain such sovereign statehood requires substantial cooperation among the people living within the territory, even if only to conduct orderly exchanges of goods and services with one another and to protect themselves against disruptive foreign intruders. Accordingly, where a particular country has persisted for generations there usually are strong bonds of identity among its people, a sense of being a *nation*. To symbolize and help maintain this sense of nationhood, each country has a distinctive flag or banner, inspirational national anthems and oaths, and other rituals of citizenship and patriotism that are performed at public ceremonies to reinforce feelings of loyalty to the country.

In each of the nation-states, ultimate authority and power normally are lodged in a central government responsible for ensuring that the basic requirements of community life are maintained—namely, law and order (particularly the physical security of persons and property), conditions that encourage industry and commerce, community norms of justice, controls on the use of natural resources and the natural environment, and a common cultural base, especially language.

Despite the existence of alternative foci of identification—religions, ethnic and cultural groups, ideological movements—the national government of the country usually has an overriding claim on the loyalty of its citizenry. Only the national government has generally recognized authority and power to require individuals to put their lives at stake, to draft them into armed forces, and to defend the common interests of the population. There are, of course, many subnational and transnational movements and organizations around the world that have members willing to die for their particular causes—for example, the Palestine Liberation Organization, the Sikhs of India, or black African liberation groups in South Africa; but according to the state-sovereignty norm of the nation-state system, violence organized by nonstate groups is almost always illegitimate unless specifically authorized by an established government. The existence of antistate violence is not necessarily a challenge to this norm; in most cases it is a challenge to the legitimacy of a particular ruling group.

It is primarily the national government that, in the name of law and order and justice, issues and implements the basic rules of community life that are to prevail throughout a country's territory. Virtually every nation-state has subordinate levels of government with which the national government shares responsibility for ensuring that law and order is maintained and essential public special fields of activity. The degree and organization of the devolution of authority vary from country to country, but in each the central government retains the ultimate authority to control the subordinate levels.

Under the assumption that each nation-state is a self-governing unit, relations between them would seem to be only a marginal feature of the system. But, in fact, "international" relations are quite prominent. Why? One basic reason is that many countries are not self-sufficient in certain goods required or desired by their peoples—including, in some cases, physical security and public order—and therefore will attempt to acquire these goods from other countries, sometimes by commerce, sometimes by conquest. Another reason is that often countries commonly use the same resource areas (oceans, rivers, the atmosphere, outer space), and the people of one country using a particular resource get in the way of or affect the condition of the people of another country; the determination of who gets what, when, and how in such contested areas necessitates international negotiation or fighting.

In an ideally functioning nation-state system, international relations would be highly circumscribed by the system's norm of state sovereignty: No country, no world or regional organization, no foreign citizen or organization would act within the territory of another country without its consent. Privileges obtained by foreigners to act within the territorial jurisdiction of a state would be negotiated. In fact, such sovereignty, although asserted as a fundamental norm of the system, is often violated in practice. Smaller and weaker countries are coerced by the more powerful into granting them privileges of access and entry—the condition since the end of the World War II of countries in Eastern Europe in relation to the Soviet Union. And to guard against unwanted intervention from hostile states, potential victims form alliances with powerful friendly countries, sometimes establishing a degree of dependence upon their protectors which, paradoxically, requires them to accept an oppressive foreign presence, as happened to the South Vietnamese during the decade of American military involvement in Indochina.

NATION-STATES AND LAW AND ORDER

Under the norms of the nation-state system, each country is responsible for maintaining sufficient law and order within its own jurisdiction to allow the inhabitants to engage in normal domestic pursuits—agriculture, industry, trade, and cultural and family life—secure from violent attacks on themselves and their possessions.

To perform this basic law and order function, the central government of the country normally maintains a monopoly of violent weapons. Short of such monopolization of violence, the central government at least tries to arm itself to the extent that it can overwhelm any private or local violence.

The central government of the nation-state is also the locus of the main capabilities for protecting the territorial unit from invasion or externally supported subversion of the country's prevailing regime. This role is often called defending the "territorial integrity" of the country.

In the nation-state system as a whole, adequate provision for both domestic order and the security of each country against external aggression requires, at a minimum: (1) clearly demarcated borders separating the countries; (2) reliable controls by each country over land, sea, and air (including telecommunications) access to its territorial area; and (3) possession by the central government of each country of the legal right and physical resources to use all means necessary, including war, to maintain the security of the territorial unit.

Because of the unequal military power of countries, some of them are unable to satisfy these minimum public order requirements without accepting material or direct help from friendly countries to balance the military power of an enemy. Thus, the nation-state system, in its public order functions, is inevitably also a system of power-balancing alliances.[2]

Historically, the nation-state/alliance system appears to have played a crucial role in preventing the planet from being convulsed by the extremes of anarchy, global empire, and world war.[3] But, as will be argued in subsequent chapters, a continued heavy reliance on the inherited mechanisms of military armaments and alliances is increasingly dangerous in the face of some of the emergent changes in world politics and threatens the very survival of the planet.

The global peace and security organizations of the twentieth century—the League of Nations and the United Nations—while conceived of by some of their champions as successors to the nation-state/alliance system, turned out, in operation, to be instruments of that system rather than its antithesis. Under the rules of the League, and now the UN, participation by members in common actions to counter threats to the peace is voluntary. Nor can any military or police forces assembled by the international organization be deployed on the territory of a country without its consent. The one notable exception to the norm of sovereign consent of affected countries was the United Nations invasion of North Korea after UN forces had repulsed the North Korean invasion of South Korea in 1950; but this "United Nations Peace Action" was actually undertaken by the military forces of the United States and a few members of its coalition, using the cover of UN resolutions to give their military operation the appearance of universal legitimacy.[4]

New forces (to be discussed in subsequent chapters) are challenging the capacity of the nation-state system to attend adequately to the peace and security needs of human society. But the responsibility for maintaining law and order between countries is still lodged in the nation-state system and its decentralized voluntary mechanisms. As yet, there is no global institution, and no process other than the formation of alliances among states to organize balances of power, that can be relied upon to restrain determined and powerful aggressor nations. Chapters 13 and 14 assay the possibilities for alternative institutions and processess in the peace and security field.

NATION-STATES AND COMMERCE

The separate nation-states also sustain the basic conditions for economic relations within and between communities. The territorial confines of a nation-state normally mark the boundaries of a highly organized trading community or "market." Except where multinational "common markets" have been negotiated (the outstanding example being the European Communities in Western Europe), foreigners usually must receive permission from the national government to sell in its market and usually must convert their own currencies into the special national currency of the market in order to pay for purchases.

As communities of coordinated economic activity, nation-states are especially responsible for providing for the construction and availability of transportation and communications networks to facilitate commerce within their jurisdictions and between them. Frequently, the national government itself owns and runs major highways, air and water transport systems, postal services, and tele-communications and broadcasting systems. In some countries, the national government monopolizes these systems (sometimes for reasons of political control of the population as well as for the effective provision of community services). In every country, the central government retains at least supreme regulatory power over the use of all but very private media of communication and transportation, even if for no other reasons than to avoid congestion, provide safe passage, and control conflict among users.

A considerable degree of coordination across nation-state lines does prevail in the commercial realm.[5] Firms that normally buy and sell outside their home countries have found it desirable, if not essential, to build some predictable order and standardization into what otherwise would be a fragmented world economy with each national market having unique rules of access, often designed to protect inefficient local producers against foreign competitors. Since World War II, those who feel they will benefit from a relatively open world market have persuaded their national governments to participate in negotiations under the General Agreement on Tariffs and Trade (GATT) to coordinate reductions in barriers to international trade, and to subscribe to International Monetary Fund (IMF) rules for stabilizing exchange rates between the currencies of various nations. Consistent with the norms of the nation-state system, however, participation in the GATT and adherence to IMF arrangements are entirely voluntary on the part of each country.

International coordination has also been found highly desirable in the transportation and communications fields, to establish "rules of the road" and to avoid congestion. Some of the most important "functional" international institutions operate in these fields—notably the International Maritime Organization, the International Civil Aviation Organization, and the International Telecommunication Union. Some of these agencies have been accorded international licensing authority; but the power to impose sanctions on violators of international rules is retained by national governments or their subunits.

The growth of the transnational economy, able to elude controls enacted by the separate national states and weak international institutions, is analyzed in Chapter 7. The opportunity this can provide for innovative institution-building is explored in Chapter 13.

NATION-STATES AND SOCIAL JUSTICE

In addition to facilitating commerce, nation-states provide the principal means for giving special help to those who cannot adequately support themselves by selling their labor, products, services, or talents in the market. The regulatory and taxing powers of national governments are the mechanisms most relied on in efforts to equalize wealth, status, power, and opportunity. And the domestic legal systems of the nation-states and their subdivisions are the sources of enforceable prohibitions and privileges of individual and group behavior—the norms that majorities impose on minorities, the rights of citizens in relation to governments, and the rights and obligations of individuals toward each other.

Efforts to develop international obligations to help the world's destitute or oppressed peoples have made little headway. Some countries unilaterally extend famine relief and even economic development assistance to others; some countries contribute to internationally organized relief efforts and to international institutions for development assistance such as the World Bank. But these efforts are voluntary acts by independent national communities, and the help usually is funneled through the national governments of the recipient nations. National governments retain their sovereignty on both the giving and the receiving ends.

Most national governments have signed international declarations and covenants of social justice and individual rights—as, for example, the Universal Declaration of Human Rights, the International Covenant on Economic, Social, and Cultural Rights, and the International Covenant on Civil and Political Rights. Twenty-one governments have signed the European Convention on Human Rights, obligating themselves to conform in fact to the Convention's detailed substantive and procedural provisions. Citizens who feel that justice is being denied them within their own nation-states can invoke such international charters in an effort to bring pressure on their national governments to respond to their grievances. But even in Western Europe, where some countries allow citizens to appeal directly to the European Human Rights Commission or Court, redress must be obtained through one of the national legal systems. There is no supranational institution that can compel a country to adhere to international human rights norms, even those that a country has formally obligated itself to implement.

As literacy and international communication intensify the perception of relatively poor and disenfranchised elements of world society that they are unjustly deprived by the existing international order (see Chapters 7, 8, and 10), new institutions for processing social justice demands are being called for. The possibilities are outlined in the final three chapters.

NATION-STATES AND THE USE OF NATURAL RESOURCES AND THE ENVIRONMENT

One of the main functions of governance is the control of access to and exploitation of the natural resources used by a community, so that members can be assured of appropriate shares, vulnerable resources are kept in usable condition, and exhaustible resources are not too rapidly depleted. Historically, strong and centralized governments have developed out of the need to perform this function—the role of ancient kingdoms in Egypt in managing the Nile being an outstanding example.

Because the location of natural resources is not always congruent with the borders of nation-states, coordination and cooperation among groups of countries has often proven to be in their mutual self-interest. Accordingly, international associations of resource users have formed in various fields, particularly where there are commonly harvested and depletable resources, such as ocean fisheries.[6]

In some fields, the responsible international institutions have been invested with limited inspection and/or licensing authority to "police" common standards. But refusals to accept international inspection or other actions that may disqualify a project from international agency certification are unlikely to be deterred by such highly limited licensing authority. A country determined to proceed with a project or action will do so without formal international blessing. Any stronger deterrent sanctions must come from other national governments.

As shown in Chapter 9, the increasing utilization of technologies and industrial activities capable of grossly disturbing the natural ecological relationships that sustain human life, let alone the growing realization that undertakings in one political jurisdiction can negatively affect the health and welfare of people in neighboring jurisdictions, is stimulating new demands for mandatory international accountability. The extent to which this may require reform of the sovereignty norms of the existing nation-state system is assayed in Chapter 13.

NATION-STATES AND THE MAINTENANCE OF DIVERSE CULTURES

One of the most important functions the nation-state performs for human society is the provision of a home for particular ways of life. Under the protection of a national legal–political system whose autonomy is respected by other countries, special rules of morality, religious practice, language, music, and artistic and architectural creation can be encouraged and preserved in the face of those who may not sufficiently value the national culture.

If such enclaves of culture were not provided with adequate protection, many of the ethnic and religious groups that now maintain their uniqueness might be homogenized into larger and more aggressive world cultures. The loss of cultural integrity is feared especially by societies that require disciplined adherence to religious rituals and specific family and sexual mores. The national governments representing these societies often attempt to prevent the dissemination of literature from other cultures and foreign telecommunications broadcasts from contaminating the local cultural purity, and frequently maintain tight restrictions on the activities of tourists and foreign commercial enterprises within their societies.

Many of the larger nation-states are multicultural. Some, like the United States, have constitutional systems and laws congenial to cultural pluralism: permissive policies toward diverse social practices, protection of minority rights, and prohibitions against official favoritism toward particular religions. Other countries—India, for example, and Canada in some of its constitutional provisions—have federal structures that devolve considerable governing authority to subunits of government ("provinces," "states") in order to accommodate the various cultural groupings within the federal union. Still others, such as the USSR, under a professed ideology of cultural pluralism, have allowed the trappings of ethnic uniqueness—languages, songs, dances, and the like—to flourish within so-called autonomous republics of the union but have imposed on top of this diversity a strict conformist regime of basic rules for everyday behavior and an unequivocal obligation for all citizens of the union to give their highest loyalty to the central state.

Not all of the cultures of the world feel adequately protected or represented in the nation-states currently in existence—the Palestinians in Israel, the Basques in Spain, and the Tamils in India being a few of the many cases in point.[7] On numerous occasions in history, civil or inter-state conflict has resulted from demands for self-determination or autonomy made by a cultural group within a society ruled by another cultural group. Indeed, the current demarcation of the globe into nation-states is in large measure the outcome of the last round of struggles between cultural groups that defined themselves as nations and insisted on their own states in which they could set the rules. Some defenders of the nation-state system as the basis for world order accept such conflicts over self-determination, viewing them as periodic shakedowns of the system conducive to the restoration of its essential equilibrium. It is questionable, however, whether human civilization can continue to survive such struggles for national self-determination as modern means of mass destruction and terror become increasingly accessible to states and stateless groups alike. The concluding chapters examine some alternative norms and instrumentalities for dealing more peacefully with the need to accommodate diverse cultures on this planet.

ENDNOTES

1. Most of the material in this chapter is adapted from my essay, "The World Polity and the Nation-State System: An Updated Analysis," *International Journal*, Vol. XXXIX, No. 3 (Summer 1984), pp. 509–528.

2. The notion that the nation-state system, relying heavily on military alliances, is the natural political system for world society is given a theoretical basis by Kenneth N. Waltz, *Theory of International Politics* (Menlo Park: Addison Wesley, 1979).

3. The best exposition of the role of the power-balancing process among nation-states in maintaining world public order remains Hans Morgenthau's classic treatise, *Politics among Nations: The Struggle for Power and Peace* (New York: Knopf, 1978).

4. The original United States Security Council resolutions authorizing the United States to conduct military operations in Korea were made possible by the temporary absence of the Soviet Union from the Council (the USSR, if present, surely would have exercised its veto). Subsequent resolutions, including the authorization to cross the 38th parallel into North Korea, were passed in the General Assembly, where the United States could mobilize a majority in the 1950s, so as to avoid the Soviet veto in the Security Council. International lawyers are still debating whether these actions were in violation of the letter and/or the spirit of the UN Charter. See Inis L. Claude, Jr., *Swords into Plowshares: The Problems and Progress of International Organization* (New York: Random House, 1984), pp. 157–158, 177–178, 268–272.

5. See Stephen D. Krasner, ed., *International Regimes* (Ithaca: Cornell University Press, 1983); see also Richard Rosecrance, *The Rise of the Trading State: Commerce and Conquest in the Modern World* (New York: Basic Books, 1986).

6. Seyom Brown, Nina Cornell, Larry Fabian, and Edith Brown Weiss, *Regimes for the Ocean, Outer Space, and Weather* (Washington: The Brookings Institution, 1977).

7. A detailed analysis of the phenomenon of the intense grievances of subnational and transnational groups against the nation-states that control them is provided by Donald L. Horowitz, *Ethnic Groups in Conflict* (Berkeley: University of California Press, 1985).

CHAPTER TWO

From Classical Balance to Cold War Bipolarity

There are at least five significantly different configurations of international relations that are sources of the traditions, norms, and power realities of contemporary world politics: (1) the "classical balance of power," usually dated from the Peace of Westphalia, 1648, to roughly the start of the French Revolution; (2) the "concert" system, beginning with the Congress of Vienna, 1815, and lasting, according to some diplomatic historians, until the immediate pre-World War I period; (3) the experiment with universal "collective security" from the establishment of the League of Nations to the first few years of the United Nations; (4) cold war bipolarity; and (5) what I call "polyarchy"—a configuration still in the process of formation, which will be analyzed in Part Three.

Some of these variants of international relations have overlapped in time. None of the temporarily dominant patterns has disappeared completely; for even while being overtaken by successor patterns, each has transmitted its own legacy to its offspring, so to speak, like genes carried through many generations. And on occasion one or another of the historical patterns has seemed to be experiencing a full-blown reincarnation.

VARIANT 1: THE CLASSICAL BALANCE OF POWER

The ideal system of international relations for many theorists, and statesmen schooled in world history, is the basic pattern of relationships prevailing in the European state system for more than a century following the Peace of Westphalia of 1648.

The Peace of Westphalia was supposed to put an end to the wars of religion that had been devastating Europe. In the numerous documents signed in Westphalia in 1648, the monarchs of the day pledged to honor each other's sovereignty over the newly demarcated or newly reaffirmed realms of territory assigned to each of them. The jurisdictional integrity of every sovereign state was to be sacrosanct. Intervention by one state into the domestic affairs of another state, especially for the purpose of aiding co-religionists, was henceforth illegitimate.

The underlying Westphalian agreement between the ruling monarchs of the time to respect one another's sovereign authority was supposed to be sustained by a flexible system of shifting alliances among the half dozen or so major dynasties of Europe to keep each other's ambitions and power in check. There would be no permanent groupings of allies. Imperialistic powers would be countered ad hoc by combinations of states. Conflicts between the various monarchies would be limited to disputes over tangible conflicting claims to land, waterways and fisheries, and new overseas imperial holdings. Disputes over ways of life and ways of worshiping God would be kept out of the inter-state arena. It would be easier to resolve conflicts through negotiated compromises. Such wars as did break out could be terminated rather rapidly short of total defeat of the enemy.

The beauty of this system—and why it still continues to have a theoretical or aesthetic appeal, if not an appeal as a practical design for world order—is that each state in servicing its overriding self-interest of survival as a sovereign political entity would thereby service the stability and durability of the system as a whole. States would adhere to rules of moderation, even in war. Self-interest and general interest would coincide.

The coincidence of the self-interest of the major states with the maintenance requirements of the system meant that the essential behavioral norms of the classical balance of power were largely self-enforcing. In this sense, the system could be thought of as self-equilibrating.

Drawing on the conceptual formulation of political scientist Morton Kaplan,[1] seven self-enforcing norms of the classical variant of the balance of power can be postulated:

1. Normally, states would attempt to increase, or at least maintain, their territory, material resources, and military strength; but as this brought them into conflict with other states, they would *prefer* negotiated settlements, and even third-party mediation, to war. (Neighboring states, such as the League of the Rhine, promised to resolve their disputes by conciliation. France accepted Swedish mediation of some of her conflicts at the end of the seventeenth century; similarly, Turkey and Austria-Hungary accepted British and French mediation in 1717–1718.[2])

2. Yet states would go to war rather than accept a major decrease in, or forego an important opportunity to increase, their resources or military strength. (Indeed, the major powers of Europe were more frequently involved in wars against each other between Westphalia and the French Revolution than during any other era of European history.)

3. States involved in warfare usually would terminate physical hostilities short of the point of total elimination of a key member of the system. (Thus, in the early 1760s, the prospect that Prussia might actually be

destroyed, which would severely destabilize the five-power European balance of the time, was a constraint even on the actions of Prussia's principal enemies, Austria, France, and Russia.[3]

4. Key states of the system that were defeated or seriously weakened in war would be permitted by the other states to reenter the system as important actors; and previously unimportant states were recognized and dealt with as important states as their changes in capability warranted this new status.

5. States would oppose, unilaterally or in combination with other states, any state or coalition that threatened to assume a position of overwhelming predominance within the system. (During the reign of Louis XIV, 1643–1715, the fear of hegemonial dominance centered on France, and Britain led in the formation of an anti-French coalition; but with the success of British overseas imperial expansion in the middle of the eighteenth century, Spain and The Netherlands, now more fearful of England's dominance, joined France in a coalition against Britain.)

6. Any state was potentially an acceptable coalition partner of any other state. Particularly during the first three-quarters of the eighteenth century, countries rapidly shifted alliances. (For example, in the War of the Austrian Succession, 1740–1748, France and Spain joined Prussia against Austria, which was supported by Great Britain; but in the Seven Years War, 1756–1763, France was an ally of Austria and Russia, while Britain was on Prussia's side.)

7. States sought to limit the inter-state or trans-state activities of states and other groups who attempted to mobilize support for themselves or to build coalitions on the basis of trans-state or universal religions or ideologies.

The first two norms are often viewed as inherent to the anarchic structure of international society: Today, no less than in the seventeenth century, the survival and well-being of a state requires that it look out for its own interests through diplomatic bargaining if possible, but be prepared to go to war to maintain its interests, since there is no reliable larger-community institution it can go to for protection.

Norms 3 through 7, however, are the products of more particular historical contexts. Most of them have not operated with any consistency since the French Revolution. Thus, to understand why all of these norms operated during the period of the classical balance of power, we must examine the collateral social and material conditions then prevailing, especially in Europe.[4]

The fact that the principal states of the last half of the seventeenth century and first three-quarters of the eighteenth century were aristocratic monarchies—the only exception being the brief Republican Interregnum in

England under the Cromwells (1653–1660)—was central to the operation of the classical balance. The monarchs of the time could arrange marriage, line-of-succession, and treasure deals with one another, form and reform alliances and counteralliances, trade colonial possessions, and even redraw the boundary lines demarcating the states of Europe, without having to worry whether the populations within their jurisdictions liked it or not. *"L'etat c'est moi"* (I am the state), France's Louis XIV is supposed to have said, giving expression to the prevailing sense that the rulers were unaccountable to the ruled.

The states, in a word, were not yet *nation*-states. Indeed, it was not unusual for the monarch to speak a different language and practice a different religion than the majority of his subjects. Monarchs often would recruit their top diplomats and generals from other countries (these valued professionals, themselves having no compelling emotional attachment to any particular country, offered their skills to the highest bidders). And the generals in turn would fill their ranks with mercenaries, hired soldiers who as often as not had no prior connection with the land and peoples they were paid to defend.

The economic and social ties between peoples within each country were still quite flimsy. Trade between different sectors of society—farmers, craftsmen, merchants—was increasing; specialization and "vertical interdependence" were growing; but the exchange of goods was largely of finished products ready for use. Country-wide or "national" markets were developing, which meant that roads and waterways had to be constructed and maintained, as public works, to link geographically dispersed communities; but as yet the larger nation that these mutually reinforcing processes of integration implied was only a thin overlay on the still relatively distinct enclaves of homogeneous ethnic/linguistic/religious subnations.

All of these social and economic conditions had a determining effect on resort by statesmen to their most important diplomatic trump card, war—on the objectives for which war was fought, and on the way it was fought.

Wars were fought by professional armies, for war aims defined by an aristocratic monarchy and its professional diplomats. The citizenry at large normally were not asked to fight or even to support the wars going on around them. Thus, wars could be conducted for any of a wide range of state interests—from vital to trivial. One war could be fought to prevent a major shift in the inter-state balance of power. Another war could be fought to establish rights to fish in a disputed area. Still another war could be fought to salvage the reputation of a particular general who was outmaneuvered by a rival general in the last war. Wars could be started quickly and turned off quickly, for the ruling elite did not have to justify their actions to anyone but themselves. A war therefore need not involve any irretrievable political or material risks. War might be an instrument of high statecraft, based on prudential deliberation and systematic strategic assessment, but it also might be an instrument of caprice.

The recruitment, organization, and provisioning of the military were important influences on the role of war in the period of the classical balance. Some mercenary soldiers fought for the glory of it. But most mercenaries were simply in the business of renting out their bodies; if they were not fed and clothed well, if the work was too hard, or if there was too much risk of their getting killed, they would desert. Consequently, the generals of the time were constrained to avoid frequent or sustained battle. In a sustained battle, not only one's soldiers, but also their supply trains, ammunition, and weapons would be lost, and all of this was very expensive to replace.

Most states still had little revenue with which to finance costly wars, noblemen being generally exempt from taxation, so the incentives all went in the direction of limiting one's war aims and fighting highly controlled and brief wars. War, like chess, was a game of maneuver; and the brilliant general not only knew how to "win" without getting into a big engagement but also knew when to concede defeat—sometimes even prior to any major exchange of gunfire. Clever statesmen could (and did) play on these incentives in order to establish a bargaining advantage over an enemy, through attempts to convince the enemy that one's own resolve and staying power had by no means reached their limits in a particular conflict.

The crucial political constraint on statesmanship in the classical balance— maintaining as much flexibility as possible in the choice of alliance partners— was highly interactive with the incentives to fight limited wars. In order to preserve the option of forming an alliance tomorrow with today's enemy, the statesman would refrain from pushing his advantage to the point of destroying or humiliating a rival power. Fortunately, because of the material and manpower constraints on warfare, there were few temptations to exceed this rule of prudence.

But underneath the admirable restraint in statecraft and the surface equilibrium of the classical balance, new forces were at work undermining the necessary conditions for its survival as the dominant pattern of inter-state relations.

It took the brutal cataclysm of the Napoleonic Wars following the French Revolution of 1789 to shock the statesmen of Europe into a recognition that the self-help, self-equilibrating features of the classical balance of power might be woefully inadequate for sustaining the requirements of civic order in the modern age. Indeed, given the new social and economic realities, the unilateral diplomacy of the classical system might well encourage the very immoderate behavior of states toward one another that nearly destroyed European civilization in the Napoleonic Wars.

Why? A short phrase sums up the complex and world-transforming metamorphosis: The state system was changing into a *nation*-state system. The territorially defined states were becoming nations, in which strong bonds were developing between ruling elites and general populace—bonds of perceived mutual material dependence between the various economic classes of the country, and the emergence of a country-wide sense of cultural identity. This general trend, as will be shown below, was to have profound effects on inter-state diplomacy and war.

Much of the change was probably inevitable, being the product of the human being's increasing and accelerating capacity to transform the natural world. This technological inventiveness was evident in eighteenth century Europe in the dramatic growth of complex manufacturing processes, which engulfed economies based on simple in-the-home craftsmen. Buildings, roads, vehicles, and instruments of war were constructed more and more out of materials and parts that were themselves made by highly specialized labor and facilities. Different sectors of society, different professions, different classes, became increasingly dependent upon each other and upon more elaborate and wide-spread systems of money and credit. Countries became internally more integrated, not only economically but also culturally. Modern "nations" were beginning to develop.

The functions of government in the various territorially demarcated countries, the controls on public order and commerce, the collection of taxes and tolls to construct and maintain commonly used roads and waterways, the raising of armed forces to enforce the rules of civic order within the country and to protect it against hostile outsiders—in short, the whole apparatus of the *state*—which heretofore were highly centralized in the monarchy would need to be adapted to the emerging social and economic complexities. The state simply could not function any longer without the cooperation of many elements of society.

The adaptation of the state to the new nation-forming forces in eighteenth century Europe proceeded at a different pace and took different forms in the various countries. In England, not wishing a repeat of the bloody Cromwellian revolution of the previous century, the monarchy gradually, if reluctantly, began to share power with a parliament increasingly representative of the commercial classes. In France, a more rigid and self-indulgent monarchy refused to accommodate sufficiently to the power-sharing demands of the emergent classes until it was too late—the result being the Revolution of 1789, the establishment of the French Republic, and a new cycle of chaos and terror leading to the takeover of the Republic by the would-be emperor of all of Europe, Napoleon Bonaparte.

In response to the imperialistic expansion of Republican and Napoleonic France, the preexisting balance of power system did come into play, but only partially, and in a way that was so distortive of its own norms that it could not be reinstituted after Napoleon's defeat in 1815.

France, especially under Napoleon, had violated the classical system's norms by using the republican and nationalistic ideologies of the French Revolution as justification for military intervention into civil conflicts of other countries; France would come to the aid of those other people fighting for the "Rights of Man" against oppressive monarchs. Understandably, the crowned heads of Europe (to repeat the famous oxymoron) were trembling in their boots! It took fifteen years for the alliance of European monarchs and England to smash Napoleon and temporarily reverse the tide of nationalistic revolutions he helped to swell; but in so defending the old order, they too violated the classical principles of nonintervention into the domestic affairs of other countries and moderation in both the objectives and conduct of war.

VARIANT 2: CONCERTS AND CONFERENCE DIPLOMACY— MANAGED EQUILIBRIUM AMONG NATION-STATES

The obsolescence of the classical balance of power was marked in 1815 by the felt need on the part of influential statesmen to come together in a group to concert their actions, to jointly steer the system, out of a fear that the unilateral pursuit by each country of its perceived self-interest would not, as in the past, guarantee a statecraft of moderate ends and moderate means.

The older system of flexible alignment and realignment among the countries of Europe to balance each other's power was being undermined by the spread of the ideology of nationalism and by new material and social forces that were transforming dynastic states into nation-states. The combustible combination of the new culture of nationalism and the new ideology of liberalism now sweeping Europe from the Atlantic to the Urals, from the Baltic to the Mediterranean, would need to be managed by the enlightened statesmen of the time if the Napoleonic Wars were not to have been only the first phase of a holocaust that would leave Europe even more devastated than had the seventeenth century wars of religion.

The post-Napoleonic statesmen differed among themselves over how much joint management was necessary—some wanting only occasional consultation, others favoring permanent institutions to formulate and oversee the implementation of new rules of inter-state conduct. All, however, were agreed on the inadequacy of the pre-Napoleonic balance of power process for containing the explosive forces of the nineteenth century.

A web of multilateral treaties and obligations to at least consult with one another before taking action of system-wide significance was now required—in contrast to the classical pattern wherein a statesman's unilateral pursuit of self-interest was assumed to serve the general interest (and in those cases where it did not, the virtually automatic workings of the balance of power would restore the general equilibrium). In the face of the rising domestic forces, which might impel governing elites to respond more to nationalistically oriented constituencies than to the requirements of world order, the post-Napoleonic statesmen, in their discussions with one another and in their treaties, attempted to forge an explicit set of understandings on the "legitimate" structure and processes of the European state system. But when it came to the specific content of the norms and the particular forms of institutionalizing the new European system, the consensus of 1815 turned out to be quite flimsy.

Czar Alexander I of Russia wanted a re-Christianized Europe, with the rulers of the countries mutually pledged to maintain the territorial status quo provided for in the treaties ending the Napoleonic Wars and to support one another in upholding the constitutional order. For the Czar, this meant coming to the aid of monarchies when they were threatened by republican revolutions. To promote these ends, the Czar persuaded his fellow rulers to sign the Treaty of the Holy Alliance of September 1815—a document long on pietistic affirmations of "Christian charity" and "indissoluble fraternity" and short on specific provisions for the conduct of inter-state relations. Behind the Czar's back, many of the other conservative statesmen of the day ridiculed the document. Austrian Chancellor Metternich made vulgar jokes about it. "A piece of sublime mysticism and nonsense," said the British Foreign Minister Castlereagh.[5]

Austria and Prussia were ready to wave the banner of the Holy Alliance as justification for their defense of monarchical principles against liberal and nationalist movements. However, Britain and France (even after the monarchical restoration) were not particularly averse to political movements that would diminish the power of the autocrats of Central and Eastern Europe. There emerged, therefore, almost as soon as the Holy Alliance was promulgated, an embarrassing East–West schism under its aegis: The three Eastern powers (Russia, Prussia, and Austria) were often inclined to intervene in other states to prevent national or political revolutions against the existing sovereign authority; while Britain and France more often than not were opposed to such interventions. This partly ideological, partly geopolitical divide was openly expressed, on the one hand, in the Pact of Munchengratz (1833), which committed the three Eastern powers to help rulers defend themselves against the forces of liberalism and revolution, and, on the other hand, in the countervailing Quadruple Alliance (1836) among Britain, France, Spain, and Portugal.[6]

But Europe was still far from polarized into two camps along either ideological or geographic lines. Britain supported Austria's imperial position in Italy in the 1820s against Italian nationalists, and in 1839–1840 supported the Turks in their efforts to suppress nationalist-reformist uprisings. As put by one British analyst, "The paradox...emerged of Britain, previously the chief liberal, antiinterventionist power, as the staunch supporter of the status quo in the Ottoman Empire, while Russia, the arch counter-revolutionary, became the main supporter of revolutionary forces in that area."[7] Throughout the nineteenth century, rivalries within the "Eastern" and "Western" blocs persisted and frequently were more salient than the East–West division: France against Britain in regard to Belgium and Italy, and especially in North Africa; Prussia against Austria over the Germanic peoples; and variously Prussia and Austria, sometimes independently, sometimes in concert, against Russia's hegemonial designs in East and Southeast Europe.

Thus the "classical" unilateral balancing system still operated under the veneer of multilateral cooperation. But both the revival of the old diplomacy and the new concert diplomacy were expressions (in the words of the subtitle to Henry Kissinger's doctoral dissertation on the period) of "The Politics of Conservatism in a Revolutionary Age." Highly elitist in conception and management, the Concert of Europe became increasingly anachronistic.

The statesmen of the nineteenth century seemed unable to fully comprehend, let alone adequately grapple with, the emerging central predicament of the nation-state system; namely, how to reconcile the requirements of a stable and moderate inter-state order with the domestic political requirements of maintaining power in one's own country. Attempts to satisfy the latter might overwhelm the former, particularly as the transformation of countries into nation-states intensified the pressures on ruling elites to be first and foremost accountable to their national constituencies.

More and more, the power of a country vis-a-vis other countries—its military and economic power—was dependent upon the ability of its rulers to gain cooperation from many sectors of the country to build modern fleets and armies, to construct and maintain nation-wide roads and transportation systems, and to foster industries that could engage in profitable international trade. This put the merchant and commercial elites in an especially strong bargaining position (particularly when it came to the mobilization of the country's resources for large projects, such as the expansion of the navy), since it was they who really controlled the country's industry and finances. Simple prudence compelled the hereditary dynasties and aristocracies to co-opt these new elites into the regime, to invite them into the chambers where policy was made. And thus were born the institutions of the nation—councils of state and parliaments—to which the monarchy had to be accountable. Inter-state diplomatic maneuverings and power plays were accordingly constrained by this need of governing elites to satisfy broader and broader segments of society that particular alliances, foreign adventures, and wars were indeed in the nation's interest.

Ruling elites could not obtain from the society at large contributions for major undertakings, especially for foreign adventures, unless these could be credibly shown to be necessary for the nation's well-being. And those who claimed a right to participate in the definition of the nation's well-being were proliferating: the business classes, newspaper editors, writers, and educated persons generally. Wars had to be fought for *national* causes or not at all.

Paradoxically, therefore, ruling elites felt it necessary to cultivate and enhance the new forces that were constraining their freedom of action, thereby even further limiting their diplomatic flexibility. In order to generate sufficient popular support for the measures, domestic and international, required to secure the country's independence, let alone to increase its power, monarchs, aristocrats, and prime ministers now had to identify with the people rather than stand aloof from them. They had to speak the peoples' languages and champion their causes. They had to embrace the ideology of nationalism—the idea of the nation-state as an organic whole.

This equation of state and nation plus the spread of the ideology of nationalism were at odds with another of the cardinal norms of the classical balance of power: moderation.

Foreign adventures, particularly wars, now being more difficult to initiate because they required a rather solid national consensus for their provisioning, would be much more difficult to keep limited in their intensity. National fear, anger, and pride had to be whipped up in order to go to war; the reasons of state for which war was required had to be reasons of nation—its survival, its honor, its glory; the enemy had to be venal, and therefore deserved to be severely punished, hobbled, if not destroyed.

Developments in weapons technology and military logistics reinforced the sociopolitical and economic factors, making for highly destructive wars. The new weapons, military transportation systems, and powerful navies required support from a militarily prepared industrial base that in turn required a virtual mobilization of the entire nation. Consequently, a belligerent country's munitions factories, transportation networks, indeed its whole industrial base, now became crucial (thus legitimate) military targets.

No longer could a country depend on hired mercenaries to fight its wars. Loyal citizens would have to be recruited to fight and to provide the generalship. This dependence on citizen armies further reinforced the requirement that wars—and military alliances—only be entered into for vital national purposes. Again, wars might be harder to start than in the previous century, but once started, there would be hell to pay.

The ideology of nationalism had another paradoxical effect even more threatening to the prospects for a stable and durable civic order in Europe. On the one hand, it helped forge the vertical integration of society within countries, the identification of rulers with the ruled, and gave "legitimacy" to the sometimes brutal suppression by national governments of dissident linguistic and religious groups. On the other hand, the ideology of nationalism (particularly when infused with the doctrines of the French and American revolutions that only those governments were legitimate that rested on the "consent of the governed") was the energizing force of groups, now claiming to be nations of their own, who resented being submerged into the dominant culture of the larger nation-state in which they resided. If states were nations, then nations had a right to states of their own. Some of these would-be nation-states transcended the existing state boundaries.

These highly combustible effects of nationalism had been exploited by the French Republic and Napoleon in their international interventions on behalf of the "Rights of Man." Napoleon, while defeated by the conservative powers, taught them a lesson they would learn all too well—that nationalism in the rival imperial power's camp could be an exploitable substance for undermining the rival's power and expanding one's own power. Henceforth, the statesmen of Europe, no matter what their own liberal or conservative ideology, would respond to temptations to expand the power and territorial base of their countries by seizing upon opportunities to help ethnic or religious dissidents in a rival state. Such interventionist temptations would be especially hard for statesmen to resist when the dissidents' causes, because of religious or cultural affinity, were popular with one's own citizenry.

Yet despite all the temptations to exploit the volatile social currents of the nineteenth century, the leading post-Napoleonic statesmen of Europe— Metternich, Castlereagh, and after them Bismarck—exhibited remarkable moderation and self-restraint. Unable to master the new forces, they at least recognized that the "bad currency" of unrestrained international power plays could easily drive out the good; and they had the recent lesson of the 20-year period of the Napoleonic Wars to remind them of the consequences of such a descent into anarchy.

While the popular image of the post-Napoleonic nineteenth century as an era of basic international peace between the great powers is surely wrong, especially for the last half of the century (witness the Crimean War of 1854 between Britain and Russia, the Italian War of 1859 between Austria and France, the war between Denmark and the German states of 1864; the Austro-Prussian War of 1866; and the Franco-Prussian War of 1870),[8] it was truly at the same time an era of creative international institution-building. The wars were a continuing reminder to enlightened statesmen that the nation-state system, left to the devices of unilateral statecraft, was now no longer capable of self-equilibration. They could no longer avoid the realization that the vaunted inter-state anarchy of the classical balance of power, carried over into the age of intense nationalism, was now, if anything, one of the stimulants to war-making and to immoderation in the conduct of war.

The verbal pledges among nineteenth century statesmen of mutual account-ability thus were more than hypocritical homages paid to virtue by vice. And the international conferences, congresses, and creation of international organizations that characterized the period were more than a diverting charade played by the diplomatic elite between their "real" power games.

The period featured serious multilateralism and international institution-building by history's arch *realpolitik* statesmen. It is the period from which the twentieth century's most noted *realpolitik* internationalist, Henry Kissinger—architect of the Nixon administration's policies of detente with the USSR and rapprochement with China—derived most of his ideas on diplomacy.[9]

Following the initial Congress of Vienna of 1815, there were a number of other congresses (the functional equivalent of today's "summits") that accomplished results of lasting significance. The London Conference of 1830–1831 established the independence of Belgium and of Greece. The London Conference of 1839 instituted the permanent neutrality of Belgium. The London Conference of 1840–1841 promulgated rules on the contentious issue of the navigation of straits; and other major navigation and sea law rules were agreed to at the Congress of Paris in 1856. The famous 1878 Congress of Berlin, orchestrated by Bismarck, resolved a bitter Russo-Turkish dispute that might easily have led to an even bloodier repeat of the Crimean War and could have directly embroiled most of the major powers. And at the Conference of Berlin in 1884, rules were negotiated on the establishment of colonial territories in Africa.[10]

The subject of war itself, its causes, prevention, and control—rather than any particular disputes among countries—was addressed at the Hague Conferences, begun in 1899. These produced a comprehensive revision and restatement of the rules of warfare and set up permanent institutions for the pacific settlement of disputes (the precursors of the system of international courts created under the League of Nations): the Permanent Court of Arbitration and the International Commissions of Inquiry. The Hague instrumentalities marked no intrusion on the sovereignty of the states who agreed to adhere to them; but they did represent the growing recognition by statesmen that agreed-upon international norms and dispute-resolution mechanisms were important, if for no other reason than to provide a notion of international "legitimacy" to invoke against immoderate nationalistic passions that might drive governments into unnecessary wars and mindless levels of destruction.

Finally, the least glamorous and yet probably the most innovative of accomplishments of the internationalist diplomats of the nineteenth century was their creation of public international "unions" for coordinating actions by countries in economic, technological, and social welfare fields where cooperation and/or standardization was necessary. Precursors of the functional specialized regional and global institutions that have proliferated in the contemporary age of "interdependence," the international unions were given mandates by their member governments to hire permanent international staffs ("secretariats") to operate between conferences in implementing agreed-upon policies, conducting research, preparing future conferences, and in general serving as administrative clearing houses. The first of these permanent international functional institutions was the Bureau of the International Telegraphic Union, established in 1868 (later to become the International Telecommunication Union). Similar organizations were instituted to coordinate activities in postal affairs, health and disease control, and labor standards and unionization rights.

The evolution of a system of international accountability for the world polity has its roots in the creative statecraft of the nineteenth century. As put by Professor Inis Claude: "Most basically, the nineteenth century contributed a broadening concept of the nature and subject matter of international relations, an evolving sense of the need for joint decisions...[and] a growing recognition of the usefulness of international machinery."[11]

However, the inter-state accountability processes and institutions, while undoubtedly an important contribution of nineteenth century statecraft to the art of human governance, were essentially conservative. They were efforts to preserve the system of cool-headed bargaining among aristocratic elites over the drawing and redrawing of territorial jurisdictions in Europe and in the colonial arena. The bargaining was constrained by the traditional power-balancing process: The European states would form alliances among themselves as required to prevent any of their numbers from overly aggressive imperialism.

German Chancellor Bismarck, the continent's quintessential conservative of the latter nineteenth century, had hoped to perpetuate the European Concert after the Franco-Prussian war by renouncing all expansionist aims and pledging to use Germany's power only to further the general peace. Perceiving correctly that a new all-European war might be catalyzed by the clash of Russian and Austrian ambitions in the Balkans, Bismarck promised St. Petersburg that Berlin would remain neutral with respect to Russian moves in the Near East but would come to the assistance of Vienna in the event of a Russian direct attack on Austria-Hungary. At the same time, he assured Vienna that Germany would use its power to help Austria-Hungary protect its present position, but not in a way that would incur strong Russian opposition.[12] The Bismarckian balancing act was prototypically "classical."

But the nineteenth century, anticipated by the American and French revolutions, was a period of radical transformation in political norms and structures *within* countries, which was turning ministers of state into the creatures of nations rather than their masters. The nations of the world were defining *their* interests, *their* borders, choosing *their* governments, and insisting that governing elites be accountable to *them* rather than to the governing elites of other countries. Inter-state conflicts, including wars, were no longer primarily caused by (and efforts to redress) disequilibria in the balance of power between countries; they were now just as much the product of domestic passions and crises demanding external release.

The state system, a product of the old forces, was unable to harness passionate nationalism, a manifestation of the new forces. Bismarck saw what was coming and warned: "If the monarchical governments do not understand the need for working together in the interests of political order and instead surrender to the chauvinistic sentiments of their subjects, I fear that the international and revolutionary social struggles, which we shall have to fight through, will become more dangerous. . . . "[13]

Approaching the twentieth century, the nation-state system was becoming a self-contradictory human invention, hardly amenable to control through traditonal balance-of-power diplomacy of either the classical or concert variety.

Yet the balance of power was still the only means at the disposal of countries in conflict to protect themselves against determined international adversaries.

Nationalism was now the driving force that set country against country, coalition against coalition. The balance of power became only an *instrument* of this immoderate force. It was the clash of rival nationalisms, aided and abetted by balance-of-power diplomats, that polarized Europe into two implacably hostile camps and brought on World War I. Moreover, what was supposed to be a solution to the problem of immoderation became part of the problem, as conservative governments, on the defensive domestically against rising liberal and socialist demands, went on the offensive internationally for nationalist causes in the hope of enhancing their popularity at home.[14]

Viewed from this perspective, World War I would not be seen, in retrospect, as a war resulting from miscalculation or diplomatic ineptitude—an unnecessary war. Rather, it can be seen as given by the system itself, a war that could have been avoided only by extraordinarily brilliant statesmanship.

It was hardly illegitimate for German nationalism to be expressed at the turn of the century in an effort to challenge British and French preponderance as colonial powers, and therefore to launch a major buildup of the German navy. Nor were the countermoves of France and Britain—their *entente cordiale* to allocate spheres of influence to themselves in the colonial world and to keep Germany out, and their subsequent link-up with autocratic Russia in the Triple Entente—inconsistent with the normal dynamics of the balance of power. Similarly, Germany's countervailing resolidification of her old Triple Alliance with Austria and Italy was in tune with "classical" principles.

This bipolarization of the European balance, when superimposed on the competitive exploitation of nationalist movements in the Balkans by Austria and Russia, put all the elements in place for the conflagration that was sparked in the summer of 1914 by the assassination of the heir to the throne of the Austro-Hungarian empire by a Serbian nationalist.

Given the overwhelming propensies in the balance of power system in

1914 for a test of strength between the Triple Entente (Britain, France, and Russia) and the Central European powers (Germany and Austria), the British effort at the last minute to convene the Concert to prevent an all-European war from breaking out was bound to be futile. Indeed, the British diplomatic maneuvering may well have had the perverse effect of convincing the Kaiser that the British might sit out the war even if, despite their warnings, Germany went ahead with its planned invasion of neutral Belgium.

This is not to say that World War I was inevitable. But the evidence is massive that the eighteenth and nineteenth century forms of the balance of power were no longer capable of adequately managing the contradictions of the nation-state system, which by now were weakening its very foundations. The crisis of the increasingly anachronistic old order is starkly rendered in a retrospective historical account:

> For the men and women who lived through the first week of August 1914, the outstanding impression was of the cheering, singing, marching masses. It was the same before the Winter Palace in St. Petersburg, on the Unter den Linden in Berlin, on the Champs Elysees in Paris, in Trafalgar Square or the Mall in London.
>
> It was as if the expanding wealth and multiplying populations, as if the unconscious boredom of peace over so many unbroken years had stored up in the nations a terrific potential, which only waited for an accident to touch it off. Far from being innocents led to the slaughter, the peoples of Europe led their leaders. Ministers of Tsar, Kaiser, King, and President watched the press and the streets during these demented days and fell victim to the hysteria as helplessly as any of the nameless multitudes about them. It was as if some historic fatality, expressing itself in a sort of elemental mass passion, for a moment had suspended all the normal processes of reason and humanity.[15]

VARIANT 3: THE LEAGUE OF NATIONS AND THE UNITED NATIONS—EXPERIMENTS WITH "COLLECTIVE SECURITY"

The immediate legacy of the failure of balance-of-power diplomacy to prevent World War I was the effort, led by US President Woodrow Wilson, to supplant the traditional self-help/alliance system with a new system of "collective security." But this would require a more fundamental transformation of the world polity than was contemplated in the new international arrangements negotiated by Wilson, the British Prime Minister David Lloyd George, and the French Premier Georges Clemenceau in the Peace Conference of 1919. (The other principal world ally at the start of the war, Russia, since October 1917 under the leadership of Lenin and his Bolshevik party, had signed a separate peace with Germany before the war's end and therefore was not regarded as one of the victor powers.)

Wilson went into the Peace Conference as a world-order idealist, asking for a peace that would be generous to the defeated countries, a peace "without victory" for either side, a peace of universal "justice." It should provide for the self-determination of peoples and for general disarmament. Above all, and of greatest urgency, the postwar arrangements should include a League of Nations to supervise the peace and promote justice through common international action to resolve conflicts and dissuade aggression.[16]

But Wilson's confreres at the Peace Conference were agents for both the historic power interests of their respective countries and for the popular nationalistic sentiments whipped up by their governments in order to sustain support for the long and bloody conflict. (The French lost over 1.5 million lives and the British 917,000, as compared with 127,000 Americans.[17]) They saw the historical moment as an opportunity to fundamentally reduce German power through a punitive peace. Lloyd George was particularly anxious to take over most of Germany's colonial commerce. Clemenceau, representing a vindictive French nation, was determined to prune Germany down to a minor weight in the new European balance by levying harsh war reparations obligations on Berlin and imposing a wholesale disarmament of the German military establishment. To discourage further collaboration between a defeated Germany and Bolshevik Russia, he insisted on establishing a *cordon sanitaire* by extending the "Polish Corridor" up to the Baltic (principally by making the ethnically German port city of Danzig a "free city" under Polish administration).

The tough negotiations between the victor powers produced the grand bargain signed at Versailles, in which Wilson got his League of Nations (somewhat watered down from his preferences) in exchange for acquiescing to a harsher peace toward Germany and her allies than he believed was just. In the bitterest of ironies, however, Wilson's own countrymen prevented him from collecting on his side of the bargain, when the Congress refused to approve the Treaty of Versailles.

The popular view has it that the League experiment with global collective security was ruined by the American failure to join. To be sure, with US participation and that of Russia and Germany when they were invited in, the international organization would have approximated its goal of universal membership. But the League's inability to significantly transcend the anarchic nation-state system was for the most part predetermined by the fact of the League's being a child of that system and carrying its progenitor's genes into its own basic structure and principal organs.

Article 11 of the Covenant reflected the collective responsibility norms of the nineteenth century Concert, stating that "Any threat of war, whether immediately affecting any members of the League or not, . . . is a matter of concern to the whole League, and the League shall take any action that may be deemed wise and effective to safeguard the peace of nations."

And Articles 12 through 15 inherited and built upon the Hague approach to conflict resolution, obligating members to submit their disputes for resolution to the League Council, the Permanent Court of International Justice or other certified international tribunals, and "in no case to resort to war until three months after the award by the arbiters or the judicial decision or the report by the Council" (the so-called cooling-off period). But, realistically, Article 15 also provided that if the appropriate League bodies were unable to render a decision in such cases, "the members of the League reserve unto themselves the right to take such action as they shall consider necessary for the maintenance of right and justice."

The heart of the League's collective security system was supposed to be Article 16, where it was stipulated that if any country resorted to war in disregard of the provisions of Articles 12 through 15, "it shall, *ipso facto*, be deemed to have committed an act of war against all other Members of the League, which hereby undertake to immediately subject it to the severance of all trade or financial relations, the prohibition of all intercourse between their nationals and the nationals of the Covenant-breaking State, and the prevention of all financial, commercial or personal intercourse between the nationals of any other State, whether a Member of the League or not." In such cases, the Council was to recommend to member countries what military forces they should contribute to a collaborative effort to protect the covenants of the League.[18]

Some of the League's basic premises were highly innovative: War, though still not outlawed, was an abnormal, last-resort method of dealing with international disputes—in contrast to the traditional *realpolitik* view of war as a normal instrument of statecraft. The resort to war before utilizing the League's international dispute-resolution mechanisms, or in disregard of their awards, was illegal. And illegal wars were acts against the whole international community and were to be countered by collective community action.

But the structure through which the new collective security premises were to be implemented was fundamentally conservative in its design and, as such, destined for self-paralysis in important cases. League collective security decisions had to be based on unanimity, excepting the parties to a dispute; but no party to a dispute, if it was a major power, would be without friends on the Council. In any event, League collective security enforcement decisions would always be in the form of recommendatory resolutions. There was a strong "moral" obligation on the part of members to conform to League resolutions, but no country in joining the League gave up a whit of its legal sovereignty.

The extent of the League's power (and impotence) was most starkly exposed in 1935, when Italy, then under the fascist dictatorship of Benito Mussolini, invaded Ethiopia. The League did brand the invasion an illegal aggression; and the Council in this case did invoke the Article 16 sanctions system, asking members to embargo sales of arms and strategic materials to Italy, excepting oil (Italy's most strategically crucial import!). Fifty-two countries made credible attempts to comply with the League's embargo resolutions, but the effects on Mussolini's ability to prosecute his bullying action were negligible.

The only two powers that might have been able to challenge Italy militarily, France and Britain, were preoccupied with domestic problems and not at all anxious to assume the burden of organizing military sanctions since none of their vital geopolitical interests were in immediate jeopardy. Within a year, Ethiopia had been totally absorbed by Italy, and the League—true to its legalistic deference to nation-state sovereignty—found itself in the anomalous position of denying a hearing to the erstwhile Ethiopian Emperor, Haile Selassie, whom it had been trying to protect from Mussolini's brutal aggression.

Other aggressor nations took note of the League's perverse role as a mechanism for mobilizing countervailing power. Not only was it unable to provide timely and decisive opposition to Mussolini's power play against hapless Ethiopia, but its existence as the world's security agency of first resort provided an excuse for countries to refrain from reacting as they might have otherwise—unilaterally or through alliances to counter acts of aggressive expansion. The Japanese invasion of China in 1937 and Hitler's moves the following year against Austria and Czechoslovakia were, if anything, tempted by the power vacuum surrounding the League's collective security system.

So irrelevant had the League become as a mechanism for managing the balance of power that when England and France finally declared war against Hitler in 1939 in response to his invasion of Poland, they did not even bother to invoke the collective security provisions of Article 16.[19]

Paradoxically, World War II, which confirmed for statesmen the irrelevance of the League, was attributed by laypersons the world over to the failure of the major powers to support and utilize the League. The United Nations embodies this paradox in its Charter, which provides for a reincarnated collective security system that is a synthesis of divergent elite and popular notions of how the balance of power should work.

Neither Winston Churchill nor Joseph Stalin nor Franklin D. Roosevelt had any desire to resurrect the League. Their preference was to project their Big Three wartime concert into the postwar world. FDR was a Wilsonian only in his belief that the democratically ascertained "self-determination" of peoples was the essential basis for a stable and peaceful nation-state system. In contrast to Wilson, he wanted the conflict-management tasks for the system to be provided by the Big Three, who would continue to act in concert as the "world's policemen" (each patrolling, as it were, a sphere of influence), joined eventually by France and China in a five-power concert.

The Big Three differed with each other in their wartime conferences mainly over precisely where the postwar spheres of influences would be drawn, how much autonomy was to be allowed each of the hegemons to control its own sphere, and how to deal with the defeated enemy countries. The design of a United Nations Organization, which they agreed to in broad outline, was worked out at a conference of foreign ministers and occupied very little of their time at the summit.

The structure of the UN surfaced as a relatively minor controversial issue at the Yalta Conference in February 1945 when Stalin asked for separate voting seats in the General Assembly for the various "autonomous republics" of the USSR. But the issue was disposed of rapidly as FDR and Churchill agreed to let Stalin have two extra seats as a compromise (one each for the Ukraine and Belorussia). The Western leaders had no qualms in allowing this without getting compensatory representation (say, for Scotland or Texas) since they regarded the Assembly as just a debating forum and assumed that only the Security Council, in which each of the Big Five would retain a veto, would have the potential for developing into a real decision-making body.[20]

There were important domestic political constituencies in Britain and the United States for a revived and strengthened universal collective security system—for a League of Nations "with teeth"—to whom Roosevelt and Churchill felt it necessary to cater, as well as to many of the smaller countries that helped the Allies in the war against Germany and Japan and whose cooperation would be important in the postwar world. Internationalists in the US State Department and in the British Foreign Ministry were therefore given encouragement to work out with their Soviet counterparts the outline of a possible weighty collective security apparatus for the United Nations, under the clear proviso that it would be directly controlled by the Security Council (where the veto still would prevail). The outcome of these deliberations was the unprecedented—but ultimately unworkable—set of provisions for a truly international military force contained in Chapter VII of the Charter.

Chapter VII stipulates that the "Security Council...may take action by air, sea, or land forces as may be necessary to maintain or restore international peace and security" (Article 42); and it obligates all members "to make available to the Security Council, on its call in accordance with a special agreement or agreements, armed forces, assistance, and facilities, including rights of passage, necessary for maintaining international peace and security" (Article 43). Anticipating such contributions of forces to UN military actions, the Charter further stipulates (in Article 47) that

> 1. There shall be established a Military Staff Committee to advise and assist the Security Council on all questions relating to the Security Council's military requirements for the maintenance of international peace and security, the employment and command of forces placed at its disposal, the regulation of armaments, and possible disarmament.
> 2. The Military Staff Committee shall consist of the Chiefs of Staff of the permanent members of the Security Council or their representatives. . . .

> 3. The Military Staff Committee shall be responsible under the Security Council for the strategic direction of any armed forces placed at the disposal of the Security Council. . . .[21]

If the Military Staff Committee were ever to receive the contributions of forces contemplated in Chapter VII of the Charter, it would be a full-blooded *supra*national military force, but quite clearly under the political control of an intergovernmental body (the Security Council) with no more supranational characteristics than existed when the nineteenth century statesmen came together, in the Concert System, for their big-power conferences.

United Nations police forces have been formed for limited "peacekeeping" actions (the interpositon of a UN presence to oversee cease-fires, truce agreements, and the like), as distinct from collective security; but these usually have been organized on an ad hoc basis under the management of the Secretary General, directly responsible to the Security Council or General Assembly, and bypassing the Military Staff Committee.

Some of the Chapter VII collective security provisions were invoked to establish the "United Nations Peace Action" of 1950 to repel the North Korean invasion of South Korea. But this was actually a US response draped in the UN flag and was possible only because of the USSR's temporary absence from the Security Council during the vote on the authorizing resolution.[22] To preserve the definition of the Korean action as a UN collective security operation even after the USSR returned to the Security Council, the United States was compelled to resort to the device of a General Assembly "Uniting for Peace Resolution" asserting the Assembly's authority to act when the Security Council was unable, because of the veto, to exercise its primary responsibility for peace and security.[23] These uses of the UN as the instrument of a particular country's or bloc's interests in opposition to one of the permanent members clearly contradict the conservative design of the Charter and, if frequently relied upon by members with a majority in either the General Assembly or the Security Council, would probably force a pullout from the organization of the countries in the minority.

The Charter's formulators explicitly anticipated the incapacity of the UN to serve traditional but still necessary power-balancing needs in the nation-state system. Article 51 accordingly legitimizes bypassing the UN in such circumstances, by allowing for "individual or collective self-defense if an armed attack occurs against a Member of the United Nations, until the Security Council has taken the measures necessary to maintain international peace and security." To garner popular support for the resort to such bypassing strategies, the United States and its allies, when forming the North Atlantic Treaty Organization in 1949, cited Article 51 to back their claim that NATO was consistent with the letter and spirit of the UN Charter, as did the Soviet Union and its allies in forming the Warsaw Pact in 1955.

The post-World War II collective security institutions, in short, were elaborated in the midst of the emergent bipolarization of international relations; more so than the institutions of the League, they were carefully designed to survive, unused if it came to that, in the basic nation-state system while more traditional balance-of-power and/or concert diplomacy took over once again.

VARIANT 4: COLD WAR BIPOLARITY

As it turned out, the bipolar configuration of world politics that developed out of World War II was in many respects a throwback to the norms of statecraft of the period of religious wars. The diplomacy of the so-called cold war differed from the diplomacy of the classical balance of power, concert, and collective security systems more than any of these previous configurations differed from each other. In the cold war, the great powers once again, as during the wars of religion, found justification for intervening in each other's internal affairs, for practicing subversion and sponsoring civil wars in the opposing camp, and for defining the rivalry between coalitions as a contest between good and evil.

The roots of this modern bipolarization of world politics were at once geopolitical and ideological.

On the "western" side (which not incidentally included the recently defeated far-eastern power, Japan) the geopolitical explanations for the emergent post-World War II bipolarity went back to de Tocqueville, the early nineteenth century French observer of American democracy, who saw the United States and Russia each "marked out by the will of Heaven to sway the destinies of half the globe."[24] More concretely, the cold war strategists sought justification for their policies in the works of the seminal Anglo-American military geopolitical theorists of the pre-World War I period—especially Captain Alfred Thayer Mahan and Sir Halford MacKinder—who had postulated a fundamental contest for global ascendancy between an expansive Russian empire and the insular states: Britain, the United States, and Japan. The cold war geopoliticians seized upon the "heartland/rimland" concepts popular before World War I to propound freshly the old imperative: Hold the rimlands around the vast Eurasian land mass, for if the resources and sea access of the rimland areas were absorbed by the power that also controlled the heartland (now the Soviet Union), that power would dominate the world.[25]

The thrust of Russian foreign policy since Peter the Great had a special clarity and meaning in light of new preoccupation with Soviet expansionism. The straits connecting the Black Sea and the Mediterranean, the approaches to the Gulf of Finland and the Baltic, nationality groups along the invasion routes from the West, the Oriental populations of Sinkiang and Mongolia, the northern Japanese territories—all of these had been periodically the direct targets of Russian military threats or diplomatic power plays. And now, having emerged from World War II a first-ranking great power, second to none on the Eurasian land mass, the Russians were at it again.

The geopoliticians in the Kremlin were themselves rereading the geopolitical classics and, knowing that their American counterparts were reviving the classical assumptions, had ample grounds for their own new worries. As is characteristic of most nation-states, Russia invariably justified its expansionist moves as dictated by minimum security needs; and, to be sure, its long history of constant suffering from attacks by enemies on all sides gave considerable credence to the posture. Added to the traditional Russian suspicions of British and French ambitions on the rimland were the Bolshevik suspicions that, being a socialist nation, the Soviet Union's continued existence was now intolerable to the capitalists. The Soviets, accordingly, were prone to see the West's containment policy as nothing less than a strategy of encirclement and strangulation.[26]

Thus, by the early 1950s, the official wisdom in Moscow and Washington reflected a set of remarkably similar geopolitical notions, presumed in both capitals to be self-evident:

1. The role of the United States as the leader of a broad anticommunist coalition was inescapable, since the Soviet Union could expand into the power vacuums of Europe, Asia, and the Middle East if the nations of these areas did not have the protection of the United States.
2. The Soviet Union, even if it abandoned or postponed its professed goal of transforming the world into a system of soviets, would continue to fear imperialist world wars and capitalist encirclement and therefore was bound to secure its borders in the West, East, and South. These fears would drive it to assure the absolute loyalty of regimes in Eastern Europe and wherever else on the periphery of the USSR allies could be signed on.
3. This historically determined power configuration—two rival superpowers separated by power vacuums—made inevitable a clash of vital interests in the areas between. War over any of these interests became an ever-present possibility.
4. Consequently, an advantageous global balance of military power and access to zones of potential combat would be sought by each superpower. This competition for military advantage created additional geopolitical imperatives—economic resources, manpower, and bases for military operations—for maintaining large and highly coordinated multilateral coalitions.

From these perspectives, national security was so dependent upon the cohesion of one's coalition that the coalition itself tended to be regarded as an end rather than a means. At the least, the strength and cohesion of the coalition were thought to be the sine qua non for the pursuit of other valued objectives.

The geopolitical incentives for polarization were reinforced by ideology. From the outset of their formation, each of the cold war coalitions was assumed to be a community of basic common beliefs no less than an alliance to marshall power for the defense of territorial objectives. Although the standard code words such as "free world" and "socialist commonwealth" were inadequate descriptions of the values adhered to by members in each camp, they did reflect a very real difference in general approach to domestic and world order that established two rival ideological centers of gravity around which most nations tended to coalesce. The collective military force of each coalition was presumed to be available to protect a "way of life" or the "rules of the international game" as well as pieces of real estate critical to the balance of power.

The socialist camp, as viewed from Moscow, was a community of communist political parties—in some countries in control of the government, elsewhere still in opposition—which represented the class interests of the proletarians. Differences in tactics and priorities that might exist between national branches of this movement were dwarfed by their common adherence to "proletarian internationalism," which put them in universal opposition to governments and parties representing the capitalist classes. The allocation of tasks for the grand struggle against the capitalists, for the time being, required all parties to support the state interests of the USSR. But specialization of effort also obligated the USSR to protect weaker elements of the community in their confrontations with locally powerful capitalists—subject to the proviso that local communist parties could not expect to be bailed out of suicidal situations that were the product of un-Marxist adventurism; namely, moves in advance of the full ripening of revolutionary conditions in particular countries.[27]

By attaching credibility to the ideological motives in Soviet foreign policy and to the international behavior of other communist regimes and parties, the leaders of most of the free-world countries—at least those in the North Atlantic region and Japan—gave serious ideological content to the non-communist coalition. The concept "free," however it might be stretched with respect to the character of domestic society, came to mean being anticommunist internationally. It became necessary to resist the assumption of power by communists or regimes willing to align themselves with the international communist movement on important international issues, as well as to resist the overt extension of communist control by military aggression. Who was in whose camp ideologically would largely determine the extent of military commitments by the superpowers and the lineup of military allies in case of general war. From the point of view of the United States, being against the extension of communism was usually sufficient to qualify a nation as a member of the free world coalition; and the ideologies of national self-determination and international pluralism countenanced the presence in the coalition of some rather curious species of free society (the Greek, Turkish, and Spanish autocracies, for example, plus various Latin American and other Third World military dictatorships).

The bipolar configuration of the balance of power seemed most natural from the late 1940s to the early 1960s—the "high cold war" period—when the rival coalitions had little interaction that was not confrontational, when the common assumption was that one side's gain was the other side's loss, when Moscow and Washington charged each other with understanding only the language of force, and when, therefore, the balance of power was essentially a balance of military power.

The equation of overall power with military power tended to reinforce the bipolar legacy of World War II, since even the reviving centers of economic and political energy in Europe and Japan and China could not hope to rival the "super" military power—particularly the strategic nuclear weaponry—of the United States and the Soviet Union. When push came to shove in any conflict between a lesser power and one of the superpowers, the lesser power would either have to capitulate or seek the military protection of the other superpower.

As long as the United States and the Soviet Union retained their unchallenged military superpower status relative to the other countries, the bipolar structure presumably would persist. Consistent with this expectation, the grand strategies pursued by both Moscow and Washington in the 1950s and early 1960s were designed to tighten the bipolar system so as to make it more controllable and predictable, and—consonant with the then-fashionable theories of deterrence— also safer.

But the two-camps world turned out to be much less cohesive and durable than the bipolarists of the 1950s and early 1960s hoped. Older relationships, temporarily suppressed by the devastation of World War II, and new forces spawned by the technological innovations of the twentieth century began to erode not only the cold war structures but also the very foundations of the nation-state system itself. These developments and what they portend for the future of world politics are analyzed in the following chapters.

ENDNOTES

1. Morton A. Kaplan, *System and Process in International Politics* (New York: Wiley, 1962), pp. 49–50.

2. Evan Luard, *Types of International Society* (New York: Free Press, 1976), p. 328.

3. Gordon A. Craig and Alexander L. George, *Force and Statecraft: Diplomatic Problems of Our Time* (New York: Oxford University Press, 1983), p. 21.

4. My account of conditions in Europe during the period of the classical balance of power is informed by the accounts of Luard, *Types of International Society*; Edward V. Gullick, *Europe's Classical Balance of Power* (Ithaca: Cornell University Press, 1955); and Richard Rosecrance, *Action and Reaction in World Politics* (Boston: Little, Brown, 1963).

5. Hans J. Morgenthau, *Politics among Nations* (New York: Knopf, 1978 [5th edition, revised]), p. 449.

6. Luard, *Types of International Society*, pp. 162–166.

7. *Ibid.*, p. 165.

8. See Gordon Craig's account of the workings of the balance of power between 1815 and 1914 in Gordon A. Craig and Alexander L. George, *Force and Statecraft*, pp. 28–47.

9. Henry A. Kissinger, *A World Restored: The Politics of Conservatism in a Revolutionary Age* (New York: Grosset & Dunlop, 1964).

10. Luard, *Types of International Society*, pp. 330–332.

11. Inis L. Claude, Jr., *Swords into Plowshares: The Problems and Progress of International Organization* (New York: Random House, 1984), p. 39.

12. Hajo Holborn, *The Political Collapse of Europe* (New Haven: Yale University Press, 1957), pp. 43–50.

13. Bismarck's warning is quoted by Holborn, *ibid.*, p. 47.

14. Rosecrance, *Action and Reaction*, pp. 149–168.

15. Frank P. Chambers, Christina Phelps Harris, and Charles C. Bayley, *This Age of Conflict: 1914 to the Present* (New York: Harcourt Brace, 1950), p. 16.

16. Arthur S. Link, *Woodrow Wilson, Revolution, War, and Peace* (Arlington Heights: Harlan Davidson, 1979); and Robert E. Osgood, *Ideals and Self-Interest in American Foreign Relations* (Chicago: University of Chicago Press, 1953).

17. Statistics on lives lost in World War I are from Francis A. Beer, *Peace against War: The Ecology of International Violence* (San Francisco: W. H. Freeman, 1981), p. 37.

18. *Covenant of the League of Nations,* Signed at Versailles 28 June 1919 (Geneva: League of Nations, 1920).

19. See the discussion of the League's collective security system in Seyom Brown, *The Causes and Prevention of War* (New York: St. Martin's Press, 1987), pp. 154–158.

20. On Big Three wartime planning for the United Nations, see John Lewis Gaddis, *The United States and the Origins of the Cold War, 1941-1947* (New York: Columbia University Press, 1972), pp. 27–30, 153–154; and Daniel Yergen, *Shattered Peace: The Origins of the Cold War and the National Security State* (Boston: Houghton Mifflin, 1977), pp. 47–48.

21. *Charter of the United Nations,* Chapter VII.

22. United Nations Document S/1587.

23. United Nations Document A/1481.

24. Alexis de Tocqueville, *Democracy in America*, Vol. I (New York: Random House, Vintage Books, 1954), p. 452.

25. The legacy of Anglo-American geopolitical thought drawn upon by the cold war strategists is found in Alfred Thayer Mahan, *The Problem of Asia and Its Effects upon International Relations* (Boston: Little, Brown, 1900); Halford MacKinder, "The Geopolitical Pivot of History," *Geographical Journal*, Vol. 23 (1904), pp. 421–441; and Nicholas Spykman, *The Geography of the Peace* (New York: Harcourt Brace, 1944). My interpretation of the essential similarities among Mahan, MacKinder, and latter-day western geopoliticians finds support in Stephen B. Jones, "Global Strategic Views," *Geopolitical Review*, Vol. 45 (1955), pp. 492–508.

26. According to the *Survey of Fifty Years of the Soviet Union*, published by the Central Committee in 1967, the socialist industrialization of the USSR, "had to be undertaken in conditions of our country's capitalist encirclement, and of constant danger of an armed attack by the aggressive power of imperialism." Quoted by Alexander Werth, *Russia: Hopes and Fears* (New York: Simon and Schuster, 1969), p. 30.

27. Zbigniew Brzezinski, *Ideology and Power in Soviet Politics* (New York: Praeger, 1962), pp. 97–113.

PART TWO

The Existing System in Crisis

The existing system of world politics—still fundamentally a nation-state system, still relying mainly on the international power-balancing process to sustain its basic norm of national sovereignty—is being assaulted simultaneously at many levels:

- With modern military technology rendering even the superpowers vulnerable to total destruction, the credibility of alliances, the system's principal equilibrating mechanism, has been cast into severe doubt. No longer can a country count on alliance partners joining it in a hot war against an enemy armed with weapons of mass destruction.

- The ability of countries to sustain orderly commerce and social justice within their borders is being undermined as national policies for the regulation of national markets are ignored or overwhelmed by buyers and sellers unaccountable to either the political and legal institutions of the nation or its social welfare policies.

- Increasingly, humans are producing large-scale and severe alterations in the natural environment—threatening vital ecosystems that traverse national lines and that are sometimes global in scope. Yet in most regions of the globe there are no legal mechanisms to assure international accountability, let alone international liability, for such transborder disturbances.

- Communications and economic activity that leap national borders are homogenizing the cultural diversity that heretofore has been one of the main contributions of the nation-state system to world society. At the same time, the new technologies for moving people, things, and information rapidly over vast distances are reviving and reuniting cultural groups whose members have been separated by political boundaries and subordinated into alien national cultures.

Cumulatively, these trends have been producing a new incongruence between, on the one hand, the inherited political-legal organization of world society—the nation-state system with its superpower-led coalitions—and, on the other hand, many of the most active and dynamic patterns of interaction, both material and human.

The chapters in Part Two examine the sources and consequences of this growing incongruence between the formal political structure of international relations and societal substance of world politics.

Chapter 3 presents an overview of the emergent challenges to the durability of the cold war coalitions and to the foundations of the nation-state system. It anticipates the more detailed analyses in subsequent chapters of the ways in which the new forces (and revived old forces) are eroding inherited military alliances, ideological bonds, and economic relationships while establishing new and more complex patterns of association.

Chapters 4 and 5 examine, respectively, the effects of these challenges in the anticommunist and Marxist coalitions. In the anticommunist coalition, the visibility and pervasiveness of the new complexities are greater, but the inherited structures of politics and government seem more capable of constructive adaptation. By comparison, the challenges to established institutions in the Marxist coalition—at least prior to Gorbachev's *glasnost*—have been infrequent and isolated, reflecting repressive policies by ruling parties fearful of the explosive potential of cultural pluralism and political liberalism.

Chapter 6 analyzes the growing cooperative interaction between the Marxist and non-Marxist countries—between the United States and the Soviet Union, between the United States and China, between the two superpowers and lesser members of the other's coalition, and between lesser members of each camp across the ideological divide. The prospects for continued expansion of East–West commerce and transideological political relationships are found to be stronger than the prospects for a reconsolidation of cold war bipolarity.

Chapter 7 is devoted to the tensions between the affluent industrialized countries and the economically disadvantaged countries. It assays attempts of the economically disadvantaged to act as a Third World coalition, in particular to pressure the affluent to enter into negotiations for a New International Economic Order that would redistribute wealth and power to the disadvantaged countries.

Chapter 8 deals with the capacity of the nation-state system to subordinate the behavior of transnational economic forces, especially multinational corporations, to the purposes and laws of the world's organized political communities.

Chapter 9 explores the extent to which modern technologies are overwhelming the ability of the separate nation-state to provide the rudiments of public order, health, and safety for the Earth's human population. The continued lack of effective international controls over threats to the natural environment and essential ecologies, it is argued, could place the survival of the entire human species in jeopardy.

The general picture arising from the analyses in Chapters 3 through 10 is of a nation-state system grossly deficient, as now structured, in its capacity to respond to the security, welfare, and justice predicaments of contemporary human society. Part Two thus establishes the need to consider plausible alternative configurations of world politics—the task of the subsequent chapters.

CHAPTER THREE

The Forces of Erosion

From the vantage point of the late 1980s, it is clear that the sporadic disintegrative rumblings in both major cold war coalitions during the past three decades have been symptomatic of growing instabilities in the bipolar structure that has lain heavily on the nation-state system since the end of World War II. The progressive loosening of coalition unity in the US-led and Soviet-led camps that began to cause each of the superpowers trouble as early as the mid-1950s, the widespread appeal of cold war *non*alignment among the new states of the Third World, and some major defections (especially China from the Soviet side in the 1960s and Iran from the US side in 1979) have been more than shifts in the surface strata of world politics. They have been the product rather of basic changes in geostrategic realities interacting with strong centrifugal political and economic forces, which together have been fragmenting the bipolar structure of the cold war system. They remind us that the "natural" condition of world politics is pluralistic—surely more pluralistic than the two-camps world implied in many of the cold war policies of the United States and the Soviet Union.

It would be a mistake, however, to view the weakening of bipolarity as indicating merely the revival of the traditional nation-state system that had been temporarily suppressed by the cold war. The shocks along the cold war fault-line emanate from deep undercurrents of change that are eroding some of the foundations of the nation-state system itself.

Some of the erosive forces are at the same time potentially integrative—in the sense of bringing together and freshly bonding various old communities as well as new communities. But the rediscovery and reconsolidation of old community ties (say, of ethnic groups dispersed among different countries) and the forging of new ones (say, among international financial elites or among peace-movement activists) are often incongruent with both the boundaries of the existing nation-states and the dominant coalitions led by the United States and the Soviet Union.

The threats to the prevailing structures of world politics have not gone unanswered by those who benefit materially and psychologically from the established system. Indeed, by the late 1970s the maturing challenges to the post-World War II order had provoked a revival of conservatism, in the sense of cold war ideological orthodoxy and the kind of patriotism that focuses on threats from the rival ideological camp. In the West, the conservative reaction was most visible in the election of Ronald Reagan in 1980 and the attempt of his administration to reforge a global "strategic consensus" against Soviet expansion. In the Soviet camp, the revival of orthodoxy was epitomized by the Kremlin's 1981 crackdown on the popular dissident worker's Solidarity movement in Poland. But by the latter 1980s, a counterreaction to Reaganism was in full swing in the West and the entire Soviet sphere was struggling to adapt to Mikhail Gorbachev's reformist efforts.

Whether the forces of erosion or the forces of reconsolidation ultimately will win out cannot be predicted. What can be confidently anticipated is the persistence into the 1990s of world-wide tension between the new forces and the old forces among and within the countries of the dominant international coalitions.

This tension between the forces for change and the forces for reconsolidation is shaking the foundations of the post-World War II order most visibly in the fields of military security and economics. The tension also is reverberating in the ideological cement of the cold war coalitions, and even in the soil of the nationalism that nourishes the nation-state system.

THE CONSTRICTION OF EXTENDED SECURITY COMMITMENTS

The new military realities experienced in the Second World War, particularly the extension of the range and destructive power of weapons and the elaborate economic base needed to sustain modern warfare, seemed to validate the prophecies of early twentieth century geopoliticians in Britain and the United States that the security of the Western countries required a globe-spanning and permanent coalition against any imperialistic Eurasian power. And Stalin seemed justified in insisting that the security of the USSR required, at a minimum, a recognized sphere of Soviet dominance covering Eastern Europe. But paradoxically, the very technologies that were thought to be making national security through national means obsolete were soon to call into question the utility of the rival extended security communities established by the United States and the Soviet Union.

Today, the superpowers are reassessing the value of forward-defense allies, and the allies are increasingly skeptical of the credibility of superpower promises of protection.

As missiles and bombers have become truly intercontinental, neither superpower needs distant allies to extend its lethal reach into the home territory of the other. Such allies might perhaps still be strategically desirable in a US–Soviet war, for confounding enemy defenses and complicating enemy offensive targeting; but they no longer provide indispensable strategic-warfare assets to the superpowers. Nor does either superpower, with reconnaissance systems in orbit around the earth, require bases near the other's frontiers to gain adequate warning of menacing deployments or impending attack.

Meanwhile, the costs and risks to the superpowers of attempting to protect their allies by direct military means has been rising. Any war between the United States and the Soviet Union, it is recognized on both sides, carries the danger of spiraling into an all-out nuclear war—a war in which there would be no winner; a war that would destroy one's own society along with the enemy's; a war that risks bringing on a global "nuclear winter" severe enough to extinguish the conditions necessary for the survival of the human species.[1]

The potential implications of the balance of terror between the nuclear superpowers for their respective allies were drawn by French President Charles de Gaulle as far back as the late 1950s, in his apocalyptic vision of a war in which Western Europe was incinerated from Moscow and Central Europe incinerated from Washington while Russia and America held back from directly attacking each other's homeland. Such anxieties have provided strategic justification for Britain to stay in the nuclear club, for France and China to build independent nuclear arsenals, and for India, Pakistan, Israel, and South Africa (among others) to develop the technical option to manufacture and deploy their own nuclear weapons.

It can be argued that the strategic standoff between the superpowers, far from nullifying the military reasons for extended alliance systems, has enhanced their importance; for without very firm and unambiguous commitments to come to the defense of one's friends, the enemy would in fact discount risks of staging faits accompli. This only states the problem without resolving it, however, since it is precisely the disproportion between the terrible physical costs of a major war against the opposing superpower and the less tangible political costs of backing out of an alliance commitment at the moment of truth that has reduced the credibility of alliances.

In theory, the credibility of alliance commitments can be sustained through doctrines, plans, and deployments for fighting "limited" wars. And indeed the prevailing geopolitical wisdom at least in the United States since the 1960s has been that mutual deterrence at the strategic level brings into prominence limited contests for local position with conventional or paramilitary forces. But suggestions from some American strategists that it would be good to institutionalize war limitations through a nuclear "no first-use" regime engender adamant protests from European strategists who worry that relieving the

Soviets of the fear that any major East–West war would turn into a global nuclear holocaust could tempt the Soviets to engage in power plays in Berlin and elsewhere in Europe, under the assumption that the risks of escalation could be controlled.[2]

In addition to engendering doubts about the credibility of US and Soviet pledges to protect their alliance partners, the realization that a limited war among the superpowers is still a distinct possibility in the nuclear age has stimulated military planners to apply the fruits of the technological revolution to conventional operations as well as to strategic nuclear ones. This in turn has led to reassessments of the importance of various locational and topographic factors in determining what foreign objectives are worth fighting for and how to fight for them—with implications that are not always positive for alliance relationships.

It is now widely recognized among strategists that communications and transportation technologies have reduced the significance of distance from the zone of battle in assessing the material costs of a military campaign. These developments have increased the ease with which military operations in remote theaters can be commenced and sustained. They have also reduced the military significance of some traditional intercontinental access routes, as improvements in air freight capabilities and economies in ocean shipping have lowered the costs of substitute routes. Today about six straits are considered geopolitically crucial whereas in the 1940s and 1950s about twenty straits were so considered. Developments in airlift, sealift, and instant communications have also reduced the military requirements for prepositioning troops and weapons in the locale of potential conflict.[3]

Simultaneously, the value of remote military bases as communication links for local wars has been declining. For conventional as well as strategic warfare, reconnaissance methods have been reassessed in the light of technological innovations—particularly the deployment of space satellites for surveillance and information relays—which can supplant battlefront or nearby observation posts and command and control headquarters. Thus, although the US military communications base in Kagnew, Ethiopia, had previously been portrayed by the Pentagon as a vital facility for gaining intelligence on Soviet activities in Southwest Asia and the Indian Ocean, its loss in the wake of a series of coups in the mid-1970s that turned Ethiopia into a Soviet client state has been adjusted to. Similarly, forward intelligence-gathering facilities in Iran, previously declared to be essential to US national security, but no longer available to the United States after the anti-United States Khomeinists deposed the Shah in 1979, have been largely substituted for by aerospace capabilities.

All in all, the new mobility and communications technologies impact ambiguously on superpower incentives to construct alliance relationships around the globe and to intervene on their behalf. On the one hand, the advanced technologies are making it less critical for the superpowers to become engaged on foreign soil and easier for them to disengage from previous commitments. On the other hand, many of these very same technologies make it physically easier to establish a presence in remote areas. The USSR has become a global commercial power, able to provide naval escort to its shipping in all theaters; and it now displays fleets in the Mediterranean, Persian Gulf, and Indian Ocean that make more creditable than ever before its capability to intervene in local conflicts. US military planning, premised on the development of huge airborne and naval transport craft for rapid deployment of troops and equipment, points toward basing US limited-war forces primarily at home and maintaining a low profile in client states without diminishing alliance security commitments. This means that while the cost of being denied access to many areas of the globe (previously defined as strategically essential) are easier to bear than the probable costs of fighting for the territory, the relative costs of getting to these places are also reduced. Both the United States and the USSR can cast their interest nets more widely, but fewer external interests merit being considered vital in a military sense.

In determining how much to invest in the protection of foreign countries, more weight must now be given to nonmilitary criteria—ideological or cultural affinity, marginal economic advantage, or simply how one's reputation for fidelity and toughness might be affected by a failure to protect even a marginal interest when challenged. In cases where such criteria still compel the perservation of a mutual defense relationship, there will be attempts by partners to assure one another of continued fidelity through symbolic deployments, joint exercises, and other visible acts that make it politically costly to renege on established commitments. But as no nation can be assumed to have an unswerving commitment to defend the interests of another nation, the major countries can be expected to incline increasingly toward postures of self-reliance when it comes to protection against military attack—self-reliance meaning mass-destruction capabilities under their own control and sufficient diplomatic flexibility to make deals unilaterally with their adversaries.

The technologically induced erosion of extended mutual security commitments cannot avoid undermining core alliance structures, especially where these involve visible deployments (weapons facilities and troops) and large budgetary outlays that become the subjects of public and parliamentary debate. As statesmen and military strategists perceive the advantages of flexible military arrangements that allow them considerable leeway to opt in or out of collective alliance actions on an ad hoc basis, they are likely to seek such flexibility by avoiding both the peacetime deployment of weapons, troops, and other military facilities on each other's soil and wartime contingency plans that depend on such foreign bases.

THE SLACKENING OF IDEOLOGICAL BONDS

The most powerful socially bonding ideas within countries and between them tend to be ideologies focusing on the malevolent character of opponents more than the principles around which one's own side is organized. The need to present a united front against "those who threaten our way of life " appears to have been the major stimulus to the coalescence of political communities throughout recorded history.[4] Conversely, the disappearance of the villain—either by his defeat, his reform, or simply the neutralization of his capabilities for doing harm—has frequently been an important cause of the disintegration of previously united communities.

This dynamic relationship between we/they ideologies and political cohesion has had different manifestations in each of the cold war coalitions, and these will be detailed in Chapters 4, 5, and 6. Here, anticipating that analysis, the international determinants of the ideological erosion evident in each coalition will be highlighted.

For Soviet and Chinese ideologists as well as other Marxists, the evident willingness of the capitalist countries, since at least the mid-1960s, to accept a relationship of coexistence has posed doctrinal problems.

According to orthodox Marxism–Leninism, the growing power of the socialist forces should have brought the world that much closer to the inevitable cataclysm, since the capitalists were not expected to come to terms peacefully with the new "correlation of forces" (Soviet term for the global balance of economic, political, and military power). The Leninists believed it was precisely out of fear of being on the losing side that the capitalists, anticipating a shift in the balance of power, would be most likely to launch an intendedly preventive but ultimately suicidal war.

But once it was admitted by the Kremlin that a world war would be mutually suicidal—the official Soviet doctrine since the mid-Khrushchev period—the prediction of a final bloody struggle to bring about the worldwide victory of socialism needed revision. In a nuclear holocaust, the workers would lose more than their chains. As the Soviet Communist Party put it in one of its doctrinal disputes with the Chinese Communist party, "The nuclear bomb does not distinguish between the imperialists and the working people, it hits great areas, and therefore millions of workers would be destroyed for one monopolist."[5] The final victory would arrive rather (the Soviet theoreticians now gleaned from Marx's own writings) through a succession of transformations of the capitalist states *from within.*

The primary diplomatic task of the leading Marxist states, therefore, has become to stabilize relations among the great powers to the degree necessary to prevent global war, while the historical revolutionary process works itself out in the varied domestic societies of the noncommunist world.[6] As explained by the American Sovietologist Marshall Shulman, the strategy of peaceful coexistence, originally a tactical response to adverse situations requiring a breathing spell, became "elongated in time" and was "extended into a long-term strategy, implying a continued acceptance of the necessity for an indirect and more political way of advancing Soviet interests than the militant advocacy of revolution and the use of force."[7]

As detente with the capitalist world was put forward by the Kremlin as a durable policy, to be capped by Soviet–American arms limitations agreements in the common interest of avoiding general war, it became increasingly difficult for Soviet Communist Party theoreticians to sustain the Marxist premise of two implacably contradictory social systems. If world politics was not simply the anticipation of the impending worldwide class war, the urgency for attaining a completely autarchic economy in the socialist commonwealth faded, as did the justification for mobilizing the camp in a rigidly hierarchical system. Indeed, the international economic policy implications of long-term coexistence were reflected in efforts by various communist countries to pursue commercial relations with the noncommunist developed world. The concept of "many roads to socialism" was elaborated in the theoretical treatises and the practice of state parties within the Soviet-led coalition—in some cases (most dramatically the Czechoslovakian "Prague Spring" of 1968) going beyond the threshold of Kremlin tolerance.

In the West, the transformation of the image of the major opponents from a monolithic band of revolutionaries into a feuding group of self-interested states also gradually eroded the ideological foundations of the extensive US system of alliances. Once it became generally accepted, as US Secretary of State Dean Rusk put it in 1964, that "the Communist world is no longer a single flock of sheep following blindly one leader,"[8] and that the Soviet Union was unflinchingly putting its state interests ahead of its missionary impulses, then it would appear unnecessary to the security of the whole noncommunist community to oppose each and every expansion of communist influence. Distinctions among communist countries would now seem to be in order, less on the basis of the internal character of their regimes than on the basis of their intentions and capabilities for major international aggression against important Western interests.

This reassessment of the importance and desirability of a global resistance to communism was well under way in the United States and other Western countries by the mid-1960s, when the Johnson administration invoked the hyberbolic ideological conceptions of the 1950s to justify its military intervention in Vietnam. Once again, US anticommunist alliances were defined by Washington policymakers as a seamless web of commitments, which if cut in one place would unravel the whole system.[9] With the failure of the American effort to prevent the communization of Vietnam and the other Indochinese countries—a failure due in part to spreading rejection within the US policy community of the cold war premise that the success of communism anywhere in the world was a threat to the American way of life—a more restrictive set of criteria would determine whether and how the United States should intervene to redress a local imbalance of power favoring the communists.[10] The importance of a particular country's alignment for the global balance of power, the degree of involvement in the local conflict by the Soviet Union, and the symbolic or emotional importance attached to the preexisting commitment— all of these would become more weighty considerations than any general obligation to support members of the "free world" against a communist takeover.

The American souring on ideological anticommunism made Henry Kissinger's classical *realpolitik* concepts palatable to President Nixon and allowed Nixon, whose past political success had been built on his anticommunist rhetoric, to preside over the distinctly nonideological policies of detente with the USSR and rapprochement with China. All high US government officials purged anticommunist rhetoric from their statements; and the President publicly allowed that "it would be a safer world and a better world if we have a strong healthy United States, Europe, Soviet Union, China, Japan; each balancing the other, not playing one against the other, an even balance."[11]

As it turned out, the Nixon–Kissinger *realpolitik* was perhaps too devoid of ideology, or at least prematurely so, to be sustained as American policy over the long run. Critics on the left and on the right called it "amoral," if not immoral. And a bipartisan majority in the Congress coalesced in 1974 to reject the economic centerpiece of the new Soviet–American detente (the extension of normal trading and credit privileges to the Soviets) as long as the Soviets continued to restrict Jewish emigration and to commit other human rights violations.

But, significantly, the revived emphases on human rights and the popular insistence that "America ought once again to stand for something in the world" which helped elect Jimmy Carter in 1976, was not accompanied by a renaissance of anticommunism as such. If anything, the Carter administration officials with responsibility for implementing the new human rights policy were more inclined to bring pressure on right-wing dictators in the US-led coalition (whose trangressions had been larely ignored by previous administrations) than on repressive regimes in the communist world. The shift in attitude was reflected in President Carter's statement that "we are now free of that inordinate fear of communism which once led us to embrace any dictator who joined us in that fear."[12] The President did write a public letter to Soviet dissident Andrei Sakharov; and US representatives in various international human rights forums were not reluctant to call the Soviets on their failure to abide by their obligations under UN covenants and the 1975 Helsinki accords (see the discussion of the Conference on Security and Cooperation in Europe in Chapter 6); but it was the Carter administration's initial policy not to let the popular human rights concerns be a drag on the negotiation of a SALT II treaty, nor to substantially inhibit the elaboration of cooperative relationships with the Soviet Union and other communist countries.

By 1981, when President Reagan—using rhetoric with a stridency not heard from the top levels of the US government since the days of Secretary of State John Foster Dulles—attempted to restore the ideology of anticommunism as a motive force for US foreign policy and coalition unity, there were already too many powerful interests in both the Soviet-led and US-led coalitions and in the Third World with a practical stake in East–West detente to countenance a full international repolarization on ideological lines. Reagan's public castigation of the Soviets as untrustworthy negotiating partners because of their adherence to Leninism[13] and his characterization of communist countries as "the focus of evil in the modern world"[14] were widely dismissed in the United States and allied countries as rhetorical excesses. Foreign diplomats were privately briefed by embarrassed administration officials to pay more attention to what the Reagan administration does than to what the President sometimes says.

CROSS-CUTTING INTERDEPENDENCE

At base, the loosening of the cohesion of the cold war coalitions along their geostrategic and ideological dimensions is the cumulative result of underlying technological and socioeconomic developments pervading the entire international system. These global, and long-term, trends are usually referred to by the catchall word "interdependence." Interdependence itself is hardly a new phenomenon. Rather, it is the changes in the scope and direction of interdependent relationships between economic sectors and between countries that are shaking loose some of the foundations of the established international order.

With the full maturing of the industrial revolution, the inputs and outputs in one economic sector more and more depend on and directly affect resources in other sectors of society. Perturb the industrial economy in any of its sectors and reverberations will be felt in many of its other sectors, often with unpredictable impact. In recent decades, this intersectoral dependence has been demonstrated most dramatically by changes in the supply and price of oil and other petroleum products used to produce the energy that drives modern industry. In addition to affecting the price of most manufactured durables (and their rate of production and thus the number of jobs available in the manufacturing sector), the petroleum supply/demand situation affects the availability of chemical fertilizers and pesticides, the costs of transporting agricultural products to market, and other factors determining the supply and price of food.

Change the price of money itself (and thereby the patterns of lending and investment) and this will affect the demand for new housing and industrial construction, and for goods, services, and labor across the whole economy. Invent a cheap synthetic for a widely used natural resource, or substitute computers for manpower in a productive process, and large communities may be compelled to make major economic readjustments.

This proliferation of connections and sensitivities between sectors has become so dense that rapidly spreading impacts across sectors now is a premise of most national planning—especially where the democratic political process compels government to provide compensatory adjustments to adversely affected regional or occupational groups. Particularly in the advanced industrial countries—whether capitalist or socialist—managing the domestic political economy with its deep intersectoral interdependencies has become a complicated art, requiring such fine tuning that there is an understandable reluctance to subject economic policies to international decision processes.

But efforts by countries to insulate the management of their own complicated economies from international disturbances are unsustainable, since the geographic scope of the intersectoral connections defies existing political jurisdictions. Intersectoral interdependence in the contemporary world is unavoidably also inter-*state* interdependence, with the linkages becoming increasingly transnational or global, cutting across alliances and blocs as well as national boundaries.[15]

The specific effects of this comingling of intersectoral and inter-state interdependence on alliance relationships will be analyzed in Chapters 4, 5, and 6, and the effects on the nation-state system itself will be assessed in Chapters 9 and 10. Here, in anticipation of those more detailed discussions, suffice it to say that many of the emerging and most durable of interdependence relationships are incongruent with many of the inherited structures of national governance and alliance coordination; and that therefore national or coalition strategies premised on a high congruence of economic interdependencies with communities of common military defense and ideological affinity (a match that did by and large prevail during the first two decades of the cold war) will be increasingly difficult to sustain.

ENDNOTES

1. Office of Technology Assessment, *The Effects of Nuclear War* (Washington, DC: GPO, 1979). For the "nuclear winter" hypothesis, see Carl Sagan, "Nuclear War and Climactic Catastrophe: Some Policy Implications," *Foreign Affairs*, Vol. 62, No. 3 (Winter 1983/84), pp. 257–292, and articles by Sagan and other scientists in *Science* 222 (December 23, 1983), pp. 1283–1300. Arguments that Sagan and his associates have exaggerated the prospects for a "nuclear winter" arising out of less than all-out nuclear

war are presented by Stanley L. Thompson and Stephen H. Schneider, "Nuclear Winter Reappraised," *Foreign Affairs*, Vol. 65, No. 5 (Summer 1986), pp. 981–1005.

2. The most prominent no-first-use proposal is that of McGeorge Bundy, George F. Kennan, Robert S. McNamara, and Gerard Smith, "Nuclear Weapons and the Atlantic Alliance," *Foreign Affairs*, Vol. 60, No. 4 (Spring 1982), pp. 753–768. A rebuttal by German strategists is offered in Karl Kaiser, George Leber, Alois Mertes, and Franz-Josef Schulze, "Nuclear Weapons and the Preservation of Peace," *Foreign Affairs*, Vol. 60, No. 5 (Summer 1982), pp. 1157–1170.

3. A seminal early assessment of the geopolitical implications for nonstrategic warfare of the new technologies was provided by Albert Wohlstetter in his paper "Strength, Interest, and New Technologies," *The Implications of Military Technology in the 1970s*, Adelphi Paper No. 46 (London: Institute for Strategic Studies, 1968), pp. 1–14.

"It was rather common until recently," observed Wohlstetter, "to talk of the comparative disadvantage to the United States in fighting eight to ten thousand miles from home against an adversary whose home base is near the scene of conflict.…This has been [challenged]…by detailed studies of the comparative logistics at present levels of technology in several areas of possible non-nuclear conflict—in Thailand, in the Himalayas, in Iran and in Lebanon—and in the *actual* conflict in Korea.

"The most striking fact displayed by these studies is that the long-distance lift capacity of each side massively exceeds its short-distance lift inside the theatre, especially in the very short ranges in which the battle would be joined" (quotation from p. 8).

4. On the history of how the existence of common adversaries has spurred political unification on previously separate communities, see Crane C. Brinton, *From Many One* (Cambridge: Harvard University Press, 1968).

5. Open letter from Communist Party of the Soviet Union Central Committee to Party Organizations and All Communists of the Soviet Union, July 14, 1963; complete text in William E. Griffith, *The Sino-Soviet Rift* (Cambridge: MIT Press, 1964), pp. 289–325.

6. For the transformations in Soviet ideology, see William Zimmerman, *Soviet Perspectives on International Relations, 1956–1967* (Princeton: Princeton University Press, 1969).

7. Marshall D. Shulman, *Beyond the Cold War* (New Haven: Yale University Press, 1966), pp. 53–54.

8. Dean Rusk, "United States Policy and Eastern Europe," address of February 25, 1964, Council on Foreign Relations, *Documents on American Foreign Relations* (1964), pp. 144–149.

9. Leslie Gelb and Richard Betts, *The Irony of Vietnam: The System Worked* (Washington, DC: The Brookings Institution, 1979).

10. The erosion of support within the US policy community for the universalistic anticommunist premises underlying the US Vietnam intervention is described in detail in Seyom Brown, *The Faces of Power* (New York: Columbia University Press, 1983), Chapter 20.

11. Interview of President Nixon, *Time*, January 3, 1972, p. 11.

12. The "inordinate fear of communism" statement appeared in Carter's 1977 commencement speech at Notre Dame University. Text in *Public Papers of the Presidents of the United States: Jimmy Carter, 1977* (Washington, DC: GPO, 1977), Vol. I, pp. 955–956.

13. Ronald Reagan, News Conference of January 19, 1981, *Weekly Compilation of Presidential Documents*, Vol. 17, No. 5, pp. 66–67.

14. Ronald Reagan, Speech of March 8, 1983, excerpts in *New York Times*, March 9, 1983.

15. On the increasing dominance of the global economy over national economies, see Peter F. Drucker, "The Changed World Economy," *Foreign Affairs*, Vol. 64, No. 4 (Spring 1986), pp. 768–791.

CHAPTER FOUR

Strains in the Anticommunist Coalition

The anticommunist coalition, like all international coalitions before it, has been subject to inherent cross-pressures. Each member has a unique combination of special international relationships that it has high incentives to maintain. These have always set limits on coalition cohesion.

Viewed in comparison with what is normal for international coalitions, the degree of cohesion exhibited by the anticommunist grouping during most of the first two decades after World War II was unprecedented. The military, ideological, and economic foundations of the coalition among the noncommunist industrial countries were mutually reinforcing and, for the most part, remarkably congruent with each other. Efforts to construct a military balance of power against the Soviet Union were sustained by the belief that the Marxist–Leninists in the Kremlin were highly motivated to expand their sphere of control even beyond Eastern Europe and if possible to Sovietize the entire world. The "free" societies therefore had to mobilize themselves into a coalition not only to maintain a balance of power against a new would-be Eurasian hegemon, but also to preserve a way of life in both its political and economic dimensions.

During this early period, the role of the United States as military, ideological, and economic leader of the anticommunist coalition was widely accepted, if not welcomed, for it was the United States, after all, that would have to contribute the largest proportion of the resources to reconstruct and militarily protect the other major members of the coalition, most of whom had been devastated by the last war. But, characteristically, the Americans overestimated the extent to which the deference by other countries to the United States as coalition leader was a product of admiration for the geopolitical wisdom and diplomatic skill residing in Washington, rather than simply a reluctant and temporary adaptation to the postwar distribution of material power.

Today, by contrast with the earlier period, coalition members unabashedly pursue many of their international relationships unilaterally and on their "merits" (meaning, according to considerations of immediate national self-interest), rather than multilaterally (meaning, on the basis of prior consultation with Washington) and with primary reference to the larger East–West balance of power. Subcoalitions and intracoalition rivalries, especially along economic lines, have become more prominent, further undermining the authority of the coalition leader and stimulating competition for relationships with members of the opposing coalition and nonaligned countries. The disintegrating forces in the larger coalition now appear to be mutually reinforcing, the unifying forces appear to be on the defensive.

Looking ahead toward the twenty-first century, the fate of the coalition is problematical. Although its complete dismantling appears highly unlikely, there is little chance—barring the emergence of a clear and present danger of a Third World War—that it can regain anything approaching its former influence. At best, the coalition will continue to be the central instrumentality for coordinating members' defense and arms control policies oriented toward the Soviet Union; at worst, coalition membership will become increasingly irrelevant to what the countries actually do in their foreign and national security policies.

The reasons for this prognosis are discussed in more detail below.

THE FLIMSY GEOPOLITICAL CONSENSUS

The post-World War II acceptance by other countries of American strategic leadership—not only the military protection but the geopolitical concepts coming out of Washington—was a function in many cases of their perception that without substantial American help they might not be able to effectively resist Soviet international power plays and domestic subversion; but other friendly governments, who themselves were not particularly exercised over international or domestic communism, deferred nonetheless to the American preoccupation with the communist threat, since this was what seemed most likely to curry Washington's favor.

By the late 1940s, the Americans had begun to subordinate virtually everything they did internationally to the overriding objective of containing Soviet power and Marxist movements around the world, which the Kremlin was assumed to be either sponsoring or likely to exploit to serve its expansionary drives. And the US foreign policy elite, convincing itself (in President Truman's words) that "force is the only thing the Russians understand," soon turned the objective of containment into a rationale for a predominantly militarized grand strategy.

Barely five years after the defeat of Germany, the western part of that country, now to be heftily reindustrialized and rearmed, was brought into the new North Atlantic Treaty Organization as a full-fledged member, and hundreds of thousands of American troops were returned to German soil. The

Marshall Plan for the economic reconstruction of war-torn Europe became the Mutual Security Program. And in the early 1950s, Washington began to prod its coalition partners in Europe to rapidly achieve a degree of political unity that would allow them to constitute themselves as a European Defense Community (subordinate to NATO), which could take over the forward containment role in Europe while the United States concentrated on strategic deterrence. In the Far East, defeated Japan was transformed by the Americans in less than five years from hated enemy into crucial partner for containing Soviet and Chinese communism in Asia—though because of the demilitarization provisions of the postwar Japanese constitution, Japan would serve primarily as the main East Asian base for deploying and servicing US military forces, and not attempt to become a regional military power in her own right. The containment chain would be linked across the Eurasian rimland by signing up other allies willing to define Sino-Soviet expansion as the overriding threat, the most important among them being Turkey, Iraq, Iran, Pakistan, and Thailand (Vietnam, Laos, and Cambodia were still French colonies), with the Philippines as the principal Pacific link.

The nonalignment posture of the holdouts—Sweden, Egypt, India, Burma, and Indonesia—was held by Washington to be naive (Secretary of State John Foster Dulles went so far as to brand it "immoral"), and ultimately unsustainable as these countries came to realize that the most serious threat to their newly won independence now came from the imperialists in the Kremlin.

As it turned out, however, it was the American assumption of a solid geopolitical consensus that turned out to be naive, as members of the coalition exploited Washington's obsession with the global communist threat to extract aid and protection in their regional and domestic conflicts, many of which really had little if anything to do with the cold war. Turkey used its American-obtained arms to stage confrontations with Greece over Cyprus. Iraq, even before its pro-Western government was overthrown in a coup, converted the asssistance it received from the NATO countries into capabilities for prosecuting its bilateral conflicts against its regional Arab rivals, against Israel, and against Iran. The Shah of Iran turned the prestige and favors bestowed on him by US administrations primarily to enhancing his own imperial grandeur. And a succession of military regimes in Pakistan extracted huge military and economic aid packages from the United States year after year for the ostensible purpose of strengthening them as the South Asian bulwark against Sino-Soviet expansion, but in fact to maintain a balance of power against India for the ever-looming war for control of Kashmir and to suppress the separatist Bengalis in East Pakistan (Bangladesh) and other dissident movements.

Moreover, even at its North Atlantic core, there were early signs that the "free world" coalition was a potentially unstable contruction with a problematical future. In the Korean War (1950–1953), America's principal NATO allies provided little tangible help to speak of, let alone major fighting contingents, to the "collective-security" action organized by the United States under UN auspices. If anything, the principal concerns of the NATO allies were that the United States was depleting resources that might otherwise go to the economic and military buildup of Europe and that the reckless Americans, having needlessly provoked the Chinese into the Korean War, might yet provoke the Soviets into World War III over this peripheral strategic area. Then in the Suez crisis of 1956, the British and the French conspired with Israel behind the back of the United States to invade Egypt in a move of momentous geopolitical importance, which provoked the Soviets to threaten to rain rockets on London and Paris and which drove President Eisenhower to publicly condemn Britain and France and to insist on their military withdrawal. The bitter Suez experience was followed by a period of assertive French unilateralism under President Charles de Gaulle, which included the development of an independent nuclear force and France's withdrawal from NATO's military command. De Gaulle also opposed Britain's entry into the European Common Market, on the grounds that the British were really proxies for America's efforts to perpetuate its economic hegemony over Western Europe.

By the middle of the 1960s, when the United States intervened militarily in Indochina against an important ally of the Soviet Union, the NATO countries and Japan were unresponsive to Washington's pleas to turn this "defense of freedom" into a coalition effort. The Europeans were mainly worried over the negative effects the Vietnam War might have on their efforts to build their own detente relationships with the communist countries.

Differences between the United States and most of its allies over the Middle East became particularly severe in the 1970s and threatened to tear apart the coalition. Japan and most of the West European countries, more dependent on Persian Gulf oil than the Americans—and anxious to not offend their Arab suppliers—distanced themselves from any US policies that might seem to favor Israel in her conflict with the Arabs. During the 1973 Yom Kippur War, various NATO countries refused to allow the use of their bases, or even overflight of their territory, to transport US military supplies to the war zone. Most of America'a coalition partners extended some form of legal recognition to the Palestinian Liberation Organization (PLO) and supported PLO requests to bring its case before various UN forums, whereas the US government made it clear that it would not recognize the PLO as long as the PLO refused to recognize Israel's right to exist. The United States also was frustrated in its efforts to forge a common front among the noncommunist industrial countries for dealing with the oil price and supply manipulations of the Organization of Petroleum Exporting Countries (OPEC), as the French, the Germans, the Italians, and the Japanese pursued their own special relationships with particular oil-producing countries.[1]

The divergent geopolitical orientations toward the Middle East and the Persian Gulf underlay the embarrassing open rift in the mid-1980s between the United States and its principal coalition partners over how to deal with international terrorism. The Reagan administration insisted on a concerted policy of sanctions against countries harboring or encouraging terrorists (much of the terrorism was presumed to be the work of militant Palestinians or groups linked to them in sentiment). Most of America's allies wanted to limit their counter-terrorist actions to improved surveillance, better security at airports and other target areas, counter-intelligence operations (including the infiltration of terrorist groups), and apprehension and legal prosecution of the individuals found to be engaged in terrorist acts. The United States was also urged by some of its allies to be more responsive to the grievances of the Palestinians.

The differences over combatting terrorism were dramatically exposed in the spring of 1986 as the United States—claiming that Libyan President Muammar el-Qaddafi had been supporting and training terrorists who were involved in various of the brutal acts in recent years in which Americans were killed or taken hostage—tried to mobilize a series of coordinated allied reprisals against Libya, ranging from economic boycotts to military retaliation. When the allies balked at joining the coercive moves and attempted to persuade the United States from locking itself into a collision course with Libya, the Reagan administration unilaterally forced the issue by sailing a US aircraft carrier task force into the Gulf of Sidra, ostensibly to assert international navigation rights against Qaddafi's claim that the Gulf was part of Libyan territorial waters, but clearly to provoke an exchange of fire with Libya.

Militarily outclassed in the Gulf of Sidra confrontation, Qaddafi announced an escalation of anti-American actions all around the globe, in response to which the Reagan administration threatened direct retaliation against Libya for terrorist acts perpetrated by the Libyans. Again most of America's allies objected that using force against Libya would give Qaddafi more visibility and would rally even moderate Arabs to his side, nor was it an effective way to deal with the problem of terrorism, which had more diverse and elusive sources.[2]

Washington went ahead anyway with its plan to give Qaddafi a bloody nose when, in reprisal for the April 1986 terrorist bombing of a West Berlin discotheque in which one American was killed and more than fifty injured, President Reagan ordered the bombing of Qaddafi's headquarters and related targets in Tripoli, using US aircraft based in Britain. In press briefings after the raid, however, administration officials were embarrassed to have to reveal that France had refused to allow the bombers to overfly its territory.[3] Public reaction to the bombing of Tripoli was overwhelmingly favorable in the United States, but highly condemnatory in Western Europe, and in Britain very negative toward Prime Minister Margaret Thatcher for permitting the Americans to stage the raid from British bases.[4] Government officials in all of the NATO countries save Britain admitted that insofar as they were consulted, they had attempted to dissuade the Americans from the Libyan raid, but to no avail. Expressions of bitterness between the United States and most of its alliance partners in the immediate aftermath were more widespread and intense on both sides of the Atlantic than at any time since the Suez crisis of 1956.

The political outcry across Europe in the spring of 1986 in reaction to the American use of military force against Libya was only the latest, event-specific expression of the more general decline in respect for the United States as alliance leader. Polls conducted by US government agencies in Europe in the early 1980s showed a substantial decline in confidence in the United States over the previous decade. In West Germany, for example, normally the country in which the United States has enjoyed the greatest popularity, the over 80 percent who expressed high confidence in the United States in the early 1970s had dropped to 65 percent by 1981. An authoritative American analysis of the survey data found that "the negative trends are more than marginal and likely to become stronger in the coming years. . . . In Europe there appears to be a substantial change in political ideas and culture, a change that is more neutralist, more skeptical of association with the United States, less sympathetic to American society, and more favorable to developing a third position separate from alliance with the superpowers."[5]

There have been two standard reactions in the American policy community to evidence of European dissension from US geopolitical leadership. The first, most prominent among the national security planners, has been to ignore the contemporary social and political reasons for the renaissance of European self-assertiveness and simply to brand it as strategically anachronistic (being inconsistent with adequate protection against threats from the new Eurasian superpower) and narrowly Eurocentric ("the Europeans have regional interests while the United States has global interests"), and to attempt to persuade the Europeans that their security increasingly requires more coalition unity rather than less. The American strategic rationale for Europeans' continuing to accept American hegemony was unequivocally asserted in the early 1960s by Secretary of Defense McNamara in response to insistent demands from the NATO allies for more of a role in decisions on the use of strategic nuclear weapons. When it came to NATO's resort to nuclear weapons, McNamara explained, there could not be conflicting targets on the part of the allies nor could there be more than one list of targets. The nuclear campaign would have to be based on strictly centralized command and control. President Kennedy backed up his Defense secretary, explaining further: "If word comes . . . that we're about to experience an attack, you might have to make an instantaneous judgment . . . Now it is quite natural that Western Europe might want a greater voice. . . . But . . . in the final analysis, someone has to be delegated who will carry the responsibility for the alliance."[6]

The second type of American reaction to European complaints and unco-operativeness has its center of gravity in the Congress and in those executive agencies most concerned with the international economic competition coming from the EEC countries. It holds that the West Europeans in the field of security have been given too much of a "free ride" for too long and that their requests for greater authority over the collective defense of the coalition need to be matched by a more equitable sharing of the burdens of defense, particularly in raising and provisioning conventional armies. From these quarters in the American policy community, hints are often given—sometimes in the form of proposed legislation—that under the new strategic realities the United States, in the face of an unwillingness by the allies to increase their own defense outlays, should substantially reduce its own 300,000 troop deployment in Europe.[7]

But these responses to the increasing geopolitical dissensus between the United States and the West Europeans deal with its symptoms rather than its underlying sources, the most important of which, as pointed out in the previous chapter, being the undeniable capacity of the Soviet Union to respond in kind to NATO's ultimate reliance on nuclear escalation to counter the Warsaw Pact's conventional force advantages. This elemental strategic predicament is also at the root of today's intense intra-alliance debates over (1) how large and long a nonnuclear war NATO should be prepared to fight to deter a Soviet attack on Western Europe, and to defend Western Europe in case deterrence fails; and (2) the circumstances under which NATO actually should begin to use nuclear weapons.[8]

The official US position, since the Kennedy administration rejected the Eisenhower administration's primary emphasis on nuclear threats to deter Soviet attacks and provocations in Europe, has been one of flexible response: Prepare to defend as far forward and as long as possible without nuclear weapons, but also be prepared to initiate nuclear warfare to prevent Western Europe from being overrun. NATO's forward-deployed conventional forces in Germany, in other words, would be more than "hostages" or a "trip wire" to assure that a nuclear response would be delivered to Soviet aggression. They would be an actual fighting force, with sufficient strength to defend Western Europe without having to initiate nuclear war.[9]

The Kennedy administration's doctrine of flexible response was accepted reluctantly by the West Germans and the French and also without enthusiasm by the British. The Europeans read more American fear than flexibility into the new US policy—fear by Americans of being compelled to place their own cities in jeopardy of Soviet nuclear attack—and suspected the existence of secret US contingency plans to confine the American military response (in the event of a Russian attack on Europe) to the European theater itself. The Americans clearly were preparing, and trying to get the Europeans to prepare, for a protracted conventional conflict in the event that deterrence failed. And whereas the American architects of the flexible response strategy claimed that this would shore up NATO's deterrence of a Warsaw Pact attack because it was more credible than nuclear retaliation, most European strategists disagreed. They argued that, on the contrary, it would undermine deterrence by signaling to the Soviets that they could engage in aggression below the threshold of the American pledge to do all that would be necessary (including a direct strategic attack on the Soviet homeland) to repel a Soviet attack. Now it looked as if the Americans were ready to equivocate on the original NATO promise of all for one and one for all.

There is no denying that the Europeans have been partly correct in their suspicions. The strategy of flexible response, to be sure, is designed to keep NATO's options open even in the face of a massive Soviet blitzkreig-style invasion of Western Europe. Some influential segments of the US policy community would even go further and attempt to foreclose the option of a US–Soviet strategic war over the fate of Europe. But other equally influential Americans have been in accord with the dominant European view that a major war confined to the European continent is not to be contemplated, and the Soviets should not be led to believe that there is the slightest chance of starting such a war without its escalating into an all-out nuclear holocaust.[10]

This fundamental debate over NATO strategy resurfaced in the spring of 1982 with the publication of a proposal for *no-first-use of nuclear weapons* by four prestigious former officials of previous US administrations: McGeorge Bundy, George F. Kennan, Robert McNamara, and Gerard Smith. Writing in *Foreign Affairs*, the four strategists argue that even the most restrained battlefield nuclear action "carries with it a high and inescapable risk of escalation into the general war which would bring ruin to all and victory to none."[11] Consequently, contend the authors, there has been a severe erosion of the credibility of a nuclear response to anything short of a nuclear attack; moreover, to the extent that any response to Soviet aggression—given current NATO war plans—puts everyone on the nuclear escalator, it is unlikely that those NATO countries not themselves already under direct attack would want to participate in any kind of collective military response to a provocation against an alliance partner. In short, NATO's nuclear reliance, far from enhancing deterrence, does exactly the opposite.

A principal benefit of an explicit adoption of the policy prohibiting the first use of nuclear weapons, say the former administration officials, is that "it would draw new attention to the importance of maintaining and improving the specifically American conventional forces in Europe." Once the military leaders of the alliance have learned to operate on the assumption that if a war has to be fought in Europe, it should only be at the conventional level, then the NATO forces "will be better instruments for stability in crises and for general deterrence as well as for the maintenance of the nuclear firebreak [between conventional and nuclear war] so vital to us all."[12]

Not surprisingly, the no-first-use proposal did not sit very well with the West European governments—particularly Germany, France, and the United Kingdom—which, in addition to the United States, make the weightiest contributions to the common defense. The very next issue of *Foreign Affairs* carried a rebuttal by four West German experts on NATO strategy (Karl Kaiser, director of the highly regarded Research Institute of the German Society for Foreign Affairs; Georg Leber, member of the Social Democratic Party and vice-president of the German Bundestag; Alois Mertes, a Christian Democratic member of the Foreign Affairs Committee of the Bundestag and foreign policy spokesman of the Christian Democratic Party; and Franz-Josef Schulze, commander in chief of Allied Forces in Central Europe from 1977 to 1979). "What matters most," argue the German strategists, "is to concentrate not only on the prevention of nuclear war, but on how to prevent *any* war, conventional as well." And the prevailing NATO doctrine and deployments, confronting the adversary with "a full spectrum of deterrence and hence with an uncalculable risk," is better able to prevent any war from starting than would the doctrine and deployments that would be associated with the no-first-use policy. "The tight and indissoluble coupling of conventional and nuclear weapons on the European continent with the strategic potential of the United States confronts the Soviet Union with the incalculable risk that any military conflict between the two Alliances could escalate to nuclear war." By contrast, contend the Germans, "A renunciation of the first use of nuclear weapons . . . would liberate the Soviet Union from the decisive nuclear risk—and therefore from the constraint that has kept the Soviet Union, up to now, from using military force, even for limited purposes, against Western Europe." Further, the proposed no-first-use policy "would destroy the confidence of Europeans and especially of Germans in the European–American Alliance as a community of risk."[13]

Although the proposal to renounce the first use of nuclear weapons came from Americans out of office, it was a measure of the anxiety it produced in West European capitals that Secretary of State Alexander Haig felt compelled to offer his own public rebuttal by way of reassurance to NATO allies that it was not an officially inspired trial balloon. "NATO has consistently rejected such Soviet proposals, which are tantamount to making Europe safe for conventional aggression," said Haig, himself a former Supreme Allied Commander for Europe (SACEUR). Those who advocate the no-first-use policy have not faced up to the implications, he argued; namely, "that the United

States reintroduce the draft, triple the size of its armed forces, and put its economy on a wartime footing." Neither do the advocates acknowledge the severe consequence to the alliances. Even if such a hefty conventional contribution could be raised, which Haig was certain would not occur, the proposed policy "would be the end of . . . Western strategic deterrence. In adopting such a stance, the United States would be limiting its commitment to Europe. But the alliance cannot function as a limited liability corporation. It can only survive as a partnership to which all are equally and fully committed—shared benefits, shared burdens, shared risks."[14]

Only partly reassured, for the handwriting was already long on the wall in the United States of a fundamental reassessment of its unequivocal NATO commitment, the European allies could not avoid their own fundamental reassessments of their continued military deference to an alliance leader from whom they were becoming increasingly estranged across a range of issues.

Evidence of transatlantic estrangement often stimulates talk among alliance geopoliticians about the possibility of a strategic "decoupling" of Europe from the United States—a recurring idea, usually rejected when the full implications are faced, that the declining credibility of a nuclear response to a Soviet attack on Europe might be restored if the West Europeans had a combined strategic deterrent force that they themselves could order into action. To a degree, of course, this already exists in the independent nuclear strike forces maintained by both France and Britain; the "decoupling" model, however, is really directed toward providing a European-operated nuclear umbrella that would extend also over West Germany and thereby make it unnecessary for the Germans, in their increasing skepticism of American reliability, to develop their own independent nuclear force. But when serious consideration is given to politics of managing such a project among governments that already find it difficult to achieve consensus on less awesome projects in the European Economic Community, few Europeans can generate much enthusiasm for it, least of all the Germans who can anticipate even greater problems with their traditional European rivals than with the Americans if it ever comes to a real sharing of the risks of nuclear war in a future German-centered crisis with the Soviets, say over Berlin or a political revolt in East Germany.

It was principally to deflect such speculation on "decoupling" possibilities—reflecting European concerns over the implications for the US strategic commitment to Europe of the continuing bilateral Soviet–American SALT negotiations and the Soviet Union's modernization of its intermediate-range nuclear forces that would not be covered by SALT II—that German Chancellor Helmut Schmidt had suggested in an October 1977 speech that NATO consider additional kinds of deployments to support the deterrent strategy of the alliance.[15] And it had been in response to these concerns that the Carter administration proposed to its NATO partners that the United States install new intermediate-range nuclear missiles on the soil of NATO countries as a counter-deterrent to the Soviet missiles targeted against Western Europe. Typically, the Americans were ready to grab the ball and run with it in a way that might only stimulate the Russians to even larger deployments of their own new Euro-strategic missiles. The result of this intra-alliance dialogue was the "Two-Track" decision of December 1979 by the NATO foreign and defense ministers to pursue "two parallel and complementary approaches to TNF [theater nuclear force] modernization and arms control." One track would be the deployment in Europe of 572 intermediate-range missiles capable of striking the USSR (108 Pershing II ballistic missiles and 464 cruise missiles). The other track was for the Americans to try to negotiate with the Soviet Union mutual limitations on the intermediate-range strategic forces. If the negotiations showed no success by the end of 1983, the US deployments were to commence. If there were success, however, NATO would reexamine its force requirements.[16]

It fell to the Reagan administration to implement NATO's "Two-Track" decision on the Euro-missiles, but to the dismay of the West Europeans it appeared that the administration was more interested in going ahead with the new deployments than in any serious Soviet–American negotiations on mutual limits. Chancellor Schmidt and other leaders, lobbying through Secretary of State Haig, finally convinced Reagan that further US foot-dragging on the arms control track would enlarge the influence of the more radical elements in the European antinuclear movement to the point where in many of their countries it would become impossible to marshall parliamentary majorities to approve the deployments anyway. These pressures from West European governments, combined with a revived peace movement in the United States, finally moved Reagan in the fall of 1981 to go ahead with intermediate nuclear force negotiations, although the early proposals coming out of Washington (notably Reagan's offer to forego entirely the planned deployments if the Soviets would totally dismantle their intermediate missiles) were at the time so obviously unacceptable to the Russians that West European leaders continued to harbor doubts about the seriousness of the administration's new commitment to arms control.[17] As it turned out, the arms control negotiations failed to register any substantial progress by the end of 1983, and accordingly the West European governments as obligated by the NATO 1979 decision, but in some countries only after major parliamentary fights, began to make ready to receive the new American missiles.

Whatever chance there might have been to meet the December 1983 deadline for progress on the arms control track was negated by the new altercation between the United States and the Soviet Union over President Reagan's March 1983 announcement of his "Strategic Defense Initiative" (SDI) and by the general hardening of Soviet–American relations following the

September 1983 shooting down by the Soviets of a South Korean commercial airliner. As the United States began to deploy the new missiles to Europe in December 1983, the Soviets suspended all arms control talks, not to resume them until 1985, at which time a Europe bristling with a new generation of strategic missiles on both sides was the new reality. All in all, the futile "Two-Track" exercise did little to arrest the dwindling confidence in America's leadership of the alliance.

Nor was alliance cohesion helped by the Reagan administration's unilateral proclamation of momentous revision in strategic and arms control concepts as part of its rationale for the new SDI program. The change from a *deterrence*-centered strategy (emphasizing the intolerable destruction to be suffered by all adversaries in a nuclear war) to a *defense*-centered strategy (that would protect the population and, in the President's words, would render nuclear weapons "impotent and obsolete"), even though fraught with implications for NATO strategies and arms control positions member governments had embraced, was sprung on the world by Reagan without prior consultation in the alliance.[18] American strategists were immediately subjected to a barrage of urgent questions from their shocked alliance counterparts. What was to happen to NATO's flexible response policy, which depended upon the threat to turn a conventional European war into a strategic nuclear war? What would be the fate of the ABM Treaty—the centerpiece of all strategic arms control since 1972? Would the new strategic defenses also be protection against the shorter-flight missiles the Soviets had aimed at the Europeans, or would the super-powers be building protective domes over themselves while leaving their respective allies exposed? Was outer space, where some of the exotic new weapons were supposed to be deployed, now to become an arena for competitive military deployments, in contravention of treaties some of the allies had been instrumental in negotiating? However coherent and convincing the American answers might be—and most of the member governments of NATO never came around to endorsing the SDI concept—the allies remained hurt and angry at being informed after the fact of the change in American doctrine. When some Reagan national security officials confessed that the President's announcement was a surprise to them too and that the new concept had not been widely vetted among administration strategists, allied officials were all the more appalled and were reinforced in their doubts about the wisdom of continuing to rely so heavily on the Untied States for the security of their own countries.

A similar reaction from America's NATO partners greeted the Reagan administration's announcement at the end of May 1986 that the United States would no longer abide by the 1979 Strategic Arms Limitation Treaty (SALT II). Signed by Presidents Carter and Brezhnev, but never ratified, and attacked as "fatally flawed" by Ronald Reagan in his 1980 election campaign, the SALT II provisions were adhered to by the Reagan administration (with the Soviet government pledging reciprocal adherence) principally as a means of restraining and keeping a closer watch on the Soviet arms program. Now, however, claiming that the Soviets were systematically violating the Treaty and, more important, that continued adherence by the United States would unduly inhibit its own strategic force modernization programs (most immediately, the impending installation of new cruise missiles on the bomber forces), the administration insisted that SALT II was no longer in the national interest.

The May 1986 decision to scrap SALT definitely did not reflect a consensus among the NATO governments, most of whom feared both the effect on overall East–West relations to which they were more deeply committed than the United States (see Chapter 6) as well as the effect of a newly stimulated arms race on their domestic economies. Some of the allied leaders headed governments resting on narrow parliamentary majorities that could be pulled out from under them by the growth in anti-American sentiment that would be engendered. Thus when Secretary of State Shultz met with his counterparts in Nova Scotia for the regular NATO foreign ministers conference a few days after the American announcement, he encountered a wall of outraged criticism—once again, not only on the substance of new US policy, but also on the unilateralist mode of its proclamation. The Canadian Minister of External Affairs Joseph Clark, in his welcoming address, called the American move "a profoundly disturbing development." And the foreign ministers of Germany and Britain were reported to have used even stronger language in their private sessions with Secretary Shultz.[19] Across the political spectrum in Europe, friends of the United States and supporters of NATO were distressed at the larger implications for transatlantic relations. "Consensus between the present American Administration and Europe is becoming an illusion," commented former German chancellor Willy Brandt. "The alliance is being drained."[20]

The erosion of the geopolitical consensus sustaining the US-led coalition has spread beyond its North Atlantic core, affecting even the presumably solid suballiance of Australia, New Zealand, and the United States, as formalized in the ANZUS Treaty. Reflecting strong antinuclear attitudes in the New Zealand electorate, Prime Minister David Lange and his Labour Government, claiming they were acting in accord with the spirit of the regional consensus among the South Pacific countries to achieve a nuclear-free zone, decided in 1985 to refuse access to New Zealand ports of the destroyer USS *Buchanan*, unless the United States could give assurances that the ship was not carrying nuclear weapons.[21]

In response to New Zealand's demand, which the US Navy said it could not honor without dangerously compromising its strategy of not revealing which of its warships carried nuclear weapons, Washington canceled the *Buchanan*'s visit and all other military exercises with New Zealand and cut the country off from intelligence information normally given allies. The Reagan administration further informed the Lange government that its implementation of legislation banning all nuclear-powered or nuclear-armed ships from New Zealand ports would cause the United States to hold New Zealand to be in violation of the ANZUS treaty. To limit the damage, the US and Australian governments have instituted arrangements to keep the mutual defense pact alive on at least a bilateral basis.[22]

In its strong reaction to the moves by the New Zealand government to deny port visits by nuclear ships, the US government was reacting less to the specific effects on its military power in the South Pacific than to the precedent that might be set for other allies—such as Japan, Norway, and Canada—who ban the deployment of nuclear weapons on their soil.

THE DISINTEGRATIVE EFFECTS OF DETENTE

There has never been any firm alliance-wide coordination of the positive side of East–West relations. To be sure, in adopting the Harmel Report of December 1967 the NATO Council gave itself the task (in addition to its primary task of deterring and defending against aggression) of pursuing "progress towards a more stable relationship [with the East] in which the underlying issues can be solved," and affirmed that "military security and a policy of detente are not contradictory but complementary."[23] But twelve years later, looking back at the problems detente caused for alliance relationships, Henry Kissinger, for one, concluded that "the theory...is totally wrong...that the Alliance is as much an instrument of detente as it is of defense....NATO is not equipped to be an instrument of detente."[24]

It had been difficult enough to develop and sustain a common definition of the military threat against which common political–military measures needed to be organized; but the effort to have all sixteen members of NATO act in harmony when it came to the diplomacy of peaceful intercourse with the communist countries—much of it involving commerce in sectors where the greatest rivalries were among the noncommunist countries themselves—was bound to result in frustration and to create extra problems even in those fields of military planning where the allies had been able to achieve a substantial amount of coordination. In pursuing detente relationships, each country typically makes the most of its own historic and cultural ties, as well as current and potential economic complementarities, in exploiting opportunities for interaction with particular members of the other camp, often with unavoidable negative implications for alliance unity and US leadership.

The pattern, to be elaborated in more detail in Chapter 6, developed essentially as follows: The West Germans unilaterally developed and practiced their policy of *Ostpolitik*, involving increasing economic and political relations with the USSR and the countries of Eastern Europe (including East Germany) in the face of official US coolness to these initiatives prior to 1971. France, too, stepped out in front of the United States to expand commercial and diplomatic intercourse with the Soviet Union and its satellites in accord with President de Gaulle's vision of a reconstructed greater European system from the Atlantic to the Urals. The United States—under the Nixon–Kissinger strategy of obtaining political concessions from the Soviets in exchange for allowing them normal trading and credit privileges in the West—was a Johnny-come-lately to the arena of detente. However, once detente was adopted as part of the US grand strategy in the early 1970s, Nixon and Kissinger were heavy-handed (but unsuccessful) in insisting that the Europeans and Japan follow the US lead. Kissinger wanted to use the prospect of enlarged East–West commerce as a carrot to supplement the stick of military containment and to combine this with US–Chinese rapprochement as means of obtaining maximum leverage on the USSR. Unilateral forays in East–West relations by America's allies would undercut the controlled and "nuanced" diplomacy that Kissinger believed he alone was qualified to direct. In the economic realm, no less than in the military realm, Kissinger would insensitively, and inappropriately, harangue the Europeans and Japanese with the grating old saw that the United States had global interests whereas the allies had merely regional interests.[25]

Later, when it became evident that the Kissinger leverage–linkage strategy (as carried forward into the Carter administration) had produced only meager, if not negative, influence over Soviet behavior, and the Americans turned sour on the detente approach in general, the European and Japanese governments with their less politicized strategy of East–West commerce found themselves subjected to new pressures from Washington to cease helping the USSR develop economic modernization and strength that could eventually be turned against the West.

The intra-alliance dissension over East–West commercial relations came to a head in 1981 and 1982 when the Reagan administration, in a determined effort to reverse the detente policies of the 1970s, objected to the natural gas deals various West European governments had negotiated with the Soviets.

The Reagan strategy was to bring maximum pressure on the Soviet system— a "full court press," in the words of Reagan's National Security Adviser, involving "diplomatic, political, economic, and informational components built on a foundation of military strength." The objective was to "convince the Soviet leadership to turn their attention inward," to "force…the Soviet Union to bear the brunt of its economic shortcomings."[26] An essential part of the strategy was tightened restrictions on the sale of technologies to the USSR that could help it overcome its economic difficulties.

Consistent with this strategy, and using the opportunity provided by new Soviet repressive policies in Poland, President Reagan added to the sanctions already imposed by the Carter administration on the Soviets for their invasion of Afghanistan by ordering the denial of export licenses to firms providing the USSR with gas pipeline equipment.[27] The problem in implementing the embargo on gas pipeline exports was that to be effective it required similar export controls by the West Europeans, since some of the components on which the Russians were crucially dependent were manufactured in Europe by subsidiaries of US corporations or by European firms. But many of the West European governments—particularly Bonn, London, Paris, and Rome—already had negotiated long-term deals with Moscow to sell the gas pipeline equipment and advanced technology in exchange for deliveries of Soviet natural gas through the completed East–West pipeline and had issued licenses to firms to proceed under these arrangements.

Predictably, the European governments refused to go along with Reagan's embargo. Indeed, at the summer 1981 seven-nation industrial summit in Ottawa they had directly expressed to the President their objections to such a policy. The Europeans cited the economic recessions in their countries and the recent cutback by the United States on steel imports from the European Community as compelling reasons for fulfilling their contracts to sell the Russians the pipeline equipment. Moreover, the Europeans were resentful at being asked to make economic sacrifices for sanctioning the Soviets when the United States, under Reagan, had removed the embargo of US grain sales to the USSR that had been imposed by the Carter administration. Why, they asked, should West European workers, instead of American farmers, bear the brunt of sacrifices required by the new cold war orientation in Washington?

The President and Secretary of Defense Weinberger (Secretary of State Haig was a dissenter from the policy within the US government) tried to persuade the Europeans that their assistance to the Soviets in building the gas pipeline would add to Soviet leverage over them since the Kremlin, with its hold on Western energy supplies, could blackmail the Western governments in a crisis. Furthermore, the $10 billion annually the USSR could expect to earn from selling the gas would free it from some of the economic pressures that were restricting its capacity to pursue an aggressive foreign policy.

But the West Europeans argued in return that attempts to use economic coercion against the Soviet Union had not worked in the past and would not work now. If the USSR were denied hard currency earnings in the West and if this produced a constriction of Soviet development plans, the Kremlin would simply take it out of the hides of the Soviet people and continue to defer satisfying their consumer needs; the last thing the Soviets would arrest would be their military buildup. Indeed, the Soviets would be confirmed in their paranoid suspicion that the West was determined to destroy the socialist experiment in Russia. The most likely result would be an even *more* aggressive Soviet foreign policy. The West Europeans also challenged the American allegation that they were making themselves vulnerable to Soviet pressures by becoming dependent on the USSR for energy. At the most, supplies from Russia would constitute 5 percent of the West Europeans' total energy consumption—a gap that could be filled from other sources in the event of a cutoff from the East.

Rebuffed by the NATO allies, Reagan moved unilaterally in the spring and summer of 1982 to prohibit US companies from transferring equipment or technology to the gas pipeline project and extended this ban to foreign subsidiaries of US corporations and even to foreign-owned companies producing pipeline items under US license. The West Europeans cried foul, pointing out that their companies were manufacturing equipment and using technology under American licenses obtained before President Reagan's 1981 sanctions against the Russians. The president then even went so far as to discipline the insubordinate allies by ordering the Commerce Department to prohibit the export of US goods and technology to foreign companies that continued to deliver items to the Soviet gas project. Even Prime Minister Margaret Thatcher, Reagan's most loyal ideological supporter among the allies, was provoked to protest angrily: "The question is whether one very powerful nation can prevent existing contracts from being fulfilled. I think it is wrong to do that."[28]

Reagan finally was convinced by his new Secretary of State George Shultz, himself an expert on economic policy, to diffuse the embarrassing and counterproductive altercation with the allies by allowing the Europeans to go forward with the gas deal as they saw fit, in return for their cooperation in forging a new consensus with the United States on a more restrictive policy for extending financial credits to the USSR and on stricter controls on the export of strategic materials.

Immediately following the death of Soviet President Leonid Brezhnev in November 1982, Reagan announced that the United States was relaxing its embargo on items for the Soviet gas pipeline project. He was willing to do this, he explained, because the Western alliance was now "fundamentally united" under a "plan of action...to give consideration to strategic issues when making decisions on trade with the USSR." The newly concerted policy of East–West trade, claimed the President, reflects "our mutual determination to overcome differences and strengthen our cohesion."[29] Actually, the new "consensus" reflected European interests in looser alliance coordination over nonstrategic items and in a narrower criteria for defining what was strategic than the Reagan administration wanted. The allies were not at all pleased at the implication in Reagan's statement that it was they who had made the important concessions. Nor did they take kindly to the impression conveyed by the President that his lifting of the embargo was *in return for* the European agreement to more closely concert East–West trade policy. French President

François Mitterrand was moved to publicly contradict the American president: The Europeans made no concessions, he insisted; statements to the contrary coming from the White House "did not correspond to reality, as far as France is concerned."[30]

The pipeline dispute has been perhaps the most embarrassing display of the centrifugal effects on the alliance of increasing peaceful interaction with members of the rival alliance, but it was by no means an idiosyncratic episode. Gregory Treverton is correct to point out that "future 'pipeline' disputes [are] altogether too predictable," given the differences in basic interests and perspectives between Americans and the West Europeans with respect to East–West commerce: "Most of American exports to the East are commodities; by contrast, the Western Europeans are heavily involved in selling capital and other industrial goods. The latter have long lead times, all the more so given the centralized planning of the European countries. Thus for the Europeans to apply sanctions is to break contracts. For them the sanctions instrument is particularly blunt, and the long-term implications of using it especially serious."[31]

Detente also has special values for various members of the coalition in the cultural and humanitarian spheres that inevitably produce a differential willingness to put detente at risk. For West Germans in particular, detente offers the immediate opportunity for families to be reunited across the border with East Germany, and the larger hope—which Americans are too ready to brand as merely symbolic—of an eventual reconstitution of the whole German nation. For the French, the Italians, the Scandinavians, and other European continentals, detente also holds the promise of a new European cultural renaissance, in which once again cross-fertilization between Eastern and Western Europe will make the continent the center of innovation in the arts and sciences. This cross-fertilization, however, cannot be managed as a coalition strategy; it must proceed pluralistically and spontaneously; and in order for this to happen, not only a relaxation of tensions with the East but also a larger tolerance for unilaterally pursued interactions are necessary. Some members of the alliance will crave these opportunities more than others, with the result that detente and alliance disintegration to a certain extent, and unavoidably, go hand in hand.

ECONOMIC TENSIONS AMONG THE ADVANCED INDUSTRIAL COUNTRIES

During the high cold war period, economic relations among the noncommunist industrial countries frequently reinforced and rarely were allowed to undermine the military and ideological foundations of the US-led coalition. But the close intercontinental economic cooperation that characterized the period might not have outlasted the postwar recovery of Europe and Japan were it not for the high priority given to countering the rising power of the communist countries.

The purpose of the coalition was never simply the containment of communism. A dominant belief among Western statesmen after World War II was that the important interests of the major industrial nations were in the main compatible, and that enlightened pursuit of economic self-interest would advance the well-being of all, provided it was carried on within a structure of mutually acceptable rules designed to reduce the barriers to international trade and payments.[32] Yet without the agreement to maintain an advantageous balance of power against the Sino-Soviet bloc, it is doubtful that Western Europe and Japan would have remained as willing as they did to defer to US concepts for organizing the world economy, or that successive US administrations could have continued to fend off domestic pressures to protect the American economy from growing European and Japanese competition.

Collective defense remains the most important task of the coalition and the primary reason most members, despite the grievances described above, still regard the United States as coalition leader. But today the need to prepare to resist communist attack is the constant concern of a rather narrow set of specialized officials; and presidents and foreign ministers only periodically concern themselves with the details of the military requirements. Compared with the earlier period, everyday diplomacy among the advanced industrial countries now is more and more involved with nonmilitary issues.

When the nonmilitary items are on the agenda, and the power of the rival ideological bloc is not a central consideration, the principle that each member of the coalition should do its part for the common good is more difficult to enforce. Those with the greatest military and economic power do not automatically exercise the greatest authority, and conflicts of interest are harder to resolve on the basis of common-denominator objectives such as balancing the military capabilities of the Warsaw Pact. Moreover, where nonmilitary matters are at issue—trade barriers, currency exchange rates, the terms of technological cooperation, access to energy supplies, environmental controls— there is more opportunity for subnational and transnational interest groups to press their demands not only upon their own governments but also upon the deliberative assemblies and bureaucracies of the coalition.

Even the debates over the size, composition, and deployment of forces by the various NATO members are now less concerned with how best to deter or defend against military attack than with the distribution of the economic burdens of alliance membership.[33] Previously when the United States insisted that economically thriving NATO countries provide more for their own defense and purchase military equipment in the United States to offset the US balance-of-payment costs of American forces in Europe, it was easier to compel agreement on the basis of the overriding imperatives of mutual security. But to the extent that questions of military burden sharing are linked to monetary and trade issues, the United States must progressively bargain against a coalition of European countries and Canada within NATO.

Similarly, Japan's hand for bargaining with the United States on both economic and security matters has been strengthened by the devaluation of cold war alignments in Asia following the 1972 Chinese–American rapprochement. Tokyo's first reaction to the dramatic changes of the early 1970s was one of shock at not having been adequately consulted, or even informed in advance, about this turnabout in US policy. But the more lasting effect has been to liberate Japan to pursue its own bilateral relationships with mainland China, the USSR, the Persian Gulf oil producers, and various Third World countries— less constrained by the need to obtain approval from Washington.

Underlying the increasingly hard bargaining among the members of the anticommunist coalition is the recognition all around that the United States has abandoned the posture of economic altruism it adopted as coalition leader during the early postwar period. By the early 1970s Washington made it clear, in trade and monetary policies and in rhetoric, that the United States was no longer inclined to make generous concessions to the countries it had helped to make its principal economic competitors. Secretary of the Treasury John Connally, speaking in Munich in May 1971, bluntly told the other industrialized nations that the United States was losing patience with them:

> No longer does the U. S. economy dominate the free world. No longer can considerations of friendship, or need, or capacity justify the United States' carrying so heavy a share of the common economic burdens.
>
> And to be perfectly frank, no longer will the American people permit their government to engage in international actions in which the true long-run interests of the U. S. are not just as clearly recognized as those of the nations with which we deal.[34]

President Nixon was a bit more diplomatic. Instead of there being just two superpowers, he observed, "when we think in economic terms and economic potentialities there are five great power centers in the world today." Western Europe and Japan , the two emergent power centers in the "free world," have become "very potent competitors of the United States—friends, yes; allies, yes, but competing, and competing very hard with us throughout the world for economic leadership."[35]

The prospect of a European economic union becoming powerful enough to compete with the United States was foreseen by the American policy community as far back as the Marshall Plan. It was widely believed that this competition would be a healthy stimulus to modernization on both sides of the Atlantic, and the United States and Europe, once the latter had completed its postwar recovery, would cooperate in freeing that competition from artificial restraints on trade—thus the U.S. Trade Expansion Act of 1962 and the Kennedy Round of tariff-reduction negotiations with Western Europe. Furthermore, a strong European partner was the keystone to the containment of Soviet expansion westward, and even if the growing economic competition would eventually involve some readjustment difficulties in the United States, it was the assumption, back in the late 1940s and early 1950s, that the temporary sacrifices would be worth the long-term gain in overall power for the anticommunist coalition.[36]

American attitudes toward the postwar recovery of Japan were more ambivalent. Unlike Germany, a rebuilt Japan could not be submerged in a regional bloc. Moreover, the war with Japan was thought to have been a direct result of the Japanese economic imperialism of the 1930s. Even when the anticommunist containment policy was extended to Asia in 1950 with the consolidation of Mao's rule in China and the outbreak of the Korean War, there was no intention on the part of the United States to help restore the Japanese "co-prosperity sphere." The future economic health of Japan, confined as it was to its home islands, would have to depend primarily on its fitting into the evolving world trading system. Thus, successive United States administrations, as a matter of high policy, paved the way for Japan's resurgence as a major competitor—but less through direct aid, as in the Marshall Plan for Europe, than through assuring fair access by Japan to the American and European markets.[37] The expectation was that once Japan recovered from the war it would reciprocate by reducing its barriers to foreign goods and direct investments and by generally helping the United States to construct a more open world economy.

Thus, the resurgence of major competitors in Europe and Asia was anticipated and encouraged by most of the cosmopolitan and liberal economists in the American policy establishment during the first decade of the cold war. What may not have been sufficiently anticipated was the degree to which economic regionalism in Europe would be accompanied by discrimination against the United States and Japan. Nor was it foreseen how weak elements in the US economy and Japanese parochial sensitivities against foreign penetration would stimulate politicians on both sides to revive the specter of a trade war.[38]

Probably the least anticipated and most significant aspect of the tripolar economic rivalry was the fact of its emergence in the detente-minded world of the early 1970s. With reduced priority accorded the global rivalry with the communists, the subordination of short-term national or special interests to the long-term goal of a stronger and more cooperative free-world community became highly problematical. Everyone's grand design for an orderly world economy began to be looked at suspiciously by everyone else as a cover for some narrow domestic objective. The whole became less than the sum of its parts.

If economic rivalry among the industrialized countries was to be the name of the game, characteristically the Nixon administration was ready to play hardball. The US economy was in deep trouble in 1971—"stagflation," it was called: Unemployment was dangerously high simultaneously with abnormal increases in prices for goods and services. US labor unions had turned protectionist, arguing that a large part of the unemployment problem was due to the influx of foreign goods produced by cheap foreign labor, sometimes in foreign subsidiaries of US multinational corporations. Trade and monetary experts were alarmed at the rapidly deteriorating US balance of payments, reflecting the lag of US exports behind the increasing outflow of US dollars in the form of overseas investments. Monetarists claimed that the dollar was highly overvalued in relation to other currencies and that this was dangerous for the health of the US economy; it artificially made US goods more expensive than they would be on the world market and made foreign goods cheaper in the United States. There were growing demands in international financial circles for the United States to devalue the dollar, but this would mean that the American domestic economy would have to absorb the first shocks of the international readjustment; moreover, such talk could cause a dangerous collapse of the whole monetary system as holders of the US dollars—the basic and most widely held of all currencies—rushed to cash them in for other currencies or, worse yet, demanded that the United States exchange their dollars for gold at the preestablished price of $35 per ounce. (There was nowhere near that amount of gold in the US treasury.)

These were the pressures that drove President Nixon on August 15, 1971, suddenly to suspend the convertibility of the dollar into gold or other international reserve assets. This technical action, dubbed by journalists as "slamming the US gold window," was taken, the President explained, to prevent international money speculators from "waging an all-out war against the American dollar." Simultaneously, Nixon imposed a temporary tax of 10 percent on goods imported into the United States. The purpose, he said, was "to make certain that American products will not be at a disadvantage because of unfair currency exchange rates. When the unfair treatment is ended, the import tax will end as well." Now that the other nations have regained their vitality and have become our competitors, argued Nixon, "the time has come for them to bear their fair share of defending freedom around the world" and maintaining a stable international order. "The time has come for exchange rates to be set straight and for major nations to compete as equals. There is no longer any need for the United States to compete with one hand tied behind her back."[39]

The European allies of the United States and Japan were outraged not only at Nixon's harsh tone and uncompromising posture but at the blatant unilateralism of the August 1971 actions. Without consulting its key coalition partners, Washington was taking it upon itself to change key structural elements of the international monetary system that had been multilaterally adopted at the Bretton Woods Conference of 1944 and was also, in contravention of the spirit of the General Agreement on Tariffs and Trade (GATT), imposing a special tariff (the 10 percent "import surcharge") on goods from its trading partners—in effect, twisting their arms until they gave in to US demands to revalue their currencies.

Although billed by the administration as part of a temporary set of measures designed to reverse the domestic inflationary spiral and the associated adverse balance of international payments, the August 1971 demarche was viewed abroad as a sloughing off by America of her special responsibility for stabilizing the world economy. The White House was somewhat taken aback by the intensity of foreign reaction to its unilateral moves and by the reactions of American firms active in the transnational economy along with influential elements of the US foreign policy community, who feared a complete unraveling of the GATT and International Monetary Fund (IMF) system.

Nixon softened the US position somewhat in subsequent negotiations with the Europeans and the Japanese by agreeing to devalue the US dollar as the others up-valued their currencies. The result was the agreement concluded at the December 1971 meeting of the IMF to realign all major currencies and subsequently allow them to "float"—that is, to have their values set by supply and demand on the world money markets within rather broad margins. Collaterally, the European Economic Community agreed to a new round of extensive trade negotiations with the United States. Japan also exhibited a cooperative attitude in implementing "voluntary" restraints on its exports to the United States and also some previously negotiated import barrier liberalizations. A tone of mutual accommodation surrounded the December 1971 meeting of the IMF, and Nixon appeared personally at the meeting to bless what he termed (with more than a little hyperbole) "the most significant monetary agreement in the history of the world." The surface sweetness and light, however, could not erase the fact that the United States had used not only economic coercion but also hints of withdrawal of military protection to compel its allies to accede to its desires.

Henceforth, the United States would lose some of its credibility in the international economy as protector of the rules, its claim to special authority as defender of the system. Other countries would feel more justified in putting their immediate self-interests ahead of the long-term general interest.

If this was the way the game was to be played, it would be harder for the United States to object on political or moral grounds to the European Community's "variable taxes" on imports such as grain, beef, poultry, and dairy products—taxes designed to make sure that foreign agricultural goods entering the Common Market would not be less expensive than European farm products. Nor could the United States convincingly claim the political high ground in objecting to the many EC nontariff devices (product standards, border taxes, and other technical restrictions) specially directed against imports from most countries in the Western Hemisphere and Asia.

Similarly, although the coercive economic unilateralist approach by the United States in August 1971 (and the overhanging threat that it might do something like this again) may have been conducive to subsequent liberalization of Japan's restrictions on imports and direct investments, the longer run effects of the new American toughness toward Japan were problematical. If the United States was going to respond to the growing Japanese competition by threatening to raise retaliatory barriers against imports and investments or by bringing pressure on the yen, Japan was not without alternatives. It could attempt to improve its global competitive position by lessening dependence on the US market. This would mean finding other major markets for its industrial products in Canada, Europe, the communist world, and the developing countries, and perhaps creating its own preferential trade and investment area in emulation of the EC's special association with Third World countries.

The coalition was hit from the outside by an even worse economic shock in the fall of 1973 when the Organization of Petroleum Exporting Countries (OPEC) instituted a series of price increases and export controls, resulting in a fourfold increase in the price of oil. To complicate matters, the Arab members of OPEC, in connection with the 1973 Arab–Israeli war, selectively embargoed oil exports to countries supporting Israel. America's coalition partners were hardly in a mood to respond positively to the Nixon administration's efforts to organize a united response on the part of the major consumer countries to break the producer cartel. Most of America's European allies and Japan, more dependent upon imported oil than the United States, unilaterally pursued their own oil purchase arrangements with members of OPEC. Except for The Netherlands, they also made it a point to disassociate themselves from US policies toward Israel to immunize themselves from the Arab oil embargo.

Intensely suspicious of the United States, and of each other, industrial country governments tended first and foremost to the anticipated domestic effects of the OPEC-manipulated oil scarcity and price rise; namely, industrial slowdown, soaring inflation, and the massive transfer of wealth out of their countries into the hands of the oil producers. Each national government, with potentially disastrous implications for the survival of any kind of world monetary order, began to print more money, which then caused them to manipulate interest rates to control inflation, inducing further instability into the pattern of international investments and money flows. And to counter the expected adverse balance of payments impact, they left the GATT rules a shambles by competitively imposing import restrictions and by offering subsidies and other incentives to key export sectors.

Despite the rebound in the late 1970s and early 1980s from the oil scarcity crisis of the early 1970s, and the emergence by the mid-1980s of an oil "glut" (in large part the result of the past decade's shortage-induced conservation policies and development of alternative energy sources), the international economic regime among the industrial countries today is characterized by the norm of domestic protection first, international system maintenance second.[40] All countries have imposed tariffs and a variety of nontariff barriers to protect sectors of their economies vulnerable to displacement by international competitors. Export subsidies are in widespread use to help agricultural and industry groups boost their foreign sales by keeping their international prices artificially low. Interest rates and currency exchange values are changed frequently by national governments to manage domestic cycles of inflation and recession without regard for the impact of such changes on international trade or the monetary system. At the annual seven-nation summits attended by the leaders of the principal noncommunist industrial countries each summer, rhetorical deference is paid to the goal of free trade and international accountability in monetary matters, but in moments of greater candor, government officials responsible for foreign economic policy admit that mercantilism is once again rife in international commerce.[41]

CUMULATIVE IMPACT ON THE COALITION

Washington is no longer *the* energizing pole of the anticommunist or, rather, noncommunist coalition. Special relationships radiate in all directions, not from a single core, but from many centers: Bonn, London, Paris, Tokyo, Ottawa, Oslo, Rome, etc. Each center is part of a number of unique webs of commercial, cultural, and political intercourse, with its own cross-pressures and its own tensions. Many of these special relationships extend into the Third World with former colonies and new client states, as will be elaborated in Chapter 7.

Given the expected persistence, even growth, of the economic and political importance of these special relationships in the years ahead, efforts by any member of the coalition to gain community-wide endorsement of its policies toward a country or bloc outside of the coalition can be expected to become increasingly difficult. If a NATO country wants the imprimatur of the Treaty Organization on its actions in bilateral conflicts—say, Britain against Argentina in another confrontation over the Falkland Islands, Italy against Yugoslavia over Trieste, West Germany against East Germany over rights in the city of Berlin, the United States against Cuba for its support of Marxist movements in Latin America—it will have to pay a higher price to co-members than previously. The change in price of obtaining coalition-wide backing itself reinforces the centrifugal tendencies described in this chapter, for it gives each member an incentive to further develop extra-coalition obligations that can then be played off against the demands of its colleagues for intramural cooperation.

ENDNOTES

1. On the sources of differences in Middle Eastern policy between the United States and its European allies see Dominique Moisi, "Tensions within the West," in Robert E. Hunter ed., *NATO—The Next Generation* (Boulder: Westview, 1984), pp. 217–226.

2. Bernard Gwertzman, "Shultz Says U. S. Rejected Allies' Advice on Libya," *New York Times*, 29 March 1986.

3. Secretary of State George Shultz, Press Conference of April 17, 1986, *New York Times*, 18 April 1986.

4. On the differences between US and European reactions to the raid on Libya, see Flora Lewis, "What Is an Ally?" *New York Times*, 27 April 1986.

5. John E. Reilly, "Citizens, Change, and Security: Sustaining the Consensus," in Hunter, ed., *NATO—The Next Generation*, pp. 179–199, quotation from p. 196. Reilly's expectation that the negative trends will continue to grow is supported by the observation of Gregory F. Treverton in his *Making the Alliance Work: The United States and Western Europe* (Ithaca: Cornell University Press, 1985), that "In most of the countries in Western Europe, but especially in the Federal Republic and Italy, younger, better educated people—presumably just those most central to shaping future trans-Atlantic relations—differ noticeably in attitude from their elders. While still favorably disposed to both NATO and the US, they are more tempted by neutralism, less impressed by the United States and less prepared to defend their country by military means" (pp. 167–168).

6. John F. Kennedy, News Conference of February 14, 1963, *Public Papers of the Presidents: John F. Kennedy, 1963*, pp. 174–175.

7. See my discussion of the amendments introduced by Senator Mike Mansfield to reduce US troops in Europe and other expressions of "Fortress America" attitudes in Seyom Brown, *On the Front Burner: Issues in US Foreign Policy* (Boston: Little, Brown, 1984), pp. 86–88.

8. The current debates within the alliance over basic nuclear strategy were foreshadowed by debates in the 1950s anticipating the Soviet development of a counter-nuclear deterrent to NATO's reliance on nuclear escalation. These earlier alliance debates, up to the period of the Kennedy administration, are penetratingly analyzed by Robert E. Osgood in his *NATO: The Entangling Alliance* (Chicago: University of Chicago Press, 1962).

9. William Kaufmann, *The McNamara Strategy* (New York: Harper & Row, 1964).

10. For an influential argument against making a robust conventional defense a central component of flexible response, see Bernard Brodie, *Escalation and the Nuclear Option* (Princeton: Princeton University Press, 1966).

11. McGeorge Bundy, George F. Kennan, Robert S. McNamara, and Gerard Smith, "Nuclear Weapons and the Atlantic Alliance," *Foreign Affairs*, Vol. 60, No. 4 (Spring 1982), pp. 753–768.

12. *Ibid.*

13. Karl Kaiser, Georg Leber, Alois Mertes, and Franz-Josef Schulze, "Nuclear Weapons and the Preservation of Peace," *Foreign Affairs*, Vol. 60, No. 5 (Summer 1982), pp. 1157–1170.

14. Alexander Haig, "Peace and Deterrence." An address before Georgetown University's Center for Strategic and International Studies, Washington, DC, April 6, 1982, US Department of State, *Current Policy*, No. 383.

15. Helmut Schmidt, "The 1977 Alastair Buchan Memorial Lecture," delivered before the International Institute of Strategic Studies, October 28, 1977, reprinted in *Survival*, Vol. 20 (January–February 1978).

16. Report on the Special Meeting of Foreign and Defense Ministers, December 12, 1979, *NATO Review*, Vol. 28 (February 1980), pp. 25–26.

17. For the pressures on Reagan to implement NATO's "Two-Track" decision, see Seyom Brown, *The Faces of Power: Constancy and Change in United States Foreign Policy from Truman to Reagan* (New York: Columbia University Press, 1983), pp. 585–590.

18. President Ronald Reagan, Address to the Nation, Washington, DC, March 23, 1983, full text in Department of State, *Current Policy*, No. 472.

19. On the reaction of NATO allies to the US renunciation of SALT II, see Bernard Gwertzman, "NATO Faults U. S. on Intent to Drop 1979 Arms Treaty," *New York Times*, 29 May 1986; and John M. Markham, "Europeans Voice Strong Criticism of U.S. Arms Moves," *New York Times*, 3 June 1986.

20. Willy Brandt quoted by Joseph Lelyveld, "On Arms Control Europe Would Prefer to Speak for Itself," *New York Times*, 8 June 1986.

21. For background on the US–New Zealand nuclear controversy see Dora Alves, *Anti-Nuclear Attitudes in New Zealand and Australia* (Washington, DC: National Defense University Press, 1985).

22. Bernard Gwertzman, "U.S. Plans End of Military Ties to New Zealand," *New York Times*, 19 April 1986.

23. "The Future Tasks of the Alliance: Report of the Council," *NATO Final Communiques, 1949–1970* (Brussels: NATO, 1971), pp. 188–192. Called the Harmel Report after its initiator, Belgian Foreign Minister Pierre Harmel, this report contains the recommendations of the study group commissioned by the Council in 1966 to examine the impact of developments since NATO's inception on the alliance's purposes and functioning. The report is often credited with paving the way for NATO's agreement to engage in mutual force-reduction negotiations with the Warsaw Pact. For analysis of the force-reduction negotiations, see Chapter 6.

24. Henry Kissinger, Speech in Brussels September 1979, quoted in Treverton, *Making the Alliance Work*, p. 59.

25. Some of Kissinger's most galling comparisons between the superpowers' interests and the interests of the lesser powers were contained in his famous "Year of Europe" address before Associated Press editors on April 23, 1973, analyzed in my *The Faces of Power*, pp. 423–424.

26. Richard Halloran, "Reagan Aide Tells of New Strategy on Soviet Threat," *New York Times*, 22 May 1982; and Saul Friedman, "Reagan Calls for Pressure on USSR," *Boston Globe*, 22 May 1982.

27. Ronald Reagan, Statement on USSR and Poland of December 29, 1981, *Weekly Compilation of Presidential Documents*, Vol. 17, No. 53, pp. 1429–1430.

28. Margaret Thatcher, speaking in the British House of Commons on July 1, 1982, quoted by James Feror, "Mrs. Thatcher Faults U. S. on Siberia Pipeline," *New York Times*, 16 November 1982.

29. Ronald Reagan, Speech on the Soviet Union, November 13, 1982, *Weekly Compilation of Presidential Documents*, Vol. 18, No. 46, pp. 1475–1476.

30. François Mitterrand quoted by *New York Times*, 16 November 1982.

31. Treverton, *Making the Alliance Work*, p. 63.

32. An excellent retrospective on the assumptions about alliance economic cooperation during the early post-World War II period is provided by William Diebold, Jr., *The United States and the Industrial World: American Foreign Economic Policy in the 1970s* (New York: Praeger, 1982), pp. 3–44.

33. A public version of the intense disagreements among NATO partners over sharing the resource burdens of their collective defense obligations was the bitterly acerbic exchange between former West German Chancellor Helmut Schmidt and former US Secretary of Defense James R. Schlesinger at a January 1984 conference on "The Future of NATO and Global Security" in Brussels, convened by Georgetown University's Center for Strategic and International Studies. The texts of the Schmidt and Schlesinger presentations are published in Hunter, *NATO—The Next Generation*, pp. 28–51.

34. John B. Connally, remarks at the International Conference of American Bankers Association, Munich, May 28, 1971 (Department of Treasury News Release).

35. Richard M. Nixon, address to midwestern newspaper and broadcasting executives in Kansas City, MO, July 6, 1971, *Department of State Bulletin*, Vol. 65, No. 1674 (26 July 1971), pp. 93–97.

36. Lawrence B. Krause, *European Economic Integration and the United States* (Washington, DC: The Brookings Institution, 1968), pp. 25–28.

37. Diebold, *The United States and the Industrial World*, p. 47–52.

38. Harold B. Malmgren, "Coming Trade Wars? (Neo-Mercantilism and Foreign Policy)," *Foreign Policy*, No. 1 (Winter 1970–71), pp. 125–126.

39. Richard M. Nixon, television and radio address on August 15, 1971, text in *Department of State Bulletin*, No. 1680 (6 September 1971), 65: 253–256.

40. For a theoretical treatment of the decline in cooperation among the industrial countries and the conditions under which cooperation might be enhanced, see Robert O. Keohane, *After Hegemony: Cooperation and Discord in the World Political Economy* (Princeton: Princeton University Press, 1984). Keohane sagely takes issue with other theorists, such as Robert Gilpen, who attribute the discord rather monotonically (and, I would add, with circular reasoning) to the decline of US hegemony and who, at least by implication, predict a continuation of discord until the emergence of another hegemon or the reemergence of US hegemony. Keohane sees considerable, although limited, economic cooperation persisting despite the decline of the hegemon and points to other crucial factors as influential in whether or not regimes of mutual accountability emerge. For more on this, see Chapter 12 of this volume.

41. See Walter Goldstein, "Economic Discord in the Atlantic Alliance," in Robert J. Jackson, ed., *Continuity of Discord: Crises and Responses in the Atlantic Community* (New York: Praeger, 1985), pp. 183–199. See also Joan Edleman Spero, *The Politics of International Economic Relations* (New York: St. Martin's, 1985), pp. 53–86, 117–125.

CHAPTER FIVE

Cracks in the Soviet Sphere

The divisions and special alignments in the Soviet-led coalition pose a more critical threat to its basic structure than do the self-assertive forces in the US-led coalition to its basic structure. In the West, even during periods of cold war tension, pluralism has been regarded as one of the essential structural principles of the coalition, subject only to the need to concert policies against the common opponent. But where strict orthodoxy and rigid hierarchy have been the central structural elements, a little dissent can seem dangerously destabilizing, and any tendencies of subunits to define and pursue their own goals may appear to risk disintegration of the whole coalition.

The strategic consequences of coalition distintegration are, of course, very different for each of the superpowers. The major allies of the United States, with the exception of Canada, are across the seas and have provided a remote forward line of containment and potential wartime bases of operations against the principal opponent. Even so, in the unlikely event that the main US allies in Europe and Asia came under hostile control, there would still be a fall-back position to "Fortress America." By contrast, most of the countries allied with the Soviets since World War II have been in the USSR's immediate security belt in Eastern Europe (and on its Siberian frontiers before the Sino-Soviet split in the 1960s)—the staging grounds for invasions of Russian territory for centuries. The development of long-range strategic striking power has only partially alleviated this historic fear of invasion, and the leaders in the Kremlin continue to be very edgy about subversion of nationality groups in border areas of the USSR, one of the reasons for their 1979 invasion of Afghanistan.

Moreover, even if the Soviets could be reassured that the United States and the other major non-Communist states have no inclination to organize attacks against or subversion of the USSR, the Kremlin leaders still would be deathly afraid of major defections from their international coalition, particularly in Eastern Europe. From their perspective, such defections would be regarded by communist parties all around the world as a severe erosion of the authority of the Communist Party of the Soviet Union (CPSU) and would be exploited by the Chinese and other anti-Soviet factions among the world's Marxists.

The ability of the CPSU to sustain its directive role in the world communist movement has been a compound of physical and nonphysical elements, the latter including the capacity to command respect on the basis of political skill, ideological vigor, embodiment of the virtues of the movement, and general social creativity—in a word, legitimacy. In the early aftermath of World War II, the legitimacy component of Soviet authority was practically immune from serious challenge within the world communist movement. The USSR's emergence from the war as a victorious superpower, along with the United States, seemed to vindicate even Stalin's excesses in his prewar consolidation of power. Leaders of communist parties the world over paid obeisance to Stalin as the great wartime leader who helped save the world from fascism. And in attempting to consolidate their own power after the war, many of these indigenous communist leaders not only sought material aid and blessings from Moscow but also often emulated their hero's brutal techniques. In their deference to Moscow and identification with Stalin, the local leaders apparently were acting with the approval of most of their party followers. There were, of course, early exceptions to this general pattern by communist leaders (Mao in China, Ho Chi Minh in Vietnam, Tito in Yugoslavia) who took over their countries largely without Soviet help and established themselves as independent authorities with whom the Kremlin had to bargain rather than command. But by and large the imperial relationship between the Kremlin and most national communist parties—in power and vying for power—was accorded broad legitimacy throughout the movement while Stalin lived.

Today, the leadership of the CPSU among the world's communist parties is no longer taken for granted. The Chinese communists openly brand the CPSU's attempts to sustain its hegemony as illegitimate and have armed rival insurgent groups against Soviet clients in the Third World. The Rumanians maintain a special relationship with the Chinese and hint at the kind of frontal defiance of the Kremlin the Yugoslavs have practiced since 1948. The Russians have intervened with troops and tanks against the fraternal communists in Budapest (1956) and Prague (1968) and more than once have threatened to use force against the Poles to keep them in line.

What are the sources of these deepening fissures? What are the prospects for the Soviet Union's continuing to contain or adapt to the pressures building up in the crucial East European core of its sphere, so that the volatile forces do not burst through the cracks to cause a chain reaction of explosions from which it will be difficult for the West to remain aloof? The answers to these questions will profoundly shape the future of world politics.

DE-STALINIZATION AND THE BACKLASH
AGAINST PLURALISM IN EASTERN EUROPE

Paradoxically, most of the erosion of the CPSU's authority in the world communist movement has its source in the effort by Premier Nikita Khrushchev in the 1950s to enhance the legitimacy of Soviet power through the de-Stalinization program. The often uncontrollable reverberations of the Khrushchev reforms throughout the Soviet sphere were a searing experience to many of the communists now in power, particularly in Eastern Europe. This memory is one of the reasons that the reforms General Secretary Mikhail Gorbachev has been attempting to institute in the USSR since 1985 have not been enthusiastically endorsed by most of the other ruling communist parties.

Following Stalin's death in 1953, the Khrushchev faction in the CPSU apparently believed that, as socioeconomic development proceeded within the Soviet Union and its satellites, attempts to induce adherence to Kremlin policy by terror would be perceived as inconsistent with Marxism–Leninism and consequently would negate the moral leadership of the Soviet party. The legitimacy of Kremlin authority was seen increasingly as requiring voluntary consensus—internationally among the diverse nation-states of the "socialist commonwealth" and internally among the domestic elite within each of the states. But when Premier Khrushchev, particularly in his address to the Twentieth Party Congress (1956), destroyed the myth of Stalin's wisdom, he also fatally weakened the Soviet party's role as the authoritative interpreter of Marxism–Leninism. The CPSU, after all, had been Stalin's main instrument for assuring ideological conformity; and many of those holding top leadership roles in the party in the mid-1950s had previously been functionaries under Stalin. Their legitimacy, too, would be undermined by the exposure of Stalin's errors.

Khrushchev also moved early in his reign to relax gradually the coercive aspects of USSR–satellite relations (symbolized by the Kremlin's reconciliation with President Tito of Yugoslavia). But when combined with the inadvertent delegitimation of CPSU authority resulting from de-Stalinization, the indication that a degree of pluralism now was to be allowed weakened the hierarchy of the bloc more rapidly than anyone, Khrushchev included, had anticipated.

The Crises of 1956

In the fall of 1956, the Poles threw off their Moscow-run regime and installed the nationalist communist, Wladislaw Gomulka. Under Gomulka's leadership, the Polish communist party was a hotbed of factionalism, with a large and growing reformist element demanding a democratization of decision making and the relaxation of state censorship. Soviet military intervention was stayed at the last moment by evidence of Gomulka's strong support in the working classes and the army.

In Hungary, however, antigovernment and antipolice rioting and a general condition of political confusion in 1956 gave the USSR the pretext for reinforcing its military garrisons. In the context of the news from Poland, the Kremlin intervention only galvanized anti-Soviet activity as revolutionary committees and workers' councils sprang up all over the country. A new nationalist government, headed by Imre Nagy and containing only three communists in its thirteen-member cabinet, negotiated a cease-fire and a withdrawal of Soviet troops from Budapest and then announced that Hungary would no longer be a one-party state and would leave the Warsaw Pact. The latter was clearly intolerable to the Kremlin, which poured military reinforcements into Hungary, set up an alternative government under Janos Kadar, and rolled tanks with heavy guns into Budapest. Massive strikes and underground resistance continued throughout the winter of 1956–1957, and some 200,000 refugees escaped into Austria.[1]

In retrospect, the significance of the 1956 crises in Eastern Europe lies not so much in the Kremlin's brutal repression of independence among its satellites. (After all, bipolarity was then the order of the day; this was the Soviet sphere of control; and not surprisingly the United States under the Eisenhower administration, despite its "liberation" rhetoric, made no threat of counterintervention.) The significance lies rather in the early sign of the USSR's inability to sustain a legitimate empire even within its own immediate zone of dominance. The Kremlin, of course, could not bring itself to view the lessons of 1956 that starkly. But it was noteworthy and portentious that in the wake of the uprisings in Poland and Hungary there was no general reinstitution of Stalinism. On the contrary, the Khrushchevian concept of "many roads to socialism" was embraced with even greater commitment in Moscow in the hope of refurbishing the legitimacy of the USSR's continued hegemony in the communist world.

The Suffocation of the "Prague Spring" of 1968

Twelve years later, the Kremlin again felt its control excessively threatened by the "Prague Spring" of 1968. In April of that year, the Czechoslovak communist party leaders announced a program of reforms to implement their concept of "socialism with a human face." There would be greater intraparty democracy; pluralism in the form of more autonomy for political parties, the parliament, and various state agencies; increased civil rights, including freedom of assembly and association; a more decentralized federal structure to accommodate the rights of Slovaks and other ethnic minorities; and comprehensive economic reforms. True to character, the Kremlin under CPSU General Secretary Leonid Brezhnev brutally suppressed the Czech reformism. But again the immediate fact of successful suppression was less important to the long-term evolution of world politics than the fact that the Kremlin felt it had to use major military force against a member of its own camp to compel conformity. The suppression of the Czechs was all the more momentous for revealing that the cracks in the Soviet sphere were manifestations of inherent contradictions in the Soviet system of organizing life within and among nations, and not attributable simply to Stalinist rigidity or the sudden thaw of the early Khrushchev period.

The August 1968 invasion of Czechoslovakia was immediately condemned by all the top officials of the Czech government and party, and for a full week Czechs and Slovaks participated in a massive show of nonviolent resistance. Over the next few months, Party Secretary Alexander Dubcek, primarily to avoid a bloodbath and secure a withdrawal of the invasion forces, gradually bargained away the popular reforms to which his regime had committed itself earlier in the year. His efforts bought mainly time, the lives of millions of his countrymen who were ready to participate in a suicidal insurrection, and perhaps some restraint on Kremlin factions anxious to stamp out all traces of anti-Soviet nationalism. But the Soviet troops stayed. Meanwhile, Dubcek's domestic backing fragmented as militant nationalists accused him of selling out to the Kremlin. Moscow no doubt was playing a different game, cajoling and coercing Dubcek himself into carrying out "normalization" measures; namely, the suppression of political pluralism and civil liberties and the reversal of market-oriented economic reforms—thus weakening his domestic support. Then, at the appropriate moment, Dubcek was replaced by a more subservient successor, Gustav Husak.[2]

Poland 1980–1981: The Rise of "Solidarity" and the Imposition of Martial Law

Unlike the uprisings in Hungary and Czechoslovakia, the agitation for reforms in Poland that most threatened the Kremlin were not initiated by leading communist party intellectuals, but by worker organizations outside of the party. This also had been the case in 1956, 1970, and 1976, when workers' strikes forced changes in party leadership and government policies.

The 1980 uprising by Polish workers was triggered by the government's announcement in July of another round of increases in meat prices. Protest strikes by workers spread all around the country. And in the port city of Gdansk, the locus of a major workers' uprising in 1970 against the Gomulka regime, the worker organization headed by Lech Walesa used the occasion to present its wider catalog of grievances and a list of twenty-one demands, some of which concerned the role of the trade union movement in the Polish political system.

The head of the government and leader of the communist party, Edward Gierek, anxious to avoid a further slowdown of the economy in a period of domestic sluggishness and soaring foreign debt, granted most of the key demands of Walesa's worker Solidarity (*Solidarnosc*) movement. Some of the provisions in the historic agreement signed by the regime and Solidarity in Gdansk on August 31, 1980, required nothing short of "revolutionary" changes in the norms of a professedly Marxist–Leninist society; notably, the governments' formal acknowledgment of an "independent and self-governing" trade union movement and willingness to grant it the status of a bargaining agent for the workers' interests (according to Marxist–Leninist doctrine the communist party is the workers' representative, and there is no class conflict in a party-run society between the managers of industry and the workers); the government's affirmation of Solidarity's right to strike; a relaxation of censorship by the regime; and a number of concessions to the Catholic church.

Hard-liners within the communist party regarded Gierek's concessions to Solidarity as a negation of Leninist principles for the organization of the socialist state. Within a month of the Gdansk agreement, Gierek was replaced as party leader by Stanislaw Kania, who continued to favor some accommodation with Solidarity. However, a few months later the defense minister, General Wojciech Jaruzelski, assumed the premiership, and in less than a year (undoubtedly with the Kremlin pulling the strings) General Jaruzelski also took over the party leadership.[3]

It was becoming obvious to Solidarity and its allies among the Polish intelligentsia and the Church that the Jaruzelski regime, as prompted from Moscow, had no intention of faithfully implementing the Gdansk agreement. But having achieved even that paper agreement with the Gierek regime, Solidarity had grown beyond the local port-city worker's organization to become the energizing center of the country's swelling nationalistic and liberal pressures for reform. Before the government's suppression of the movement in December 1981, Solidarity claimed a membership of some 10 million (out of a country of 35 million), one million of whom were members of the communist party (which meant that about one-third of the party belonged to Solidarity!).

Given such a massive polarization of the nation, the Soviets could not sit idly by. Yet just as in the 1956 crisis, direct military intervention would carry enormous risks. It would surely arouse an intensely nationalistic reaction within the Polish military itself; and many units might well fight for the honor of the country against the Russians regardless of General Jaruzelski's stance.

The Kremlin decided rather to play on the Polish fears of a Soviet invasion by conducting major military maneuvers along Poland's borders starting in the spring of 1981. Jaruzelski was thus able to appeal to the common sense of wavering party members and broad segments of the Polish public by way of presenting himself as, at the same time, a Polish nationalist and someone the Soviets would have sufficient confidence in to maintain public order against the irresponsible elements pressing for overly rapid change.

The stage was thereby set for Jaruzelski to declare martial law on December 13, 1981—in the freezing cold of winter when Solidarity would have difficulty getting the masses to take to the streets in protest. The military moved quickly to arrest Walesa and the rest of the movement's leadership, and throughout the country purges were conducted of "unreliable elements." There was little more than token resistance. Jaruzelski was now in a position of unchallenged power to "normalize" the political and economic situation, ostensibly without intervention by the Russians but, in fact, on the basis of substantial Kremlin direction.

Jaruzelski's imposition of martial law was widely condemned as a moral outrage by Western observers; and most of the governments in the industrial world imposed trading and financial restrictions on Poland. Mainly to curry favor with the West, Jaruzelski released Lech Walesa from jail in November 1982 (but Solidarity was not restored to legal status). Martial law was lifted at the end of December 1982. Some Western countries thereupon reduced their economic sanctions against Poland, but the Reagan administration wanted more evidence of a genuine let-up in political repression by the Jaruzelski regime.

When a general amnesty was at last extended to all political prisoners in September 1986, the United States lifted most of its economic sanctions against Poland. Opportunities of Polish citizens to form political groups to express views in opposition to government policies, however, still remained more circumscribed than they were prior to the imposition of martial law; and large segments of the populace remained deeply alienated from the regime and the ruling party.[4]

THE EMERGENT PATTERN OF SOVIET-EAST EUROPEAN RELATIONS

The declining authority of the Kremlin in the world communist movement has become particularly evident in the reactions of communist officials throughout Eastern Europe to Mikhail Gorbachev's post-1985 domestic *glasnost* reforms ("openness" in criticism of officialdom, gradual liberalization of the economy, and limited democratization of the political process). Perhaps fearing a contagion effect—in the form of excessive expectations on the part of citizens in their own countries—party leaders in most of the satellite countries have greeted Gorbachev's reformism with skepticism, indifference, and even ridicule.[5]

Despite the continuing diminution of the Soviet party's authority over other parties, however, the likelihood of major overt defections from the Soviet-led coalition in Eastern Europe still is considered low by most policymakers in the West—at least for the next five years or so.[6] This prognosis rests on the following assumptions: (1) The Kremlin continues to believe that it would be a threat to the security of the USSR itself to have other than subordinate allies in Eastern Europe. (2) The economic and political weakness of the East European countries allows the Kremlin to maintain control at relatively low cost to the USSR. (3) Wherever and whenever the Kremlin decides it is necessary to apply overwhelming force to maintain its European security belt, it will not shirk from doing so.

The emerging geopolitical, economic, and cultural realities, however, point toward significant changes in the Soviet imperial relationship over Eastern Europe in the long run.

Even the Soviet Union's presumably decisive security interest in having a belt of loyal allies in Eastern Europe may be in line for some revision. Since military threats to the security of the USSR are seen to come less from invasion by Germany and other Western powers across Eastern Europe and more from remotely based strategic striking forces, and since the ability to deter or defend against such strategic attacks depends primarily on Soviet strategic capabilities deployed on Soviet territory, in the oceans, or outer space, the East European security belt assumes at least a relatively reduced *military* priority. And as the prospect of a war between NATO and the Warsaw Pact for the control of Germany (let alone for the whole of Europe) becomes an ever more remote fantasy (see the discussion of the 1971–1972 agreements on Berlin and Germany in the following chapter), the need for the Soviets themselves to maintain a secure invasion and military-logistic route through Eastern Europe is correspondingly reduced.

Moreover, the need to keep Eastern Europe as a major theater for potential large military operations takes away from resources that may be needed for more plausible military encounters the Soviets may need to anticipate on the Chinese border and in South and Southwest Asia.

This is not to say that the USSR will no longer *prefer* to maintain a belt of military allies around its western frontiers, but only that from a military planning perspective it may want to search for alternative means of guaranteeing its own security, especially with a rise in the political costs of attempting to maintain reliable military allies in Eastern Europe. On the basis of such calculations, a belt of cooperative but militarily nonaligned states in Eastern and Central Europe, perhaps on the model of Finland's circumscribed neutrality, might begin to look attractive—particularly if there was a collateral Western willingness to explore all-European neutralization arrangements.

The hope of such a Soviet recalculation of its military priorities is one of the reasons that the East Europeans are committed to detente. There are few illusions in Eastern Europe, however, that the waning of the geostrategic rationale for heavy Red Army deployments in the region would be sufficient to effect a substantial diminution of the Soviet presence. But it would bring the more embarrassing reasons for the USSR's overbearing hegemony more into focus: (1) Moscow's prideful desire to maintain its newly acquired empire; (2) the CPSU's fear that a revival of nationalism in Eastern Europe will combine anti-Russian xenophobia with a rejection of Soviet-style socialism and that these subversive tendencies will spread to the non-Russian nationalities of the USSR; and (3) the advantages obtained by a number of the orthodox communist leaders in Eastern Europe, for purposes of keeping themselves in power against domestic opposition, of being able to request or invoke the specter of Soviet military intervention.

As the underlying political reasons for the continuation of a heavy Soviet presence come into focus, they become a clearer target for nationalists and reformists. In most of the East European countries, the growing unpopularity of the Soviet presence confronts the domestic regime with a most delicate balancing task: If it becomes openly the spokesman of anti-Soviet nationalism and reformism, as did the Dubcek government in early 1968, it risks being forced out of power by the Kremlin; yet if it fails to be adequately responsive to the growing popular pressures, it risks becoming the target of progressive agitation and even detemined subversion. Clever politicians—and there are many in power today in Eastern Europe—can turn this delicate situation into a major bargaining asset vis-à-vis the USSR. They must be able to bring home the bacon, so to speak, especially on intrabloc economic matters, to demonstrate to their countrymen that constructive participation in the socialist common-wealth has its rewards.

Political leverage by the satellite leaders has been increasing concurrently with the rise in intrabloc economic issues, which result from the uneven progress in economic development throughout Eastern Europe during the past two decades. The bargaining within COMECON is now very tough, and Russia by no means always gets its way.

Observers of economic relations among the COMECON countries report that the primary issues concern the pricing of goods exchanged among the members; the design and management of multilateral projects, such as the development of nuclear energy or cooperation on the Danube; and economic intercourse with the noncommunist countries.

Coalitions within COMECON for bargaining on these issues tend to follow the natural economic cleavages within the region. The most pervasive, natural coalition derives simply from the overweening size and diversity of the Soviet economy, which establishes a colonial type of tension between the USSR and the rest of the COMECON members. Attempts by the Soviet Union to institutionalize a "socialist division of labor" within the group exacerbate this cleavage between superpower and small power. As economic modernization proceeds throughout the region, the concept of the socialist division of labor also tends to open up other cross-cutting cleavages: between the developed and less-developed countries of the alliance, essentially the northern and southern tiers; and between the traditional international traders (Hungary, Poland, and possibly again Czechoslovakia), which are more interested in moving toward a greater reliance on market forces, and the others who are inclined to insulate their national economies from outside disturbances.[7]

The USSR cannot simply command conformity with its preferences on these issues; nor can the Kremlin apply gross economic or military pressure when its preferences are resisted, without drastically undermining the already weakened legitimacy of its claim to supreme authority in the international communist movement. As economic growth, nationalism, and the declining external military threat reinforce each other in Eastern Europe, the big question is whether the Soviet Union will gradually raise its threshold of tolerance for pluralism.

Additional perspective on this still essentially unpredictable region can be gained by a brief country-by-country survey—starting first in the geopolitically crucial "northern tier" of Poland, East Germany, and Czechoslovakia, and then moving into Hungary, Rumania, and Bulgaria.

The Potential of Polish Nationalism

The communist lid over Polish nationalism has been threatening to blow off in Russia's face ever since World War II. As indicated above, this nearly happened in 1956 at the time of the Hungarian revolution when Gomulka triumphantly faced down the threat of Soviet military intervention; and it was narrowly averted in 1981 by the imposition of a martial law regime under General Jaruzelski.

The Warsaw–Moscow compromises under Gomulka and the Moscow-directed incarceration (and subsequent release) of dissenters by Jaruzelski are symptoms of deep anxiety in the Kremlin over the eruptive potential of swelling Polish discontent with both the economic and political aspects of life as a Soviet satellite.

The pressures for change in the Polish status quo have been building up simultaneously on three fronts: against overdependence on the Soviet Union on economic matters, against economic planning on the Soviet model, and against restrictions on civil liberties and political pluralism. All of these pressures are mobilizable under the banner of Polish nationalism, and any regime that ignores them risks being overturned as insufficiently patriotic. This was precisely the source of Solidarity's strength in 1980, when, as put by Sarah Terry, "widespread social discontent, which elsewhere has remained largely unfocused and unorganized, coalesced spontaneously and almost overnight into a nationwide mass organization with a coherent program."[8]

Although in the early 1970s the desire of the Poles for more economic independence was compatible with the Kremlin's desire to bring more dollars and advanced technology into the Eastern bloc, the results—a crushing Polish indebtedness to the West, exceeding $20 billion by the early 1980s—in turn led to drastic measures to alleviate the hard currency deficit and provided the Kremlin with an excuse for sustaining the Soviet oppressive economic hegemony over the Polish economy. The Poles, along with other members of COMECON, were required to attempt to reduce their debt by maximizing exports to the West while minimizing imports from outside COMECON, which required them to rely more on imports of inferior quality and often higher price (including, significantly, purchases of Soviet oil above the world market price). But these constrictive policies of the late 1970s and early 1980s only made things worse. Terry describes the negative dynamics:

> With shortfalls in energy supply acting as the key bottleneck multiplier, disruptions in transportation, raw materials supply, equipment and spare parts, as well as many other consumer items, set off a viscious downward spiral whereby shortages of inputs led to declines in production and product quality, which in turn reduced export capacity, leading to more cuts in imports, increased strains on domestic markets, deterioration of public services, further pressure on living standards and a weakening of labor incentives and discipline. Attempts to stem the tide—for example by forcing up coal exports (Poland's premier hard-currency earner) or curbing grain imports—led only to longer term structural problems, such as massive damage to power generating equipment (from low-quality or adulterated coal delivered to domestic consumers) or stress slaughtering of breeding stock (for lack of feed grains). In a very real sense, then, the increases in retail meat prices which set off the events of August 1980 were merely the catalyst, but not the root cause of the crisis.[9]

The Soviets are caught on the horns of a dilemma here (and elsewhere in Eastern Europe): Any expansion of exports to bring more hard currency into the COMECON area (which is necessary to pay off accumulated debts and to pay for needed high-technology imports) requires an ability to respond rapidly to demand changes in Western markets; and this requires not only more flexible economic mechanisms (like Hungary's, which will be described below) and more imports from the West, but also considerable contact with Western societies. Eastern Europe cannot be expected to be a region of modernization and economic growth without becoming more and more open to the goods, people, culture, and, inevitably, the political ideas of the noncommunist world. But as this happens, the influence of the Soviet Union over the region is bound to suffer a decline.

In Poland, in particular, efforts to quarantine the effects of East–West economic intercourse from the cultural and political realms cannot succeed over the long run. This now would take a pervasive society-wide repression against not only the workers' movement and the intellectuals but also the Church.

However, an attack on the Church, which in allying itself with the workers and intellectuals has become the bastion and symbol of Polish nationalism, would totally delegitimize any regime that tried it.

Jaruzelski, recognizing that the required revival of economic relations with the West was incompatible with an attempt to reimpose a harsh Stalinist totalitarianism (which would probably have been futile anyway), was evidently able to persuade the Kremlin that martial law should be rescinded, and the repression of dissent should gradually be relaxed.[10] The graffiti scrawled on the walls in 1980 and 1981 may have been scrubbed off, but its message remains indelible: The beginning of the end of the Sovietization of Poland is at hand.

Portentous Stirrings in East Germany

As the reliability of Poland becomes more and more problematical, the role of the German Democratic Republic in the Soviet scheme of things in Eastern Europe gains in importance—both geopolitically and economically. This enlarges the bargaining power of the GDR within the Warsaw Pact and COMECON and has required expanded contacts with the West. Consequently, it has also generated increased Soviet hovering and anxiety over any stirrings toward greater autonomy and Westernization.

Today, the GDR maintains the highest defense burden of any of the Soviet Union's Warsaw Pact partners, as well as the most modern and well-equipped army. The primary responsibility for defending the Baltic area along with the Soviets has been transferred from the Polish military to the East Germany army and navy; and the Soviets and the East Germans, since the 1980–1981 crisis in Poland, have been accelerating the construction of lines of communication and transportation that bypass Poland.[11]

East Germany is also the largest trading partner of the USSR, supplying over two-fifths of Soviet imports of agricultural machinery, two-thirds of its rail vehicle imports, and nearly a quarter of its imports of ships. In return, the GDR obtains most of its energy supplies from the USSR (oil, natural gas, and coal), 80 percent of its sheet metal, 85 percent of its cotton, and nearly all of its cut timber.[12] However, not all of this economic interdependence is entirely congenial to the GDR. Soviet energy prices have often been higher than world energy prices, but the GDR has been prevented from taking advantage of the lower prices. The GDR's efforts to increase its foreign exchange earnings and reduce its external indebtness by exporting microelectronics and consumer goods to the West has met with Kremlin complaints and pressure to stop ignoring Soviet needs.[13]

The biggest worry of the Soviets, of course, is that the strong ethnic and national affinity among Germans will prove to be a stronger force than the "class" loyalty of the GDR to the Marxist–Leninist cause, and that the center of gravity for such a pan-German revival will be located in the westernized and capitalist FRG. This worry has been exacerbated by the evolution over the past decade of a flourishing economic relationship between the two Germanies, making the FRG the GDR's most important trading partner other than the Soviet Union itself. West Germany has also become East Germany's most important source of credit outside the Soviet sphere.

By 1984, when the FRG prepared to accept the deployment of new intermediate-range US missiles following the breakdown of the Soviet–American negotiations to limit superpower "Euromissiles," officials in both Germanies worked assiduously to insulate the inter-German relationship from the new NATO–Warsaw Pact tension. And the Kremlin was surprised and disturbed to find that its threat to deploy Soviet intermediate-range missiles in East Germany to counter the new deployments in West Germany served only to stimulate the fledgling unofficial East German peace movement to protest against the arms policies of *both* superpowers and to demand that the GDR government refuse to accept nuclear weapons on East German soil.

The Soviet anxiety over revived pan-German nationalism was evident in the Kremlin's veto of an agreement between East German party leader Erich Honecker and FRG Chancellor Helmut Kohl to have Honecker visit Bonn in September 1984. In the summer of 1987, however, consistent with Gorbachev's policy of maximizing East–West diplomatic exchanges, and growing cordiality in the Moscow–Bonn relationship, the Kremlin endorsed a new plan to have the East German leader visit West Germany in the fall—despite uncertainties over the pan-German emotions the event would stimulate.[14]

Conformity and Stagnation in Czechoslovakia

Among the northern tier countries, Czechoslovakia and East Germany have exchanged places from where they stood two decades ago in relation to the Soviet Union on the autonomy vs. subordination spectrum. Czechoslovakia, then headed toward its "Prague Spring," was the focus of dynamic self-directed experimentation within the Soviet-dominated socialist commonwealth, while the GDR was in dutiful lock-step with the Kremlin on virtually every item on the agenda of the Warsaw Treaty Organization and COMECON. Today, it is the East Germans who, along with the Hungarians, are in the forefront of economic change (while rather openly criticizing the USSR's sudden belated attempt, under Gorbachev, to combine political and economic reforms), and it is the Czechs, deathly afraid of being burned twice, who have crouched down into sullen conformity.

A Rand Corporation report describes the sad condition into which this once-hopeful enclave in Sovietized Eastern Europe has sunk:

Today...Czechoslovakia is still ruled by men who experienced, survived, and then helped Moscow crush [the Prague Spring]. And what for most Czechs and Slovaks remains but a memory, often irrelevant to their daily lives, is for their rulers an immobilizing trauma. The immobilism affects all important aspects of their rule: relations with the Soviet Union and with Czechoslovakia's allies; relations with the West; and domestic policy in the political, economic, and cultural spheres. It is prompted by a fear of change, because change might, in some way or to some degree, set in motion again those trends that operated in the 1960s and coalesced so dramatically in 1968.[15]

Modernization is feared, as is contact with the West, the result being a sluggish economy and cultural grayness. Czechoslovakia has avoided the staggering Western debt that afflicts Poland and East Germany, but also therefore the Western technological inputs with which to sustain industrial growth and a modern society.

Even under the repressive regime and socioeconomic immobilism, however, the flame of liberalism has not been completely suffocated. Two small groups, Charter 77 and the Committee for the Defense of the Unjustly Accused—despite frequent harassment by the authorities, searches and surveillance, and 48-hour detentions—exist as self-appointed monitors of the government's adherence to the Helsinki Final Act of 1975, especially its "Basket III" provisions on human rights (see Chapter 6, pp. 119–120), which Czechoslovakia signed along with 34 other countries. Charter 77, the best known and internationally admired of the "Helsinki watch" groups in Eastern Europe, takes its name from a charter signed in February 1977 by several hundred Czechoslovakian citizens appealing to the regime in Prague to obey its own laws and international commitments. The Charter 77 group is always careful to assert its adherence to the Czechoslovak constitution and its intention to operate within the law; within this constraint, it has publicly dissented from government policies on a wide range of topics in addition to civil liberties, including: living standards, destruction of the environment, and the stationing of Soviet troops on Czechoslovak territory.[16]

Charter 77 forged links with the Polish Solidarity movement in 1980 and 1981 and like Solidarity became a target of the harsh crackdown at the end of 1981. Since then, the churches have become a haven for those wanting to express their dissatisfaction with existing conditions, but in response, the state has tightened its supervision of religious institutions and publications.

In short, Czechoslovakia stands out today as perhaps the greatest embarrassment to the Soviet way of running things in Eastern Europe. Afraid of the economic experimentalism and political pluralism that are the conditions for dynamic modernization, the Kremlin ordered conformity and docility and received stagnation—this in the country that prior to World War II was the center of East European enlightenment.

Hungary's New Economic Mechanism

In contrast to the way Czechoslovakia has been treated since 1968, the Kremlin, having brutally repressed the Hungarian deviationism in 1956, gradually allowed Budapest, under the leadership of Janos Kadar, considerable leeway to experiment with hybrid socialist/market economy forms of organization. But Hungary's success with its new experimentation was also an embarrassment to the Soviets, for it further undermined the CPSU's pretentions to be the authoritative center for progressive change in the world.

Surely in the economic realm the most venturesome of the COMECON countries during the 1970s and early 1980s, Hungary differed dramatically from the Soviet Union in the degree to which it has dismantled the system of centralized planning and command of the economy and replaced it with a system of indirect controls. Budapest's New Economic Mechanism (NEM) provided a larger role for the market—including more reliance on supply and demand to determine prices and measurement of enterprise performance by profit—than was allowed anywhere else in the Soviet sphere. Citizens had more opportunities to engage in a "secondary economy" of private enterprise to increase their income. By the 1980s, factory employee councils in large and medium firms were choosing their general managers (instead of having them appointed by the central planning ministry in Budapest) and were given authority to decide on investments and production strategies—a move toward management on the Yugoslav model, which the Kremlin heretofore castigated.[17] The NEM, particularly because of its more flexible pricing system, has been conducive to a broadening of commerce with the noncommunist industrial countries. In the mid-1980s, 35 percent of Hungary's trade was with the West (a higher percentage than any other East European country), and, unlike the USSR, it belonged to the International Monetary Fund, the World Bank, and the General Agreement on Tariffs and Trade.

The ability of the Kadar regime to depart from the Soviet model as much as it did in the pre-Gorbachev era can be attributed to its policy—plausibly part of an explicit bargain struck with the Kremlin—of keeping the economic experimentalism from spilling over into the political realm.

But continuing economic modernization has produced new middle classes skeptical of the elitist basis of one-party dictatorship and the ideological orthodoxy that sustains it. More than 25 percent of the population is now composed of white collar workers and intellectuals who, according to studies by Hungarian sociologists, are typically nonideological and individualistic. To avoid isolating the communist establishment from the most dynamic elements of Hungarian society and to prevent the latter from being so alienated that they refuse to lend their best energies to further national development, the Kadar regime has gradually expanded civil liberties (with some setbacks in the repression in 1981 of Hungarian supporters of the Polish Solidarity movement) and cautiously increased opportunities for special interest groups to participate in the political process. In the spring 1985 parliamentary elections, two candidates competed for each seat. These are still only token concessions, however, by a regime premised on the depoliticization of the populace and on the effort to maintain "legitimacy" by the satisfaction of material needs.[18]

Such pragmatic accommodation to the values of the expanding middle class may not be enough to stave off the nationalistic revival that always lurks around the corner in Hungary. The country's traditional fierce nationalism has strong anti-Russian overtones. But this is precisely the source of the deeper dilemmas of the Kadar regime, for in Hungary, like the other countries of Eastern Europe, popular politics inevitably means nationalism—thus the reluctance to open up the governing ranks to extensive popular participation. The present regime or any post-Kadar regime the Soviets would find acceptable must therefore be prepared to deal with the fact of the existing system's increasing unpopularity unless and until there is a substantial loosening of Soviet control over the Warsaw Pact countries generally. The continued presence of 60,000 troops on Hungarian soil is a reminder of the consequences of any inability in Budapest to keep the nation relatively quiescent.

The Rumanian Deviation

Under President Nicolae Ceausescu, Rumania has been the most overtly independent of the Soviet East European satellites—condemning the Soviet invasions of Czechoslovakia (1968) and Afghanistan (1979); not allowing Soviet troops to be stationed in the country; refusing to participate in Warsaw Pact maneuvers; maintaining cordial diplomatic relations with China, Israel, and Albania even during periods of Soviet confrontationist policies toward these countries; sustaining more trade outside the Soviet bloc than any other East European country except Hungary (like Hungary, Rumania has been rewarded by the United States for its independent-mindness by being granted most-favored-nation trading privileges in the US market); and objecting to virtually any Soviet move in COMECON designed to tighten the economic interdependence of the members.

Bucharest early saw the contemplated socialist division of labor as unpalatable. If Rumania were to restrict its commerce with its COMECON partners according to the principle of comparative advantage within the bloc, it would be the supplier of petroleum products, hard minerals, and grains in exchange for machinery and finished consumer goods provided by the more industrialized East Germans, Czechs, Poles, or the Russians themselves. As put by Premier Ion Gheorghe Maurer, "Why should we send our corn to Poland? So Poland can fatten its pigs and buy machinery from the West? We can sell the corn directly and buy the machinery we need ourselves."[19]

The standards by which Rumania would henceforth conduct its relations within and outside of the Soviet sphere were trumpeted boldly in its party Central Committee declaration of 1964 that

> The sovereignty of the socialist state requires that it hold...in its hands all the levers of managing economic and social life. Transmitting such levers to the competence of superstate or extrastate bodies would turn sovereignty into a meaningless notion....Bearing in mind the diversity of the conditions of socialist construction, there are not nor can there be any unique patterns or recipes; no one can decide what is and is not correct for the other countries or parties. It is up to every Marxist–Leninist party, it is a sovereign right of each socialist state, to elaborate, choose, or change the methods of socialist construction....There does not and cannot exist a "parent" party and a "son" party, or "superior" parties and "subordinate" parties, but there exists the great family of Communist and workers' parties, which have equal rights.[20]

Why has the great Soviet Union put up with such frustrations and public embarrassments from its small neighbor without resorting to the coercive bullying tactics it has against Hungary, Czechoslovakia, and Poland?

The failure to apply major force against Ceaucescu's deviance is an indication of the recognition in the CPSU that such interventions are a profound admission of impotence in the noncoercive elements of authority and constitute costly setbacks to its efforts to strengthen its noncoercive authority not only internationally, but at home. Any contemplation of such military interventions involve intense debates within the Politburo and need to be justified by "last resort" or "no tolerable alternative" arguments.[21]

Little Rumania's dissidence, even its defection, constitutes nowhere near the geopolitical threat to Soviet security that would be feared from the defection of either Poland (the USSR's major victory prize in World War II) or Czechoslovakia (traditionally the main invasion corridor from Germany). Thus, Rumania's international diplomatic deviance could be dismissed by the Kremlin as the posturing of a relatively insignificant power.

Moreover, unlike the other cases of more threatening deviation within the bloc, Rumania has hardly been a model of heresy in matters of socioeconomic and domestic political organization. Except for having a less restrictive emigration policy than the other countries in the Soviet sphere, the Ceausescu regime has a poor reputation on human rights, specifically for its persecution of unauthorized Christian denominations (the regime favors the Rumanian Orthodox Church which has been unswervingly loyal to the state). And its organization of its internal economic system is the most rigidly centralized and Stalinist of any of the socialist states. In November 1985, reacting to Gorbachev's initiatives, Ceausescu told his party Central Committee that any move toward private ownership or market economics was "in total contradiction with socialist principles, and we will never permit it to happen under any circumstances."[22]

Thus, even though Rumania is an irritant to the Soviets, it is neither an exemplar of an alternative way of life that could be contagious to others, nor a sufficiently influential energizer of general centrifugal tendencies within the Soviet empire. If, however, in some major East European eruption, or East–West crisis, Bucharest were to allow Rumanian soil to be used as a base of significant operations by anti-Soviet groups, the Kremlin undoubtedly would be unconstrained in applying overwhelming force against its small southwestern neighbor.

Bulgaria's New Economic Self-Assurance and Revived Nationalism

Overtly the most obedient satellite, Bulgaria during the 1970s began to assert itself more within intrabloc affairs. Sofia's new self-confidence appears to result partly from its rather surprising success in developing its economy and partly as a result of a revived pride in its cultural heritage and national identity.

A competent technocratic elite has risen within the government to prod the country to institute reforms on the model of East Germany, if not yet on the model of Hungary's NEP. The Bulgarian planners, in addition to promoting decentralization and limited experimentation with market mechanisms, are evolving their own approach to development based on relatively small projects appropriate to the size and resources of the country. As compared with the economic contraction experienced by the other members of COMECON since the middle 1970s, Bulgaria has been doing remarkably well. Her hard-currency debt has been manageable, and therefore she has not had to implement the kind of drastic import-reduction policies that have generated consumer short-ages in the other countries. And her overall economic growth, though at a somewhat reduced rate from that of the 1970s, has been sustained.

Meanwhile, largely in response to the enthusiasms of Lyudmila Zhikov, the Bulgarian president's daughter (who died prematurely in 1981), the Bulgarians have been rediscovering and taking pride in their historic contributions to European civilization. While in its recent anti-Macedonian and anti-Turkish manifestations, it has not been averse to Soviet policies in the Balkan area, the new nationalistic pride in this small but strategically located country is another significant indicator of the underlying and largely irreversible erosion of the Soviet East European empire now underway.[23]

THE FUTURE OF SOVIET HEGEMONY OVER EASTERN EUROPE

By fits and starts, and sometimes with brutal responses by the Soviet hegemon that temporarily seem to reverse the process, the countries of Eastern

Europe—each in their own way—have been transforming their status from subordinate satellites of the USSR to relatively independent countries with whom the Kremlin must bargain.

Efforts to command obedience to directives of the CPSU will alienate not only citizens who have regained a sense of their nationhood, but also the government and party leaders of the various countries who know that modernization and economic growth cannot be achieved with a demoralized and sullen citizenry, let alone under conditions of martial law or military occupation. Few domestic elites remain in positions of influence in the region who are simply local satraps for the Kremlin, acting to implement policies conceived in Moscow. More and more, they have become just the opposite: agents for their national constituents, acting to extract the best deals they can get in the region from the Soviets and the other members of the coalition, and attempting to enhance their bargaining power by cultivating relationships outside of the coalition.

How far and how fast this evolution will progress in the years ahead, and how much blood will be shed before the Soviets fully readjust their expectations of control, cannot be forecast. What can be forecast is that the direction of the change is irreversible short of the outbreak of a general war for the control of Europe; but this apocalyptic possibility is an event that the Soviets cannot with any degree of sanity regard as better for them than having to accommodate to the new (and old) centrifugal forces.

THE SINO-SOVIET SPLIT: ITS DEPTH AND DURABILITY

The cracking in the monolithic sphere of control the Kremlin had hoped to establish in Europe is, as it were, geologically connected to the split between the People's Republic of China and the Soviet Union. Shocks along the immense Eurasian faultline reverberate into the East European fissures and vice versa. The disturbances radiate outward to communist movements in Western Europe, Africa, South and Southeast Asia, and Latin America.

The intensity of the animosity between the two communist giants is difficult to fathom for anyone not a national of either country. It is partly a product of historic antipathies with racist overtones and of imperial ambitions which overlap, literally and symbolically, at a 4,000 mile common frontier. On the one side lies a sprawling Eurasian multination determined to assimilate the "backward" peoples on its Middle Eastern and Asian peripheries; on the other side are the proud descendants of the glorious Middle Kingdom, bitterly resentful of the cannibalization of their territory and culture by the Russians among others during centuries of Caucasian colonial expansion. Overlay these ancient antagonisms with the contemporary rivalry between Moscow and

Beijing over which is the authoritative center of Marxism–Leninism, and the only surprise in the Sino-Soviet relationship is that they were able to effectuate a working alliance for a decade following Mao's assumption of power in China in 1949.[24]

The real heresy, from the point of view of the Kremlin, has lain not so much in the substance of the Chinese party's open doctrinal disputes with the CPSU as in Beijing's attempts to be an alternative pole of attraction within the world communist movement. When Khrushchev proposed "many roads to socialism" in the 1950s, Mao argued for unity in the camp. In the late 1960s, Brezhnev insisted on only limited sovereignty for smaller communist countries in the coalition, but the Chinese were now champions of absolute sovereignty. While the Kremlin was still cool to neutralism in the Third World, Chou En-lai was warmly courting India's Nehru, Egypt's Nasser, and Indonesia's Sukharno. During the 1960s, Mao bitterly castigated the USSR for becoming a status quo power anxious to be accepted by the West; but in the early 1970s, the toasts to coexistence in Beijing's hall of mirrors set the tone for East–West diplomacy.

The Kremlin has been particularly galled by China's manipulation of the centrifugal tendencies in the East European segments of the Soviet sphere to prosecute its rivalry with the Soviet Union. China publicly chastened the Soviet Union for invading Czechoslovakia in 1968; it has issued joint statements with Rumania against big power hegemony; and it has interpreted the Polish crises of 1970 and 1980–1981 as a reaction against "Soviet social imperialism." The Chinese have also encouraged separatist movements among the Ukranians and other nationalities of the USSR.

From the Chinese perspective, the Soviets have been blatantly protective of their power over other members of the Marxist coalition—even exploitatively so.[25] The leaders in Beijing harbor deep grievances over the Kremlin's withholding of capital for China's industrialization in the 1950s, the failure of Khrushchev to make counter-deterrent threats against US threats to attack China with nuclear weapons during the the Taiwan Straits crisis of 1954 and 1958, and for refusing to help China develop her own nuclear capability.

The continuing deterioration of Sino-Soviet relations during the 1960s, expressed most dramatically at the end of the decade in a series of military clashes along their common border, was the principal reason for Mao's willingness to explore the possibilities for rapprochement with the United States. Although China now had her own nuclear weapons, they were no match for the huge and sophisticated Soviet arsenal, and the Chinese had got wind of the soundings Soviet strategists were taking in the United States of how the Nixon administration might react to a Soviet "surgical strike" to remove the fledgling Chinese nuclear facilities. In the early 1970s, in addition to initiating limited commercial negotiations with the United States, Chinese leaders began to drop hints of possibilities for a major geopolitical realignment, obliquely quoting ancient Chinese aphorisms such as "the enemy of my enemy is my friend." These themes struck a responsive chord in the Nixon administration which, because of domestic isolationist pressures stimulated by the unpopularity of the Vietnam War, was searching for new diplomatic counterweights to the Soviet Union to compensate for the coming reduction in forward-based US military forces, particularly in Asia.

The visible expressions and impact of the simultaneous revision of geopolitical priorities in Washington and Beijing—Nixons's historic 1972 visit to China, the Shanghai Communique, and the ensuing flowering of commercial and diplomatic intercourse—will be discussed in Chapter 6. Here the subject is the sources and durability of China's movement out of the Soviet orbit; and all signs are that within the post-Mao leadership, despite some rather profound struggles over domestic policy, there is no inclination to restore anything even approaching a political–military alliance with Moscow.

China's diplomacy in the 1980s, however, has featured efforts to reduce tensions with the USSR, looking, perhaps, toward eventual "normalization"— but cautiously and pragmatically, so as not to reduce the American incentives for cooperation, and certainly not to restore any substantial dependence on the Soviets. Sino-Soviet trade doubled between the early 1980s and the mid-1980s, reaching a level of over $2 billion for 1986 (still far behind the nearly $8 billion China–US trade). And official delegations in fields of commerce and science and technology are constantly exchanging visits.[26]

In their high-level diplomatic meetings with the Soviets to explore the possibilities for fuller "normalization" of the relationship (these meetings typically are initiated by the Kremlin), the Chinese consistently demand the fulfillment of three stringent preconditions: Soviet military withdrawal from Afghanistan, cessation of Soviet aid to Vietnam's occupation of Kampuchea (Cambodia), and a major reduction in the Soviet military deployments along the Sino-Soviet border. As of this writing, the Chinese apparently do not feel the Soviets have given sufficiently credible indications of their readiness to satisfy these preconditions. Meanwhile, according to Michel Oksenberg, one of the West's most knowledgeable experts on contemporary China,

> The basic Chinese strategy appears to be to foster a stable relationship in which rancor and personal animus are minimized. Beijing wishes to deprive Moscow of pretexts for returning to the volatile, tension-ridden confrontation of the 1960s and 1970s. Cooperation can arise in those realms where compatibility of interest exists, most notably in trade and cultural relations. But Deng [Xiaoping] and his followers, especially in the military, have asserted that the adversarial dimensions of the relationship outweigh the constructive elements.[27]

Whatever the degree of reconciliation between the two communist giants that does take place, it is virtually certain to be limited by China's deeper determination to preserve its political independence and cultural uniqueness.

All indications are that China's leaders are more convinced than ever that such autonomy in the modern world is best pursued by a diversification of international relationships (see Chapter 6) rather than by a return to a reconsolidated Marxist coalition—even under Kremlin assurances of a co-equal Moscow–Beijing partnership.

ENDNOTES

1. Adam B. Ulam, *Expansion and Coexistence: The History of Soviet Foreign Policy* (New York: Praeger, 1968), pp. 589–596.

2. For a thorough and comprehensive analysis of the 1968 Czech crisis and the Soviet response, see Jiri Valenta, *Soviet Intervention in Czechoslovakia, 1968: Anatomy of a Decision* (Baltimore: Johns Hopkins University Press, 1979).

3. My account of the situation in Poland during the 1980–1981 period relies heavily on Andrzej Korbanski's chapter "Poland" in Teresa Rakowska-Harmstone, ed., *Communism in Eastern Europe* (Bloomington: Indiana University Press, 1984), pp. 50–85. See also Jiri Valenta, "The Soviet Union and East Central Europe: Crisis, Intervention, and Normalization," in *Soviet Intervention in Czechoslovakia*, pp. 329–359.

4. Michael T. Kaufman, "Patience Is Paying Off for Poland's Jaruzelski," *New York Times*, 15 February 1987; and John H. Cushman, Jr., "Reagan Lifts Polish Trade Curbs Citing Progress on Human Rights," *New York Times*, 20 February 1987.

5. Michael T. Kaufman, "Gorbachev Draws a Mixed Reaction from Soviet Bloc," *New York Times*, 12 February 1987.

6. William Zimmerman, "Soviet–East European Relations in the 1980s and the Changing International System," in Morris Bornstein, Zvi Gitleman, and William Zimmerman, *East-West Relations and the Future of Eastern Europe: Politics and Economics* (London: George Allen & Unwin, 1981), pp. 87–104.

7. On the cross-cutting cleavages within Eastern Europe see Vernon V. Aspaturian, "Eastern Europe in World Perspective," in Rakowska-Harmstone, *Communism in Eastern Europe*, pp. 8–49.

8. Sarah M. Terry, "The Implications of Economic Stringency and Political Succession for Stability in Eastern Europe in the Eighties," in US Congress, Joint Economic Committee, *East European Economies: Slow Growth in the 1980s*. Vol. 1. *Economic Performance and Policy*, 99th Cong., 1st sess. (Washington, DC: GPO, 1985), p. 519.

9. *Ibid.*, pp. 518–519.

10. Korbanski, "Poland," pp. 57–69.

11. F. Stephen Larrabee, *The Challenge to Soviet Interests in Eastern Europe* (Santa Monica: The Rand Corporation, 1984), R-3190-AF, pp. 99–100.

12. Angela E. Stent, "Soviet Policy toward the German Democratic Republic," in Sarah Meiklejohn Terry, ed., *Soviet Policy in Eastern Europe* (New Haven: Yale University Press, 1984), p. 45.

13. Larrabee, *Challenge to Soviet Interests*, p. 104.

14. James M. Markham, "Soviet Calls the Tune in a Duet Set in Germany," *New York Times*, 19 July 1987.

15. J. F. Brown and A. Ross Johnson, *Challenges to Soviet Control in Eastern Europe: An Overview* (Santa Monica: The Rand Corporation, 1984), R-3189-AF, p. 22.

16. Michael T. Kaufman, "Are Things Looser in the Eastern Bloc? Yes and No," *New York Times*, 4 August 1985; and Otto Ulc, "Czechoslovakia," in Rakowska-Harmstone, *Communism in Eastern Europe*, pp. 115–136.

17. Larrabee, *Challenges to Soviet Interests*, pp. 56–82; and Laura D' Andrea Tyson, *Economic Adjustment in Eastern Europe* (Santa Monica: The Rand Corporation, 1984).

18. Bennet Kovrig, "Hungary," in Rakowska-Harmstone, *Communism in Eastern Europe*, pp. 86–114; Kaufman, "Are Things Looser in the Eastern Bloc?"

19. Premier Maurer quoted by Anatole Shub, *An Empire Loses Hope: The Return of Stalin's Ghost* (Norton: New York, 1970), p. 204.

20. Statement of the Rumanian Workers' Party Concerning the Problems of the International Communist and Working Class Movement, April 1964. Text in William E. Griffith, *Sino-Soviet Relations 1964-1965* (Cambridge: MIT Press, 1967), pp. 269–296.

21. See Valenta, *Soviet Intervention in Czechoslovakia*.

22. Ceausescu remark of November 1985, quoted by Paul Lewis, "Economy Tight, Rumanians Face a Long Winter," *New York Times*, 15 December 1985.

23. For recent developments in Bulgaria, I have relied on Brown and Johnson, *Challenges to Soviet Control in Eastern Europe*, pp. 19–22.

24. O. Edmund Clubb, *Twentieth Century China* (New York: Columbia University Press, 1964).

25. A. Doak Barnett, *China and the Major Powers in East Asia* (Washington: Brookings Institution, 1977), pp. 20–87.

26. Michel Oksenberg, "China's Confident Nationalism," *Foreign Affairs*, Vol. 65, No. 3 (Special Annual Issue: *America and the World 1986*, published February 1987), pp. 501–532.

27. Oksenberg, *ibid.*, p. 510. See also International Institute for Strategic Studies, *Strategic Survey 1985-1986* (London: IISS, 1986), pp. 152–159.

CHAPTER SIX

Spans across the Ideological Divide

Some of the most contentious disputes within the US-led and Soviet-led coalitions are over what kinds of cooperative relations are to be pursued with members of the rival coalition and over the extent to which such relations ought to be based on a concerted coalition strategy. Inevitably, as East–West contacts proliferate, common coalition strategies are more and more difficult to sustain; indeed, for some countries in each of the cold war coalitions an independent cultivation of relationships across the ideological divide has been a means of getting out from under the hegemonial grip of the coalition leader. Thus, today's overall East–West "bridge-building" activity, even though the superpowers are constructing spans of their own, is both a symptom of and stimulus to the centrifugal forces disintegrating each of the cold war coalitions.

On the Soviet side, there has been considerable worry that opening up contact with the West, like applying fresh oxygen to boiling liquid, can strongly increase the chances of major eruptions in the communist countries. As incentives and opportunities for cross-alliance interactions rise, the risks— particularly to the Soviet Union's control over Eastern Europe and over its own restive nationality groups—also rise. The Kremlin has been well aware of these dangers, at times obsessed by them, as demonstrated by its military interventions in Hungary in 1956 and Czechoslovakia in 1968, by its political bludgeoning of Poland to suppress the Solidarity trade union movement in 1981, and by its on-again, off-again tightening of restrictions on dissidence within the USSR. Yet despite the obvious risks to its hegemonial control, the Soviet leadership seems to have rejected for the foreseeable future a return to the policies of economic autarchy and tightly sealed political isolation for the Socialist Commonwealth. The reasons for this shift in Soviet policy—which since the mid-1960s appears to be a firmly implanted grand strategy—will be explored below. Communist China's emergence from an even more severe xenophobia will also be analyzed.

In the West, particularly in the United States, there usually is a deep wariness of the Kremlin's motives whenever Moscow indicates a willingness to facilitate cooperative arrangements across the divide. (Most of the top US officials breathed sighs of relief after World War II when the Soviets rejected the Baruch Plan for the international ownership and control of nuclear energy and weapons, and when Stalin refused to allow Soviet or East European participation in the Marshall Plan for economic reconstruction of Europe.) In some quarters of the US policy community, including high officials in the Reagan administration, the policies of political detente, arms control, and expanded East–West economic intercourse that had been initiated by the Europeans in the late 1960s and embraced by the Nixon administration in the early 1970s have been viewed as naive in their assumptions about Soviet intentions and dangerous in their encouragement of military retrenchment in the West at the very time the Soviets were embarked on a major military buildup. But it was the Reagan administration's attempt to revive a militarized anti-Soviet policy that turned out to be unrealistic, for the elements in the world situation that led to detente were deeply cutting structural developments that would take more than cold war rhetoric to reverse.

THE PAN-EUROPEAN IMPETUS

East–West bridge-building first got going in earnest in Europe, a good five years before the United States and the Soviet Union decided in the early 1970s to construct their own substantial ties of bilateral communication and cooperation. And the intra-European activity continued to expand even during the 1978–1984 period as the superpowers in a revival of cold war animosity were reducing their cooperative interaction.

From the standpoint of the Europeans, the continent's bifurcation is an aberration—a temporary condition superimposed on them by World War II and its immediate aftermath. Prior to the war, about 60 percent of Eastern Europe's trade was with Western Europe, and about one-fourth of this was with Germany. Accordingly, the revival of the economic and political health of the European nations ought to be part and parcel of the reestablishment of a vigorous pan-European economy and civilization, and a sloughing off of their relationships of subordinate dependency on the essentially non-European superpowers.

Although neither superpower has been particularly anxious to hasten the full maturing of European self-reliance on its side of the divide, it has attempted to stimulate pan-Europeanism as well as nationalism in its rival's sphere of influence. But for both superpowers this stratagem has proven to be a two-headed hammer, also dislodging the cement of its own hegemonic alliance system.

The West European allies of the United States, to be sure, have had much more leeway to forge their own East–West links than the Soviets have allowed their allies. This asymmetry has affected attitudes in Washington toward Kremlin proposals for all-European security conferences and economic intercourse since the 1960s. The United States has been apprehensive that the Soviets have been trying to create opportunities to gain legitimacy for their sphere of control in Eastern Europe while playing off the Western countries against one another. The West Europeans, by contrast, have discounted the American perceptions of a political asymmetry in the East's favor, emphasizing instead how increased opportunities for diplomatic contact and commerce with the countries of Eastern Europe can help enlarge the fissures in the Soviet sphere, and how genuine detente—rather than sealing the permanent division of Europe—deligitimizes the Kremlin's insistence on maintaining its tight hierarchical control over its neighbors.

These transatlantic differences over the risks of dealing with the East were temporarily suppressed in the late 1940s and early 1950s when the crucial role the United States had assumed in the economic reconstruction of Western Europe also put the United States in the driver's seat when it came to the coalition's grand strategy. However, as alluded to in Chapter 4, one of the means by which America's European partners have been able to express their revived international power has been through the exploration of opportunities for East–West cooperation on their own without waiting for the United States to endorse their efforts.

Under the leadership of President Charles de Gaulle, France was the first to candidly assert a French and all-European interest in more intensive interaction between the West and East Europeans that might not be congenial to *either* superpower. His concept of a revived and flourishing Europe "from the Atlantic to the Urals" underlay his diplomatic demarche of 1966, which included his own visit to Moscow, visits by his foreign minister to Warsaw, Prague, Bucharest, Budapest, and Sophia, and the withdrawal of France from the integrated NATO military organization. Grandly pursuing his European idea, which he sometimes referred to as a "third force," he visited Poland and Rumania with great fanfare in 1967 and 1968, and would have visited most of the other countries in Eastern Europe during the next few years had he not resigned the presidency in 1969.[1] All of de Gaulle's successors carried forward his basic Eastern policy of weaving an ever-thickening web, particularly of commercial relations, with the USSR and the other members of COMECON.

De Gaulle's demarche made it legitimate for West Germany to experiment with a policy of enlarging contacts and commerce with the East—a reversal of Chancellor Konrad Adenauer's policy of making Soviet agreement to a reunification of Germany through free elections a precondition for detente. While still not ready to recognize the government in East Germany, Adenauer's successors (Chancellors Ludwig Erhard and then Kurt Kiesinger) in 1966 began to promote trade with Eastern Europe and, somewhat ambivalently, with the USSR. The Erhard government also sent a "Peace Note" to all other governments, including the communist governments in Eastern Europe, proposing an exchange of declarations to refrain from using force in international disputes.[2]

Thus, a modest *Ostpolitik* was already in place in Bonn by 1969 when Chancellor Willy Brandt, as head of the coalition of his Social Democrats and the Free Democrats, launched a more assertive Eastern diplomacy—producing the 1970 FRG–USSR Non-Aggression Pact, the 1970 treaties with Poland and Czechoslovakia recognizing the post-World War II borders, the 1971 Quadrapartite Agreement on Berlin (signed by the United States, the USSR, Britain, and France), and finally the Basic Treaty of 1972 between the FRG and the GDR.

Under Willy Brandt's leadership, West German *Ostpolitik* became the catalyst of the larger movement toward East–West detente resulting in the Nixon–Brezhnev summit of 1972. But Brandt was highly sensitive to concerns in Moscow and the United States that the European equilibrium not be destabilized. The FRG's first normalization agreements were with the Soviet Union; only then did Bonn negotiate directly with Warsaw and Prague, thus deferring to the Soviet Union's compulsion to retain authority over the detente policies of its allies. Brandt was also insistent that his program of increasing interaction with the communist countries was fully compatible with Germany's continuing support for economic and political unity in Western Europe within the larger framework of the NATO alliance. Typical was his April 1972 article in *Foreign Affairs* reassuring the Americans, and not incidentally reminding the Russians, that "as far as security is concerned, the United States and Western Europe will retain their close connection and remain dependent on each other." Any substantial reduction of the American armed presence in Europe, he said, "must be part as well as a result of decreasing tension between East and West."[3]

SOVIET-AMERICAN DETENTE AND COLLABORATION

The notion prevailing in both Washington and Moscow for roughly two decades after World War II that interests of the country and its coalition partners could best be maintained by a policy of disassociation from, and coercive deterrence of, the other superpower was perhaps essentially flawed at the outset. It did not correspond with the reality that their spheres of control did not encompass many areas of the globe in which their interests might come into severe conflict and lead to war. It failed to take into account the dramatic changes in military technology that made imperative a certain amount of cooperation between the rival superpowers in their arming and deterrent strategies if they were not to inadvertently provoke a mutually suicidal holocaust. It did not sufficiently address the need of the United States and the Soviet Union to concert their actions in certain fields—such as the international dissemination of nuclear materials or weapons, or new rules for using the ocean—in which as superpowers they might have common interests different from many of the other countries. Nor was the perpetuation of the basic cold war alienation sensible in the economic realm, where the well-being of each side might be advanced by removing some of the political barriers to commercial intercourse between them.

Accordingly, even within the essentially polarized world system that coalesced after 1947, the superpowers by fits and starts attempted to supplement their arms-length relationship with some minimal cooperative efforts to keep their rivalry, and dangerous developments in the world at large, from exploding into another world war. Although the general presumption among US policymakers before the 1970s was that the Kremlin was furthering the idea of peaceful coexistence mainly to sow dissension in the anticommunist coalition, there were some notable US–Soviet agreements that in some ways prefigured the Nixon–Brezhnev detente: the Austrian Peace Treaty of 1955 providing for a mutual withdrawal of troops, demilitarization, neutralization, and a Western-style political democracy; the Nuclear Test Ban Treaty of 1963; the 1963 agreement (growing out of the Cuban missile crisis) to establish a direct communications link, the so-called Hot Line, between the two governments; and the Nuclear Nonproliferation Treaty of 1968.

It was not until the early 1970s, however, that substantial credit was given by US policymakers to the hypothesis that the Soviet leadership, while not abandoning the goal of communizing the world, might have made a historic shift in grand strategy away from isolation and antagonism vis-à-vis the West and toward securing and developing the USSR through cooperation and commerce with the noncommunist industrial world.

Actually, the Soviets had made such a shift in grand strategy by 1966, and there had been signs even earlier that they were preparing for such a reorientation of their global policy. Signals of the Soviets' shift were picked up by European statesmen such as de Gaulle and Brandt and gave them to believe that efforts to help move the Soviets in this direction might be worth a serious try.

A strong indication that a major change was in the works in at least Soviet foreign economic policy was the Kremlin's public revision, at the Twenty-Third Party Congress in 1966, of its standing doctrine that the Socialist Commonwealth ought to produce all its own economic requirements. To be sure, the Soviets since Stalin's death in 1953 had made periodic forays into the capitalist marketplace to purchase machinery and technology and in 1963 had to negotiate a huge wheat deal with the United States and other grain producers to make up for some disastrous crop failures. Such shopping excursions had been officially defined by the Kremlin as ad hoc and stop-gap measures not in any way inconsistent with the policy of COMECON self-sufficiency.[4] But now, before the representatives of most of the world's communist parties, Premier Aleksei Kosygin was admitting that "It is becoming more and more evident that the scientific and cultural revolution under way in the modern world calls for freer international contacts and creates conditions for broad economic exchanges between socialist and capitalist countries."[5]

This historic Soviet decision to participate in the capitalist international economy appears to have been dictated by the following considerations: A technological gap between the two halves of the industrialized world (communist and noncommunist) was threatening to negate much of the international influence the Russians gained as a result of their rapid modernization, industrialization, and strategic buildup. Continuing modernization now required the Soviet Union to make a substantial reallocation of resources into many of the high-technology, largely civilian areas which, until recently, had been given low priority in comparison with military and space needs. But taking off into a kind of advanced industrialization that would allow the Warsaw Pact countries to maintain military parity *and* satisfy rising consumer demands would require substantial inputs from the West, especially in the fields of information technology and electronics. These expensive inputs could not be had for nothing. They would have to be purchased in the world economy, and this in turn would require flexible economic decision making capable of responding to demand changes in the world market. Only a fully creditable Soviet policy of peaceful coexistence, however, would induce the noncommunist industrial countries to extend credits, liberalize their strategic embargo lists, and otherwise let down their political barriers to East–West commerce.[6]

Henceforth, Soviet decisions about whether to produce a commodity or to purchase it in the world market would be based heavily on calculations of the cost of production relative to the cost of importation. In a complimentary move, producers in the USSR were to have their quotas and product specifications formulated with greater sensitivity to the world market than previously.

At the Twenty-Fourth Party Congress, General Secretary Leonid Brezhnev called special attention to the "economic, scientific, and technical ties, in some instances resting on a long-term basis," being developed "with the countries of the capitalist world." And he labeled as "*basic* concrete tasks" cooperative projects for "conservation of the environment, development of power and other natural resources, development of transport and communications, prevention and eradication of the most dangerous widespread diseases, and the exploration and development of outer space and the world oceans."[7]

The Kremlin also developed a geostrategic rationale to justify their shift toward peaceful interaction with the capitalists: The Soviet Union's attainment of parity with the United States in strategic nuclear forces had changed the overall "correlation of forces" (the Soviet term for the global balance of military, economic, and political power) from one in which the capitalists might contemplate initiating another world war in order to prevent the global ascendancy of socialism, to a situation in which this was no longer a real option for the capitalists. Consequently, they—the capitalist countries—now might be willing, however reluctantly, to accept the necessity of the peaceful coexistence with the socialists.

Meanwhile, on the American side there was a parallel revamping of the cold war doctrines that, prior to the 1970s, had prevented normal commerce with the Soviets and members of their coalition.

Of crucial importance to the change in US policy was the information on the Soviet policy changes revealed at the Twenty-Third and Twenty-Fourth Party Congresses and corroborated by intelligence data on the new pattern of Soviet international commercial activities. It became an accepted premise within the Nixon administration that the Soviets, because of seriously lagging modernization efforts, were sorely in need of substantial long-term economic intercourse with the noncommunist industrial countries and that the Kremlin therefore really did want a protracted period of peaceful coexistence—not (as it was previously assumed) for the purpose of destabilizing the West, but rather to allow the Soviet Union access to the advanced technologies of the leading capitalist countries and to earn the foreign exchange needed to purchase the inputs necessary for modernizing the Soviet economy.

By the late 1960s, there was also heavy lobbying by the exporting sectors of the US economy to normalize trade with the Soviet Union and its allies. As US producers faced increasingly vigorous competition globally (and in the American market itself) from the West Europeans and Japanese, the US merchandise trade balance was rapidly deteriorating. This loss of markets to US competitors was partly due to the American involvement in the Vietnam War and the resulting inflation that increased the price of US goods; it was partly the inevitable result of the revival of the economic strength of the war-devastated countries. In this context, US self-denial of access to willing importers in the Soviet sphere seemed economically foolhardy.[8]

The readiness of the National Association of Manufacturers and the US Chamber of Commerce and large segments of American labor to support efforts to penetrate the beckoning Eastern market provided the Nixon administration the opportunity it was seeking to convert the Soviet hunger for commerce with the United States into a US political asset.

Back in the 1960s, former Vice President Nixon and the scholarly strategist Henry Kissinger had been among those disparaging attempts to alter Soviet international behavior through trade. And during the first two years of the Nixon administration, it appeared that the president and his national security adviser were giving short shrift to any such nongeopolitical notions. Consistent with this posture, the administration in 1970 pressured the Ford Motor Company to back out of negotiations to participate in the construction of a huge Soviet truck factory on the Kama River near Moscow, on the grounds that some of the trucks might find their way to North Vietnam for use in the war.

But in 1971—rather suddenly, it seemed—firms anxious to cultivate new commercial relationships with the USSR began to experience success in getting the US government to approve East–West commercial deals previously denied them. Prior to a highly publicized visit to the Soviet Union of the American Secretary of Commerce, the government granted more than a billion dollars' worth of export licenses to American firms attempting to obtain orders from the Kama River plant and other Soviet projects.

Collateral moves on both sides during the fall of 1971 indicated that the logjam in their commercial relations was loosening. Having suffered a very poor harvest, the Russians arranged a $1 billion purchase of American surplus food grains; the State Department said it was ready to reduce advance notification required from Soviet ships entering US ports; and bilateral talks were scheduled to effect additional mutual easing of shipping restrictions. Other prospective agreements were revealed in numerous background stories from government ministries in both countries. The most lucrative deals were foreseen in cooperative efforts to develop and market the copper deposits and other raw material sources in Siberia including natural gas. Given the facts that in 1971 the US merchandise trade balance was running a deficit and that the administration had been driven to extreme measures to reverse the trend (devaluation of the dollar, refusing to convert dollars into gold, a 10 percent import surcharge), these measures to increase exports to the East were hardly unpopular.

Nixon and Kissinger conceived of the change in US East–West commercial policy as part of the larger grand strategy they had been developing. They had by no means adopted the purely economic rationale of the industrial and agricultural interests lobbying for a removal of the political barriers to trade with the communists. Two of the basic premises of the emerging grand strategy were: (1) the Soviet Union's *economic* need to open up commerce with the industrial countries was greater than the latter's need for commerce with the Communist countries; (2) if the United States and its allies wisely bargained with the Soviet Union from this position of economic strength, the Russians, if not openly backed into a corner, could be made to pay a *political* price for an expansion of East–West commerce. As Kissinger more delicately put it in a public explanation of the US policy shift, "We have approached the question of economic relations with deliberation and circumspection and as an act of policy not primarily of commercial opportunity."[9] The containment of Soviet aggressive expansion would henceforth need to be accomplished more by "carrots" than by "sticks." The big stick of nuclear deterrence of Soviet expansion had lost most of its utility as the Soviets attained essential nuclear parity with the United States, and the nonnuclear sticks were being whittled down by an antidefense majority in the Congress reflecting the popular isolationist reaction to the war in Vietnam. The lever of expanded economic intercourse, combined with the new US ability to worry the Kremlin about how far the developing US–China rapprochement would go (another essential feature of Kissinger's new international "mosaic"), could supplant the previous policy of threatening US military counteraction against Soviet international power plays and threatening major increases in the US military budget to dissuade the Kremlin from provocative buildups of Soviet military forces. East–West commerce would thus be linked to Soviet international moderation and seriousness in negotiating arms limitation agreements.

The very different purposes of the two superpowers in laying economic spans across the ideological divide was artfully finessed in the central plank of the declaration on "Basic Principles of Relations" signed by President Nixon and General Secretary Brezhnev at their May 1972 summit:

> The USA and the USSR regard commercial and economic ties as an important and necessary element in the strengthening of their bilateral relations and thus will actively promote the growth of such ties. They will facilitate cooperation between the relevant organizations and enterprises of the two countries and the conclusion of appropriate agreements and contracts, including long-term ones.[10]

The joint communique at the end of the Moscow summit cleared the way for accelerated negotiations to remove some of the still-standing barriers to Soviet–American economic intercourse. "Both sides...agree that realistic conditions exist for increasing economic ties," said the communique. "These ties should develop on the basis of mutual benefit in accordance with generally accepted international practice" (a phrase particularly important to the Soviets in their effort to have the United States remove the special tariffs and quotas on imports from the USSR and other COMECON countries). Detailed negotiations were to be responsive to guidelines developed by a Joint US–Soviet Commercial Commission, which was also charged with the responsibility of working out a comprehensive bilateral trade agreement.[11]

This omnibus economic accord was linked to the general agreement between the United States and the Soviet Union to moderate their political competition. The capstone on this framework for the Soviet–American relationship was the SALT agreement to mutually limit their strategic armaments. In the May 1972 Declaration of Principles signed by Nixon and Brezhnev, the governments of the United States and the Soviet Union agreed:

First. They will proceed from the common determination that in the nuclear age there is no alternative to conducting their mutual relations on the basis of peaceful coexistence. Differences in ideology and in the social systems of the USA and the USSR are no obstacles to the bilateral development of normal relations based on the principles of sovereignty, equality, noninterference in internal affairs, and mutual advantage.

Second. The USA and the USSR attach major importance to preventing the development of situations capable of causing a dangerous exacerbation of their relations. Therefore, they will do their utmost to avoid military confrontations and to prevent the outbreak of nuclear war. They will always exercise restraint in their mutual relations, and will be prepared to negotiate and settle their differences by peaceful means. Discussions and negotiations on outstanding issues will be conducted in a spirit of reciprocity, mutual accommodation and mutual benefit.

Both sides recognize that efforts to obtain unilateral advantage at the expense of the other, directly or indirectly, are inconsistent with these objectives.

The prerequisites for maintaining and strengthening peaceful relations between the USA and the USSR are the recognition of the security interests of the parties based on the principle of equality and the renunciation of the use or threat of force.

Third. The USA and the USSR have a special responsibility, as do other countries which are permanent members of the United Nations Security Council, to do everything in their power so that conflicts or situations will not arise which would serve to increase international tensions. Accordingly they will seek to promote conditions in which all countries will live in peace and security and will not be subject to outside interference in their internal affairs.

[The Declaration of Principles contained twelve clauses in all.][12]

The arms control agreements signed at the 1972 summit—the ABM Treaty and the Interim Agreement on strategic offensive weapons—marked the culmination of the first round of Strategic Arms Limitation Talks (SALT) begun in November 1969. Going into the summit, the SALT negotiators still were struggling to come up with mutually acceptable texts; but it was so important to be able to show that significant arms control was integral to the new detente between the superpowers that Henry Kissinger and Soviet Foreign Minister Gromyko simply took over the SALT drafting process from their respective negotiating teams and, running back and forth between Nixon and Brezhnev, themselves conducted the final detailed bargaining.[13]

In combination, the ABM Treaty and the Interim Agreement on strategic offensive forces constituted a Soviet–American suicide pact against a nuclear World War III. The SALT accords reinforced the Mutual Assured Destruction (MAD) basis of the balance of nuclear terror by virtually eliminating (in the ABM Treaty) the deployment of defensive weapons on either side that could substantially reduce the massive destruction each would suffer in a strategic war, and allowing each side (in the Interim Agreement) sufficient strategic offensive weapons to survive even an all-out first strike by the other superpower and still to retaliate in a massively destructive second-strike. Each side, in effect, was to hold the other's population "hostage" against any attempt to start a strategic nuclear war.

By the end of 1972, the tally of successful Soviet–American negotiations included the following breakthroughs: (1) agreement by the Russians to pay back $722 million, by the year 2001, of their wartime Lend Lease debt, in return for which President Nixon would now authorize the Export-Import Bank to extend credits and guarantees for Soviet purchases of US goods; (2) a commitment by the Nixon administration to seek congressional extension to the Soviet Union of most-favored-nation (MFN) tariff rates; (3) provision for the United States to set up government-sponsored and commercial offices in Moscow to facilitate the work of US businessmen seeking contracts, and similar provisions for Russians in Washington; (4) the delivery of 440 million bushels of wheat to the Soviet Union; (5) a maritime accord opening forty ports in each country to the other's shipping; (6) an agreement between the navies of the two countries to take steps to prevent high-risk incidents at sea; (7) the start of joint work on a combined space flight planned for 1975 of the US Apollo and the Soviet Soyuz; (8) a series of projects to solve environmental problems in which Soviet and American experts would work together in both countries; (9) an agreement to set up the International Institute of Applied Systems Analysis, a multinational think tank involving social and systems scientists from both countries, as well as from Britain, France, Japan, West Germany, East Germany, Czechoslovakia, Poland, Italy, Canada, Rumania, and Bulgaria, to study problems of industrialized society; and (10) joint US–Soviet projects in medical research, oceanography, and environmental problems.[14]

The Soviets during this period played to the rising fears in the West and Japan of an impending energy shortage by offering secured deliveries of Siberian natural gas to countries that would help them—through financial credits and technology transfers—build some mammouth trans-Siberian pipelines. One contemplated project was to involve three-way cooperation between American companies, the USSR, and Japan for construction of two eastward-flowing pipelines, associated liquification plants, and tankers to carry natural gas from the USSR to Japan and the United States. Another giant project, on which negotiations were successful, involved long-term agreements with West European firms to supply important high-technology components on long-term credit arrangements for the construction of westward-flowing pipelines to carry natural gas from Soviet energy fields to Western Europe. This latter project, as recounted in Chapter 4, was to become the focus during the first Reagan administration of a new divergence between the United States and many of its coalition partners over the role and conduct of relations with the Soviet-led coalition.

CSCE AND MBFR: MULTILATERAL NEGOTIATIONS ON PEACE AND SECURITY ISSUES

Suspicions in the West that the Soviet interest in detente was motivated in substantial part by the aim of reducing the presence in Europe of the United States—leaving the USSR as the European hegemon—were fueled by the Soviet campaign in the late 1960s and early 1970s for an all-European conference on security and cooperation. Simultaneously with the intensification of Soviet commercial negotiations with France and Germany in 1966, the Warsaw Pact countries issued calls for all the European states, including the USSR, to meet to finally legitimize the post-World War II order in Europe (which would include recognition of the two Germanies) and thus end the East–West confrontation, which would allow for the dissolution of the two alliances and the withdrawal from the continent of all foreign (meaning American) troops. The West Europeans were by no means ready to dispense with the American presence as a counterweight to Soviet power, and the Kremlin knew this; so these Eastern proposals were generally dismissed as exercises in propaganda. In any case, the possibility of convening an all-European conference was precluded for a time by the Soviet invasion of Czechoslovakia in 1968.

But by the fall of 1969, the campaign for such a conference was back in full swing, and with a new seriousness, for this time the Warsaw Pact countries indicated a willingness to accept the participation of the United States and Canada. The basic counterthrust of the NATO countries was to call for negotiations to achieve Mutual and Balanced Force Reductions (MBFR), a call they made repeatedly over the next three years, while the Warsaw Pact continued to press for a Conference on Security and Cooperation in Europe (CSCE).[15]

The Soviets were, in effect, saying to the West: Remove the political cause of war in Europe—your refusal to recognize the legitimacy of the territorial status quo, including the existence of two Germanies—and then we can make progress in the field of arms reduction. The West was saying to the Soviets: Reduce your overbearing military presence and be satisfied with an essentially equal military balance in Europe, and then we can begin to have a meaningful dialogue with you and the East Europeans about an all-European system of security and cooperation.

The impasse over which occurs first, the European Security Conference or MBFR negotiations, was broken in the new mood of optimism generated by the successful conclusion of East–West negotiations on Berlin in the fall of 1971 and the agreements achieved between Nixon and Brezhnev on strategic arms limitation and economic cooperation in the spring of 1972. The European Security Conference CSCE and MBFR negotiations would convene at about the same time: the preparatory conference for the political and economic forum in Helsinki at the end of November 1972, and the preliminary meetings on the troop negotiations in Vienna two months later.

Initially, the thirty-five member Conference of Security and Cooperation in Europe appeared to be a more important instrument for the Soviets than it was for the West. It was to be the functional equivalent of a World War II peace conference (which never took place) and would legitimize the USSR's wartime territorial gains, the division of Germany, and, by implication, the Soviet sphere of influence in Eastern Europe. But by the time the CSCE concluded on August 1, 1975, it had been partially transformed by the Western participants into a forum for calling the Soviet and East European governments to account for their failure to accord their citizens many of the basic human rights that members of the United Nations, including the USSR, had subscribed to in the Universal Declaration of Human Rights and various corollary protocols.

The *Final Act* of the CSCE (sometimes referred to as the Helsinki accords) reflects these conflicting Eastern and Western concepts of the basis for a legitimate and durable peace in Europe.

The provisions on "Security in Europe" (Basket I) contain what the Soviets most wanted: clauses affirming respect for the sovereignty of states, the inviolability of their frontiers, and their territorial integrity. At Western insistence it also has a clause affirming respect for human rights and fundamental freedoms. In addition, the West was successful in getting the Soviets to agree to a special document on "Confidence-Building Measures," providing for advance notification and international observation of large military exercises. The provisions on "Cooperation in the Field of Economics, of Science and Technology and the Environment" (Basket II) are rather straightforward endorsements of what was already transpiring in the atmos-phere of detente. The Western delegations, however, made their acceptance of Basket I and Basket II conditional upon the acceptance by the Conference of the Basket III provisions on "Cooperation in Humanitarian and Other Fields" which enumerated various human rights that needed improvement, giving special emphasis to the free movement of people, ideas, and information within and between countries.[16]

The ability of the Western delegations to turn the CSCE into an instrument of face-to-face official pressure on the USSR and East European governments on human rights issues converted the US Department of State from a cool, if not reluctant, supporter of this ideological extravaganza into a rather enthusi-astic supporter. Accordingly, when President Ford flew to Helsinki for the signing of the Final Act by heads of state, he came armed with ringing rhetoric connecting what had been accomplished at the CSCE to the American rededication to the universal cause of human liberty then being celebrated in the Bicentennial of the Declaration of Independence. (In the Reagan wing of the Republican Party, however, "Helsinki" continued to be viewed as a Western "sell-out" to the Russians, typifying all that was wrong with the detente policy.)

The periodic CSCE follow-up conferences have been in many respects recapitulations of the East–West bargaining that went on in the foundational conference of 1973–1975, with the West attempting to hold the East to account on the human rights provisions of Basket III and the Soviets attempting to separate out and give special emphasis to projects for commercial and technological cooperation.

In the field of military "confidence-building" measures, however, the CSCE follow-up process has resulted in a significant arms control accord: the 1986 Stockholm agreement (signed by the thirty-five original signatories of the Helsinki Final Act of 1975) obligating the governments to inform each other of substantial military exercises and troop movements, allowing mutual observation of military exercises, and allowing signatories to carry out inspections on each other's territory of military activities suspected of violating the accord.[17]

The European force reduction negotiations, which at American insistence were to run parallel to the CSCE, have still (at this writing) to produce an agreement. The principal reason for the lack of success is symbolized by the debate over the official name of the enterprise: The NATO countries, insisting that the Warsaw Pact countries hold a military advantage in the European theater, have wanted the negotiations to *achieve* a balance (thus *Mutual and Balanced Force Reductions*); the Warsaw Pact countries, insisting that essential equality already exists in the theater, have maintained that the negotiations are supposed to *stabilize* the balance (thus *Mutual Reduction of Forces*).

Gradually, over the course of more than a dozen years, the differences between the two sides over initial specific MBFR measures have been considerably narrowed by the negotiators, to the point where political decisions at the highest levels in Moscow and Washington could well produce an agreement at any time. The Soviets have conceded to asymmetrical reductions (more of their forces to be withdrawn in the first phase than the United States would withdraw) to reach a common ceiling of 900,000 military personnel deployed by each alliance in Central Europe. And the United States has indicated a willingness to allow such mutual troop reductions to proceed prior to resolving the differences between the Western estimates of currently deployed Warsaw Pact troops and the Pact's own count, in return for Soviet willingness to allow for appropriate post-reduction verifications.[18]

THE AGREEMENTS ON BERLIN AND GERMANY: POLITICAL STABILIZATION OF THE PRECARIOUS CENTER

Just as the central confrontations of the cold war have taken place over the Berlin and German issues, so the hopes for a durable East–West detente have depended on being able to avoid these confrontations and to resolve the underlying German "problem." The most dangerous confrontations have occurred over Western access rights to the city of Berlin and the roles and jurisdictions of the various governments responsible for the administration of the city; but the successive Berlin crises of the last few decades have been only symptoms of the presumably irreconcilable ideological/geopolitical visions in the East and the West for the future of Germany as a whole, and the consequent clashes over the legitimacy of existing political arrangements.

Both sides, accordingly, view the crucial 1971 international agreement on Berlin access and administration as a *modus vivendi* (way of living with the situation) during the evolution of the larger set of arrangements for all of Germany.

The nailing down of the Berlin stabilization arrangements *prior* to the negotiation of a permanent peace treaty for Germany represents a major concession on the part of the Soviets—by implication—to the fundamental stance of the West that there is a continuing US, British, French, and Soviet responsibility for the administration of Berlin, even though it is located 110 miles inside the "sovereign" German Democratic Republic. The Soviet position had been that since there were now two separate and sovereign Germanies, the Western control of half of Berlin is an anomaly; and, in any case, whatever foreign presence is established in any part of the city should be with the permission of the GDR and negotiated with them and them alone. The 1958–1959 and 1961 Berlin crises in particular had been provoked by Soviet efforts to force their definition of the situation on the West, and the United States' standing firm on behalf of West Germany's position; namely, that the division of Germany was only a temporary legacy of the Second World War, that it was still one nation destined to become one state again on the basis of free all-German elections, and that the continuing shared Soviet–US–British–French control of Berlin (which would again be the capital of a reunited Germany) was both a symbol and guarantee of this, the only legitimate concept for a German peace treaty.

The diplomatic maneuverings of 1970–1971 that broke the impasse were catalyzed and masterminded by Chancellor Willy Brandt, with Henry Kissinger (who at first was resentful of Brandt's running with the ball) providing his own deft pressure tactics on the Russians. Brilliant diplomacy, including that of Soviet foreign minister Andrei Gromyko, was responsible for the set of successful negotiations on Berlin and Germany; but these centerpieces of detente would not have been laid without the prior emergence in the principal countries of strong interests in breaking out of the cold war rigidities.

There was a convergence of basic interests in the early 1970s among the United States, the Soviet Union, and West Germany when it came to the overall relaxation of East–West tensions and a recognition that this required either a resolution or a suppression of the German division/unification issue, particularly as it came to a head in Berlin.

The Soviets appeared to favor a suppression of the division/unification issue, deferring for a time their standing insistence on the formal recognition of the GDR as a sovereign nation-state by the international community. The Kremlin, as a part of its new *Westpolitik*, now put a higher priority on establishing a flourishing Moscow–Bonn relationship than on gaining full legitimacy for the GDR; indeed, letting up on the latter was the condition for the former—and the Soviet–West German renunciation of force agreement of August 1970 and follow-up efforts to negotiate an overall commercial agreement were testimony to this priority.

For the West Germans, however, East–West normalization and a postponement of the issue of Germany's future was acceptable, and even welcome, as long as it did not imply settling for the political status quo of a divided Germany, or seeming to confer legitimacy on Soviet–GDR policies in Berlin (the wall between the Eastern and Western sectors, and the establishment of East Berlin as the capital of the GDR while denying the Federal Republic the right to incorporate West Berlin into its political system). Accordingly, the Brandt government informed the Soviets that it would hold back on ratification of the Soviet–West German normalization agreement until a satisfactory agreement on Berlin had been reached.

The US government under Nixon and Kissinger, anxious for detente to materalize, but not wanting to appear more anxious than the Kremlin, was pleased at Brandt's hang-tough attitude on Berlin. It strengthened the American hand in the on-going quadrapartite (Soviet–US–British–French) negotiations over Berlin and gave Kissinger an even stronger basis for implementing his "linkage" approach to Soviet–American relations: cashing in on the Soviet desire to get a quick Berlin settlement by making it clear to the Kremlin that President Nixon's willingness to facilitate a rapid consummation of the negotiations would be affected by how cooperative the Soviets were across the broad field of Soviet–American issues, including Vietnam (where the Soviets presumably had some leverage on Hanoi's war efforts and peace policy) and SALT. Characteristically, when Kissinger was ready for a rapid and successful conclusion of the Berlin negotiations in order to lay the groundwork for the Nixon–Brezhnev summit, he preempted the Department of State and conducted his own bilateral secret negotiations with top-level Soviet officials, while consulting with the Brandt government, also through a secret "back channel," on what he was doing.[19]

The Quadrapartite Agreement on Berlin (signed by the United States, the USSR, the United Kingdom, and France, on September 3, 1971) provided an explicit written four-power guarantee—which heretofore had been lacking—for surface access to West Berlin from West Germany by civilians (explicit guarantees for air access had been provided in the postwar agreements). The Soviets were thus freshly bound, and even more firmly than in the past, to take responsibility for maintaining such access through GDR territory and could not play with Berlin access controls as a device for compelling the West to deal with the GDR. To get this basic Soviet concession, the three Western powers marginally compromised some of the West German interests in politically linking West Berlin to the FRG, including the right of the West German parliament periodically to convene in the city. But the Soviets did give formal recognition, also for the first time, to West Berlin's cultural, economic, and consular ties with the Federal Republic. While not entirely satisfactory to either of the Germanies, the 1971 agreement, by defusing the Berlin issue at least for the time being, made it much easier for other normalization tracks to be laid between East and West Europe and even betweeen East and West Germany.

A decade earlier, it would have seemed an absurd proposition to most politically aware people on both sides of the ideological divide that with Berlin still split by the ugly wall, and with each of the two Germanies integrated into the political, economic, and military systems of their respective superpower protectors, the FRG and the GDR would voluntarily, on the basis of their own bilaterally initiated negotiations, agree to normalize their own relations. Yet that is exactly what they did in their Basic Treaty of November 1972. The West Germans still held back, however, from extending full diplomatic recognition to East Germany as a sovereign state. The FRG and GDR would exchange "permanent representatives" instead of ambassadors. The Brandt government explained that it was simply adapting to the current reality of "two states in one nation." The justification for this demarche was elegantly expressed by Foreign Minister Walter Scheel in a Bundestag debate over the *Ostpolitik*: "If there is any way towards the unity of the nation, then it is only through a general relaxation of tension in Europe which can bear the burden of pushing in the background everything that separates us from the GDR."[20]

The Bundestag's ratification of the Basic Treaty with East Germany in May 1973 opened the way for other countries, who had not wanted to offend Bonn, to extend recognition to the GDR. In September 1973 both German states were admitted to the United Nations.

A flourishing economic relationship has since developed between the two Germanies, with trade doubling in a decade to reach its mid-1980s level of about $5 billion a year. West Germany is now the GDR's largest trading partner next to the USSR itself. And some 6,000 West German firms specialize in business with East Germany. Much of this involves substantial credit arrangements backed by the West German government. Meanwhile, on the more sensitive issue of contacts between the citizens of the two German states and the reuniting of families, the regime in the East has been more cautious, but gradually loosening up on its restrictions. During 1984, for example, an unprecedented 30,000 East Germans were allowed to emigrate to the West.[21] However, the rapprochement between the two Germanies at times has proceeded at a pace that makes the Kremlin nervous. The Soviets vetoed the plans of the East German leader Erich Honecker to visit Bonn in September 1984, but did allow the visit in September 1987, making it clear that the Kremlin still intends to stage-manage the scenario of East–West reconciliation in the center of Europe.

THE CHINA CONNECTION

The Soviet Union's efforts to consolidate its detente with the Western countries and to enlarge its global commercial activities were in no small degree stimulated by the intensification during the 1960s of its rivalry with Communist China. Soviet resources were being strained by the need to maintain a balance of military power against China in the east while simultaneously maintaining a balance in the West; and the Kremlin's worst nightmare was someday having to fight a two-front war.

The Sino-Soviet conflict was an even heavier determinant of China's western policy. In the PRC's active courtship of western relationships in the late 1960s and 1970s—emerging from the extreme isolation China had imposed on itself during the period of the Cultural Revolution—other considerations were secondary to the objective of building a world-spanning structure of diplomatic counterweights to the Soviet Union. China's new international priorities were displayed in its negotiations to establish diplomatic relations with Canada and Italy, especially in its surprising flexibility on the Taiwan issue. Previously, Peking had demanded from any country with whom it was to have diplomatic relations an unequivocal endorsement of its claim to rule over Taiwan. But now it was willing that Canada and Italy simply "take note" of its claim without requiring their explicit endorsement.

As with the Soviet Union's detente policies, the PRC's new openings to the West were first explored with Europe and Canada. Many of the West European countries, including France and Britain, had recognized the PRC as the government of China soon after the victory of the Maoists in 1949. Those who refused to extend recognition were mainly deferring to the US policy of continuing to support the "Republic of China" on Taiwan. Any possibility of an early cordiality developing between the United States and the PRC was precluded by the escalation of the Korean War in 1950 into a Sino-American conflict and by their brink-of-war confrontations in the Taiwan Strait during 1954–1955 and 1958.

But in 1969 the signs of a significant attempt by China to become once again an active participant in international diplomacy coincided with the Nixon administration's search for new leverage on the Soviet Union to compensate for adverse changes in the East–West military balance. Nixon and Kissinger came quickly to the realization that Beijing's needs might mesh with their own. In the tradition of classical European balance-of-power diplomacy (one of Kissinger's academic specialties), moves toward rapprochement with China could be means of pressuring the Kremlin to be more accommodating to US demands. There was nothing to lose (except the affection of the Nationalist Chinese on Taiwan) by trying. And if a genuine Sino-American detente did result, it could also serve other priority objectives of the administration: an early end to the Vietnam War; a reduction in overseas deployment of American troops; a dismantling of military commitments to Asian regimes that might be unstable or reckless; and simply the need to do something dramatic to convince the American public and international audiences (discouraged by US impotence in Vietnam) that the government, under Nixon's leadership, did have the capacity to act impressively on the world stage.[22]

In March 1969, a renewed outbreak of border hostilities between Soviet and Chinese forces laying claim to a disputed island on the Ussuri River indicated that the time was ripe for some American gestures. Over the next 15 months the administration announced a series of unilateral steps "to relax tensions and faciliate the development of peaceful contacts."[23] In July 1969 many travel and trade restrictions that had been applied to China since 1950 were relaxed. In November, US naval patrols in the Taiwan Strait (deployed by President Truman at the start of the Korean War) were terminated, removing the most visible symbol of support for the Nationalist Chinese exiles. In February 1970, in a "State of the World" message to Congress, President Nixon, calling the Chinese "a great and vital people who should not remain isolated from the international community," announced that it was now the policy of the United States government to "attempt to define a new relationship" for the future."[24]

Meanwhile in China a struggle for the mind of Mao over how to deal with the United States was being resolved in favor of Chou En-lai who urged moves toward rapprochement, over Defense Minister Lin Piao who insisted that the United States, particularly in light of its heavy military involvement in Indochina, was still very much an enemy.[25]

In the fall of 1970, Nixon and Kissinger, communicating with the Chinese leaders indirectly through the Rumanians and Pakistanis, let it be known that the American president would like an opportunity to visit China. The subsequent events, from China's hosting of a US ping-pong team, to Kissinger's secret travels to Beijing to arrange for Nixon's historic February 1972 visit, need not be retold here.[26] In diplomacy, modalities and substance are inextricably intertwined, and it is quite possible that without the artistry of both Chou En-lai and Kissinger, the opportunity to begin the process of Sino-American rapprochement might have been lost; but the underlying cause of the opportunity was deeply geopolitical on both sides, and this has sustained the 1972 rapprochement for well over a decade, despite the election of an American president in 1980 pledged to restore US support for the Chinese regime on Taiwan. President Nixon phrased it euphemistically in his statement announcing his planned trip to China: "There can be no stable and enduring peace," he said, "without the participation of the People's Republic of China and its 750 million peoples." Mao gave the more candid explanation in an old article he had reprinted to help his followers understand what to many of them must have seemed like a 180-degree turnabout, given the 20-year legacy of intense anti-American propaganda. Mao's article, defending the wartime collaboration of the Chinese Communist Party with the "imperialists" in order to resist the Japanese invasion, defended the wisdom of "uniting with the forces that can be united while isolating and hitting at the most obdurate enemies."[27]

The parameters of the new Sino-American relationship that were established in 1972—the areas of common interest and the major issues in dispute—persist to this day. They are nowhere better articulated than in the Shanghai Communique, issued by President Nixon and Premier Chou En-lai upon the conclusion of Nixon's first visit.

The two sides agreed to "facilitate the progressive development of trade between their two countries" and to "broaden the understanding between the two peoples" by the further development of contacts and exchanges in such fields as science, technology, culture, sports, and journalism. They committed themselves to maintaining diplomatic contacts at the senior level "to further the normalization of relations" (full diplomatic relations were established six years later during the Carter administration); and, despite "essential differences...in their social systems and foreign policies," to conduct their relations "on the principles of respect for the sovereignty and territorial integrity of all states, non-aggression against other states, non-interference in the internal affairs of other states, equality and mutual benefit, and peaceful coexistence. *International* [my emphasis] disputes should be settled on this basis, without resorting to the use or threat of force."

The agreed formulation on excluding force in the settlement of "international" disputes was carefully crafted to exempt the Chinese from having to dispense with military means to dispose of the Nationalists on Taiwan—which the PRC held to be an "internal" problem. The Taiwan issue remained unresolved between them and was handled in the Shanghai Communique by the device (suggested by Chou En-lai) of explicitly including the different positions of "each side": Thus,

> The Chinese side reaffirmed its position: The Taiwan question is the crucial question obstructing the normalization of relations between China and the United States; the Government of the People's Republic of China is the sole legal government of China; Taiwan is a province of China which has long been returned to the motherland; the liberation of Taiwan is China's internal affair in which no other country has the right to interfere; and all US forces and military installations must be withdrawn from Taiwan.

But just below this paragraph,

> The U. S. side declared: The United States acknowledges that all Chinese on either side of the Taiwan Strait maintain there is but one China and that Taiwan is a part of China. The United States Government does not challenge this position. It reaffirms its interest in a peaceful settlement of the Taiwan question by the Chinese themselves. With this prospect in mind, it affirms the ultimate objective of the withdrawal of all US forces from Taiwan. In the meantime, it will progressively reduce its forces and military installations on Taiwan as the tension in the area diminishes.

The agreement to disagree in this way on such an important matter was a remarkably clear testimony to the overwhelming advantage, in the calculations of both countries, of cooperating to forge a global balance of power against the Soviet Union. But Nixon and Kissinger, in anticipation of the forthcoming detente summit in Moscow, wanted to play down any statements that could be interpreted as a Sino-American collusion against the USSR, while not totally relieving the Kremlin of anxiety that such collusion could be forced upon the Americans and Chinese by uncooperative Soviet behavior. Chou and Mao, on the other hand, had their own anxieties about the new detente Nixon and Brezhnev were about to conceive. The result in the communique of this convergence, yet divergence, in grand strategy was the following exquisitely nuanced section:

> [The two sides agreed that] neither should seek hegemony in the Asia-Pacific region and each is opposed to efforts by any other country or group of countries to establish such hegemony; and... neither is prepared to negotiate on behalf of any third party or to enter into agreements or understandings with the other directed at other states.
>
> Both sides are of the view that it would be against the interests of the peoples of the world for any major country to collude with another against other countries, or for major countries to divide up the world into spheres of influence.[28]

Since 1972, the evolution of the Sino-American relationship has been mainly elaboration of what was laid down in the Shanghai Communique. Full mutual recognition was extended in December 1978, at which time the United States withdrew its formal diplomatic recognition of Taiwan and agreed to the complete withdrawal of its military personnel and to terminate the Taiwan–US defense treaty; but under the Taiwan Relations Act of 1979, Congress provided that US arms of a "defensive character" could still be sold to Taiwan. Beijing's strong objections to such arms sales were deflected somewhat in 1980 and thereafter as the United States, in the wake of the Soviet invasion of Afghanistan, began to develop a closer military relationship with the PRC simultaneoulsy with a substantial expansion of commercial intercourse.

Today the principal international commercial activity of the People's Republic is with the capitalist world, reflected in trade statistics that show Hong Kong to be China's largest trading partner. Despite efforts begun in the early 1980s in Beijing and Moscow to reduce Sino-Soviet tensions, China shows no signs of wanting to cool its still-warming relationships with the West and Japan.

In 1985, China's trade with the United States was $7.7 billion (compared with only $1.9 billion with the USSR), and nearly 17,000 students and scholars from the PRC were attending American universities (compared with a mere 200 in Soviet universities). And China welcomes the American military presence in Asia as a balance to the Soviets.

The dramatic improvement in relations between the United States and China has not been free of conflict, however—even in the commercial realm. The American textile industry's claim to be injured by low-priced imports from China has stimulated protectionist legislation in the Congress, angering Beijing. And the US government has expressed strong objections to the PRC's reluctance to restrict its export of nuclear materials (with weapons potential) to countries in the Third World.

Not wanting to kowtow to the United States any more than it would to the Soviet Union, the PRC has been active in constructing a diversity of international relationships. The European Community is now China's second largest trading partner (after Hong Kong), and China has become Japan's second largest trading partner (after the United States). Beijing also relies heavily on Tokyo for low-interest loans. China's other major trading partners are West Germany, Australia, Canada, Singapore, Rumania, France, and Italy.[29] Moreover, the PRC is now a member of more international organizations than is the USSR—including, among others, the International Monetary Fund, the World Bank, the International Atomic Energy Agency, the Food and Agricultural Organization, the International Maritime Organization, the International Telecommunication Union, and INTELSAT.

In short, the prospects are very high for a continued thickening of China's ties with the advanced capitalist world, if only to offset the possibility of the Kremlin's once again attempting to subordinate the PRC to Soviet hegemonic ambitions in Asia. However, a full-blown alliance with the United States does not seem to be in the offing, short of the outbreak of a major Sino-Soviet war, for the related basic reason that this would surely reduce the PRC to the status of a junior partner, thus diminishing its bargaining leverage with both superpowers; nor would it be consistent with Beijing's efforts to enhance its influence among the countries of the Third World.

US–SOVIET DETENTE IN EARLY DIFFICULTY: THE SURFACING OF STRUCTURAL PROBLEMS

Because the rationale in Western capitals for building bridges to the East has been partly commercial and partly political, and because the Kremlin in particular has worried about the loss of centralized control that could accompany the rapid opening of borders, the expansion of commercial intercourse has been inhibited by special restrictions and manipulations on both sides. Moreover, the politically imposed inhibitions, when added to the inherent difficulties in attempting to expand commerce between market-oriented economies and state-run economies, have not yet allowed East–West commercial interdependencies to grow to the point where they can be relied on to prevent a dangerous escalation of cold war conflicts.

Soviet–American commerce perhaps might have expanded more were it not for the premature effort by the Congress (strongly but unsuccessfully opposed by Henry Kissinger) to use the commercial lever on the Kremlin on the issue of Jewish emigration from the USSR. The congressional acts of 1974 denying the Soviets most-favored-nation tariff reductions on their exports to the United States (the Jackson–Vanik Amendment) and limiting US Export-Import Bank credits to finance Soviet purchases from US firms (the Stevenson Amendment) were motivated on human rights grounds by some of the supporters of the restrictions, and simply as a means of scuttling detente by others. Kissinger argued that it was wrong to assume that the Kremlin's motivation for commerce with the United States was so high that they would modify Soviet *internal* policies to obtain it, and certainly not under a public ultimatum from the United States. "We have accomplished much," he said, "but we cannot demand that the Soviet Union, in effect, suddenly reverse five decades of Soviet, and centuries of Russian history." He argued further, but to no avail, that if the commercial lever was to work at all, even on less sensitive matters, trade should not be subject to such political restrictions before it was permitted to achieve the level that economic market conditions would allow.[30]

The Soviet leaders were angry at the American reneging on the 1972 Moscow deal of MFN and new credits arrangements in return for Soviet payment of their wartime Lend-Lease debt. They responded by summarily renouncing their side of the bargain. But as it turned out, neither the denial of MFN or Ex-Im Bank credits has had much effect on the actual volume of Soviet–American commerce. Soviet government-manipulated pricing policies can largely evade the effects of US tariffs and, in any case, most of what the Soviets have to sell in the US market is in categories subject to very low tariffs (or none). Furthermore, credit is available from private financial sources even without the official Ex-Im Bank backup.

The reason Soviet–American commerce did not expand to the levels expected by some early enthusiasts for opening up relations has just as much to do with the "economic structural factors" as with the thaws and freezes in the cold war since 1972. A core problem has been the inability of the Soviet system (and most of the countries in its economic bloc), with its highly bureaucratized central organization for determining production quotas and product specifications, to respond flexibly to demand changes in the international market. If the

Soviets and their COMECON partners cannot earn sufficient foreign exchange to pay for their imports from the West, they must incur overly large amounts of indebtness, which at a certain point results in a drying up of further Western credit, even from private lending institutions not using political criteria. Even under the impact of the Gorbachev economic reforms, there still are very different ways of doing business in Moscow and Prague and Bucharest from the ways business is done in New York and Bonn and Tokyo that prevent commercial transactions between the particular advanced capitalist countries and particular COMECON countries from attaining the levels they do between comparable trading partners within the two economic worlds.

In addition to the failure of East–West commerce to burgeon, especially between the United States and the Soviet Union, there have been other—political—sources of disappointment with detente on both sides:

On the part of the Soviets, as noted, the souring was largely in reaction to Western efforts to use the enlarging opportunities for intergovernmental and people-to-people contact to pressure them on human rights. Kissinger had tried to soft pedal the human rights issue in the face of growing congressional demands that he link cooperation desired by the Soviets to changes in their behavior toward dissidents. But the popular human rights constituency found some powerful champions in the Carter administration—most notably Zbigniew Brzezinski—who insisted that the Soviets ought not to be in any way exempted from the new human rights emphasis. In response, the Soviets in the spring of 1977 nearly called off the resumed SALT II negotiations. The Russians also regarded their virtual exclusion from the peace process in the Middle East after the 1973 Arab–Israeli war as inconsistent with the superpower-consultation groundrules of detente.

On the American side, within a year of the 1972 Nixon–Brezhnev summit, Kissinger himself was losing hope that the Soviets would indeed honor their commitment in the Soviet–American Declaration of Principles to forgo "efforts to obtain unilateral advantage at the expense of the other, either directly or indirectly." He faulted the Kremlin for giving aid and encouragement to the Vietnamese communists in their violations of the 1973 Agreement on Ending the War—cynically taking advantage of the congressional restrictions on further US military assistance to the South Vietnamese.[31] And he was doubly angry at them in 1975 and 1976 for exploiting the post-Vietnam isolationist syndrome in the United States to create new client states for the USSR in southern Africa upon the withdrawal of the Portuguese from Angola and Mozambique.[32]

Despite the mutual disillusionment of the superpowers with how the other was attempting to exploit detente at the economic and political levels, the Soviet–American dialogue and on-again, off-again negotiations continued through most of the 1970s at the most crucial level of their relationship: the balance of nuclear terror. The SALT II Treaty signed by Leonid Brezhnev and

Jimmy Carter in Vienna on June 18, 1979, was held by both presidents to represent "a mutually acceptable balance between the interests of the sides based on the principles of equality and equal security...[and] a substantial contribution to the prevention of nuclear war and the deepening of detente."[33] But this time, in contrast to the general public approval that greeted SALT I, opponents of the treaty in the United States had marshalled their forces to put in doubt its approval by the Senate. Led by the Committee on the Present Danger, whose analyses purported to show that SALT II would result in "a large imbalance in Russia's favor," the opposition argued that the treaty was a sellout of America's security and that President Carter and his negotiators had, in effect, been duped by their Soviet counterparts.[34] Even Henry Kissinger, the architect of the SALT process, expressed serious reservations and testified that he did not believe it would be wise for the Senate to approve the treaty until the administration had proposed and Congress approved a beefed-up five-year defense plan.[35] Thus, the ratification of SALT II was already in serious doubt when the Soviet Union invaded Afghanistan at the end of 1979. Now Carter felt he had no choice but to ask the Senate to defer action.

AFGHANISTAN AND THE CLOSING DOWN OF THE SOVIET–AMERICAN BRIDGES

The Soviet invasion of Afghanistan put virtually all of the US–Soviet detente relationship on ice. Saying that "While this invasion continues, we and the other nations of the world cannot conduct business as usual with the Soviet Union," President Carter imposed a wide range of sanctions: the licensing of high technology exports to the USSR was suspended, and some recently granted licenses were revoked; fishing privileges for Soviet ships in US waters were severely curtailed; an embargo was placed on 17 million tons of grain already purchased by the Soviets but not yet shipped to them; planned openings of new American and Soviet consular facilities were canceled; most of the Soviet–American economic and cultural exchanges then under consideration were deferred; US athletes were not permitted to compete in the Olympics being hosted by Moscow; and visa criteria were tightened for Soviet officials wanting to visit the United States.[36] Secretary of State Vance announced that "the sanctions we have undertaken in response to the Soviet invasion will remain in force until all Soviet troops are withdrawn from Afghanistan."[37]

These immediately tangible moves were accompanied by a stiffening of the US rhetorical stance and puffing up of the military posture reminiscent of the Truman Doctrine and Korean War periods of the cold war.

"The implications of the Soviet invasion of Afghanistan," said President Carter in his January 23, 1980, State of the Union address, "could pose the most serious threat to world peace since the Second World War....Let our position be absolutely clear: Any attempt by any outside force to gain control of the Persian Gulf region will be regarded as an assault on the vital interests of the United States. It will be repelled by the use of any means necessary, including military force."[38] The White House was pleased at the media's labeling of this statement as the "Carter Doctrine."

The administration's defense budget submission to Congress for fiscal 1981 requested a real (after inflation) increase of 5 percent. Plans to organize a Rapid Deployment Force (RDF) were accelerated as were negotiations with Kenya, Oman, Somalia, and Egypt to provide service facilities for the RDF and other expanded US naval units in the region. Pakistan, presumably threatened by the Soviet military operations in Afghanistan, was offered $400 million in military aid.[39]

The anti-Soviet basis of the Sino-American connection was allowed to surface more openly. National Security Advisor Brzezinski conducted negotiations with Pakistan and China for concerting aid to Afghan insurgents (dramatized in the world's press by a photo of Brzezinski at the Khyber Pass holding a Chinese-made automatic rifle). Secretary of Defense Harold Brown's January 1980 trip to China, although planned before the Soviets marched into Afghanistan, was now accorded heightened strategic significance in both Washington and Beijing. Following Brown's discussions with Chinese defense officials, the administration announced approval of previously restricted exports to China, including air defense radars, electronic counter-measure devices, military-type helicopters, long-distance communications equipment with military potential, and hundreds of items of advanced technology and military support equipment. The news media throughout the remainder of 1980 featured reports of this or that high-level defense delegation from China visiting the United States and vice versa. "What had started as an exercise in evenhandedness [toward the USSR and China]," recalls Brzezinski, "by 1980 became demonstrably a tilt, driven by stark strategic realities."[40] Congress did its part by approving MFN trading status for China (a status still denied the USSR), giving a major filip to Sino-American commerce, which rose to the unprecedented level of $5 billion in 1980.

The Soviet leadership apparently was taken aback by the intensity of the American reaction to Afghanistan, but not so much as to accede to Washington's demands for military withdrawal. Brezhnev charged that "the forces of imperialism have gone over to a counteroffensive against detente," but made it known to most of the other noncommunist governments that they needn't be affected by the new estrangement between Moscow and Washington. Although strong voices were raised in the internal Soviet debate on behalf of reducing the USSR's economic dependence on the West, the basic Soviet policy adjustment to the American sanctions was simply to redirect the lost American commerce to other Western countries.[41] The Europeans and Japanese, anxious for detente to continue and angry at the United States for unilaterally announcing the sanctions policy as if it were speaking for the whole coalition, were more than happy to respond to the new Soviet overtures.

The results were hardly what the Carter administration wanted. The Soviets continued to pour more troops and heavy military equipment into Afghanistan. Meanwhile, as Soviet–American trade dropped in the early 1980s to nearly a third of what it was in the late 1970s (US exports falling from $3.6 billion in 1979 to $1.5 billion in 1980), Soviet–West German trade expanded by nearly two-thirds, and Soviet–French trade increased 100 percent! The Japanese also increased their trade with the USSR by 35 percent.[42] And in the food grains sector, the Canadians and Australians were taking up the sales opportunities now denied to American farmers.

Ironically, the United States in attempting to punish the Soviets for their invasion of Afghanistan ended up punishing itself, at least in the commercial field. Even at the level of international politics, an event which might have been expected to reconsolidate the US-led coalition (the first direct use of Soviet military force since World War II outside of its immediate sphere of control) had precisely the opposite effect. It exposed the divergent interests in detente within the US coalition and provided the Soviets with new opportunities to attempt to decouple the West Europeans from the United States.

1981–1984: THE REAGAN POLICY OF KNOCKING DOWN THE BRIDGES

Despite the negative effects of Carter's sanctions policy on the US economy and international political leadership, the Reagan administration during most of its first term continued not only to dismantle the remaining material bridges but also the geopolitical foundations of detente. This was the declared intent of the new administration, consistent with the Republican Party platform of 1980 and numerous public pronouncements by Ronald Reagan himself during his 12-year campaign for the presidency.

US military superiority over the USSR rather than the *mutual* deterrence championed by the arms controllers would be once again the basis from which to confront the Soviets with the consequences of attempting to impose their will on others. If the Kremlin was foolish enough to take up the challenge of a new arms race, so much the better, for this would deeply strain available Soviet resources, compel the USSR to dispense with long-delayed domestic modernization, and deny it the economic wherewithal to sustain its empire. It should not be the job of the West to relieve the Kremlin of its resource allocation crunch by providing the Soviets with access to the relatively inexpensive quality goods and technologies produced in the capitalist world (especially those technologies that have potential military applications), and surely not to provide them with financial credits to make purchases beyond their current ability to pay. It was time to return to the predetente prohibitions on "trading with the enemy" and to restrictions on scientific and technological exchanges that provide the Soviets a legitimate cover for espionage. These people in the Kremlin, after all, profess to be the heirs of Lenin, who advised lying and cheating to undermine the Western democracies, and who gleefully prophesied that the capitalists would sell their executioner the rope by which they would be hanged. The atheistic Marxists of the Soviet communist party are today the "focus of evil" in the world; they must have their international activities severely curtailed and themselves be eventually strangled by the constricted bottlenecks in their own system.[43]

The incoming Reagan administration made a heroic try during its first few years in office to translate its ideologically conceived grand strategy into concrete policy: Arms control negotiations with the USSR were to be officially suspended until the United States (under a projected military buildup to cost $1.7 trillion over the next five years) was again in a position to "negotiate from strength." As it turned out, however, this criterion would not be strictly adhered to, as popular and allied pressures compelled the administration to resume arms control negotiations in the fall of 1981. Reagan's earliest arms proposals, however, were transparently unacceptable to the Russians.

On the trade-restriction front, the Reagan administration moved swiftly after inauguration to tighten export controls on various categories of high-technology goods and attempted to get the allies to adopt similar stringent controls, in particular to stop selling the Soviets equipment for their 2,600 mile gas pipeline project. The only significant exception to the policy of economically isolating the USSR was Reagan's removal in April 1981 of the grain embargo imposed by the Carter administration and his pledge not to use grain as a tool of foreign policy. (This was a payment by Reagan of his political debt to the farm lobby, which supported him in the election in return for his pledge to remove the embargo.)

Reagan needed a new popular cause, however, akin to the Afghanistan invasion, to move decisively to implement his grand strategy of containment *plus* economic strangulation of the Soviets. At the end of 1981, the Kremlin (for their own reasons, as described above, pp. 88–90) obliged, by their sponsorship of the martial law regime in Poland and its arrest of Solidarity leaders including Lech Walesa—who had become something of a folk hero to the American public.

The administration's immediate moves in the Polish crisis were directed against the Jaruzelski regime in Warsaw and included a suspension of the US government's food shipments to Poland; denial of Export-Import Bank credits; withdrawal of Poland's permission to fish in US waters; and a denial of the right of the Polish airline to operate in the United States. "These actions are not directed against the Polish people," explained Reagan. "They are a warning to the Government of Poland that free men cannot and will not stand idly by in the face of brutal repression." He also warned the Soviets that he was ready to take measures against them if there was no letup in the repression, contending that "The Soviet Union, through its threats and pressures deserves a major share of the blame for the developments in Poland." Ironically, in light of Reagan's past attacks on the Ford–Kissinger endorsement of the Helsinki accords, Reagan also announced that the had written directly to President Brezhnev demanding that he "permit the restoration of basic rights in Poland as provided for in the Helsinki Final Act."[44]

The following week, on December 29, 1981, Reagan dropped the other shoe on the Soviet Union "for its heavy and direct responsibility for the repression in Poland." The already long list of prohibitions on US exports to the USSR was extended to additional high-technology items, including oil and gas pipelaying equipment (this especially aimed at preventing the completion of the Soviet pipeline to Western Europe). Soviet Aeroflot privileges to use US airports were withdrawn. New restrictions were put on the access of Soviet ships to US ports. Soviet purchasing offices in the United States that had survived the Carter sanctions were ordered to close. And all existing energy, science, and technology agreements with the USSR were placed under review, with the clear implication that any or all of them might be summarily suspended. There was even a postponement of negotiations on a new US–Soviet long-term agreement on the purchase of US grains, but—at least in partial adherence to Reagan's earlier promise not to restrict grain exports for foreign policy purposes—no postponement or suspension of existing short-term agreements for Soviet grain purchases.[45]

Once again, as with the various Carter embargoes at the time of the Afghanistan invasion, most of these new sanctions, to be effective, required that other technologically capable countries and grain-exporting countries join in the restrictions. But once again, the other relevant countries, including America's principal allies, had their own priorities and strategies; and Reagan's impatient efforts to coerce the West Europeans into a concerted policy for restricting East–West commerce produced the most serious crisis in the coalition since the Suez crisis of 1956.

Also, contrary to its initial attitude on arms control negotiations, the Reagan administration made an effort to insulate the recently begun Euro-missile talks and the Strategic Arms Reduction Talks (START), scheduled to begin in the spring of 1982, from the otherwise virtually complete revival of the cold war between Washington and Moscow.

There are grounds for suspecting, however, that neither the Reaganites nor the Kremlin at this point seriously expected concrete progress to be made in the arms control negotiations in any case and that each side was playing political games to convince particular arms control and disarmament constituencies that the other was to blame for the lack of progress. The Reagan administration, having inherited NATO's "Two Track" decision of 1979 to try to negotiate mutual limitations on intermediate-range nuclear force (INF) deployments before proceeding to deploy new American Pershing and cruise missiles on European soil, was worried that the West Europeans would refuse to accept the new missiles unless the United States made a credible effort to achieve such a mutual-limitation agreement with the Soviets.

When the failure to achieve agreement in the INF talks by the end of 1983 resulted in the on-schedule start of the deployment of American Pershing IIs and Tomahawk cruise missiles in Europe, the Soviets (as they had threatened in advance) walked out of both the INF and the START negotiations. The expressions in Washington and Moscow of anger and disappointment at the other side were only one more act in the arms control charade that had been performed over the past few years by both.

THE LIMITED RESTORATION OF SUPERPOWER DETENTE

The posture of seriousness on arms control in the Kremlin and the White House, even if largely determined by the "constituency politics" of each leadership group, has become a constraint on their cold war policies. What politicians feel they must do and say to garner public support and the cooperation of other politicians—domestic and foreign—may start out as only "public relations," but when the public relations impact becomes one of the determinants of policy, the distinction between mere posturing and sincerity blurs.

As shown in Chapters 4 and 5, the increasing need of the cold war coalition leaders to take into account and cater to the demands of constituent members of their coalitions as well as the nonaligned has become a central feature of world politics since the middle 1960s. The demands from the majority and most influential of the international constituents on both sides are overwhelmingly in favor of (1) expanding relationships across the ideological divide, which they have shown they will pursue on their own even if the superpowers are estranged from one another; and (2) arms limitation regimes that will reduce the likelihood of a globally destructive nuclear holocaust, allow for a greater allocation of resources to domestic development tasks, and, not incidentally, lessen the dependency of smaller powers on one or another of the superpowers for protection.

Simply in order to retain the respect as worthy leaders from their various international constituents, and to preserve a modicum of authoritative control over the inevitable loosening of their coalitions, the superpowers must, each in their own way, demonstrate a credible determination to rebuild detente between themselves and limit their arms race. Thus, even while seeming to be dismantling detente in the early 1980s, the superpowers began to search for ways to avoid its full demolition.

Primarily motivated by the need to mend his rift with the West Europeans over their gas pipeline deal with the Soviets, Reagan in November 1982 conceded to their demands (and pressure from the proponents of East–West trade in the US Congress) for a less restrictive policy on technology sales. He was willing to do this, he explained, because the allies had agreed to "a plan of action...to give consideration to strategic issues when making decisions on trade with the USSR," in return for an agreement by the NATO countries to work out a new "more efficient" common position on the control of technologies that would "contribute to the military or strategic advantage of the USSR."[46]

Then in November 1982, the Polish regime, with Kremlin endorsement, released Lech Walesa and other Solidarity leaders from prison—while continuing to define Solidarity as an illegal organization. And on the last day of the year, Jaruzelski suspended the state of martial law. These actions provided the Reagan administration with another excuse for removing some of the sanctions imposed the previous year on Poland and for further lifting of the restrictions on trade and diplomatic and people-to-people exchanges with the USSR (as if the restrictions on Soviet–American intercourse had been applied only as sanctions for the Russian bullying of Poland and not also as part of the grand strategy of weakening the Soviet economy). Clearly, Reagan was now interested in allowing a new thaw to develop in the Soviet–American relationship, at least in the commercial field. And so even when US public and international outrage at the Russians became intense in response to the Soviet shooting down of the Korean commercial airliner on September 1, 1983, the administration confined its reactions to strong verbal condemnations.

By the end of Reagan's first term in office, US–Soviet and US–Eastern European economic relations were subject to about the same legal restrictions they were in the Carter administration prior to the Soviet invasion of Afghanistan: still no MFN or Ex-Im Bank credits for the Soviets; a reluctance to grant export licenses for computers and other high-technology items with obvious military applications; but otherwise a generally permissive go-ahead for American businessmen and Soviet planners to negotiate contracts and for scientists, academics, and performing artists to develop their transideological relationships.

Somewhere along the way to the 1984 presidential elections, Reagan also seems to have become a convert to the idea that it might be possible to negotiate arms control agreements acceptable to the Soviets that would also serve US security interests. There were hold-outs within his administration against this notion, most notably Secretary of Defense Weinberger and some of his key aides; but other trusted associates of the president, including Secretary of State George Shultz and various of Reagan's economic advisers, apparently won him over with arguments about the international and domestic political gains *and* possible expenditure reductions that might result from some genuine arms limitation agreements. The 1982 election had strengthened the pro-arms control coalition in the Congress. In eight states the voters had approved ballot propositions calling for a negotiated freeze on further nuclear weapons' tests, deployments, and production. Eleven state legislatures, 195 city councils, and over 400 town meetings across the country had endorsed freeze resolutions; and the administration on a number of occasions had to lobby hard in the Congress to prevent that body from passing its own freeze resolution. The enormous defense outlays were the main cause of the embarrassing yearly increase in the federal budget deficit, which was the biggest blot on the Reagan domestic economic program. Moreover, the president had nothing to lose by becoming a genuine champion of arms control; for if his serious bids to the Russians did fail, he would then be in a much stronger position to go to the country and the Congress for approval for additional military modernization programs.

A few weeks before Reagan's second inaugural in January 1985, Gromyko and Shultz announced that arms control negotiations would resume in Geneva that spring in three categories: (1) intercontinental missiles and bombers, (2) intermediate-range nuclear forces in Europe, and (3) space weapons. Still, it was unclear—not only to observers, but seemingly to the governments themselves—whether they were reentering the negotiating arena to seriously bargain toward a new mutual limitation of their arsenals or to score propaganda points off each other.

This basic question about the real objectives being pursued by each side in the arms control negotiations persisted after the succession to power in the Soviet Union of a new and younger leadership group, headed by Mikhail Gorbachev. Secretary Gorbachev indicated that his highest priority was attending to neglected domestic modernization tasks within the USSR, which implied a desire to shift resources away from the military sector; but he also showed himself to be a master public relations artist—even a match for the "Great Communicator" in the White House—and this portended a temptation to play directly to public opinion in the West as a means of getting the United States and the NATO countries unilaterally to reverse their arms buildup.

The first summit meeting of Gorbachev and Reagan in November 1985 produced plenty of opportunities for the two media-conscious leaders and their photogenic wives to exhibit a mood of mutual respect and cordiality and to present themselves to an anxious world as statesmen dedicated first and foremost to international peace. Like the first detente summit between Nixon and Brezhnev, the meeting produced a joint statement of common aims and cooperative intentions: Recognizing "the special responsibility of the USSR and the US for maintaining peace,"

> The sides...have agreed that a nuclear war cannot be won and must never be fought. Recognizing that any conflict between the USSR and the US could have catastrophic consequences, they emphasized the importance of preventing any war between them, whether nuclear or conventional. They will not seek to achieve military superiority.

The joint statement called for early progress in various fields of arms control and conflict control, including nuclear arms reductions (agreeing to the "principle of 50 per cent reductions"), preventing "an arms race in space," the establishment of "nuclear risk reduction centers," strengthening the nonproliferation regime, banning chemical weapons, mutual force reductions in Europe, and "confidence building measures."[47]

But unlike the May 1972 summit, the November 1985 summit did not produce any specific and concrete agreements. These would have to emerge from the specific negotiating forums, now presumably energized to succeed by the ringing joint endorsement of their efforts at the highest level.

The professional negotiators, it was generally assumed, would now be given a mandate to narrow their differences beyond the glare of the media and hammer out the very complex and detailed arrangements that make up serious arms control agreements. Instead, their efforts were derailed once again in the months following the summit by a grandiose proposal from Gorbachev for eliminating all nuclear weapons on earth by the year 2000, requiring, of course, a prior renunciation by Reagan of his Strategic Defense Initiative (SDI). The consensus among Western arms control experts was that Gorbachev was simply playing to the public galleries.

Not to be outdone in the new propaganda game, Reagan, in his October 1986 meeting with Gorbachev in Reykjavik, Iceland, countered with a proposal to eliminate all ballistic missiles in ten years. But Gorbachev stuck by his position that all such arms control measures were still linked to Reagan's willingness to forgo SDI.[48]

Fruitful negotiations did resume, however, on the intermediate nuclear missiles with ranges from 300 to 3,400 miles deployed mainly in Europe. In September 1987 as this book went to press, the two governments announced an agreement in principle to eliminate these politically controversial (but militarily not-too-important) forces. A signing of the completed treaty—despite efforts by opponents to link it to a removal of the Warsaw Pact's conventional force advantage—was being planned for the late fall as the centerpiece of another Washington summit between Reagan and Gorbachev.[49]

Despite the periodic setbacks to detente, and what for a time in the early 1980s seemed to be a full-blown revival of the cold war, the world in the last quarter of the twentieth century—in contrast to the first two decades after World War II—is pervaded by transideological bridges between and within all continents, with more groups committed, out of pragmatic self-interest, to maintain them and widen them rather than to tear them up. Moreover, because the setbacks have occurred mainly in the bilateral superpower relationship and have been resisted by most other countries, the majority of the bridges and the largest volume of traffic over them are between allies and clients of the superpowers. This further weakens the bargaining power of each of the superpowers with members of its own coalition, particularly when what the superpower wants is a concerted coalition position against the other side. A higher price often needs to be paid other members to gain their support on cold war issues, and this, in turn, only further increases the value to lesser members of engaging in their own bridge-building.

Thus, not only do detente and coalition disintegration feed upon one another, but attempts by the superpowers to substantially reverse either process at particular times and places, even if they seem immediately successful, are likely to intensify the overall global trend toward a more pluralistic, post-cold war international system.

ENDNOTES

1. On de Gaulle's Eastern demarche, see Raymond L. Garthoff, *Detente and Confrontation: American-Soviet Relations from Nixon to Reagan* (Washington: The Brookings Institution, 1985), pp. 106–107.

2. See Angela Stent, *From Embargo to Ostpolitik: The Political Economy of West German-Soviet Relation, 1955-1980* (New York: Cambridge University Press, 1981).

3. Willy Brandt, "Germany's *Westpolitik*," *Foreign Affairs*, Vol. 50, No. 3 (April 1972), pp. 416–426, quotations from pp. 418–420.

4. On the pre-1966 period, see Marshall Goldman, *Detente and Dollars: Doing Business with the Soviets* (New York: Basic Books, 1977), pp. 21–31.

5. Kosygin's remarks before the Twenty-Third Party Congress are quoted by Samuel J. Pisar, *Coexistence and Commerce: Guidelines for Transactions between East and West* (New York: McGraw-Hill, 1970), pp. 33–34.

6. On the doctrinal and practical considerations underlying the 1966 Soviet shift in international economic policy, see Richard V. Burks, *Technological Innovation and Political Change in Communist Eastern Europe* (Santa Monica: RAND Corporation, 1969), RM-6051-PR; Richard W. Judy, "The Case of Computer Technology," in Stanislaw Wasowski, *East-West Trade and the Technology Gap: A Political and Economic Appraisal* (New York: Praeger, 1970), pp. 43–72; Ivan Berenyi, "Computers in Eastern Europe," *Scientific American*, Vol. 233, No. 4 (October 1970), pp. 102–108; and Goldman, *Detente and Dollars*, pp. 35–39.

7. *Report of the Central Committee of the Communist Party of the Soviet Union*, delivered by Leonid Brezhnev, March 30, 1971 (Moscow: Novosti Press), pp. 33, 37.

8. Goldman, *Dollars and Detente*, pp. 73–76.

9. *Ibid.*, pp. 353–359.

10. "Basic Principles of Relations Between the United States of America and the Union of Soviet Socialist Republics," *Department of State Bulletin*, Vol. 66, No. 1722 (29 June 1972), pp. 898–899.

11. Text of the final communique of the May 1972 summit, *New York Times*, 30 May 1972.

12. *Department of State Bulletin, op. cit.*

13. Henry Kissinger, *White House Years* (Boston: Little, Brown, 1979), pp. 1229–1246.

14. *US-USSR Cooperative Agreements*, Hearings before the Subcommittee on International Cooperation in Science and Space, House Committee on Science and Astronautics, 92d Cong., 2d sess. (1972). See also Bernard Gwertzman, "U. S. and Russians Sign Agreements to Widen Trade," *New York Times*, 19 October 1972.

15. Garthoff, *Detente and Confrontation*, pp. 113–114. The Nixon administration's call for MBFR negotiations was only partly designed as an alternative to the Soviet-sponsored CSCE; it was also designed to undercut support in the Congress for the Mansfield Resolution for unilaterally withdrawing half of the some 300,000 US troops deployed in Central Europe.

16. Department of State, *Conference on Security and Cooperation in Europe, Final Act* (Washington, DC: Department of State, 1975), Publication 8826.

17. "Key Sanctions of Document at Stockholm Meeting on Security," *New York Times*, 22 September 1986. The military significance of the "confidence-building" accord is analyzed in Seyom Brown, *The Causes and Prevention of War* (New York: St. Martin's Press, 1987), pp. 193–197.

18. For details on the MBFR negotiations, see John G. Keliher, *The Negotiations on Mutual and Balanced Force Reductions: The Search for Arms Control in Europe* (New York: Pergamon Press, 1980); Congressional Research Service, *East-West Troop Reductions in Europe: Is Agreement Possible*, Report for Subcommittee on International Security and Scientific Affairs of the House Committee on Foreign Affairs (Washington, DC: GPO, 1983); and William R. Bowman, *Limiting Conventional Forces in Europe* (Washington, DC; National Defense University Press, 1985).

19. Kissinger, *White House Years*, pp. 823–833.

20. Walter Scheel, quoted by Stent, *From Embargo to* Ostpolitik, p. 185.

21. James M. Markham, "For Both East and West Two Germanies Is Better," *New York Times*, 24 August 1984; and "German Detente: Soviet Quandry?" *New York Times*, 5 September 1984.

22. See my account of the calculations by Nixon and Kissinger underlying their China policy in *The Faces of Power*, pp. 344–353. See also Henry Kissinger, *The White House Years*, pp. 163–194.

23. *Department of State Bulletin*, Vol. 61, No. 1573 (18 August 1969), p. 126.

24. Richard M. Nixon, *US Foreign Policy for the 1970s: A New Strategy for Peace* (Washington, DC: GPO, 1970), pp. 140–141.

25. Garthoff, *Detente and Confrontation*, p. 225.

26. The preliminaries to Nixon's 1972 visit to China are detailed by Kissinger in *White House Years*, pp. 684–763.

27. Mao's article was reprinted in September 1971 in one of the regime's official journals and also broadcast over Radio Peking. Tillmann Durdin, "Peking Explains Warmer US Ties," *New York Times*, 22 August 1971. See also Garthoff, *ibid.*, p. 235, for a slightly different, but essentially the same, translation of Mao's words.

28. Text of Joint Communique Issued at Shanghai, February 27, 1972, *Department of State Bulletin*, Vol. 66, No. 1708 (20 March 1972), pp. 435–438.

29. Michel Oksenberg, "China's Confident Nationalism," *Foreign Affairs*, Vol. 65, No. 3 (Special Annual Issue: *America and the World 1986*, published February 1987), pp. 501–532.

30. *Department of State Bulletin*, Vol. 71, No. 1842 (14 October 1974), pp. 505–519.

31. Henry Kissinger, *Years of Upheaval* (Boston: Little, Brown, 1982), pp. 301–370, *passim*.

32. Henry Kissinger, Statement of January 19, 1976, before the Subcommittee on African Affairs of the US Senate Committee on Foreign Relations, *Hearings on US Involvement in Civil War in Angola*, 94th Cong., 2d sess. (Washington, DC: GPO, 1976), pp. 14–23.

33. Joint US–Soviet Communique in Connection with the Signing of the SALT II Treaty, Department of State, *Vienna Summit* (Washington, DC: Department of State, 1979), General Foreign Policy Series 316, Publication 8985.

34. Committee on the Present Danger, *Does the Official Case for the SALT II Treaty Hold up under Analysis?* (Washington, DC: Publication of the CPD, March 14, 1979).

35. Brown, *The Faces of Power*, pp. 544–548.

36. For the various presidential announcements of sanctions on the USSR for its invasion of Afghanistan see *Weekly Compilation of Presidential Documents*, Vol. 16 (Washington, DC: GPO, 1980), issues of 14 January, 28 January, 18 February, and 14 April 1980.

37. Cyrus Vance, "Afghanistan: America's Course," *Department of State Bulletin*, Vol. 80 (April 1980), p. 12.

38. Jimmy Carter, State of the Union Address, January 23, 1980, *Weekly Compilation of Presidential Documents*, 28 January 1980 issue, pp. 194–203, quote on p. 197.

39. On the US military measures in reaction to Afghanistan, see Brown, *The Faces of Power*, pp. 559–563; and Garthoff, *Detente and Confrontation*, pp. 972–975.

40. Zbigniew Brzezinski, *Power and Principle: Memoirs of the National Security Adviser 1977–1981* (New York: Farrar-Strauss-Giroux, 1983), p. 423–425, quote on p. 425. It should be noted that Secretary of State Vance was opposed to such a blatant playing of the China card, even after the Soviet move into Afghanistan, but the views of Brzezinski and Secretary of Defense Brown, also supported by Vice President Walter Mondale, carried the day with President Carter. See Cyrus Vance, *Hard Choices: Critical Years in America's Foreign Policy* (New York: Simon and Shuster, 1983), pp. 390–391.

41. Garthoff, *Detente and Confrontation*, pp. 990–1002.

42. *Ibid.*, p. 977; and Joan Edleman Spero, *The Politics of International Economic Relations* (New York: St. Martin's, 1985), p. 377.

43. The most candid and comprehensive authoritative statement of the underlying philosophy of the Reagan administration during its first few years for dealing with the Soviets was contained in an address by the National Security Adviser, William Clark, on May 21, 1982, at the Center for Strategic and International Studies of Georgetown University. The Clark statement, which was not published as an official document, was reported on in detail by Richard Halloran, "Reagan Aide Tells of New Strategy on Soviet Threat," *New York Times*, 22 May 1982; and Saul Friedman, "Reagan Calls for Pressure on USSR," *Boston Globe*, 22 May 1982. Reagan's own comments about the Soviets' practice of lying and cheating to gain their ends appear in the text of his first presidential press conference, *Weekly Compilation of Presidential Documents*, Vol. 17, No. 5, pp. 66–67. His "focus of evil" remarks were made in a speech on March 8, 1983, reported in the *New York Times*, 9 March 1983.

44. Ronald Reagan, Statement on Polish crisis, December 23, 1981, *Weekly Compilation of Presidential Documents*, Vol. 17, No. 52, pp. 1404–1407.

45. Ronald Reagan, Statement on sanctions being applied to the Soviet Union, December 29, 1981, *Weekly Compilation of Presidential Documents*, Vol. 17, No. 53, pp. 1429–1430.

46. Transcript of Reagan's Speech on the Soviet Union, November 13, 1982, *Weekly Compilation of Presidential Documents*, Vol. 17, No. 53, pp. 1429–1430.

47. Text of joint US–Soviet statement, issued in Geneva, November 21, 1985, at end of Reagan–Gorbachev meeting, *New York Times*, 22 November 1985.

48. Leslie Gelb, "The Summit: New Issues," *New York Times*, 26 October 1986.

49. Fred Kaplan, "Pact Alters Terms of Arms Debate," *Boston Globe*, 21 September 1987.

CHAPTER SEVEN

North–South Tensions

Located largely south of the Tropic of Cancer, for the most part considerably less developed economically than the countries to the north, predominantly nonwhite, the countries of the so-called Third World are more exercised by "North–South" issues than "East–West" issues—principally the disparities in wealth and power between the more affluent and poorer countries rather than the geopolitical and ideological rivalry between the coalitions of the United States and the Soviet Union. Approximately 130 countries in all, the Third World countries have formed their own coalition to press common demands upon the affluent countries for international redistributions of wealth and power.

Third World demands that rectification of North–South disparities be accorded high, if not the highest, priority on the international agenda are at considerable tension with the still-prevailing cold war preoccupations of the superpowers; and through the Nonaligned Movement (whose members profess neutrality toward the US–Soviet rivalry), to which most of the southern coalition belongs, many Third World leaders are purposefully working to accelerate the disintegration of cold war bipolarity.

Some of the Third World's proposals for internationally redistributing power and wealth also imply a substantial modification of the nation-state system, turning universal membership institutions of the United Nations into authoritative rule-making agencies with supranational licensing, taxing, and resource allocation functions.

NORTH–SOUTH VS. EAST–WEST

The cold war is not easily dislodged from the Third World, however. Including most of the rimland of classical geopolitics, most of the former colonial empires of the European members of NATO, and (in the Western Hemisphere) the region covered by the US Monroe Doctrine, the Third World continues to be viewed by many influential American and Soviet policymakers as an arena still largely up for grabs—comprising countries that are bound to gravitate toward or be coerced into one or the other side's sphere of influence. Indeed, at various times since World War II, the competition for client relationships in the Third World has been of the very essence of the cold war. Some governments in the Third World play upon this competition by offering closer association with one side or the other, in some cases hinting at either nonalignment or a switch in alignment, in order to extract concessions from Washington or Moscow.

The basic trend since the 1960s, though, has been away from political alignment with either cold war coalition, for throughout the Third World only those leaders capable of mobilizing intense nationalist loyalty are able to sustain their power and authority. Most of the Third World countries have achieved independence from their colonial overlords only since the end of World War II, and their governments are wary of seeming to accept a new semicolonial (or *neo*colonial) dependency on one of the superpowers.

The need to perpetuate nationalist fervor in order to sustain viable government is particularly great in the multiethnic, multicultural countries carved out of the old colonial empires—which, indeed, describes virtually all of the new states. In these countries, a visible amount of xenophobia toward the new imperialists in Washington and Moscow is a necessary ingredient of domestic political leadership, especially as popular aspirations for economic development remain unsatisfied and frustrations mount. No leader could hope to be seen as a puppet of an external power and still survive.[1] Moreover, the most sagacious indigenous leaders have come to realize that their countries are not well suited to regimes imitative of those prevailing in either the affluent West or the Soviet sphere, but rather are best governed through hybrid ideologies and constitutional structures more suited to the traditional cultures of their particular nations.

The superpowers, too, have become more cautious in signing up allies in the Third World and locking themselves into "mutual security" obligations to help client regimes sustain themselves against their internal and external enemies. Regimes that survive primarily as wards of one of the superpowers, however successful they might look in terms of gains in gross national income, often can turn out to be political and security liabilities. Both Washington and Moscow have had to distance themselves from particular Third World clients who, using weapons and other resources obtained from their superpower ally and claiming to be fighting on behalf of shared ideological causes, have moved unilaterally against local opponents in brutal or rash power plays adverse to the interests of their benefactor.[2] US problems with client regimes in Argentina, Turkey, Pakistan, South Vietnam, Taiwan, the Philippines, South Korea, and Indonesia are cases in point. The Soviets have had to pull the reins on, or disassociate themselves from, moves they considered reckless made by China (when they were allies), North Korea, Vietnam, Libya, Iraq, Syria, Ethiopia, Algeria, and Cuba.

Restraining actions by the superpower often carry their own high price, since the client's acquiescence to more cautious strategies usually requires the superpower to increase tangible signs of fidelity—meaning more military and economic assistance—which carry the risk of a stickier identification with the client's fortunes in the next crisis. The Kremlin has had to wrestle especially with this dilemma in its relations with Middle Eastern countries, where Soviet Arab clients, frustrated or defeated in an encounter with Israel, blame their failure on insufficient support from Moscow.

In a 1986 publication, the American sovietologist Marshall Shulman characterizes the general evolution over the past three decades of superpower relations with the Third World as a movement from a situation dominated by strategic bipolarity to one in which "events in the Third World took on a life of their own, subject only to a limited degree to the will of the great powers."[3]

Along with the increasing geopolitical distancing between the superpowers and many of their southern economic and military clients, there has been a growing realization all around that the causes of the persisting poverty and economic underdevelopment in many countries are much less tractable than had been supposed by either Marxist or non-Marxist development economists. And to compound the difficulties, just when the magnitude of the Third World development problem was beginning to be appreciated, the industrially advanced countries were becoming less inclined to allocate resources to the problem.

The Third World countries have resented their status as pawns in the bipolar rivalry, but the alternatives may not be much better. The emerging reality was described some years ago by an Indian commentator: "With the loosening of the two blocs and the beginning of a certain measure of multipolarity, the nations of Asia and Africa suddenly found themselves reduced to the position of the 'Fifth (or Sixth) World,' in terms of their importance in world politics."[4]

THE THIRD WORLD AS A COALITION

Sensing their weakness in bilateral bargaining with their affluent patrons, the Third World countries have been attempting to concert their demands on the industrialized countries. As far back as 1955, twenty-nine African and Asian countries convened in Bandung, Indonesia, to proclaim their nonalignment from the superpower blocs and their common opposition to colonialism and neocolonialism. But the emergence of the Third World's determined effort to bargain as a coalition can be dated from 1964, when seventy-seven countries at the first United Nations Conference on Trade and Development (UNCTAD), over the objections of the Western countries in attendance, turned the conference into a continuing institution for confronting the North on economic issues. (The UNCTAD southern coalition has expanded to well over a hundred countries, but the designation "Group of 77" has been retained in commemoration of their dominance of the 1964 conference.)

Since the 1964 UNCTAD session, the Group of 77 has attempted to bargain as a coalition in all international forums dealing with matters affecting the developing countries—including the GATT, the International Monetary Fund, various specialized UN agencies, the Law of the Sea Negotiations, and UN environmental conferences. It has been caucusing before and during virtually all international meetings on economic development and relations between the rich and poor countries in order to present a common front both to the industrial North and the East.

Demands for a New International Economic Order

The 1964 UNCTAD session also marks the origin of the basic common set of demands by the developing countries for what they call a New International Economic Order (NIEO). These demands, specifically and cumulatively, constitute a rejection of the established "liberal" international economic order of Bretton Woods and the GATT premised on the belief that everyone will benefit from a global market as free as possible from barriers to buying, selling, and investing across national borders. As seen from the South, the prevailing order was a regime of the already industrialized countries instituted for their benefit. The developing countries came to regard the insistences from the North that the South join this order as at least "benign neglect" of their interests, if not a malign conspiracy to keep out new competition; for international free trade, historically, was opposed by the United States and other now-developed countries when they were at a competitive disadvantage and wanted to diversify their economies.[5]

The principal NIEO demands include:

Commodity agreements to stabilize world prices of primary product exports at remunerative levels, preferably with built-in price increases indexed to price increases in industrial goods. The standard Third World argument is that it is grossly inequitable for poor countries with economies highly dependent on export earnings from one or a few basic commodities to be thrown into severe depressions because of slackened international demands for these commodities or a decline in real earnings from their exports in relation to goods they must import. The more diversified economies of the affluent countries are better able to absorb demand and price changes for vulnerable exporting sectors: and, in fact, most of the industrial country governments provide such sectors with subsidies, such as agricultural price supports and government purchasing arrangements. Simple fairness, it is contended, requires international guarantees to poor countries against disastrous export-income losses that are no fault of their own.

Orthodox free traders object to commodity price stabilization agreements, however, as too much of an interference with the market. Everyone loses over the long run, they argue, by making purchasers of goods pay more than they would if prices are allowed to reflect supply and demand. Especially where price declines reflect the entry into the market of new producers, the development of more efficient means of production, or the use of better substitutes, efforts to prop up commodity prices are unfair to the consumers—many of whom may also be poor. Free market economists also argue that artificial pricing arrangements either feed on themselves, by attracting even more producers into a particular commodity line and thus requiring even heavier controls on prices and production, or else they will collapse when the number of new producers extends supply beyond the point where restraining competitive selling underneath fixed prices is feasible.[6]

The objections of the orthodox free traders tended to determine the responses of most of the industrial countries toward the idea of commodity agreements until the 1970s, when the oil producers in the Organization of Petroleum Exporting Countries (OPEC) acted as a cartel to compel the oil importers to purchase oil at prices the OPEC members decided upon among themselves. Recognizing the enhanced bargaining clout the Group of 77 derived from the success of OPEC, and worried that other commodity producers might try to emulate such cartelization, France tried to stimulate a North–South dialogue on the international management of raw material markets. And at the 1975 meeting of the Commonwealth Heads of Government, the United Kingdom proposed a "new deal" in the world trading system that would include agreements to stabilize commodity export earnings and that might even include indexing the prices of raw materials and manufactured products.[7]

The new European responsiveness was reflected in the Lomé Convention of 1975 between the European Economic Community (EEC) and the forty-six former European colonies in Africa, the Caribbean, and the Pacific (the ACP states) associated with the EEC. The Lomé Convention of 1975, succeeded by a second Lomé Convention of 1979, established a compensatory finance scheme, STABEX, to stabilize the export earnings of the APC states in twelve commodity groups.[8] The Lomé accords also responded positively to many of the other southern demands, as discussed below.

The United States initially objected to international pricing arrangements for commodities. But Secretary of State Henry Kissinger, not wanting to see the United States isolated from the North–South dialogue, got President Ford to authorize a shift in US policy (over strong objections from the Treasury Department) in the direction of greater responsiveness to the Third World's NIEO demands, including commodity agreements.[9] This demarche in US policy was revealed in Kissinger's September 1975 speech to the Seventh Special

Session of the United Nations (actually read to that body by Ambassador Daniel Patrick Moynihan).[10] Still the United States would negotiate only on specific commodities individually, on a case-by-case basis. In addition to signing international commodity agreements on tin and coffee (but refusing to sign one on cocoa), the US government at the omnibus North–South Conference on International Economic Cooperation, held from December 1975 to June 1977, departed from its ground rule on case-by-case negotiations only and agreed in principal to establish a common international fund for commodity price stabilization.

The agreement in principle on the Common Fund for commodities took another three years of difficult negotiations to translate into a specific accord. As provided for in the 1980 articles of agreement, a meager $400 million will be made available by the international community for maintaining buffer stocks but only for commodities covered by international commodity agreements. When the price of a covered commodity falls below a stipulated level, the common fund is drawn upon to purchase stocks of that commodity in the open market to support its price. On the other hand, if the supply–demand situation for a commodity is driving prices too high, some of the buffer stocks in that commodity will be sold to keep its price within a predetermined range.[11] Even these concessions to the South's position on commodities have been made reluctantly, however, particularly by the United States, where the dominant view among government and private economists is that commodity agreements distort the natural efficiency of the market in determining who should produce what and how much.[12]

Open access to the markets of industrial countries for goods from the poor countries, and in some fields preferential access, without reciprocal access to poor-country markets. The Third World coalition has been challenging not only the sluggish pace at which industrial countries are reducing the barriers to imports from developing countries (particularly on semimanufactured textile, wood, and metal products), but also the central reciprocity principle of the GATT. The developing countries see no way of diversifying their economies to provide them with the basis for more balanced economic growth unless they are allowed special markets for the goods and services of their new industries where they will not have to compete with similar goods and services produced by the affluent countries.

In order to head off the formation by the South of a counter-GATT (which it looked like the Group of 77 was trying to do in UNCTAD), the Northern countries in 1964 added a new section on trade with the developing countries—Part IV—to the General Agreement. Part IV calls on members of the GATT to give priority to the reduction of trade barriers of special concern to the developing countries. Of greater significance, because it contradicts the under-lying philosophy of the liberal economic order, is the allowance of exceptions for developing countries to the most-favored-nation (MFN) rule and other reciprocity principles that are supposed to prevail in the GATT's mutual tariff reduction regime.

Part IV is only a statement of a willingness of the leading GATT countries to respond to the special circumstances of the developing countries; it is hardly a binding commitment. The Northern countries are constrained from implementing it by their own industry and labor groups who fear their products will be undersold by subsidized developing-country industries with cheaper labor costs, fewer environmental regulations, and less onerous tax burdens.

Even so, a number of West European governments have supported the Group of 77's more extreme demands for a general system of preferential entry into industrial country markets; that is, goods from developing countries are to be exempt from tariffs and other barriers the industrial countries otherwise apply to foreign imports, but the developing countries need not institute reciprocal concessions. The Scandinavian countries, The Netherlands, and West Germany have been most supportive of this general system of preferential trade with the poorer countries, with France and Belgium willing to endorse a more selective system of preferences. Under the terms of the Lomé Conventions of 1975 and 1979, the EEC does allow preferential entry into the Common Market of a considerable range of goods from the ACP countries.

The US government continues to object in principle to preferential trading access agreements and is particularly critical of the EEC–APC arrangements, contending that in providing privileged access to the European Community for only a subset of the developing countries, the EEC preference system discriminates against all the rest of the developing countries, and thus not only contradicts the free trade principles of the GATT but stimulates the development globally of rival trading blocs dangerous to stability and peace. Yet the United States has followed suit, arguing with some validity that it has been forced to do so in extending to selected Caribbean Basin countries preferential access to the US market. Japan has also joined in the preferential access game, negotiating special trading agreements with various countries in Asia.[13]

By and large, particular developing countries are willing to pay the price of being discriminated against by some regional preferential arrangements if this gains them preferential access to other industrial country markets. The Group of 77 continues to argue for a globally extensive system of general preferences covering all of them, but this appears to have become more of a rhetorical posture.

Commitments by each affluent country to allocate a minimum percentage of its GNP for the transfer of resources to developing countries. Official development assistance, bilaterally from donor governments directly to recipient governments or multilaterally through the World Bank or any of the regional development banks, is now of lesser importance in the South's coalition strategy for reforming the international economic order than it was in the early UNCTAD years. In the 1980s, such foreign aid provides only about 10 percent of total financial flows to the developed countries as compared with the 70 percent accounted for in export earnings.[14] Yet for many countries, the official assistance they receive from other countries, whether in the form of direct grants or international bank loans at concessionary rates, provides the margin between a minimal hope of bettering their economic condition and sliding backward into abject poverty. For others—newly industrializing countries that are beginning to approach self-sustaining growth—it can provide that crucial boost toward success. Thus, the Group of 77 and its champions in the affluent countries, despite growing reservations about the demeaning dependency relationships often associated with official development assistance, continue to press the affluent country governments for pledges of 1 percent of their GNP (up from the .7 percent asked for in previous decades). But very few countries have met this target; and the United States refuses to subscribe to it.

Official development assistance has been found to carry special problems for both donors and recipients. Because it involves transfers of resources that would not occur naturally in the market, donor governments extending the special help usually expect special favors in return: political alignment, votes in international forums, military base rights, a hospitable environment for their corporations, and concentration of their imports in purchases from the donor country rather than from other foreign sellers. Donor governments generally assume the right to ask for such things and may get angry when they fail to materialize. From the point of view of the recipients, however, these expectations by donors can be viewed as a kind of neocolonial intervention; and if a recipient government itself doesn't vigorously object, there are likely to be plenty of opposition politicians around ready to charge those in power with selling out the country's independence and national dignity.

The misunderstandings and resentments between donor and recipient countries experienced by many countries in the bilateral aid relationships of the 1950s (among the most notorious were the falling out between the United States and Egypt over the Aswan Dam project and the bitter hostility that developed between Moscow and Beijing) led to a greater reliance by Western donor countries in the 1960s and 1970s on multilateral institutions.

But the new multilateralism spawned its own tensions and animosities, as the donor countries in control of the international and regional institutions dispensing financial and technical assistance required greater specificity in applications for assistance, imposed stricter performance criteria, and insisted on closer monitoring by the aid-dispensing institutions.

The World Bank and its affiliates gave increasing emphasis to funding particular *projects* as opposed to general support for country development programs; and under the bank presidency of Robert S. McNamara, there was an effort to induce developing countries to give priority to "basic human needs" projects for alleviating the destitution of the poorest elements of society, which many Third World governments resented as an intrusion on their sovereign prerogatives to fashion their own development plans.[15]

The International Monetary Fund's gradual move into the business of supporting development, while favored by the Group of 77, has occasioned bitter North–South disputes. Particular tensions surround the question of allocating Special Drawing Rights (SDRs) to Third World governments in need of financial resources for development projects. The SDRs had been originally created by the IMF as a special monetary reserve to help members over temporary imbalances in their payment accounts to trading partners (a problem that afflicts the affluent as well as the poor countries), and there continues to be reluctance by many members to dilute this special purpose.

Moreover, as the IMF took on a development-supporting role, it imposed the conservative bankers' criteria and market-oriented philosophy of its Directors—most of whom are from the advanced capitalist countries—in the form of stipulations that the developing-country governments institute austerity measures, such as high interest rates (to restrict consumer borrowing and consumption and bring down inflation) and reductions in social welfare programs (to free up resources to invest in basic development projects). More often than not, developing-country economists have considered the IMF conditions excessively reflective of the Fund's preoccupations with financial stability and debt repayment rather than development, and not responsive to local needs and sensibilities; but they have reluctantly accepted the conditions anyway rather than forfeit urgently needed resources.

The multilateral mode of transferring resources, while at first welcomed by developing countries as a way of removing *politics* from donor–recipient relationships, had the unintended effect of reducing the *political will* of the affluent countries to help the world's disadvantaged peoples. The indifference also reflected the waning of the superpower rivalry for Third World allies and clients in the late 1960s and early 1970s.

To make matters worse, the decline of the North's attention to the South's development problems coincided with a time of increasing preoccupation by the industrial countries with a new set of economic problems of their own. Northern remedies for their own problems not only were indifferent to Southern difficulties but often exacerbated them.

The energy supply and pricing crisis of the 1970s (induced by a subset of the Group of 77, the OPEC countries)—rather than giving the Southern coalition new leverage over the North—gave rise to inflation and inflation-control policies in the industrial countries that adversely affected the terms of trade and balance of payments condition of most of the developing countries and worsened their international debts. Moreover, the industrial country recessions of the late 1970s gave rise to a new protectionism that further hurt the ability of the developing countries to earn foreign exchange by exporting to the North and forced them to restrict imports crucial to their own development programs.[16] The non-oil producing Third World countries were left with little choice but again to become supplicants for loans at the windows of the World Bank and the IMF in addition to commercial lenders at a time when they were least able to meet the repayment obligations on their past debts.

Special debt and balance-of-payments relief. Even with the availability of low-interest loans and other concessionary resource transfers, many a developing country is unable to pay its debts, often not even the interest charges of its debts, at previously negotiated rates. By 1987, the outstanding debts of the developing countries totaled over $100 trillion, more than half of this incurred by governments with major debt-servicing difficulties.[17] For most of these countries, the repayment of debts at the originally agreed rates would substantially wipe out the debtor country's annual margin of economic growth or, in extreme cases, cause the country to suffer a disastrous decline in national income.

The countries with their backs against the wall have been pleading for payments moratoria, in some cases even debt forgiveness, on their accumulated debts. Their argument is that without such additional concessions, the purposes of the original loans—to allow the recipients to generate development investments that would be unavailable out of current earnings—would be negated, and they would be unable to sustain their economic growth. Worse yet, they would have to default and might fall into total bankruptcy.

But moratoria on outstanding debt obligations create problems for the international lending community and also for some of the relatively more successful developing countries that have been servicing their obligations. They tend to dry up sources of future credit, much of it from nongovernmental contributors to the resources of the international financial institutions, who fear the precedent of rewarding weak economic performance and loan repayment delinquency. As lenders are driven away from the international development banks and funds, the better risk borrowers, many of whom are still not ready to pay market rates of interest, have fewer funds available to them.

By the later 1980s, the declining hope that adequate debt relief would be provided through the multilateral institutional network was driving many developing countries back into the bilateral mode of seeking relief from particular benefactors in the North. Mexico was compelled to pursue this strategy and succeeded in obtaining a major renegotiation of loans from the United States in 1986. But the developing country coalition is unhappy with this need to return to the bilateral framework, fearing it will tempt Northern countries to pursue divide-and-rule strategies vis-à-vis the Group of 77. It also revives opportunities for the reinjection of the cold war and neocolonial relationships into development financing.

To alleviate the severe balance of payments deficits incurred by many developing countries when their export earnings drop far below their expenditures on imports, the industrial countries have been generally willing to provide temporary relief through the Special Drawing Rights of the International Monetary Fund and regional financial facilities. For such situations, each developing country member of the IMF is supposed to have access to SDRs equal to its share of world trade or world production. But the Group of 77 has urged that a substantially larger proportion of SDRs be allocated to the poorer countries, not only for relief of balance of payments deficits but as an additional source of credit for basic economic development. The industrial countries, especially the United States and the Federal Republic of Germany, have objected to the proposed SDR-development link, arguing that the resulting diversion of SDRs to development purposes may reduce their availability for their primary purpose of avoiding severe international recessions that might accompany constrictions in trade when there are liquidity bottlenecks in the system. In recent years, however, while not yet granting the development link in principle, the industrial countries have agreed to increased allocations of SDRs to developing countries—beyond what they would have received under the older income percentage formulas.[18]

The elimination of weighted voting procedures favoring the affluent countries in international agencies, especially those dealing with development problems, and wherever possible the institution of one-country/one-vote procedures. This demand is adamantly resisted by most of the Northern governments, particularly because it would affect the functioning of institutions that play a prominent role in the global economy such as the IMF, the World Bank, the GATT, the International Maritime Organization, and the International Telecommunication Union. Power in these bodies characteristically rests with those countries with the most real resource power in the economic sector to be regulated. The IMF and the World Bank, for example, give primary weight to paid-in contributions in the allocation of votes among member countries.

Moves in the direction of one-country/one-vote decision processes allegedly will lead to irresponsible decisions and will only drive away the holders of real resources whose participation in any case is voluntary. If the World Bank, for example, no longer represents the preferences of the affluent contributors when it sets the terms on loans, then the sources of the bank's assets will dry up because the contributors will either revert to bilateral negotiations with recipients or form new multilateral lending consortia under the control of the donor countries.

Yet there has been some movement in the direction of Group of 77 demands for greater sharing of decision power. In the World Bank today, the developing countries hold about 35 percent of the voting power, while their subscriptions amount to about 4 percent of the bank's resources. And in the IMF, the developing countries' share of votes is over 35 percent in contrast to their 22 percent in 1948. Moreover, certain key policymaking committees have accorded greater representation to the developing countries: Most notably, the IMF Committee of Ten (which initially contained no members from the Third World) was expanded in the 1970s to the Committee of Twenty (containing nine Third World members).[19]

The Southern coalition is not satisfied with these concessions, however, and has been agitating for the UN General Assembly and its affiliated one-country/one-vote bodies to pull back authority on devlopment matters from the specialized bodies and to be the directing institution for global negotiations on reforming the world economy.

An important precedent for the Group of 77 is the decade-long negotiations on the Law of the Sea, involving more than 100 countries, that produced a new treaty in 1982. But for the US government under the Reagan administration, the Law of the Sea negotiations are precisely the model of what is wrong with universal-membership, equal-voting, international forums.

The Law of the Sea negotiations provided for the establishment of an International Sea-Bed Authority to control the mining of minerals on the deep ocean floor. The Sea-Bed Authority, while operating under the direct control of a Council of thirty-six members chosen from five different classes of states, would be under the basic authority of an Assembly that would be a replica of the Law of the Sea forum itself. Moreover, the new Sea-Bed Authority would contain its own "Enterprise" for engaging in the exploitation of the sea-bed resources. It would assign a portion of the mining sites to state and private corporations, but even on these it would collect taxes and have the right to regulate production and prices. The Reagan administration reversed the intention of its predecessors to have the United States sign the Law of the Sea Treaty and to participate in the new deep-sea mining regime, branding the mining Enterprise in particular an intolerable example of the kind of "international socialism" that is likely to be forced upon the world by universal-membership bodies deciding matters of substance on a one-country/one-vote basis.

THE NIEO AS A CHALLENGE TO
THE NATION-STATE SYSTEM

Much of the reaction by the more affluent countries to the planks in the New International Economic Order reflects apprehension by those relatively well off in the prevailing system that concessions even to some of the specific demands of the Third World coalition will set in motion a radical unraveling of not just the existing international economic order but the political order as well. In fact, many leaders among the developing countries are themselves worried about the larger political implications of some of their demands, especially the consequences for national sovereignty and the norm of nonintervention in domestic systems; indeed, this Southern ambivalence is behind some of the anomalies and contradictions in Third World rhetoric and behavior. Even those Southern countries engulfed by starvation and disease, and desperately in need of outside help to ameliorate these conditions, are determined that whatever help they accept shall not be at the cost of their newly won independence.

Thus, with respect to the basic structure of the world polity, the "Magna Charta" of the NIEO—the *Charter of Economic Rights and Duties of States*, passed by the UN General Assembly in December 1974—is at the same time radical and conservative. Article 1 affirms that "Every State has the sovereign and inalienable right to choose its economic system as well as its political, social, and cultural systems in accordance with the will of its people, without outside interference, coercion or threat in any form whatsoever." But in numerous other provisions (especially Articles 8, 17–18, and 22–29), the Charter asserts a firm international "social welfare" obligation, as it were, on the part of the more economically prosperous countries to transfer real resources to the less advantaged countries beyond what occurs in the international market; and it contemplates major institutional and structural changes in the world political economy to facilitate these resource transfers.[20] Were the new equitable distribution norms to become the basis of the international economic order, and were the institutions required to apply these norms given sufficient legal power to achieve the distribution objectives, there would inevitably need to be radical changes in the norms and structures of the inherited state system contrary to the philosophy expressed in Article 1.

The radical implications of efforts to institute an effective worldwide regime to assure that economic opportunities and amenities are distributed equitably have been explicitly recognized and embraced by a prestigious group of authorities from the industrialized and developing countries alike in the Independent Commission for International Economic Cooperation, chaired by the former West German Chancellor Willy Brandt.[21]

In a highly controversial but groundbreaking series of reports, the Brandt Commission endorsed most of the planks of the NIEO and supported the Group of 77's call for a series of global negotiations, including periodic summit meetings among the world's leaders, to help design an "equitable world order." In the view of the Brandt Commission, these global negotiations should be open to proposals heretofore dismissed as too radical, including certain forms of automatic international taxation to raise funds from those with great wealth to be transferred to the world's poor. Such measures might include taxes on international trade, especially arms exports, and taxes on users of the international "commons" areas—the ocean beyond national jurisdiction, Antarctica, the atmosphere, the moon and other celestial bodies, and outer space. "What is now on the international agenda," said Chairman Brandt, "is a rearrangement of international relations, the building of a new order and a new kind of comprehensive approach to the problems of development."[22]

There is yet another school of thought and set of interests, however, that has its center of gravity primarily in the Northern headquarters of private concentrations of economic power, particularly the multinational corporations, whose views and bargaining power need to be taken into account in any global dialogue on radically restructuring the world's political economy. As the discussion in the following chapter shows, they have a legitimate claim to be counted among the world's leading agencies, since the demise of the colonial empires, for transferring resources from the affluent North to the poor South as well as for transcending barriers imbedded in the nation-state system to the free exchange of goods, people, and ideas.

ENDNOTES

1. For an analysis of the domestic sources of xenophobic foreign policies in Third World countries, see W. Howard Wriggins, *The Ruler's Imperative: Strategies for Survival in Asia and Africa* (New York: Columbia University Press, 1969).

2. See Francis Fukuyama, "Military Aspects of U. S.–Soviet Competition in the Third World," in Marshall D. Shulman, ed., *East-West Tensions in the Third World* (New York: Norton, 1986), pp. 181–211.

3. Marshall Shulman, "Overview," in Shulman, *ibid.*, p. 7.

4. Sisir Gupta, "The Third World and the Great Powers," *Annals of the American Academy of Political and Social Science*, Vol. 386 (November 1969), p. 56.

5. On the evolution of developing country attitudes toward the established "liberal" regime, see Jagdish N. Bhagwati, "Rethinking Global Negotiations," in Jagdish N. Bhagwati and John Gerard Ruggie, eds., *Power, Passion, and Purpose: Prospects for North-South Negotiations* (Cambridge: MIT Press, 1984), pp. 21–31.

6. For the arguments of market-oriented economists against commodity agreements and other NIEO measures, see Richard N. Cooper, "A New International Order for Economic Gain," *Foreign Policy*, No. 26 (Spring 1977), pp. 65–120.

7. Joan Edleman Spero, *The Politics of International Economic Relations* (New York: St. Martin's Press, 1985), pp. 244–245.

8. *Ibid.*

9. On the Kissinger shift toward responsiveness to NIEO demands, see Seyom Brown, "The New Legitimacy," *International Journal*, Vol. 31, No. 1 (Winter 1975–76), pp. 14–25.

10. Henry A. Kissinger, Address read by Daniel P. Moynihan to the General Assembly of the United Nations, September 1, 1975, *Department of State Bulletin*, Vol. 53, No. 1891 (21 September 1975), pp. 425–441.

11. Spero, *The Politics of International Economic Relations*, pp. 249–250.

12. Stephen D. Krasner, *Structural Conflict: The Third World against Global Liberalism* (Berkeley: University of California Press, 1985), pp. 290–292.

13. Spero, *The Politics of International Economic Relations*, pp. 236–264.

14. David H. Blake and Robert S. Walters, *The Politics of Global Economic Relations* (Englewood Cliffs: Prentice-Hall, 1983), p. 134.

15. See Krasner, *Structural Conflict*, pp. 19–20, 144, 273–274.

16. For the economic crises of the 1970s and early 1980s, see Spero, *The Politics of International Economic Relations*, pp. 197–207.

17. International Monetary Fund, *Annual Report of the Executive Board for the Financial Year Ended April 30, 1987* (Washington, DC: IMF, 1987).

18. Krasner, *Structural Conflict*, p. 138.

19. *Ibid.*, pp. 138–139, 145.

20. *Charter of Economic Rights and Duties of States*, Dec. 12, 1974, U.N.G.A. Res. 3281 (XXIX), 29 U.N. GAOR, Supp. (No. 31) 50, U.N. Doc A/9631 (1975).

21. The other members of the Brandt Commission were Edward Heath (Conservative Prime Minister of the United Kingdom, 1970–1974); Olaf Palme (Prime Minister of Sweden, 1969–1976, 1982–1986); Peter G. Peterson (US Secretary of Commerce, 1972–1973); Eduardo Frei Monyalva (President of Chile, 1964–1970); Adam Malik (Vice President of Indonesia, 1977–1978, and Minister of Foreign Affairs, 1966–1979); Layachi Yaker (Minister of Commerce of Algeria, 1969–1977); Antoine Kipsa Dakouré (Minister of Commerce of Upper Volta, 1970–1976); Rodrigo Botero Montoya (Minister of Finance of Colombia, 1974–1976); Lakshmi Kant Jha (Indian Ambassador to the United States, 1970–1973); Haruki Mori (Japanese Ambassador to the United Kingdom, 1972–1975); Joe Morris (Canadian labor leader and Chairman of the International Labor Organization Governing Body, 1977–1978); Abdlatif Y. Al-Hamad (prominent Kuwaiti economist); Khatijah Ahmad (prominent Malaysian banker and economist), and Katherine Graham (publisher of the *Washington Post*).

22. Independent Commission for International Economic Cooperation, *North-South: A Program for Survival* (Cambridge: MIT Press, 1980), p. 75.

CHAPTER EIGHT

Economic Transnationalism

Contemporary international commerce is in many respects antithetical to the basic norms of the nation-state system—national sovereignty and noninterference by foreigners into a country's domestic affairs. More than the legal-constitutional forms of national sovereignty are at stake. The ability of a country to ensure that public safety, orderly commerce, social justice, and cultural integrity are sustained within its territory is undermined when national policies for regulating the national market can be ignored or overwhelmed by buyers, sellers, and investors unaccountable to the legal institutions of the country.

Most countries today attempt to regulate and moderate their cycles of inflation and recession through alterations in interest rates and currency value—usually administered by a national central bank—in order to affect the availability of money domestically as well as the country's ability to sell goods and services abroad and to attract foreign investments. But tremendous amounts of money held by private institutions can now change national hands so fast that the whole thrust of even a country's domestic economic policy can be overthrown by nongovernmental financial transactions.

The multinational banks and production and marketing enterprises with branches in many countries have knowledge of and financial ties to all major money markets and often obtain information early on contemplated shifts in interest rates or currency values. They will frequently transfer huge financial investments in and out of countries to take advantage of higher rates of return and, in anticipation of currency devaluations or upward revaluations by particular countries, will move massive amounts of funds from weaker to stronger currencies—thus further aggravating the international trading and monetary instabilities that triggered the sudden shifts of money flows in the first place.[1]

The inability of national governments to regulate the transnational economy does not bode well for the effectiveness of social policies designed to transfer resources and other benefits from the more successful competitive members of society to those handicapped for competition in the market. If corporations are able to relocate production facilities to avoid paying high wages and other benefits to workers, or if they can avoid local taxes by transnational relocations of financial assets within the corporation, then in many countries the fruits of decades of domestic political struggle to legislate "progressive" redistribution of income will be left to wither.

The principal political responses to the growing contradictions between the expanding transnational economy and the nation-state system run in opposite directions: One response, prevalent among the internationally mobile elements of society, is to go with the rising tide of economic transnationalism and to intensify pressures on national governments to eliminate barriers to the free flow of international commerce. The other response is centered among those elements of society with less access to and ability to exploit the fruits of the technological revolution in transportation and communications who believe themselves to be at a competitive disadvantage in the open global market and who therefore want to preserve niches they have carved out for themselves in the national market. Some public-interest constituencies also want to assure that the transnationally mobile elements do not evade their responsibilities to the national society by shifting investments, funds, and operations to other countries to avoid having to pay the higher taxes, wages, costs of environmental protection, and other social overhead charges levied on the affluent in the modern nation-state.

There is yet another response, but it still lacks the political clout of either the market expanders or the protectionists. This response is to devise international instruments and institutions with spans of effective control more congruent with the spans of activity of the highly mobile actors. The purpose of such international mechanisms would be to assure that economic actors with an international reach are accountable to those whom these actors substantially affect.

THE MULTINATIONAL CORPORATION AS THE PRIMARY AGENT OF ECONOMIC TRANSNATIONALISM

The most prominent players in the game of eluding nation-state controls are large corporate enterprises such as Exxon, Royal Dutch/Shell, General Motors, General Electric, Unilever, Fiat, International Telephone & Telegraph, and Hitachi—the so-called multinationals. Constituting a family of firms located in different countries and joined together by a parent corporation usually located in one of the advanced industrial countries, many a contemporary multinational enterprise has greater impact on the world economy than do some of the important nation-states themselves. Exxon, for example, sells over $100 billion in goods and services each year, which is considerably more than the annual gross national product of any of 140 countries. Using this comparison, Royal Dutch/Shell outranks Argentina, General Motors has more economic clout than Norway, General Electric is more powerful than Portugal, Unilever than Hungary or Israel, and so on.[2]

A principal reason for the phenomenal proliferation of multinational enterprises since World War II has been the growing industrialization of many countries, often on the basis of subsidies and other protections to local producers of goods and services that would otherwise be imported; paradoxically, efforts to protect national industries from competitive imports have impelled foreign firms to establish branch manufacturing and marketing enterprises *within* such countries rather than be displaced from previous markets.[3]

The global dispersal of manufacturing and marketing subsidiaries has been facilitated by the application of high-speed communications and information processing systems to product manufacture, business management, and banking. The ability to transmit, receive, and store swiftly vast amounts of technical and accounting information has allowed for centralized, standardized, yet flexible direction of far-flung and diverse operations. Where barriers are erected around particular national or multinational markets to intercept the inflow of foreign products, today's communications technologies allow for the avoidance of such barriers through the virtually instantaneous audio or video transfer of financial resources from country to country which then can be converted into tangible goods and services for local sale. Highly sophisticated information systems even allow for the remote command and control of manufacturing processes. American computers are sold in Europe or French automobile tires in the United States, for example, not on the basis of their having been shipped across the ocean but on the basis of international communications, including financial capital transfers, that have allowed IBM to produce goods and services on the Continent and Michelin to manufacture its products in the United States. A related factor has been the revolution in high-speed transportation that shrinks distances and allows for the unprecedented transfer of personnel and product components among subsidiaries.

Currently, as many as 20,000 corporations have subsidiaries in two or more countries, amounting to some 100,000 firms around the world that are controlled from corporate headquarters in a foreign country. These transnational firms are estimated to be responsible for marketing at least three-fourths of all the world's goods and services that traverse national borders.[4]

It is not merely in international trade and finance, however, that the multinational corporations are dominating the world economy. By the year 2000, it has been estimated, well over half of the world's industrial production within countries probably will be by firms with manufacturing plants in a number of countries.[5]

Some commentators see this phenomenon of transnational business as the means by which humankind creates the global city of abundance. By striving to maximize returns on their investments, multinational enterprises presumably promote the growth of most of the national economies in which they operate. Peter Drucker, a prominent management consultant and popular writer, portrays the multinational corporation as an institution that represents "the interests of the world economy...against all the partial and particular interests of the various members. It [is]...an institution that has a genuine self-interest in the welfare of the world economy, an institution that, in pursuing its own goals serves the world economy rather than any one of the individual national economies....Its development...may well be the most significant event in the world economy, and the one that, in the long run, will bring the greatest benefits."[6] Some leaders in the advanced corporate sector also view the multinationals as important for world public order—"a strong force for world peace," as the president of the Bank of America put it, having "a direct, measurable, and potent interest in helping prevent wars and other serious upheavals that cut off its resources, interrupt its communications, and kill its employees and customers."[7]

Over the long run, it may well be true that the most efficient allocation and management of the Earth's resources could be brought about by those enterprises large enough and mobile enough to respond to technology-induced changes in the factors of production and consumer preferences on a worldwide basis. Free competition among such corporations, unencumbered by artificial national restraints on trade and investment, would allow for the location of production and service facilities close to markets, making needed goods available to more people at reduced costs. Capital markets would be linked, increasing the global availability of financial resources. Through these proc-esses, the multinational enterprises would substantially contribute to the economic development of the poorer regions of the globe through the transfer of technology and income-earning capacities from the highly industrialized to the less industrialized countries.

The most intense contemporary debates over the role of the multinationals, however, have less to do with the presumed long-term global effects of unfettered economic transnationalism—for as Lord Keynes observed, "In the long run we'll all be dead"—than with the specific, here-and-now advantages and disadvantages they bring to particular countries and economic sectors.

On the *advantages* side of the ledger, the following claims are often made:

- Multinational firms bring financial resources into countries that the host governments and indigenous private sectors would otherwise not be able to obtain. Thus in the 1980s, some 15 percent of all funds flowing into the developing countries were in the form of investments by the multination-als.[8]

- Because of the risk capital, advanced technology, and skilled personnel a large multinational firm can move into a host country, it can establish facilities in previously underdeveloped areas—constructing roads, bringing in electricity and water, setting up local suppliers of goods and services—thereby generating new centers of industry, employment, and economic growth.
- The multinational subsidiaries, by locally hiring and training workers, technologists, and managerial personnel, contribute to the diversification of skills and talents within the host-country population and thus to the country's overall development.
- By creating indigenous markets and consumer demand for new lines of goods and services, the multinationals provide an established, relatively low-risk environment for indigenous entrepreneurs (with less risk capital at their disposal) to start their own businesses.

The *disadvantages* side of the ledger includes the following frequently voiced complaints:

- The managers of local subsidiaries of multinational corporations, appointed by and expected to maximize returns to the parent company, have no compelling sense of responsibility or accountability to the host society and therefore are prone to make investment, production, and marketing decisions distortive of the host country's national economic planning.[9]
- The multinational subsidiaries often develop sectors or localities in the host country that draw local talent and financial resources away from sectors and localities that may be in greater need of development.
- The new industries brought by the multinationals into a host country frequently use advanced capital-intensive technologies whose effects can be pernicious in at least two respects: (1) Their greater efficiency over indigenous industries in similar product lines destroys local competition and discourages the development of local technological capabilities; and (2) their reduced need for human labor worsens unemployment problems that are particularly severe in most of the developing countries.
- The multinational enterprises provide a funnel and mechanisms for an excessive outflow of capital from the host countries, through repayments of loans extended to local public and private enterprises by the multinationals, special royalties and fees paid to the subsidiary, the disguised repatriation of profits to avoid host-country taxes, and intercorporate trade (purchases of goods and services among the various national divisions of a multiproduct multinational instead of purchases within the host-country market)—the latter accounting for about 25 percent of all trade in the noncommunist world.[10]

- Because a congenial host-country political and economic environment is the key determinant of whether a multinational will transfer in its capital and technology, the corporations have a high interest in the makeup of host-country governments and their policies; they often will exploit their strategic position within the host-country's economy and among its elite elements to assure the passage of favorable legislation and the perpetuation of friendly regimes. Occasionally, this intervention goes as far as financial bribery and/or covert conspiracy to install or destabilize particular ruling groups (as in the notorious activities of the International Telephone & Telegraph Company in Chile in the early 1970s to prevent the election of the Marxist Salvador Allende and then to encourage the overthrow of his government).[11]

- Finally, the transnationalization of economies through the agency of multinational corporations carries along with it the cultural mores and values of the advanced industrial societies that are the locus of the parent corporations. In the process, indigenous ways of life—including religious practices, languages, arts and crafts—are often overwhelmed. The euphemism for this impact is "modernization." The negative characterization is "neoimperialism," which is also a connotation carried in the Latin American term *dependencia*.

But despite all these criticisms of the pernicious effects of multinational corporations on balanced development, and despite the claim by Third World countries (in the Charter of Economic Rights and Duties) of the right by host countries to nationalize the property of multinationals in their jurisdictions and to determine themselves what is fair compensation, most developing countries are anxious to attract the investments and resources the multinationals have to offer. The postures struck against them by Third World leaders are more rhetorical—a politically necessary element of nationalism—than real, as evidenced by the ubiquitous existence of subsidiaries enjoying local tax breaks and other incentives designed to attract and keep them.

Indeed, some of the toughest constraints on the freedom of the multinationals to invest, produce, and market wherever and whenever they choose have been legislated in the affluent industrialized countries in response to pressures from smaller businesses and labor unions. The smaller firms (unable to take advantage of the reduced factor costs obtainable by producing product components abroad) often ally with organized labor (which fears a loss of jobs resulting from the multinationals' transfers of operations to low wage-rate countries with nonunionized workers) to sponsor special surcharges, nontariff barriers, or other penalties on foreign-produced goods reentering the country.

THE NEW PROTECTIONISM

In the Third World, the backlash against economic transnationalism has been most pronounced against the multinational corporations involved in the extractive industries. The example of successful nationalizations of the extractive subsidiaries of many oil multinationals by the oil-producing countries in the 1960s has stimulated a new assertiveness by host-country governments, particularly when it comes to negotiating for shared ownership, but also for greater information and control over the subsidiaries' capital, technology, and markets. The tough host-country bargaining is also a function of the spawning of multinationals by many countries in recent years, in competition for licenses and privileged access to local markets, as contrasted with the period of the 1950s and 1960s when this form of economic transnationalism was dominated by the Americans and the British.[12]

The new Third World assertiveness, however, has not always redounded to the benefit of the host countries. Thus the Japanese, who are the largest new investors, while ostensibly adapting to the push by developing countries for increased control, have fashioned a counterstrategy: Taking advantage of the fact that many developing countries have become dependent on Japanese purchases of their raw materials, the Japanese have been diversifying their sources of supply; they have also kept control for themselves of the most profitable transportation and processing stages of raw material industries, and—rather crassly—have located some of their most environmentally damaging processes in developing countries with lax regulations. The Americans and the Europeans, not to be outdone, are following suit. All in all, observes Stephen Krasner, "there have been substantial changes in the rules of the game for direct foreign investment....International corporations have come to accept, tacitly if not always explicitly, the legitimacy of greater national control of multinational corporate activity. Sovereignty is not at bay. However, these new rules of the game have made corporations very wary of putting large amounts of capital at risk in the Third World."[13]

Efforts to limit the freedom of action of multinationals in the industrialized market economies—which still is where 75 percent of their affiliates operate—emanate less from governments anxious to preserve their sovereignty than from particular industry and labor groups anxious about their survival in the face of competition from the internationally mobile giants. As put by three prominent spokesmen for US labor unions in some of the affected industries,

> The age-old theory of comparative advantage...assumes that the factors of production remain fixed. This assumption no longer holds true....U. S. multinational corporations have been investing overseas at phenomenal rates in recent years. The U. S. labor force, on the other hand, is not mobile. The result—

products produced overseas that take advantage of cheap labor using the most modern of the U. S. or world's technology enter the world market and seriously disrupt job opportunities in the United States. Today, the comparative advantage is, in most cases, simply, cheap labor.[14]

Reflecting similar concerns, organized labor in Sweden and Canada, joined by vulnerable business interests, have sponsored legislation requiring reviews of the effects on domestic employment of the outward investment and importing policies of multinational firms. The Canadian movement toward stricter controls was buttressed by a Royal Commission study showing that multi-nationals operating in Canada preferred to seek supplies and services from foreign branches of the company instead of from within Canada. The federal task force concluded that this could retard the development of Canadian industry to the extent that it overbalances the positive effects on Canada's economy of foreign—principally US—direct investments.[15]

The growing Canadian resentments at becoming economically dependent on US-owned multinational enterprises that were unaccountable to Canada's own determination of its needs were reflected in the Canadian Foreign Investment Review Act of 1972 requiring that new investments in Canada be screened for their benefit to Canada; namely, for their contribution to employment oppor-tunities, to Canadian exports, to increased sales of goods and services produced by Canadian-owned industries, and to Canadian access to advanced technologies, in addition to the opportunities afforded for Canadian equity participation in the ownership of the involved multinational firms. A Foreign Investment Review Agency (FIRA) was established with a broad mandate to conduct such reviews and issue or deny licenses on the basis of its findings.[16] The US government reacted strongly to the new Canadian restrictions and in 1983 obtained a GATT determination that some of FIRA's policies, particularly those requiring companies investing in Canada to buy specified proportions of their goods and services from Canadians, were in violation of the GATT rules.[17]

The most restrictive policies toward multinationals operating within its jurisdiction have been pursued by Japan, principally through stringent percent-age limitations on foreign ownership of Japanese industries (liberalized somewhat in the late 1970s and early 1980s) in addition to careful review of all foreign investments to screen out any adverse effects on domestic business. The Japanese barriers to foreign investment have become a major source of friction in the US–Japanese relationship, especially as the Japanese, leapfrogging US restrictions on Japanese imports, have dramatically increased their US-based production and marketing operations and direct investment in US industry and financial institutions.

France and Britain also have systems of prior review of direct foreign investments to screen out those that might distort national economic plans, but in the 1970s and 1980s, the general trend in both of these countries has been to encourage the foreign capital. Their review procedures have become mostly positive, concentrating on ways of assuring that new foreign investments contribute to the growth of employment and export earnings and devising arrangements for their own nationals to maintain substantial managerial influence in multinational subsidiaries located within their jurisdictions.

REGIONALISM AS AN ALTERNATIVE RESPONSE

Efforts to organize countervailing power to economic transnationalism can also be organized regionally by groups of countries to subject intraregional movements of capital and labor to public interest regulation and to control economic access to the region. Intergovernmental accords need not merely impose constraints but can also stimulate the flow of economic factors across national lines within a region and attract constructive foreign investments.

These have been some of the animating purposes in the formation and elaboration of the European Community. Community-wide procedures were established to encourage the freer circulation of resources, people, and management among member countries and to ensure that the socioeconomic effects of the enhanced mobility were consistent with the members' national goals. The EC was also designed to control penetration of its market by outsiders. In the 1950s and 1960s, the latter purpose caused divisions among the members, with France being the most insistent on curbing the entry of externally owned funds and firms as opposed to Germany, which was more receptive to the inflow of external risk capital, particularly from the United States. France's turnaround on this issue in recent years has allowed the Community, while still often intensely divided over trade and import issues, to coalesce around the Caborn Report, adopted by the European parliament in 1981, which was essentially hospitable to foreign investments, recommending that member nations develop multilateral codes and guidelines on transfer pricing, mergers, and the like, and in general coordinate their monitoring of multinational corporations to assure accountability to common European interests.

The regional approach has had particular appeal to Latin American economists as a way of attempting to match the economies of scale enjoyed by the giant multinationals. Limited success along these lines has been achieved in the Andean Common Market (comprising Bolivia, Colombia, Ecuador, Peru, and Venezuela). The members have agreed on a common foreign investment code that, in addition to maintaining substantial local control over all foreign subsidiaries, is an attempt to prevent competitive bidding among the Andean group and to rationalize production among them. Multinational subsidiaries are required to share at least 15 percent of their ownership with indigenous investors by the end of three years and must phase out their holdings over specified terms averaging about twenty years. Firms must adhere to these provisions to qualify for various market access and trading privileges of the Andean customs union.[18] However, in the larger hemispheric-wide association of Latin states, the Latin American Free Trade Association (LAFTA), efforts to develop a common approach to the problem of direct foreign investment in general and the multinationals in particular have not borne fruit. The member countries are too diverse in size, product concentrations, industrialization, special relationships with extra-hemispheric powers, and political economic systems. Nor have other Third World regions been able to emulate the coordination achieved by the Andean group.

POSSIBILITIES FOR GREATER INTERNATIONAL ACCOUNTABILITY

The ability of the giant multinational firms and international financial networks to affect who gets what, when, and how in world society—often without being accountable to those whom they most affect—naturally stimulates efforts to bring them into greater accountability. But the spans of control of many of the existing nation-states and regional multilateral institutions are simply not wide enough to encompass the global scope of operations of the most active and powerful multinationals.

Accordingly, there are increasing attempts on a global level, both intergovernmentally and in the nongovernmental sectors, to monitor and develop at least common codes of conduct for activities in the transnational economy. Some of these efforts are contributed to by enlightened members of the multinational corporate sector, as a better approach to the problem of nonaccountability than the confiscations and extreme restrictions on their activities that may otherwise eventually gain popularity among alienated populations.

The United Nations Center for Transnational Corporations has become an important source of information and study on the patterns and problems created by multinational corporations and, in consultation with corporate executives as well as host countries, has been developing codes of conduct for direct investments. UNCTAD has been attempting to formulate a common code on technology transfer, and the International Labor Organization has produced a code on restrictive business practices. Stimulated by these efforts, the International Chamber of Commerce has set to work to develop guidelines for relationships between multinational corporations and governments.[19] These codes, once formulated, can be passed as resolutions of international organizations; more important, they can be included as clauses in commercial treaties between national governments and between governments and the corporations they license to conduct business within their jurisdictions.

Some international economists, most notably Charles Kindleberger, suggest the creation of a permanent international forum on the model of the GATT where governments can harmonize their policies for dealing with multinational corporations. Companies and countries could submit their grievances to the secretariat of the international forum, or perhaps to experts appointed by the forum, who would issue recommendations. Compliance would be voluntary, but if the institution were widely used and its decisions respected over time, it might perform a very important role as international "ombudsman for corporations and countries seeking relief from oppressive policies."[20]

Even more ambitiously, but clearly designed to look out for the interests of the corporations, former Undersecretary of State George Ball advocates a "supranational body, including representatives drawn from various countries, who would...enforce antimonopoly laws and administer guarantees with regard to uncompensated expropriation...[and to other] restrictions nation-states might be permitted to impose on companies."[21]

Another potential for bringing some international accountability to the multinational giants exists in international labor unions. Most labor unions, heretofore international in name only, have been prone to agitate automatically for national protection when their industry's productivity in other countries lessens the demand for labor in their own country. Even when foreign goods are produced by a subsidiary of the firm with whom they are engaged in collective bargaining, and by labor belonging to the same international union, the national unions usually try to protect themselves by pressuring their own government to keep out the products.[22]

However, some labor unions—frustrated by the ease with which the large multinational firm can close down a local subsidiary or transfer production and investments to other nations—have been trying to coordinate action with fellow workers in foreign subsidiaries of the same industry. Regional and international trade union secretariats, traditionally serving mainly as information clearing houses, are becoming more aggressive in sponsoring industry-wide consultation and strategy planning on a transnational basis. The European Metalworkers' Federation has been instrumental in coordinating meetings between unions of various countries and various multinational employers. As a portent of things to come, the Geneva-based International Federation of Chemical and General Workers Union (ICF) representing workers in the US rubber industry has intervened with multinational rubber companies in Akron, Ohio, on behalf of demands being made by an otherwise powerless union in Turkey. Such interventions are in the self-interest of the better-organized unions with higher wage-rates and benefits, who stand to lose their own bargaining power if management can get away with ignoring the demands of weaker unions in their foreign corporate subsidiaries.

The types of demands that the international unions, more and more, are attempting to coordinate on a global basis, especially with newly organizing sister unions in the industrializing countries of the Third World, include job classifications, work speeds, safety standards, and even wages and fringe benefits. In addition to the ICF, the most active labor organizations in this movement to develop a global counterpoise to the multinationals are the International Conference of Free Trade Unions, the International Metalworkers Federation, and the International Transport Workers Federation. Some international union officials have predicted that collective bargaining agreements on a world scale, backed by the sanction of coordinated transnational strikes, will be a feature of international relations in the twenty-first century.[23]

To the extent that unions eventually do obtain collective bargaining clout on a transnational basis within certain industries, the effects can impinge on consumer interests and the general safety and welfare of various populations. Higher prices might result from successful bargaining, or essential public services could be disrupted during a bargaining impasse. It may well be, however, that this anarchic potential of transnational labor-management strife will need to materialize in a number of large, socially disruptive crises before transnational legal structures for regulating the transnational economy in the public interest become salable.

This set of developments, speculate the authors of one of the leading international political economy textbooks, "is leading to the emergence of a more truly international economic and political system. Processes and procedures limited formerly to nations are being introduced at the regional and international level because of the international nature of these [multinational] firms. Although this trend is just developing, evidence suggests that it may well be one of the most important long-run effects of the multinational corporations."[24] The realism of such speculations will be analyzed in Chapter 13.

ENDNOTES

    1. Lawrence B. Krause, "The International Economic System and the Multinational Corporations," in *Annals of the American Academy of Political and Social Science*, Vol. 403 (September 1972), pp. 95–100.

    2. United Nations Center on Transnational Corporations, *Transnational Corporations in World Development: Third Survey* (New York: United Nations, 1983).

    3. Raymond Vernon, *Sovereignty at Bay: The Multinational Spread of U. S. Enterprises* (New York: Basic Books, 1971).

    4. United Nations Center on Transnational Corporation, *Third Survey.*

    5. Robert L. Heilbroner, "The Multinational Corporation and the Nation-State," in Stephen Spiegal, ed., *At Issue: Politics in the World Arena* (New York: St. Martin's Press, 1977), pp. 338–352.

    6. Peter F. Drucker, *The Age of Discontinuity: Guidelines to Our Changing Society* (New York: Harper & Row, 1969).

7. A. W. Clausen, "The International Corporation: An Executive's View," in *Annals of the American Academy of Political and Social Science*, Vol. 403 (September 1972), pp. 12–21; quotation from p. 21.

8. Joan Edleman Spero, *The Politics of International Economic Relations* (New York: St. Martin's Press, 1985), pp. 274–275.

9. Stephen Hymer, "The Multinational Corporation and the Law of Uneven Development," in Jagdish N. Bhagwati, ed., *Economics and World Order: From the 1970s to the 1990s* (New York: Macmillian, 1972), pp. 113–140. The thesis that the multinationals in league with the advanced capitalist states, contribute to the under-development of the poor countries is a central argument of Immanuel Wallerstein, *The Modern World System* (New York: Academic Press, 1974).

10. Spero, *The Politics of International Economic Relations*, 276–278; see also OECD, *International Investment and Multinational Enterprises: Recent International Direct Investment Trends* (Paris: OECD, 1981).

11. On the ITT's intervention in Chilean politics, see US Senate, Subcommittee on Multinational Corporations of the Committee on Foreign Relations, *Hearings: Multinational Corporations and United States Foreign Policy* (Washington, DC: GPO, 1973), 93rd Cong., 1st sess; and US Senate, Select Committee to Study Governmental Operations with Respect to Intelligence Activities, *Final Report* (Washington, DC: GPO, 1976), 94th Cong., 2nd sess.

12. Stephen D. Krasner. *Structural Conflict: The Third World against Global Nationalism* (Berkeley: University of California Press, 1985), pp. 185–188.

13. *Ibid.*, pp. 187–188.

14. Rudolph Faupl (International Association of Machinists), Thomas Hannigan (International Brotherhood of Electrical Workers), and Howard Samuel (Amalgamated Clothing Workers of America), in National Planning Association, *U. S. Foreign Economic Policy for the 1970s: A New Approach to New Realities* (Washington, DC: National Planning Association, 1971), pp. 44–45.

15. Royal Commission on Canada's Economic Prospects, Task Force on the Structure of Canadian Industry, *Foreign Direct Investment in Canada* (Ottawa: Information Canada, 1972), pp. 183–211 (cited in Spero, *The Politics of International Economic Relations*, p. 166).

16. Stephen Clarkson, *Canada and the Reagan Challenge* (Ottawa: Canadian Institute for Economic Policy, 1982), pp. 13–14, 83–107.

17. Spero, *The Politics of International Economic Relations*, p. 155.

18. Krasner, *Structural Conflict*, p. 181.

19. On the development of international codes of conduct, see David H. Blake and Robert Walters, *The Politics of Global Economic Relations* (Englewood Cliffs: Prentice-Hall, 1987), pp. 135–137.

20. Paul M. Goldberg and Charles P. Kindleberger, "Toward a GATT for Investment: A Proposal for Supervision of the International Corporation," *Law and Policy in International Business*, Vol. 2, No. 2 (Summer 1970), pp. 295–323, quotation from p. 323.

21. George Ball, "Cosmocorp, the Importance of Being Stateless," in Courtney Brown, ed., *World Business* (New York: Macmillan, 1970), pp. 330–338.

22. Elizabeth Jager, "Multinationalism and Labor: For Whose Benefit?" *Columbia Journal of World Business*, Vol. 5, No. 1 (January–February, 1970), pp. 57–64.

23. For a catalog of devices available to transnational labor organizations, see Robert

W. Cox, "Labor and Transnational Relations," in Robert Keohane and Joseph Nye, *Transnational Relations and World Politics* (Cambridge: Harvard University Press, 1972), pp. 554–584.

24. Blake and Walters, *The Politics of Global Economic Relations*, p. 129.

CHAPTER NINE

The Impact of Technology on Community

The expansion of transnational economic activity analyzed in the previous chapter is an expression of the more general and fundamental increase in human power to change and exploit nature. The location, population, culture, and organization of communities are highly determined by nature's "givens"— the planet Earth's material makeup and environment and human biology. But the basic dimensions of community also are profoundly affected by the remarkable capacity of humans, as distinct from other creatures, to transform what has been given to them by nature or god.

Who can communicate with whom, who can easily exchange goods and services with whom, who can injure or destroy whom will at any point in history substantially define the shape of human communities and their durability. It is hardly surprising, therefore, that the twentieth century revolutions in the technologies of communications and transportation, industrial processes, and warfare have been playing havoc with the traditional national-community basis of the world polity.

THE MOBILITY OF PEOPLE, MATERIALS, AND INFORMATION

Many of the scientific advances and new technological applications of the twentieth century have had their most dramatic cumulative or synergistic effects in the fields of transportation and communication, radically altering the role of location, distance, and topographic barriers in human affairs. From the standpoint of the physics of moving persons, things, and ideas, the whole Earth is already a community. The degree to which the Earth community has been activated to form concrete cooperative relationships, however, lags far behind what now is physically possible and rapidly becoming cost-effective in economic terms. The reasons for this sluggish response are almost all political, not physical.[1]

Transportation

If distance is measured by the time it takes to move from place to place, then the size of the world has indeed been shrinking at a phenomenal rate since the emergence of the modern nation-state system (dated roughly from the time of the French Revolution and the inauguration of George Washington as the first American president). In 1789, it still took a few years to circumnavigate the globe with the fastest sailing ships; horses were the principal means of rapid overland transit, and traveling 25 miles a day in a horse-drawn carriage was considered to be very fast. By the 1880s, steam engines had compressed the distance–time ratio to as much as 250 miles a day over the ocean (about two weeks from New York to London) and some 500 miles a day by rail locomotive. Now it takes only a day to fly around the world in a jet aircraft, and astronauts in space vehicles can orbit the Earth 16 times each 24 hours.[2]

But even though the movement of people and goods between countries and continents today can be virtually as rapid as between neighboring cities, international travel is frequently still a time-consuming and expensive operation—mainly for political reasons: Countries remain determined to keep control over who and what enter their territory, for to lose such control would be in effect to lose control over fundamental social and economic processes.

Indeed, the expanding international mobility of persons and things is the principal stimulus to the thickening apparatus of inspections and controls at most points of entry to and exit from countries: Relatively unpoliced national borders, such as among countries of the European Community and between Canada and the United States, are rare. National land frontiers are fenced, and transit between countries is funneled through a few officially manned checkpoints. The physically accessible ocean coasts of most countries are heavily patrolled and guarded. Aircraft are not allowed to penetrate the airspace above a country without prior authorization from that country's aviation agencies (though some spy planes fly high enough to elude the controls). National governments retain sovereign control over all landings and takeoffs from their territory. International travelers must submit to sometimes elaborate procedures of identification and inspection of themselves and their baggage when entering and/or leaving. Almost all countries require foreign visitors or even those simply in transit to produce proof of citizenship of their country of origin and may deny entry to citizens of countries with which they do not maintain friendly relations. Some governments require considerable advance application for foreign visitors and will frequently deny visas for unspecified political and security reasons. In the 1980s, responding to the increase of terrorist acts by transnationally mobile militants, there has been a tightening of these various controls worldwide on national ingress and egress.[3] Commercial cargo transport is subject to even more elaborate systems of national surveillance and permissions at points of entry—applying customs charges, rigid product and packaging specifications, and other nontariff barriers to implement national policies designed to protect various economic sectors from unwanted foreign competition.

Such tension between the mobility technology allows and the mobility societies will countenance has become a central issue in both international and domestic politics. Everywhere, the physical ease with which people and goods can circulate among countries presses against the barriers to their free circulation, with the result that the barriers have become more and more costly to maintain. The costs of maintaining the barriers, particularly the opportunity costs of contact and commerce foregone, bear differently on various sectors of society (as shown in Chapter 8); and thus the subject of international transportation controls and barriers has become highly contentious in most countries.

Especially where tourism has become a large earner of foreign exchange, which is the case in many developing countries, visa and customs regulations that may discourage foreign visitors are matters of intense debate in national parliaments and bureaucracies, often pitting cultural traditionalists and xenophobes against the entrepreneurial middle classes and cosmopolitan elites.

Those who favor taking maximum advantage of the technological revolution in transportation constitute, as it were, a new transnational community that cuts across not only national boundaries but the larger regional and East–West, North–South coalitions. Where controls on the international mobility of people and goods are obviously required for reasons of safety, orderly commerce, and environmental protection, powerful interest groups representing the internationally mobile sectors tend to prefer assigning a greater role to the specialized international organizations operating in the transportation field: the International Maritime Organization (IMO) for sea transport and the International Civil Aviation Organization (ICAO) for air transport. The national and industry delegates to these institutions, while looking out for the interests of their home industries, are motivated to facilitate and expand international transportation and therefore do work cooperatively—knowing that if they do not resolve their differences at the international level, uncoordinated and unstandardized domestic regulations, often reflecting protectonist interests, will proliferate to constrict international mobility and increase transportation costs.

The IMO, created in 1958, is mandated by its charter to promote standards of safety, efficiency, and fair competition in the maritime industry and to facilitate international cooperation in technical and operational matters. It has formulated navigational rules of the road—particularly navigational lanes, traffic separation schemes, improvements in ship-to-shore communications, and internationally standardized license and training requirements for ships' officers.

An increasingly important function of IMO has been to serve as a negotiating forum for international conventions regulating ocean-going oil tankers: rules for how far from shore tankers must be when discharging their waste oil and special requirements for ship design and navigational procedures to avoid collisions and other sources of accidental oil spills.

Although the implementation and enforcement of IMO-formulated standards and regulations negotiated under its auspices remain with the national governments, the organization is looked to as the source of workable international arrangements in the field of sea transport, and national bodies operating in this field and member governments try to maintain operations consistent with IMO-sponsored regulations. Its central role is attested to by efforts in the early 1970s by environmental groups to assure that their interests are also represented, not only in their national delegations but also in the deliberations of IMO itself. These pressures resulted in the creation within IMO in 1973 of a Maritime Environmental Protection Committee to assure that attention would be given to the environmental impact of various shipping practices.[4]

In the field of civil aviation, ICAO is responsible for formulating standards and rules for use of the increasingly congested international air corridors. It is active in standardizing members' rules governing the overflight of their countries, air traffic control procedures for takeoff and landing, pilot licensing, aircraft design, on-board passenger safety, and the like. Although the organization has no direct enforcement powers, members are required to notify ICAO of differences between their practices and its rules, and ICAO then gives this information to all members.[5] ICAO also conducts investigations of aviation disasters with an international dimension, such as the Soviet shooting down of Korean Airlines flight 007, in response to which new rules for signaling and handling off-course flights were formulated.

Communication

The compression of spatial relationships, as dramatic as it has been in the transportation field, is even more dramatic in the field of communication. Before the invention of the telegraph in 1840, all information had to be transmitted on material documents carried by people or shipped in containers, so the distance–time ratios were exactly the same for communication as they were for transportation. Today, using Earth-orbiting communications satellites as relays, electronically processed sounds and visual imagery can be sent almost instantaneously from any point on Earth to any other point.

International broadcasting.   Politically, the most consequential development is the Direct Broadcast Satellite (DBS), which, along with improvements in reception technology, allows an international broadcaster to transmit programs directly into individual households. Using as few as three of these satellites, appropriately positioned 22,300 miles above the surface of the Earth (in the so-called geostationary orbit where the inertial motion of the spacecraft keeps it roughly over the same spot on the revolving Earth below), a broadcasting corporation or country with the required advanced technologies could beam a program simultaneously to the populations of every country in the world. International Telecommunication Union rules adopted in 1979 put some constraints on such unlimited broadcasting through the assignment of particular orbital slots, broadcast frequencies, and "cones of transmission" to each country, which provide the basis for mutual restraint and accountability. But the new technologies now coming into use by powerful broadcasters allow those who want to receive their broadcasts to pull them in across any such assigned electronic jurisdictions.

As put by the Director of the British Broadcasting System,

> DBS will, in effect, create proximity between far-flung points; all countries across oceans and cultures could become as Canada to the United States, as Ireland to Britain, as the other islands of the Caribbean to Cuba. The economics of communications satellites...destroy geography....
>
> With a working DBS, we could all become each other's neighbors, with everything that implies, to be enriched, influenced, and irritated by each other. In that sense, we may all become Canadians now.[6]

Countries that for cultural, political, or economic reasons want to maintain control over the broadcasts received by their populations have three options: electronic interference with unwanted broadcasts ("jamming"); controls on the reception equipment they allow their own citizens; or international regulations that the powerful broadcasters will respect.

While the technology of jamming has also been making strides, effective interference with broadcasts from space requires expensive and complex equipment. Only a handful of advanced countries appear capable of developing electronic anti-DBS capabilities. The developing countries, among which are many of the governments most worried about the harmful political or cultural effects of foreign television programs, would have difficulty in obtaining jamming capabilities without outside help.[7] A government lacking effective means of jamming unwanted broadcasts can still counter the new DBS technology by allowing individuals to possess only specially altered television receivers that filter out all broadcasts on unapproved networks; but this approach puts the government visibly in the role of censor and requires intrusive and heavy inspection of households by officials to suppress the inevitable black market in illicit receiving sets—a policy hardly conducive to the popularity of a government with its citizenry.

The third course—that of trying to develop an internationally acceptable regime to regulate direct broadcasting across national borders—is favored by a majority of countries. The principal holdout against such a regime is the United States, on the grounds of international "freedom of information."

The essential feature of most of the regulatory regime proposals under consideration in the UN Committee on the Peaceful Uses of Outer Space is the requirement of prior consent by the government of a country that would receive broadcasts. The consent requirement might be applied to an overall arrangement between the broadcaster and receiver country to allow relatively unrestricted broadcasting and reception; alternatively, the receiving country's government might be accorded prior consent rights on program content.

The most vociferous proponents of a rigid prior consent regime are the Soviets and many of the Muslim theocratic states of the Middle East. Some Western democracies—notably Canada and Sweden—are also part of the coalition in favor of receiver-country choice, fearing inundation by broadcasts from the technological giants. The United States, virtually isolated on this issue but whose cooperation is needed for any consent regime to be viable, takes the doctrinal highroad, invoking Article 19 of the Universal Declaration of Human Rights, which asserts the right "to receive and impart information and ideas through any media regardless of frontiers."

Meanwhile, the diplomatic impasse tends to favor those with powerful broadcasting capabilities. US broadcasters already have what amounts to worldwide coverage. The signal of the Soviet Horizon satellite is now technically available to households in Western Europe served by cable systems. The East and West Germans see each other's television programs. Israel and Jordan compete in beaming news broadcasts to each other.[8] At the technological level in the field of telecommunications, the global neighborhood exists. At the legal, political—and moral—levels, however, there are hardly any global community norms (analogous to the broadcasting rules in national communities) for assuring that users of the electromagnetic spectrum are mutually respectful and accountable to each other for what is seen and heard.

Observation technologies.   Synergistic developments in communications, photography, and other observational techniques, combined with advances in space satellite technology, have also made it possible for those in possession of the advanced capabilities to obtain detailed information on human and natural activities and phenomena the world over. The increases in remote sensing power, similar to the increases in broadcasting power, are having both positive and negative effects on how the world's peoples relate to each other.

The powerful new sensing technologies can identify a wide range of electromagnetic energy emissions from the Earth's natural features and from human activity and artificial structures. The energy is emitted, reflected, or scattered at distinctive wavelengths by each particular surface or atmospheric feature; and each of these unique "signatures" can be minutely analyzed with cameras and other instruments sensitive to radiation to detect changes in structure or activity.

The technological breakthroughs in this field since World War II have greatly facilitated the remote surveillance of the following phenomena:

- Military deployments and activity (reducing the opportunities for surprise attack and enhancing the prospects for verifiable arms limitation agreements)

- Meteorological conditions (allowing for better forecasting of weather and climate patterns, including timely warnings of hurricanes, blizzards, and other damaging occurrences)

- Ocean surface and subsurface conditions (providing for better ocean resource management, particularly in fisheries and petroleum exploitation and for the control of ocean pollution)

- Geologic characteristics of land masses (permitting more accurate mapping and location of commercially exploitable minerals and fossil fuels)

- Soil conditions, pest infestation, and the availability of irrigation (when combined with better weather and climate forecasting, allowing for more comprehensive and accurate forecasts of crop yields)

- Patterns of urban, rural, and coastal-zone land use (providing the basis for economically sound and ecologically responsible development plans and projects)

Ideally, the availability of continuous information on threatening military deployments and on the condition of the Earth's ecologies, geology, and environment should be to everyone's benefit. But the reality of the uneven possession among countries of the sensing and information-processing technologies, as with direct broadcasting technologies, has led to fears on the part of the technologically less-developed countries that their relative lack of access to the information can hurt them militarily and economically; and these fears have been translated into demands for restrictions and international management of remote-sensing technologies—demands that the technologically well-endowed countries, especially the United States and the Soviet Union, are stoutly resisting.

Many developing countries fear a loss of their newly won sovereignty. Traditionally, nations have been able to control information about their military preparations, land use, and natural resources by controlling foreign access to their territory. Even with the advent of surveillance from aircraft, host-country prerogatives were retained: Airspace was considered an extension of landspace; and foreign overflights, whatever their purpose, were considered illegal unless the state under surveillance consented—a principle embodied in standard international legal theory and practice.

The increasing reliance on surveillance from spacecraft, however, has rendered anachronistic the traditional international law on territorial sovereignty. There is no way of drawing lines of territorial jurisdiction up into space from the continuously revolving Earth and therefore no way of determining just when foreign spacecraft are engaged in "overflight" of national territory. Yet the sovereignty of countries under surveillance from space surely *is* being violated. And the negative consequences to some target countries indeed can be tangible and substantial.

A developing country in negotiations with a mining corporation for exploratory drilling rights in its territory can be at a major bargaining disadvantage if the corporation initially knows more about the local geology and location of mineral deposits than do the indigenous experts, particularly if the host country is ignorant even of the fact that the corporation has such knowledge.

Moreover, reconnaissance that is supposed to be primarily for producing information on resources and environmental conditions will also—by design or simply as a byproduct—obtain information on the observed country's military capabilities.[9] Much of geodesic and military information thus obtained can be incorporated into the guidance and targeting programs of ICBMs and cruise missiles.

A similar fusion of civilian and military functions is inherent in the reliance on navigational satellites to control the routing of ships at sea. Information received by the satellites on the location of ships is not only used to steer other ships, commercial and naval, but can be fed into the computers that direct offensive weapons to their targets in the ocean.[10] Even so, and in part to ward off international efforts to block the use of preferred frequencies and orbital slots for their own maritime satellites, the United States and the Soviet Union have joined some thirty countries in establishing the International Maritime Satellite Organization (INMARSAT) under the overall supervision of the IMO. INMARSAT, which started operations in 1982, is supposed to provide navigational assistance to all member countries, eventually utilizing its own equipment but meanwhile linking into some of the nationally established navigational satellites of its more technologically advanced members.[11]

Understandably, countries unable to deploy or rent surveillance time on another country's observational spacecraft see many of the innovations in remote-sensing technology as enlarging the gap between the affluent and the poor countries and even as dangerous to their security. As in the direct broadcasting field, resolutions have been introduced in the United Nations to prohibit satellite sensing of a country's land areas and zones of ocean jurisdiction without that country's consent.[12] But just as understandably, countries with a head start in the relevant technologies claim that a prior-consent regime is both retrogressive and unworkable.

The United States and the Soviet Union have attempted to cater to developing-country concerns by selling the nonmilitary information obtained from their reconnaissance satellites and by providing assistance in photo interpretation and other information processing to countries that need it. The space powers have also helped other countries to build and launch their own observational satellites. These technical assistance measures, however, have only partly overcome the deep-seated suspicion by the technologically lagging countries that they are being continually spied on from space and that much of the information thus obtained can be used against them—commercially and militarily.

Responding to these divergent interests, the UN General Assembly in 1979 requested the Secretary General to undertake a study of the legal and financial implications of establishing an international satellite monitoring agency, along lines ·suggested by France, with operational capabilities (contributed by the advanced space powers) to service the remote sensing needs of all members and with the additional mandate of verifying arms control agreements. A committee of experts appointed by the Secretary General endorsed the concept; but the US government has made known its opposition, and the Soviet Union, although it has not made its position explicit, appears equally against it.[13]

Congestion on the frequency spectrum and geostationary orbit. The proliferation of communications satellites in outer space has been turning preferred segments of the electromagnetic broadcasting spectrum and slots on the orbit 22,300 miles from Earth into scarce resources. The users of these resources have not been able to escape the realization that they constitute an interdependent community, since if the pressure continues on the resources unabated, there will be too much mutual interference with broadcast signals from closely positioned spacecraft to allow any of them to function efficiently. Accordingly, current users and prospective users, acting through the International Telecommunication Union, have adopted detailed rules for allocating the spectrum and preferred orbits and for the design of space communications systems so as to prevent unnecessary use of these resources.[14] The ITU's frequency and orbit allocation regime is described in Chapter 13.

GLOBAL AND REGIONAL "COMMONS"

The realizations among users of the electromagnetic spectrum and geostationary orbit that they comprise an interdependent community and that all of them will suffer unless they devise a rational regime to prevent overuse or abuse of the resources are but two manifestations of the more general realization—

stimulated by the technological revolution—that all humans are interdependent users of numerous global and regional "commons" that they cannot escape sharing across national borders and ideological groupings. The term *commons* was applied in nineteenth century English village life to the open cattle grazing land shared by the villagers. It is applied in contemporary international discourse to resource areas or ecological systems that are shared by the people of various countries and are not parceled out to the separate national jurisdictions.

The principal international commons are outer space; the moon and other celestial bodies; the Earth's biosphere; the atmosphere; the oceans and internationally used seas, lakes, and river systems; interlinked plant and animal ecologies; and Antarctica. Modern technologies have made these realms susceptible to intensive use and exploitation by humans and therefore subject to the kind of "tragedy of the commons" that befell the English village grazing lands when individual villagers increased the size of their herds to the point where the commons was severely overgrazed and everyone suffered.[15]

A number of disastrous modern commons tragedies are in the offing—if humans do not alter their prevailing industrial and technological habits— including a dangerous thinning of the Earth's ozone envelope, the excessive "greenhouse" warming of the Earth's climate, the death of major aquatic ecosystems, the degradation of previously fertile croplands, and the poisoning of the air breathed by large populations.

Threats to the Ozone Layer

In the 1980s, atmospheric scientists discovered an alarming depletion of the layer of ozone concentrated in the stratosphere nine to thirty miles above the Earth that shields the planet's living organisms from harmful ultraviolet radiation. The ozone gas, which screens out most of the sun's biologically damaging rays, is being assaulted by industrially produced chlorofluorocarbons (CFCs). The scientists are most worried by the accelerating growth of a huge hole in the ozone layer over Antarctica, which could widen to reach the populated areas in the Southern Hemisphere; such ozone depletion could also occur at the North Pole and affect the Northern Hemisphere. Without sufficient filtering by the ozone layer, the ultraviolet rays reaching the Earth's surface will dramatically increase the incidence of skin cancer and damage DNA cells. The unscreened rays also will wipe out varieties of plankton and fish larvae floating near the ocean surface and diminish crop yields.[16]

The CFCs that, along with natural phenomena, have been thinning out the ozone are injected into the atmosphere by aerosol propellants used in hair sprays, spray paints, perfumes, deodorants, and lubricants; by refrigerators, freezers, and air-conditioners; by fire extinguishers; by solvents used in dry cleaning and in the manufacture of computers and other electronic products;

and by the blowing agents used to produce foam cushions and packaging substances.[17]

Some governments have been exercised to legislate controls on the ozone-destroying agents. The United States, Canada, and the Scandinavian countries have banned at least the aerosol propellants that rely on CFC gases. In the fall of 1987, official delegates from forty countries meeting under the auspices of the UN Environmental Program agreed on a treaty to freeze the production of all CFCs at 1986 levels starting in 1990 and to cut production by 50 percent before the year the year 2000. Some environmentalists criticized the accord as inadequate, insisting that at least an 85 percent reduction in current CFC production should be mandated; discontent was also voiced at provisions allowing developing countries to postpone abatement so as not to inhibit industrial development; but others hailed the accord as a major step in the right direction and an unprecedented international commitment by such a large group of sovereign countries to pass specific laws in the environmental field.[18] Implementation would, of course, depend on subsequent legislation and regulatory action by each signatory country, which could yet prove problematical; indeed, in some countries that had pushed for the accord, including the United States, interest groups opposed to the contemplated controls on industrial activity were intensively lobbying their governments to refrain from finally ratifying it and were preparing domestic legislation designed to inhibit its effective enforcement.

The "Greenhouse Effect"

The injection of fluorocarbons into the atmosphere is also one of the sources of the cumulative assault on another of the biospheric conditions that sustains life on the surface of the planet; namely, the Earth's temperate climate. The temperate climate results from the balance between the heat from the sun that is absorbed by the Earth's surface and the heat that is reflected back out of the atmosphere. For decades, however, scientists have been warning that the buildup of an atmospheric belt of concentrations of chemical substances, predominantly carbon dioxide (from the burning of fossil fuels on Earth) and methane, is changing the planet's basic temperature balance by blocking the escape of heat back into space—the so-called greenhouse effect. Other causes of the buildup of carbon dioxide in the atmosphere are large-scale deforestation (the foliage absorbs carbon dioxide) and, potentially, the pollution of the oceans (which serve as a major sink for carbon dioxide and a source of oxygen). The principal worry of the concerned scientists is that the resulting warming of the Earth could melt the polar ice caps sufficiently to produce a rise in the level of the oceans that would inundate many of the world's major cities. Some previously frigid regions might benefit by having more moderate temperatures, but others would experience desertification.[19]

In 1985, scientists from twenty-nine countries met to pool their knowledge on these phenomena under the auspices of the World Meteorological Organization, the UN Environmental Program, and the International Council of Scientific Unions. Their deliberations, plus reports of international scientific panels convened by the US National Academy of Sciences and the National Aeronautics and Space Administration, have produced a rather solid universal consensus among meteorologists and atmospheric scientists that man-made effluents have contributed significantly to an appreciable greenhouse warming already, and that the rate of warming will accelerate in the future—probably at as much as twice the rate in the next thirty years as the rate of the previous 130 years.[20]

The international political implications of the emerging scientific consensus were drawn by astrophysicist Carl Sagan in his December 1985 testimony before a Senate committee considering possible legislative responses to the threat of excessive global warming:

> The nations to deal with this problem have to make a change from their traditional concern about themselves and not about the planet and the species, a change from the traditional short-term objectives to longer-term objectives and would have to bear in mind that problems like this, the initial stages of global temperature increase, one region of the planet might benefit while another region of the planet suffers, and there has to be a kind of trading off of benefits and suffering....
>
> I think that what is essential...is a global consciousness, a view that transcends our exclusive identifications with generational and political groupings into which, by accident, we have wandered. The solution to these problems requires a perspective that embraces the planet and the future, because we are all in this greenhouse together.[21]

Such consciousness-raising will have to be translated into governmentally imposed sanctions, however, if there is to be sufficient abatement of the buildup of carbon dioxide and other climate-altering effluents. Accordingly, environmental scientists and policy analysts, such as those at the World Resources Institute in Washington, DC, are urging governments to levy taxes on fossil fuels and to use the revenues to support the development of alternative energy sources, particularly solar energy.[22]

Acid Rain

Coal-burning power plants, the combustion of gasoline by automobiles, oil refineries, smelters, and a host of other industrial operations emit sulfur oxides and nitrogen oxides into the air where they are exposed to sunlight and water vapor; the resulting acidic compound falls to the ground in rain, snow, or fog (sometimes even as a dry dust). If this "acid rain" falls into freshwater lakes, it can deplete the calcium in the bone structure of fish and can interfere with their reproductive processes; the acidity can also cause chemical reactions in the subsoil of lakes that inject aluminum and other heavy minerals into the water, clogging up the gills of fish and suffocating them. On land, acid rain can damage the foliage of crops and arrest the growth of trees; it can also corrode steel bridges and railroad tracks and the marble and limestone surfaces of buildings.

Ironically, efforts by particular countries in the 1970s to reduce the concentrations of acid rain within their borders, by requiring industries producing the dangerous oxides to build high smokestacks and thereby disperse the effluents over a large area, have been primarily responsible for converting it from a local issue of concern to a few highly industrialized and coal-burning areas into a general national and international issue. The higher altitude emissions remain suspended in the air long enough to be carried thousands of miles in moving weather fronts. Consequently, much of the acid rain falling on eastern Canada originates in the American midwestern industrial heartland. And the Scandinavian countries have had to absorb substantial amounts of acid rain originating in Germany, France, and especially Britain.[23]

The principle that countries must be accountable to one another for such obvious transboundary pollution has been affirmed in numerous international environmental conferences, beginning with the Stockholm declaration of the 1972 UN Conference on the Environment. And many countries have now formally assumed such an obligation in subscribing to the International Treaty on Long-Range Transboundary Air Pollution, which entered into force in 1983. Working out the respective responsibilities for corrective action and liabilities for damage is often a delicate and controversial diplomatic job among particular sets of countries; but at least in this field there is now a widespread recognition that the problem must be dealt with on an international community basis.[24]

Marine and River Ecosystems As Vulnerable Commons

The proliferation of new technologies for using seas and rivers and the concurrent growth of scientific knowledge about ocean and river ecologies have undermined the traditional assumption that the Earth's great bodies of water and river systems are essentially self-equilibrating and will rebound to their normal conditions no matter what is done to them. From mountain streams down to the farther reaches of the continental shelf and out to the high seas beyond national jurisdiction, from the airspace above the water, through the water itself, on and beneath the seabeds and riverbeds—living and nonliving resources of high value to much of the world's population are being used, abused, and used up.

Paralleling the technological/industrial assaults on basic marine and river ecosystems, a worldwide consciousness has been emerging, sparked by the publication in 1962 of Rachel Carson's book *Silent Spring*, that ocean ecologies, no less than land ecologies, can be critically unbalanced to the detriment of vast segments of the Earth's population simply through the narrow unregulated pursuit of national and private self-interests by the major ocean users. The new consciousness was heightened in 1967 by reports of the widespread death of aquatic animals and plants from the oil spill caused when the supertanker *Torrey Canyon* ran aground. Finally, the rise of a full-blown environmentalist movement in the United States can be dated from 1969 and the media coverage of the lethal effects on ocean ecology along the Pacific coast resulting from a leak in the Union Oil Company's rig in the Santa Barbara Channel. The decade of the 1960s may well be looked back on as the period when human society experienced a "paradigmatic shift" in its view of the sea. As put by the oceanographer Edward Wenk, Jr., "The Community of nations began to recognize that all peoples cluster on continental islands embedded in the vast ocean, that man's activities are intimately linked to the sea, and that the planet represents a closed ecological system wherein ostensible local events may have widely distributed effects."[25]

To be sure, for centuries the major powers have considered the great seas as essential highways for commerce and war, and many populations have obtained important food and income from marine fishing. Clashes among nations over rights of passage through straits and over fishing grounds and disputes over the jurisdiction of coastal waters have been a prominent feature of world politics. Naval encounters have often decisively altered the outcome of major wars. And maritime law, well before the Law of the Sea Treaty of 1982, was perhaps further advanced than any other field of international law.

What is new in the current perspective is the awareness that: (1) the waters and seabeds beyond recognized national jurisdictions are wealthy not only in food but in industrially usable materials; (2) physically, not just politically, the vast seas, even though covering more than 70 percent of the Earth's surface, are not able to accommodate all users; and (3) the maritime environment is a key component of the total biospheric ecosystem and of a number of very important subordinate ecosystems.

It is the third of these elements in the new perspective that is potentially the most massive in its political implications and yet remains the least understood. The conclusion of a study published in 1972 by Resources for the Future still pertains in the later 1980s: "We know all too little of how the sea and its biotic communities impinge on the global ecology, but there is every reason to treat this relationship with great respect. Instead we utilize the sea thoughtlessly as the ultimate sink for all sorts of debris and chemicals generated on land and transported by air and water."[26]

The strain humans have been putting on sea-centered ecological relationships is most evident in semienclosed parts of the planet's larger marine ecosystem.

The following vivid account of the degradation of the Mediterranean Sea illustrates the problem:

> Surely Neptune never anticipated that Homer's fabled "wine dark waters" would one day become a colossal toilet bowl and waste tank. Every year, 85 percent of the raw sewage from 44 million residents and 100 million tourists is dumped directly into the Mediterranean Sea. Inundated as they are, the Mediterranean waters that under normal circumstances could purify and oxidize human wastes now breed infectious diseases such as cholera, typhoid, viral hepatitis and dysentery. Pollutants from land-based industry smother sea floor organisms in a deadly gray ooze. Overfishing, water and noise pollution have dramatically reduced fish stocks and threatened species. The food chain is thoroughly contaminated. The Mediterranean is dying.[27]

But because the death of the Mediterranean would be an unmitigated disaster to the nations surrounding it, the littoral-country governments, with help from the UN Environmental Program, have been able in the 1980s to transcend some of their intense political conflicts (Greece vs. Turkey; Arabs vs. Israel, etc.) at least to the point of formulating a plan of coordinated national actions to save the great sea from irreversible putrification. (The so-called Med Plan is discussed in Chapter 13.) Dire necessity, it seems, can be the mother of constructive political invention—even in the most anarchic regions of the nation-state system.

Other examples of technology's impacts on common water resources leading to at least a modicum of constructive community responses among the surrounding governments can be found in the Rhine River–North Sea region, where effluents from upstream industries in France and Germany have been dangerously polluting the waters that flow into coastal cities and ports along the North Sea; in the Danube River Basin, where countries belonging to rival cold war coalitions cooperate under the aegis of the Danube Commission to coordinate navigation, flood control, hydroelectric planning, and water pollution control; in the Niger River Basin, where nine not always friendly African countries have established a commission to integrate planning for use of the river's resources; and, of course, on the lakes and rivers along the US–Canadian border where the International Joint Commission of the United States and Canada supervises a wide range of transboundary environmental issues.[28]

MEGA-TECHNOLOGICAL ACCIDENTS AND THE QUESTION OF INTERNATIONAL ACCOUNTABILITY

The growing expectation, resulting from the expansion of knowledge about ecological interdependencies, that countries and nongovernmental actors shall be held accountable for the peacetime injuries they inflict upon foreign populations and property has been enhanced by two disastrous accidents in the mid-1980s: the release of poison gas in December 1984 from the Union Carbide pesticide plant at Bhopal, India; and the explosion and meltdown in the Soviet Union's Chernobyl nuclear power facility at the end of April 1986.

In the Bhopal disaster, about 2,000 people in the immediate vicinity of the Union Carbide pesticide factory were killed by an escaping gas cloud of methyl isocyanate, which fortunately was blown away from the city of Bhopal itself (where nearly 1,000,000 people live); however, an additional 30,000 people downwind were exposed to the lethal substance, and a considerable percentage of them would suffer serious long-term effects in the form of pneumonia, emphysema, asthma, or bronchitis.[29] Preliminary investigations by the government of India supported allegations that negligence on the part of Union Carbide was responsible for the disaster. The next question was in which country's court system should the company be sued: India, the location of the accident, or the United States, the location of the home offices of the multinational chemical corporation? Lawyers representing the victims finally decided to press the claims of the victims in the US courts in the expectation of being awarded more substantial damages. In this case, the US courts granted that they had jurisdiction (and finally awarded damages); but they might have refused jurisdiction, as they have in roughly analogous cases; nor could it be expected that other countries would allow such international litigation in their courts.

The gap between the harms people can suffer across international boundaries and human society's means for assuring the accountability of those responsible for the injuries was even more starkly exposed by the Chernobyl nuclear power plant accident. Neighboring countries in the path of the radioactive cloud escaping from the fire raging at the Soviet nuclear facility did not even know that a terrible accident had occurred until two days after the explosion when scientists in Sweden and Finland discovered abnormal levels of radioactivity in their own atmosphere. As the Soviet government over the next few days reluctantly revealed details on the nature of the disaster, West European health authorities advised their populations about the dangers of consuming milk and fresh produce, and the European Community banned agricultural imports from the Soviet Union and Eastern Europe. In Finland, radiation levels reached ten times the normal amounts, in Sweden and Denmark five times the normal, and in Norway 60 percent above normal. The radioactive fallout in Paris some 10 days after the accident was as high as it was during the period of most intense nuclear weapons testing in the atmosphere in 1963.[30]

Though fewer than 100 people working in and near the Chernobyl facility died from immediate exposure to lethal doses of radioactivity, American physicists and medical experts expect that tens of thousands of deaths in the USSR and Eastern Europe over the next several decades will have been caused by the nuclear accident.[31]

The heightened sense of intersocietal vulnerability to such accidents as Chernobyl was reflected in various unilateral actions by national governments in 1986: Austria dismantled its Zwentendorf nuclear power plant and Vienna brought pressure on Bonn not to start work on a planned West German nuclear power plant at Wackersdorf. The Saarland government and the city of Trier initiated legal action against Electricité de France to ensure that France would apply safety standards as rigorous as West Germany's in the French company's nuclear plant just across the Franco-German border. The Danish parliament demanded that the Swedes close down a nuclear facility barely twenty kilometers from Copenhagen. Observing these reactions, the British publication *The World Today* commented: "Thus for many countries and especially individual cities the policies of foreign neighbours may be as important as their own governments."[32]

One positive result of the Chernobyl disaster has been a greater willingness of the Soviet Union to concert with the United States and other Western governments in tightening up International Atomic Energy safety standards and safeguard procedures in nuclear power plants. There have been new efforts in cognizant international agencies, such as the World Health Organization and the Food and Agricultural Organization, to improve their reporting and information dissemination on accidents and natural disasters of international scope.[33]

The old adage that sometimes things need to get worse before they can get better is apparently being borne out with respect to the imperatives of harnessing the technological revolution. Gradually and fitfully—more in after-the-fact-responses to tragic accidents than on the basis of rational foresight—the human species may be beginning to realize that its survival depends on creating communities of mutual political and legal accountability to match the communities of mutual vulnerability its technological genius has created. Whether or not even such limited optimism is warranted, however, will be crucially determined by the international limitations countries are willing to accept on the development and application of military technologies.

THE TECHNOLOGY OF WARFARE[34]

The ability of the nation-state system to maintain world public order and to preserve the sovereign independence of its members, large and small, has depended upon credible alliance commitments designed to redress imbalances of military power that might tempt aggressor nations. The viability of this equilibrating mechanism of the system has been cast into severe doubt, however, by the development of weapons that have made all states—even the superpowers—unconditionally vulnerable to virtually total destruction, and by the prospect that the use of these weapons of mass destruction in war would bring on a "nuclear winter" that would severely jeopardize the capacity of the human species to survive.[35]

The bare facts of the lethal power capable of being unleashed by the two superpowers alone is now commonplace information to statesmen and laypersons all around the world: Assuming roughly 10,000 strategic nuclear warheads on each side, if only 10 percent impact on the other's territory, the Soviet Union would be exploding 1,000 weapons on the United States, with each one on the average over 60 times more powerful than the bomb the United States dropped on Hiroshima in 1945; and the United States would be exploding 1,000 weapons on the Soviet Union, with each one on the average over 30 times more powerful than the Hiroshima bomb—all in all, equivalent to more than 1.2 billion tons of TNT being exploded, or about 5,000 pounds of TNT for each man, woman, and child in the Soviet Union and the United States.

Given this stark reality, it is also now widely recognized, even though rarely admitted explicitly by alliance statesmen, that no country can count on its alliance partners joining it in a hot war against either of the nuclear superpowers. As pointed out in Chapter 3, this has been one of the principal causes of the disintegration of cold war bipolarity, and—ominously—of the incentives for countries currently without nuclear weapons to obtain their own nuclear arsenal.

Thus the nuclear age, which at its dawning seemed as if it might bring a more integrated nation-state system, has only intensified the structural contradictions of the system—figuratively and literally increasing the likelihood of its eventual atomization.

The socially integrating impact of nuclear weapons now appears to be taking place *outside the system*, so to speak. The fear of a species-destroying holocaust has been perhaps the greatest stimulant in history to the emergent countercultures of *anti*nationalism and pacifism, which are profoundly antithetical to the cultural and political norms of the nation-state system. The antinuclear movements in Western Europe, Japan, the United States, Canada, and even (in their suppressed form) in Eastern Europe are linked not only in their opposition to The Bomb but also in their animosity toward the inherited state system itself. The antinationalism is often amorphous and somewhat deceptive in its inchoateness, for it is frequently combined with vigorous opposition to one's country becoming the lackey of one of the superpowers, and as such can appear to be an expression of nationalism. But the nationalism usually goes only so far as opposition to oppressive dependence on the external power; it does not extend to a worship of the national flag and other symbols of patriotism—my country right or wrong. Quite the contrary.

The fate of the new pacifists and other nationalist cultural movements—their intersection with various transnational and subnational cultural movements, and the strength of nationalistic and patriotic backlashes against them—is the subject of the following chapter.

ENDNOTES

1. A wide-ranging survey of developments that are turning the world into a community at the material level is provided by Lester R. Brown, *World Without Borders* (New York: Random House, 1972).

2. On the transportation revolution, see John McHale, *The Future of the Future* (New York: George Braziller, 1969), Chapter 1; and Hal Hellman, *Transportation and the World of the Future* (New York: M. Evans and Company, 1968).

3. In response to the flareup of terrorism in France in the summer and early fall of 1986, the French government on September 14, 1986, joined the ranks of those governments requiring visitors to France (except from co-members of the European Community) to first obtain visas from French consulates. Richard Bernstein, "France to Require Visas for Visitors to Combat Terror," *New York Times*, 15 September 1986.

4. Seyom Brown, Nina W. Cornell, Larry L. Fabian, and Edith Brown Weiss, *Regimes for the Ocean, Outer Space, and Weather* (Washington, DC: The Brookings Institution, 1977), pp. 38–40.

5. Harold K. Jacobson, *Networks of Interdependence: International Organizations and the Global Political System* (New York: Knopf, 1984), p. 240.

6. David Webster, "Direct Broadcast Satellites: Proximity, Sovereignty and National Identity," *Foreign Affairs*, Vol. 62, No. 5 (Summer 1984), pp. 1161–1174, quotation from p. 1161.

7. Brown et al., *Regimes for the Ocean, Outer Space, and Weather*, pp. 153–154.

8. Webster, "Direct Broadcast Satellites," p. 1166.

9. On the overlapping military and civilian uses of observational space satellites, see Antony Dolman, *Resources, Regimes, World Order* (New York: Pergamon Press, 1981), pp. 310–313.

10. See discussion of maritime satellites in Brown et al., *Regimes for the Ocean, Outer Space, and Weather*, pp. 165–175.

11. Lynton Keith Caldwell, *International Environmental Policy: Emergence and Dimensions* (Durham: Duke University Press, 1984), pp. 235–236.

12. A typical prior consent rule was proposed in 1974 by Brazil and Argentina. See United Nations Document A/AC. 105/22, February 4, 1974 (cited in Brown et al., *Regimes for the Ocean, Outer Space, and Weather*, p. 139).

13. Dolman, *Resources, Regimes, World Order*, pp. 314–315.

14. Brown et al., *Regimes for the Ocean, Outer Space, and Weather*, pp. 176–196.

15. Garrett Hardin, "The Tragedy of the Commons," *Science*, 3 December 1968, pp. 1243–1248. See also Hardin's *Exploring New Ethics for Survival: The Voyage of the Spaceship Beagle* (New York: Viking, 1972), p. 254.

16. James Gleick, "Hole in Ozone over South Pole Worries Scientists," *New York Times*, 29 July 1986 (science section).

17. Dianne Dumanoski, "Scientists Say Ozone Threat Is Worsening," *Boston Globe*, 15 September 1986 (science section).

18. Dianne Dumanoski, "Ozone, Arms and Politics," Boston Globe, 20 September 1987.

19. Kenneth A. Dahlberg, "Environment As a Global Issue," in Kenneth A. Dahlberg, Marvin S. Soros, Anne Thompson Feraru, James E. Harf, and Thomas Trout, Environment and the Global Arena: Actors, Values, Policies, and Futures (Durham: Duke University Press, 1985), pp. 25–27.

20. United States Senate, Subcommittee on Toxic Substances and Environmental Oversight, Global Warming: Hearings, December 10, 1985 (Washington, DC: GPO, 1985). See also Philip Shabecoff, "Scientists Warn of Effects of Human Activity on Atmosphere," New York Times, 13 January 1986.

21. Statement of Dr. Carl Sagan, U.S. Senate, Global Warming: Hearings, p. 8.

22. "Study Urges Steps to Curb Earth's Warming," New York Times, 12 April 1987.

23. Dahlberg et al., Environment and the Global Arena, pp. 109–112.

24. Caldwell, International Environmental Policy, pp. 224–225.

25. Edward Wenk, Jr., The Politics of the Ocean (Seattle: University of Washington Press, 1972), p. 423.

26. Sterling Brubaker, To Live on Earth: Man and His Environment in Perspective (New York: New American Library, 1972), p. 148.

27. Douglas LaValle, "Mediterranean Sea: Just How Much Can It Take?" Greenpeace Examiner, Vol. 11, No. 2 (June 1986), pp. 13–14.

28. Caldwell, International Environmental Policy, pp. 112–115.

29. Sanjy Hazarika, "India Police Seize Factory Records of Union Carbide," New York Times, 7 December 1984; Walter Sullivan, "Health Crisis Could Last Many Years, Experts Say," ibid.

30. Ellen Dudley, "In the Aftermath of Chernobyl: Contamination, Upheaval, and Loss," Nucleus, Vol. 8, No. 3 (Fall 1986) (publication of the Union of Concerned Scientists), pp. 3, 5.

31. See the New York Times from 29 April 1986 to 15 May 1986 for extensive reporting on the Chernobyl nuclear accident.

32. "The Chernobyl Effect," The World Today, Vol. 42, No. 7 (July 1986), p. 110.

33. John F. Ahearne, "Implications of the Chernobyl Nuclear Accident," Resources, No. 86 (Winter 1987) (publication of Resources for the Future), pp. 10–12. See also Bennett Ramberg, "Learning from Chernobyl," Foreign Affairs, Vol. 65, No. 2 (Winter 1986/1987), pp. 304–328.

34. Much of the discussion in this section on the impact of weapons technology appeared originally in Seyom Brown, "The World Polity and the Nation-State System: An Updated Analysis, International Journal, Vol. 39, No. 3 (Summer 1984), pp. 509–528, especially pp. 519–522.

35. National Research Council, The Effects on the Atmosphere of a Major Nuclear Exchange (Washington, DC: National Academy Press, 1985).

CHAPTER TEN

Cultural Pressures on the Nation-State

With contemporary economic and technological forces penetrating the material foundations of the territorial state, it falls to the culture of nationalism to reinforce the structures of state sovereignty. But the cultural foundations of the type of nationalism that identifies with the territorial state are themselves under assault in many countries. Countervailing cultural pressures, many of them also stimulated by the new economic and technological forces, are pounding against the walls of nation-state sovereignty on three levels: subnational, transnational, and supranational.

The various countercultures intersect in many places—sometimes working at cross-purposes, sometimes reinforcing each other in their erosion of loyalty to the institutions and symbols of the national state. Such antinationalism usually produces a nationalistic backlash from economic classes, regions, and ethnic and religious groups who believe that their material and/or psychological well-being depends on the cohesiveness of the national polity.

From the vantage point of the latter 1980s, there is no telling which of these antithetical broad cultural movements—those challenging the authority of the nation-state or those reasserting its primacy—will be ascendant during the first half of the twenty-first century. What can be forecast, however, is the high likelihood that increasingly, over the coming decades, the basic issue of the authority of the nation-state will define the political alignments and ideologies of peoples—competing with and perhaps eclipsing the Marxist vs. capitalist, East–West, North–South antagonisms that have dominated world politics in the last half of the twentieth century.

THE REVIVAL OF SUBNATIONALISM

The nation-state system is being undermined from within by the concept of nationhood itself. The idea of the state as a nation has always contained the seeds of profound trouble for the established state system—from the insistence by leaders of both the French and American revolutions that governments derive their just powers from the consent of the governed, to Wilsonian concepts of national self-determination, to the doctrine professed by many of today's dissatisfied minorities that each nation has a right to its own state.

The root of the trouble lies in the fact that the nation is a state of mind. There is no permanent basis for dividing the people of the world into national communities. New subjective definitions of nationality may gain prominence among some groups, making them intensely uncomfortable with an existing government premised on older definitions. Groups who feel themselves to be culturally unique, by virtue of their particular set of traits and traditions— whether language, religion, physical characteristics, or other emanations of shared historical evolution—have chronically threatened international and domestic stability since medieval times.[1]

In the contemporary postcolonial period, the highly subjective and volatile basis of nationalism has been a particularly acute problem for most of the new states, which have only recently gained independence under the banner of national self-determination. Following independence, with the necessity of maintaining solidarity in their struggle against the colonial power no longer compelling, the ethnic heterogeneity of the populations of most of these states has turned the issues of postindependence constitutional and representational structure into explosive contests over which internal "nations" shall now lord it over others.[2]

Many social analysts, however, expected to see a decrease in subnationalist dissidence within the modern industrialized states in the second half of the twentieth century. Consolidation of the polity was thought to be a necessary condition for industrialization, which in turn would reinforce the homogeniza- tion of populations within the nation-state, as transportation and communica- tion networks made for a rapid interchange of goods and ideas.[3]

In free enterprise societies, it was supposed, the expanding economy and desire for jobs in the technological sectors would encourage national integration by stimulating internal migrations to the urban centers, demands from all segments of society for education in the new knowledge and skills, and attempts by ethnic subcultures to assimilate the general culture of the dominant society. In more authoritarian societies, where human and material resources can be commandeered, it was expected that the assimilation process would be accelerated by compulsory language and literacy programs and sometimes by the direct suppression of subcultural and religious institutions and mores that might interfere with complete loyalty to the central state. Once industrialization had proceeded beyond a certain point, however, cultural integration was supposed to proceed on its own momentum.

Neither of these variants of the assimilation process in the industrialized states has worked out according to expectations.[4] The increased mobility of people and information has tended to give the technological centers of society greater potential attraction and control. But the same developments have enabled special cultural elites to mobilize sentiment and support for their own communities, especially when their communities feel discriminated against by the central state apparatus.

Relatively underprivileged ethnic groups become more receptive to the idea that they are indeed victims of unjust discrimination when they are daily exposed via the mass media to the apparent privileges of the majority. The fact that industrialization has also raised the absolute level of goods and services available to all groups in the society does little to relieve this sense of injustice and often exacerbates it. It is the perception of *relative* deprivation that is crucial to the mobilization of group jealousies; and the realization that, even in an economy of abundance, the room at the top is limited, and the competition for status and power increases the higher one climbs, engenders intense bitterness among cultural groups that are upwardly mobile. Often their bitterness is reflected in systematic discrimination against those on the status rungs just below.[5]

When grievances against the material and status privileges of others emanate from a group that is differentiated by a number of cultural factors— say, language, religion, and concentration in certain occupations; or physical traits and geographic clustering—the situation is ripe for the ethnic group to be politicized and demand greater autonomy or even full independence.

The following capsule summaries of conflicts between aggrieved subnational groups and defenders of the prevailing regime in particular nation-states comprise only a sample of the wide variety and ubiquity of this phenomenon.

Catholics vs. Protestants in Northern Ireland

Constituting less than 40 percent of a population more than 60 percent Protestant, the Catholics in Northern Ireland ("Ulster") have been agitating, often violently, for a rectification of their minority status, which they regard as being artificially imposed on them by predominantly Protestant Britain. If all of Ireland were one nation-state (that is, if Northern Ireland were merged with the predominantly Catholic Irish Republic), the Catholics, constituting 76 percent of the entire island's population, would provide the ruling majority for the whole country. Thus, from the perspective of the Catholics, the 1921 "solution" to the eight-century long—often bloody—history of Anglo-Irish and religious conflict was unjust from the start: Under the 1921 partition, the southern and western two-thirds of the country, over 90 percent Catholic, was granted the status of a self-governing dominion; but the northeastern one-third of the country where 85 percent of Ireland's Protestant minority resides was kept out of the Irish Republic and preserved as a Protestant-majority province of the United Kingdom. Understandably, from the point of view of the

Protestants the 1921 partition was an eminently fair resolution of the otherwise interminable civil war between the two religious groups.

As it turned out, however, the 1921 partition only deflected the violent civil conflict from the whole island (where the Protestant minority would be battling for its rights against the Catholic majority) into Ulster where the now-minority Catholics have been battling against the province's Protestant majority, whom they charge with preempting the best living areas and jobs and in many other ways perpetuating a regime uncongenial to the Catholic way of life. Extremely militant Catholics in both parts of Ireland, who have never reconciled themselves to the 1921 "solution," have conspired in outlawed societies to make Northern Ireland ungovernable—often resorting to terroristic acts and harassments to provoke violent encounters between the two religious communities.[6] The situation deteriorated so severely in the late 1960s and early 1970s that the British government was driven to reinstitute direct rule from London in 1972; and concerned people in England and abroad were compelled to reconsider whether or not the only way of avoiding intensified rounds of intercommunal terrorism and even full-scale civil war would be to acquiesce to the militant Catholic demands for the separation of Northern Ireland from Britain and some sort of federation with the South.

In 1985, after more than a decade of failed mediational and diplomatic efforts, the British government and the Republic of Ireland signed an agreement that would give the government in Dublin a consultative voice on a wide range of policy decisions affecting Ulster. The 1985 accord was denounced by Protestant party leaders from Northern Ireland sitting in the British parliament as providing the Southern Catholics with "covert joint authority" with Britain over the northern countries; they also charged that it was transparently a first step toward the united Ireland that the Protestants could not accept. Militant Catholics denounced the agreement for the opposite reasons: In signing it, the Irish Republic recognized British sovereignty over Ulster and in return got a consultative role that in reality was responsibility without appropriate power.[7]

As of this writing, fall 1987, the tensions between the two rival religious communities still are explosive. In Ulster's capital, Belfast, the major Protestant and Catholic residential areas are separated by an ugly cinder block and steel wall topped by barbed wire, and the city is patrolled continuously by British troops and helicopters. A nation-state? The idea remains out of reach and inappropriate.

The Flemish–Walloon Rivalry in Belgium

In Belgium, a bitter historic polarization of society along ethnic and linguistic lines periodically threatens to overwhelm other bases of political alignment that sustain the authority of the unified nation-state. The 5.5 million Dutch-speaking Flemings in the traditionally agricultural north have for centuries resented the dominance of the 4 million French-speaking Walloons of the more industrialized south. Their linguistic differences became the central political issue between the two communities in the 1830s when French was made the official language of the new kingdom of Belgium. Henceforth, facility in the French language, to the disadvantage of the Flemings, was essential to professional advancement in both the public and private sectors. The post-1950 industrialization of some of the Flemish areas and the accompanying northward migrations of the Walloons into Flemish border areas and cities exacerbated the interethnic animosities.[8]

During the 1970s, various proposals were debated in the Belgian parliament to transform the centralized government into a federal system. One of these, the Egmont Pact—which called for three autonomous regions (Flanders, Wallonia, and an independent federal city at Brussels)—was at first supported by broad segments of the public in the north and the south and by four-fifths of the members of parliament. But Flemish militants mobilized sentiment in the Dutch-speaking areas against the Egmont Pact, charging that the plan to make Brussels (where the population was more Walloon than Flemish) an independent federal province was really a ruse to give the French speakers a two-to-one advantage in the new federal system. Ensuing elections did not return a parliament with a sufficient majority to pass the new federal plan.

Modified versions of the Egmont Pact finally produced agreement on a degree of regional autonomy, which took effect in October 1980. Flanders and Wallonia, each with its own assembly and executive, would legislate and implement their own laws on matters of public health, the economy, urban projects, and culture. The federal government would retain predominant power in the fields of defense, foreign affairs, education, finance, and justice.[9] It remains to be seen whether the devolution of governing authority to the regional level where there is no ambiguity about which linguistic group is in control will defuse the country's interethnic conflict or whether the retention of authority by the federal government in the still-divisive issues of education, finance, and justice will generate agitation for additional control of these fields by the regional governments. Of course, such a further decentralization would come close to breaking up Belgium into two nation-states.[10]

Basque Separatism

The traditional resistance to assimilation into larger nation-states by the Basques, a linguistically and culturally distinct population of over 2 million living just north and south of the Pyrenees mountain range between Spain and France, also has been stimulated by economic modernization and literacy.

Exposure to the outside world, including the examples of the Irish, Flemish, and French Canadian independence movements, and the universal affirmation of the right of national self-determination have had the most intensive political impact on the four Spanish Basque provinces, where contemporary demands for autonomy echo Spain's long history of regionalist–centralist conflict.[11]

As part of Spain's evolution toward full democracy after the death of dictator Francisco Franco in 1975, the Constitution of 1978 divided the country into 17 regional "autonomies." Under the new Spanish constitution, the Basques, like the peoples of other regions, have increasingly assumed power over schools, taxation, and local economic development in their provinces. But Basque political extremists, worried that their compatriots would settle for half a loaf, particularly during the economic depression the region was suffering, escalated their demands for total independence and stepped up terrorist attacks against Spanish officials and local industrialists and businessmen who wanted constructive cooperation with the new democratic modernizers in Madrid.

The militants' terrorist strategy is designed both to provoke the Spanish government into repressive reactions, so as to justify the claim that fair treatment of the Basques can never be had from Madrid, and to take credit for whatever additional concessions to local autonomy the central government may choose to make to avoid further extremism. As of this writing, however, it appears that the Basque moderates who believe autonomy within the Spanish state makes more economic and political sense than full independence have the ascendancy in the Basque provinces.[12]

Separatism among Canadians of French Ancestry

The facts that approximately 6 million Canadians out of a total Canadian population of 21 million trace their ancestry back to France and continue to regard French as their first language, and that 5 million of them live in Quebec (which has a total population of 6 million) have been a persisting source of potential disruption of the Canadian federal system. Beginning in 1963 with the founding of the *Rassemblement pour l'independence nationale*, Quebec's secession from the Canadian federal union has been an openly proclaimed objective of influential elements of the province's elite.

The high point, but also the beginning of the decline, of secessionist agitation was the election of the Parti Quebecois (PQ) into power in 1973 under the leadership of Rene Levesque. Now faced with the practical problems of just when and how to effect secession, the economic and political costs of the rupture and then of going it alone compelled the PQ to modify the objective to "sovereignty/association"—political independence but economic association with the rest of Canada in a common market. Put to the vote in a plebescitory referendum in May 1980, the concept of secession, even with continuing economic association, was rejected by 60 percent of the voters. In 1985, the PQ lost control over the provincial government to the Liberal Party, also a champion of greater autonomy for Quebec, but within a reformed Canadian federation rather than through full independence.[13] In 1987, the Quebec Liberals negotiated an all-Canadian agreement granting Quebec and each of the other provinces an effective veto over matters substantially affecting Canadian federal institutional arrangements. There has been no backtracking whatsoever, however, from the policy instituted by the PQ of Quebec's pursuing a wide range of international relationships—particularly in the commercial field—sometimes in parallel with, but sometimes independently of, the relationships conducted by the Canadian federal government. In virtually every important commercial city in the world, the province of Quebec has its own offices, puts on commercial and cultural fairs, and conducts its own negotiations on trade and investments.[14]

Ethno-Nationalism in Eastern Europe

Within the Soviet sphere of influence in Eastern Europe, ethnic rivalries seethe beneath brittle political structures—a deep historic legacy that communist state authoritarianism has been unable to dissipate. (World War I was catalyzed by Serbian nationalist resistance to subordination by Austria-Hungary and triggered by the assassination of the Austrian Archduke by a Bosnian nationalist student.) Today, the greatest eruptive potentials, which the USSR is tempted to exploit to retain its hegemonial control, are found in Czechoslovakia and Rumania. In Czechoslovakia, Slovak (actually ethnically Magyar) animosities against the more modernized and urbanized Czechs have produced a succession of vitriolic Slovak independence movements since these two peoples were amalgamated by the peace settlement after World War I.[15] In Rumanian Transylvania, too, the ethnically distinct Magyars are discontent with subordination to Bucharest and are susceptible to appeals that Transylvania be detached from Rumania and joined with the Magyars in Hungary.[16]

The Soviet Union itself is a conglomeration of about one hundred linguistically distinct ethnic groups, most of whom harbor historical grievances against domination by greater Russia. The USSR is therefore especially vulnerable to and anxious about the global recrudescence of ethnic nationalism. Lenin proclaimed the right to national self-determination, and in the 1920s the Soviet regime granted formal autonomy to the major national minorities, creating constituent republics. The Bolsheviks, of course, viewed full national self-determination as disruptive of the socialist state. Formal autonomy was merely a characteristic Leninist stratagem of co-optation. In each case, in strict interpretation of Marxist–Leninist orthodoxy, the language, symbols, and folk art of the nationality were brought into the service of the communist party, which remained highly centralized and uniform throughout the USSR.

In reality, the policy was one of the russification and compulsory assimilation where the Marxist believes it counts: the socioeconomic infrastructure. The constitutional recognition of cultural differences, however, has allowed the regime to excuse uneven development of the various regions on the grounds that they are incompletely assimilated. This has always been a transparent formula to the non-Russians and has been a target of periodic discontent. Fanned by knowledge of events in the noncommunist world, ethnic ferment appears to be on the rise once again, not only among Jews who identify with Israel but also among the 40 million Ukrainians, the Lithuanians, the Estonians, the Soviet Muslim peoples, and the Crimean Tartars.[17]

The viability of nonaligned but Marxist Yugoslavia as a multinational state is jeopardized by Croatian, Slovenian, and Albanian agitation for national autonomy against the champions of a strong federal center, led by the Serbs. The richer northern regions, Croatia and Slovenia, are autonomist–confederalist, not wanting to share their wealth with their historic rival Serbia and the poorer regions to the South.[18]

A Global Phenomenon

The situations briefly described above are just a sampling of the politicizing of ethnicity that has become a worldwide challenge to the authority of existing nation-states. We need only mention the chronic Turko-Greek conflict on the island of Cyprus; the unhappiness in South Tyrol with Italian rule; the agitation of the French-speaking population in Berne, Switzerland, for autonomy from the German-speaking population; the resentment of the Bretons at being a part of France; the American Indian rights and Puerto Rican independence movements in the United States; the upsurge of Scottish and Welsh nationalism; and the demand of the Palestinians on the West Bank and in the Gaza strip for an independent state not under the control of Israel (the Palestinian cause is also partly a manifestation of Islamic transnationalism, to be discussed below).

The secessionist movements in the Third World—most prominently the successful Bangladesh independence movement; the militant, often violent, uprising of the Punjab Sikhs against the government of India; the demands of the Tamil-speaking population of Sri Lanka for political autonomy; the unsuccessful Biafran secession from Nigeria—are too numerous to catalog, and in any case have not been unexpected.

It is the worldwide scope of the ethnic militancy and its tendency to persist, if not increase, with modernization that warrants analysis here—especially in light of the reality that only one in ten of the world's 165 countries are ethnically homogeneous; three-quarters of the countries have ethnic minorities that make up over 5 percent of the population; and in one-tenth of the countries at least 40 percent of the population is distinct from the dominant ethnic group.[19]

In almost every modern nation-state industrialization and economic development have visibly benefited some regions, ethnic groups, or classes more than others. In the early post-World War II period, the promise of equalization—leveling up through universal education and leveling down through progressive taxation and other redistributive policies—was still fresh, and temporary inequalities could be accepted as part of the process of equalization itself. But with each passing year, the failure to realize the promise results in greater impatience by the relatively disadvantaged, and it then becomes subjectively valid for them to see themselves as victims of systematic discrimination by the privileged groups. The situation thus ripens for indigenous regional, ethnic, or class leaders to step forward and demand power in addition to programs and to promote the heady notion that things would be better if the distinctive group, even with more limited material resources, designed and operated its own sociopolitical system. In some countries where the poorer ethnic elements are in the majority or are special beneficiaries of redistribution programs, the better-off ethnic groups can be aroused to agitate for their own autonomy.

Few of the would-be separate nations, however, are strong enough in numbers or command enough resources to carry through a full-blown secessionist revolution on their own. Consequently, although ethnic self-reliance is the ideal that holds them together, many militant vanguards are tempted to seek allies among other aggrieved groups at home or abroad that are severely alienated from the dominant culture, or with separatist movements in other countries, or sometimes with foreign nation-states that also oppose the existing national government.

THE REEMERGENCE OF RELIGIOUS AND ETHNIC TRANSNATIONALISM

The contemporary robustness of religious and ethnic *transnationalism* also has been a surprise to many social scientists and cultural historians, let alone to leaders of national governments. Rather than being subordinated to the state-based nationalism of the modern polity, geographically dispersed transnational cultural groups, brought into contact again by the new technologies of communciation and transportation, are vigorously reweaving their bonds across and between continents.

The modern state system, with its foundational norms of state sovereignty and mutual noninterference across territorial borders, had emerged largely in reaction to the religious wars between Protestants and Catholics and between Christians and Muslims that nearly destroyed the European and Middle Eastern civilizations in the sixteenth and seventeenth centuries. The Treaty of Westphalia (1648), legally codifying the new norms of interstate restraint, was supposed to have contained religious proselytizing and conflict within the confines of the sovereign territorial states or their imperial holdings. Even the Universal (Roman Catholic) Church accommodated pragmatically to the imperatives of the emerging civil state system and urged the faithful to respect and loyally serve the authorities of their sovereign territorial states in matters secular.

Then in the eighteenth and nineteenth centuries, the rise of capitalism, the money economy, and industrialization, in forging cohesive *nations* out of the diverse religious and ethnic groups populating each of the larger territorial states (see Chapter 2), seemed to have reduced further the prospect that transstate cultural or religious movements could seriously challenge the viability of the state system. Even the eighteenth century American and French revolutions on behalf of the principle that governments must rest on the consent of the governed, and Napoleon's imperialistic exploitation of the republican-nationalist ethos, have been viewed by historians of nationalism as merely shakedowns, as it were, of the inevitably evolving *nation-state system*. There might yet be periodic readjustments in territorial jurisdictions occasioned by war or other important reasons of state. And at times minority cultures in states run by other groups might attempt to force such readjustments by insisting on national self-determination, as in the Balkans prior to World War I, or in the Third World after World War II where the devastated older imperial powers had to grant national self-determination to the non-European peoples they had previously colonized. But the long-term trend—the basic congealing of nations into permanent states and states into permanent nations—was regarded as essentially irreversible.

A potentially serious transnational threat to the foundational norms and structure of the nation-state system germinated in the middle of the nineteenth century from a highly intellectualized materialistic philosophy of historical progress that true believers translated into a justification for seizing political power on behalf of the "working class." The nineteenth century followers of Karl Marx and the twentieth century Marxist–Leninists saw themselves as leaders of a worldwide revolution of the proletarians against their capitalist exploiters. Accordingly, when the Bolsheviks seized power in Russia, they proclaimed the Kremlin to be the directing center of proletarian internationalism. But the very success of the Leninists in establishing a Soviet state in Russia had the paradoxical effect of generating suspicion on the part of Marxists in other countries that henceforth the Communist Party of the Soviet Union, while still claiming to be the vanguard of the world revolution, would really put what it perceived to be the state interests of the USSR ahead of the interests of fraternal parties. This suspicion, notoriously borne out by the Hitler–Stalin pact of 1939, was in many countries fatal to the efforts of Marxist–Leninists to organize the proletarians on a transnational basis—an effort that in any case was running aground on the basic religiosity, cultural ethnocentrism, and sociopolitical conservatism of the working and lower middle classes.

The revival following World War II of Marxist–Leninist transnational bonds (centered in the Soviet-run Communist International) among the communist parties of war-devastated Europe and between the Soviets and national liberation movements in the Third World, and the organization by the capitalist powers of a countervailing coalition led by the United States, seemed to many analysts and statesmen in the first two decades after the war to be the beginning of a great transformation of the world polity into two rival societies that might well supplant the nation-state system. The reversal of this ideological bipolarization of the world and (as detailed in Chapters 3 through 7) the emergence of a multipolar, perhaps even polyarchic, pattern of alignments has not, however, led simply to the reconstitution of the traditional nation-state system. Rather, the receding of the ideological class-conscious basis of trans-national affinities and antagonisms has opened the field to fresh communica-tion, contact, and political bonding among transnationally dispersed religious and ethnic groups.

Politically, the most significant of the contemporary transnational religious and ethnic groups are the Muslims, world Jewry, the Roman Catholics, and the black Africans (including those who live outside the African continent). Other widely dispersed ethnic groups, such as the Latins of the Western Hemisphere or the ethnic Chinese throughout Asia, are potentially mobilizeable on behalf of political causes transcending nation-state lines, but up to now have shown no inclination to act as transnational coalitions.

The Transnation of Islam

The Islamic religion, at its founding in the seventh century and until the abolition in 1924 of the caliphate (which had been the highest civil as well as religious authority for all Muslims and was located in Turkey) by the secular Turkish nationalist Mustafa Kemal Ataturk, was explicitly and aggressively opposed to the territorial (and later national) state system. Believing them-selves to be the carriers of the mission Allah gave to Muhammad to unite all of humankind under the one true religion—at times by violent *jihad* (holy war) against the Christians and other infidels, often in combination with the armies of imperial powers (such as the Ottoman Turks, the Persians, and the Indian Mughals)—the prophet's disciples fanned out from their Arabic core to establish major Muslim communities as far west as Morocco and Spain, as far north as Siberia, as far south as Tanganyika (today Tanzania), and as far east as the Philippines and Indonesia. Muslim leaders reacted to the maturing of the nation-state system in the nineteenth century by promulgating the pan-Islamic theory that Islam, now embraced by one-eighth of the world's peoples, must be united under a strong unitary authority centered in the caliph. But this global supranationalist concept remained only a theory in the face of the division of most of the world into the imperial domains of the European powers and the progressive secularization of the still independent Ottoman and Persian empires.[20]

Today, although the nation of Islam has been parceled out into separate (often rival) states, a transnational competition for loyalty is being waged between the largest minority, the Shiites (centered in Iran), and the majority Sunnis. The militant Shiites are not only virulently antisecular and anti-Western fundamentalists, but also vigorous proselytizers. Their successful overthrow of the Shah of Iran in 1979, their efforts to sponsor a Shiite uprising against the Sunni regime in Iraq, their sponsorship of Muslim fundamentalism throughout the Islamic world (in Afghanistan, Saudi Arabia, and Egypt), their efforts to determine the political future of Lebanon, and their championing of the Palestinian cause, including terrorism, against Israel has made the transnational Shiite–Sunni rivalry one of the principal political realities that all powers with interests in the Middle East must now contend with.

One of the rallying points for Middle Eastern Muslims with transnationalist aspirations, such as the Shiites, is that some of their Arab Muslim brothers, the Palestinians, have been denied the right that all other nationalities claim—namely, statehood—by a Jewish transnational movement, Zionism, that with the aid of the Western "imperialists" (Britain, France, and the United States) has driven the Arab Palestinians from their homes and subjected those that have remained on the West Bank of the Jordan and in the Gaza strip to rule by an alien culture and religion.

Zionism and World Jewry

Zionism's impact extends beyond the Arab–Israeli conflict in the Middle East. It is a transnational political phenomenon with considerable impact on the normal functioning of the nation-state system, operating simultaneously within the system and at cross-purposes with some of its basic norms. Drawing on the religioethnic identification of Jews around the world as still one nation, destined to return to their biblical homeland in Palestine, some branches of the Zionist movement in the late nineteenth and early twentieth centuries began Jewish resettlement of the area in the form of small agricultural communities, while other branches led by Jews influential in the governments and commercial sectors of the Western countries tried to convince the great powers to carve out a new nation-state for the Jewish people.

Zionist activism on behalf of a reconstituted homeland was both a unifying force among world Jewry and a divisive force, for it compelled Jews the world over to determine for themselves, first, whether their Jewishness was primarily religious or politically nationalistic, and second, whether they could best express their self-definition by remaining citizens of the nation-states of their current domicile or by emigrating back to the ancient Hebrew homeland. The establishment of the state of Israel after World War II and the influx of more than 2 million Jews from throughout the diaspora did not resolve these fundamental questions for the transnational Jewish community. Today only 3.3 million of the world's 15 million Jews live in Israel; over 6 million live in the United States alone, and nearly 3 million live in the Soviet Union. The vast majority of the 12 million Jews outside of Israel are at the least somewhat ambivalent in their political loyalties to their country of citizenship and to the state of Israel, especially in cases of clashing policies between the two countries.

Particularly in the United States, the Jewish community constitutes a significant electoral force and legislative lobby for assuring that anti-Israeli policies are avoided. Expectations that a severe divergence of national interests between the United States government and Israel could produce a traumatic crisis in American politics operates as a subtle, yet profound, constraint on the international behavior of the United States, which the Soviet Union and other international actors must also take into account.

The Catholic Church As a Transnational Force

A more amorphous kind of ambivalence than the dual national loyalties of many non-Israeli Jews affects members of the Roman Catholic Church. No longer, as during the period of the Holy Roman Empire, does the Church aspire to institute a worldwide and centralized theocracy; nor, as in medieval and early modern Europe, is it actively in the political business of assuring that as many countries as possible will be governed by loyal Catholics and of subverting non-Catholic regimes. Yet some of the enduring features of Catholic doctrine and organization do rather deeply cross-pressure Catholic citizens of particular nation-states in the contemporary world.

Catholicism reaches into some of the most basic and intimate levels of human life: defining permissible and impermissible sexual behavior in and out of marriage; prohibiting most kinds of artificial birth control and abortion. Church doctrine on these matters, promulgated by the Pope—who is regarded as infallible—is supposed to be taught faithfully by all prelates and obeyed by all good Catholics the world over (in some countries where the dominant social mores and laws contradict Catholic doctrine) under threat of excommunication.

And although the Church professes to restrict its intervention in human affairs to matters sacred and to leave matters secular to the secular governing authorities, many of the deliberations by national councils of bishops and by the College of Cardinals in recent years have been over world economic and political development issues, disarmament, arms control, and even alternative military strategies—since policies being pursued (or not being pursued) by governments and international agencies in these fields today raise the most profound questions of morality.

The Church's jurisdiction covers the entire surface of the Earth, which is divided into territorial administrative units: dioceses, abbacies, vicarates, and apostolic prefectures.[21] These are congruent with or overlap the existing jurisdictions of the nation-state system; and while they are not legally empowered to enforce the Church's edicts in civil society, the instructions to the faithful transmitted through the Church's hierarchial structure can significantly affect the positions of lay Catholics active in the secular institutions of governance.

Thus when the Pope travels to predominantly Catholic Latin America and speaks about "social justice" or pronounces on the rights of workers during a visit to Poland, or when the American Council of Bishops issues a Pastoral Letter on nuclear weapons policy, the powers that be in the world of statecraft pay close attention. Moreover, the highest officials of government—communist as well as capitalist—frequently call on the Pope in the Vatican, not simply out of courtesy, but out of the pragmatic calculation that the views of one who has substantial influence over what one-eighth of the world's population views as right and wrong need to be given careful consideration in the formulation of state strategies.

Pan-Africanism and the Black Diaspora

The sense among the world's "blacks" (those with negroid physiological characteristics) that they are one nation has had a number of diverse yet interrelated manifestations: pan-Africanism among the independence movements and postindependence nation-states on the African continent; the desire of black people in the African diaspora (largely the descendants of former slaves) to return to Africa; black separatist movements within non-African nation-states; and political support by blacks outside of Africa for the causes of their "brothers" and "sisters" in other countries—today, in particular, the overthrow of the *apartheid* regime of South Africa.

The early leaders of independence for the African peoples from colonial rule (most notably the American W. E. B. Du Bois following World War I and the West African, London-educated Kwame Nkrumah after World War II) were also pan-Africanists in their advocacy of mutual help among the black liberation movements and in their vision of a postindependence union, or at least federation, of the African continent. But this pan-African ideal was overtaken by (1) the reality prior to independence of the physical separation, varying colonial situations, self-contained leadership groups, and different pacing of African anticolonial movements; and (2) the priority accorded by the postindependence governments to consolidating their own nation-states out of feuding religious, ethnic, and tribal groups who in many cases have used their ties across national borders to subvert the new national governments, and which in turn has generated intense suspicion and hostility between many of the neighboring countries of contemporary Africa.

The ancestral connection of American blacks with Africa was translated by Marcus Garvey during the period 1915-1925 into a popular movement for creating a special homeland in Africa to which the descendants of former slaves could return. Garvey's movement was unable to survive the demise of its charismatic leader after his conviction for financially defrauding thousands of his followers;[22] but his ideology of black separatism and ultimate secession from the United States found an echo in the radical black nationalist movements of the 1960s and 1970s.

Many Americans were shocked in the 1960s to find that the United States, the prototypical melting pot of diverse cultures, was regarded as an alien country by many of the most educated and upwardly mobile of the 22 million black Americans—this following a decade of legal progress (Supreme Court decisions outlawing separate educational facilities and other forms of racial discrimination, and legislation removing inhibitions to black participation in the electoral process). The new black nationalism was in part the result of the earlier decade of progress—enlarged educational opportunities, exposure to the anticolonial and other revolutionary movements energizing blacks in other countries—which heightened the sense of relative deprivation among a new generation of blacks, while giving them new confidence that through organizational work and militancy they could effect radical change.

The new militancy—though expressed in diverse ways by different strands of the new black nationalist movements (the Black Muslims led by Malcolm X, the antiwhite racism of the Black Power movement led by Stokely Carmichael, the neo-Leninism of the Black Panthers led by Bobby Seale and Eldridge Cleaver)— was determinedly subnationalist, in holding that American blacks had a distinct culture and ought to be granted substantial autonomy (albeit with financial help from the larger society) to run their own affairs in their own communities without interference from the white majority culture. But it was also determinedly transnationalist in its identification with Africa—reflected in efforts by the new American black militants to establish bonds with the independence movements and new states of Africa, the widespread adoption by American blacks of African hairstyles and dress, their efforts to learn African languages, and pressures to include courses in both African and Afro-American history and contemporary culture in the core curricula of American schools and colleges. Survey research data for 1970 showed that nearly half of all blacks in the United States viewed the growing interest in African culture as important to black identity and pride.[23] This was more than an expression of benign cultural awakening, for, as collateral surveys revealed, over 60 percent of all American blacks believed that "the system is rotten and has to be changed completely for blacks to be free"; and nearly one-third maintained that the black community "would probably have to resort to violence in order to gain their rights."[24]

The separatist features and implications of the Africanization of the American black consciousness have waned since the early 1970s—in part because of the maturing realization on the part of the young militants that even the demographics alone of the American black community (its wide geographic dispersal beyond improverished central-city ghettoes) made it impossible to territorially demarcate the black nation within the American nation; in part because of the increasing success by blacks in getting elected to political office on the municipal, state, and federal levels; and in part because of continued progress in the integration of blacks into the fabric of social life generally in the United States, including the highly visible fields of television journalism (not just entertainment) and professional sports where the role models for young blacks work cooperatively "in the system" with whites, often in highly prestigious and superordinate roles.

Meanwhile, however, the transnational identification with Africans has not waned, despite the drop in enthusiasm for Afro hairdos and dashikis—perhaps a manifestation of a general trend in the larger society away from the popular counterculture lifestyles of the late 1960s and early 1970s and back toward conventional looks and behavior. Indeed, the very assimilation of blacks into American political party, governmental, and private-sector establishments that has undercut black separatism has provided more opportunity for influencing US policy toward Africa—particularly toward the *apartheid* regime in South Africa—analogous to the influence American Jews have on US policy toward Israel. The sanctions against the South African government by the American Congress in 1986, over the veto of President Reagan, was not simply an expression of popular American sentiment on human rights. It was by many, including the majority of members of Congress from the president's own party, the product of the practical realization that the South African issue is highly salient for the blacks in their constituencies and, moreover, that the black political leadership is now in a position to swing the election in many key districts against candidates who cross them on this issue, and might even be able to determine the outcome of senatorial and presidential elections.[25]

OTHER TRANSNATIONAL GROUPINGS

The ease with which people geographically remote from one another can come into contact, coupled with the universalization of the notion that no ethnic group, religious community, economic class, gender, or even age-cohort group has presumptive superiority over any other group, has led to all manner of mutual-support movements formed transnationally among people with particular characteristics trying to bring pressure on their respective national government to improve their lot.

As transnational bonds are established between special subgroups, particularly on the basis of a shared characteristic that heretofore has been regarded as a badge of inferiority in their own countries, the new affiliations often attain a positive emotional salience that intrudes upon and reduces the affective bonds between group members and their nation-state of domicile.

Many feminists are convinced that the nation-state system and its principal bargaining instruments—coercive diplomacy and war—are quintessentially male and part and parcel of the system of male dominance over females: Patriotism and patriarchy are seen to be mutually reinforcing; accordingly, women's liberation requires that they both be undermined. There are, of course, some highly nationalistic, even militaristic, feminists (for example, Indian Prime Minister Indira Gandhi and Israeli Prime Minister Golda Meir); but in the gravitational center of the feminist movement—the relatively affluent female intelligentsia in advanced industrial societies—feminism and antiwar internationalism more often than not walk hand in hand.

Gay liberationists, both male and female, tend to exhibit attitudes similar to those of the feminists in their disparagement of the traditional "macho" traits of patriotism and militarism, and in their accordance of higher value to camaraderie with other gays than with the "straight" and "homophobic" types perceived to be the loyal constituents of the national state.

In the late 1960s and early 1970s, a youth "counterculture" emerged in the United States, centered in the affluent and upper middle classes, opposed to "the system." In the United States during the high point of opposition to the Vietnam War, attitudinal surveys showed that more than 45 percent of all university students believed that the United States was "a sick society," and three out of ten indicated they would prefer to be citizens of some other country.[26]

Its strongest overt stimulus, surely, was the Vietnam War and the military draft, but the youth counterculture had its origins in the "free speech" movements among students at Berkeley and other mammoth state multiuniversities and pre-dated US military intervention in Vietnam. The targets of youth antipathy included not just foreign policy and military and educational establishments but also institutions of law and order, patriotic symbols generally, financial institutions, the Protestant work ethic, traditional sexual mores and roles, and the family unit—in short, virtually everything in the mainstream American culture of the older generation that was presumed to be antithetical to authentic and spontaneous human relationships. Moreover, the counterculture rapidly spread to the youth of other countries not involved in the Vietnam War, especially France, West Germany, The Netherlands, Scandinavia, and Japan.[27] The lifestyle manifestations of the youth counterculture also spread into the countries of Eastern Europe and the USSR, where Western fads in dress, hairstyle, popular music, literary forms, and even attitudes toward work became substitutes for overt political forms of expressing dissatisfaction toward ruling communist party establishments.

Following the American withdrawal from Vietnam in 1973 and the development of economic conditions in the United States that constricted the disposable income and leisure time of upper middle-class youth, there was a distinct diminution of dissidence among American youth—at least on the surface. Some observers were quick to conclude that this confirmed the supposition that the youth counterculture movement was a transitory phenomenon, mainly caused by the college students' fear of being drafted into military service. But the youth counterculture still is vigorous in the later 1980s in other countries, where it is often targeted on armaments and environmental issues. And in the United States, while dissident college students are not objecting as frontally to "the system" and are focusing mostly on specific political issues (policies relating to *apartheid*, nuclear weapons, and nuclear power plants), some of the apolitical manifestations of the counterculture (especially drugs and nihilistic popular music) have, if anything, spread more widely among the country's economic classes.

Deeper explanations and prognoses for the counterculture phenomenon must be sought in the basic transformations wrought by fast-paced technology-induced change on popular attitudes toward inherited institutions of authority and power.

Authority—the capacity to influence others by virtue of their recognition of the authority's special command over knowledge, resources, or people—is disintegrating in numerous fields simultaneously. The accelerating rate of scientific, technological, and socioeconomic change is disrupting allegiance to traditional influences; and faith is waning that the traditional authority does indeed retain command of significant knowledge, resources, and groups of people. When these doubts are exacerbated by evidence of moral culpability in high places, disrespect for all establishments tends to spread.

Concurrently, the impermanence of residence, jobs, friendships, and even familial obligations—the culture of mobility and transience—is destroying the cohesion of community structures through which authorities are given their legitimate power and by which they are held accountable to the general public interest.[28]

The operators and guardians of the established structures of society are themselves transients and unsure of their ability to command respect by virtue of their social, professional, or political positions. The young, anxious to discover any weakness in authority, are bound to sense such confusion in their elders, their teachers, their bosses in the bureaucracy, and their commanding officers in the military and to take considerable delight in provoking a "crisis of legitimacy" wherever this can be done.

Anthropologist Margaret Mead's thesis that all of this reflects the emergence of a "prefigurative culture"—one in which the children teach their parents what the future holds in store—need not be accepted completely to credit her observation that

> a profound disturbance is occurring in relationships between the strong and the weak, the possessors and the dispossessed, elder and younger, and those who have knowledge and skill and those who lack them. The secure belief that those who knew had authority over those who did not has been shaken.[29]

To the extent that the deauthorization of established institutions spreads throughout a society, it undermines the capability of the national government to speak for the people within its territorial jurisdiction or to commit the nation to major, particularly long-term, international undertakings. No democracy, certainly, could hope to mobilize its population to fight on behalf of others if there was little confidence throughout the land in the judgments exercised by the nation's official leadership.

While a full counterculture paralysis is highly unlikely in either the advanced capitalist or socialist countries in the decades ahead, it is particularly in the most modernized parts of society that stable authority structures and moral codes are becoming difficult to sustain. Bases of community other than the nation-state are increasingly vying for the affection and loyalty of individuals. To the extent that this cultural pluralism exists in many countries simultaneously, transnational bonds between peoples who share the same values are likely to thicken as the authority of nation-state institutions weakens.

THE RENAISSANCE OF SUPRANATIONALISM

From time to time in human history, often following periods of devastating warfare, the idea gains currency among philosophers, theologians, other intellectuals, and occasionally statesmen that world society, like domestic society, requires authoritative and powerful institutions of governance capable of subordinating the behavior of states, nations, and other assertive groups to world community laws and norms. The basic arguments for such a tranformation of world society, as well as the opposition by those whose power for independent action would have to be subordinated, have been well rehearsed.[30] On the basis of the historical record, the prospects for the supranationalist idea having much practical effect would seem dim.

But the contemporary renaissance of supranationalism appears to have a broader array of prominent advocates than was the case in the past, many of them with considerable practical experience in public statecraft and large nongovernmental organizations. Although neither the more grandiose proposals for world government nor the cautious experimentation now going on with limited-function supranationalist arrangements in international financial institutions and specialized agencies have generated large popular constituencies, many of the more popular schemes for disarmament or arms control championed by influential elements of the peace movement and for ecological protection championed by environmentalist and conservationist groups do imply unprecedented supranational monitoring and enforcement.

The thesis that there are unavoidable requirements for supranational political structures to assure that the human species does not destroy itself in a nuclear holocaust is supported today not only by an elite group of world federalist intellectuals but also by the leaders of major religious institutions. Thus the American Catholic Bishops, in their widely disseminated 1983 Pastoral Letter *The Challenge of Peace: God's Promise and Our Response*, argue that

> An important element missing from world order today is a properly constituted political authority with the capacity to shape our material interdependence in the direction of moral interdependence....
>
> Just as the nation-state was a step in the evolution of government at a time when expanding trade and new weapons technologies made the feudal system inadequate to manage conflicts and provide security, so we are now entering an era of new, global interdependence requiring global systems of governance to manage the resulting conflicts and ensure our common security.[31]

Similarly, the United Methodist Council of Bishops, in their 1985 statement *In Defense of Creation*, maintain that "The transformation of the nation-state systems into a new world order of common security and interdependent institutions offers the only hope for enduring peace."[32]

The supranational political implications of the new ecological consciousness are drawn in a book that is a virtual bible for many in the environmentalist movement: *Only One Earth* by Rene Dubos and Barbara Ward. Many of the world's essential biospheric and even local ecological balances, observe Dubos and Ward, lie beyond the protection of individual governments.

> It is no use one nation checking its energy use to keep the ice caps in place if no other government joins in. It is no use the developed nations suggesting lower energy use just at the moment when the developing nations see increased use as

their only exit from the trap of poverty. The global interdependence of man's airs [and waters] and climates is such that local decisions are simply inadequate. Even the sum of all local separate decisions, wisely made, may not be a sufficient safeguard....Man's global interdependence begins to require, in these fields, a new capacity for global decision-making and global care. It requires coordinating powers for monitoring and research. It means new conventions to draw up ground rules to control [activities affecting the shared environment]....It requires a new commitment to global responsibilities. Equally, it needs effective action among the nations to make responsibility a fact.[33]

A supranationalist vision also infuses the work of the Independent Commission on International Development Issues, chaired by former West German ·Chancellor Willy Brandt. Brandt himself makes this explicit in discussing the implications of some of the Commission's proposals for raising revenue for economic development through taxes on international trade, travel, and communications and special levies on users of international commons resources:

One might argue that it is hard to imagine international taxation without international government. But we believe that certain elements of what might be called international government are already called for to meet both mutual and national interests, and that by the end of this century the world will not be able to function without some practicable form of international taxation; and a decison-making process which goes a good deal beyond existing procedures.[34]

Notably, the Commission advancing these supranationalist views was comprised mostly of recent top-level government ministers of industrialized as well as developing countries—including, for example, Edward Heath (Prime Minister of the United Kingdom, 1970–1974; and leader of the British Conservative Party, 1965–1975); Olaf Palme (Prime Minister of Sweden, 1969–1976 and 1982–1986); Peter G. Peterson (US Secretary of Commerce, 1972–1973); Eduardo Frei Montalva (President of Chile, 1964–1970); Adam Malik (Vice President of Indonesia, 1977–1978; Minister of Foreign Affairs, 1966–1977; and Minister of Commerce, 1963–1965); Amir H. Jamal (Tanzanian Minister of Finance, 1965–1972 and 1977–1979) and Layachi Yaker (Algerian Minister of Commerce, 1969–1977).

In their December 1982 follow-up report, the Brandt Commission expressed disappointment that not enough attention was given to their 1980 proposals for international taxes to generate development revenue. Reacting to what seemed to be a revival of unilateralist nationalism stimulated by the Reagan administration, the Commission lamented that "The pendulum of internationalism has swung rather a long way from this ideal." But they reiterated their admittedly "futuristic" recommendations, insisting that "We do not accept defeat; we hope others do not either."[35]

An energizing center for contemporary supranationalist thinking has been the World Order Models Project of the Institute for World Order.[36] The most prominent of the new world order models developed under the Institute's auspices, Richard Falk's "Preferred World Polity," is one of the plausible alternative futures discussed in Chapter 11.

A potentially large constituency for supranationalist proposals can be seen in the growing cosmopolitanism among the more mobile and educated elements of society in all countries. Cosmopolitanism refers here not to any particular political philosophy, but rather to an *attitude* characterized by relatively low emotional or affective identification with particular national or local jurisdictions, institutions, and symbols, and relatively high identification with worldwide, or potentially worldwide, associations and symbols. Those classes and professions that often travel internationally or change domicile and whose primary peer reference groups and information networks span the world tend to be receptive to concepts such as "the global city" and "spaceship earth." To be sure, mobility per se or contact with foreigners does not always result in wider community identifications. Some people return from tours abroad more patriotic than before they left; indeed, where there are already deep cultural dissonance and jealousies, contact will frequently exacerbate hostility. But the available sociological data support, in the aggregate, the proposition that frequent exposure to other cultures breaks down preexisting parochialisms and creates new transnational commitments and loyalties.[37]

CONSERVATIVE BACKLASH

The most uncompromising defenses of the authority of the nation-state and its institutions, domestically as well as internationally, have come from the Soviets and their satellite regimes in Eastern Europe and from Third World governments. In the noncommunist industrialized world, the conservative supporters of the nation-state have also been regrouping since the 1970s. National flags are increasingly on display and proudly saluted; but subnational and transnational themes and symbols continue to proliferate.

The countercultures of subnationalism, transnationalism, and supranationalism have been regarded by the ruling parties of Eastern Europe and the USSR as potential threats to their survival as much as any aggression by Western countries. The specter of Western-sponsored antistatism has reinforced the reluctance of the most paranoid factions in these parties to allow Western commerce and communications and any but the most marginal access to their societies. But the exposure of their peoples, particularly the youth, to developments in the West cannot be completely suppressed nor can efforts to constrict such access be hidden; and the suppression of popular ideas is bound over the long run to undermine further the authority of these regimes with their peoples. Aware of this, the Gorbachev regime in 1987 not only called off official condemnations of manifestations of an incipient youth counterculture in dress and popular music, but also began to sponsor even "heavy metal" rock concerts featuring Western and home-grown performers.[38]

Many Third World governments, especially in newly independent states, are terribly afraid of the contagious effects on their own ethnically diverse populations of the stimulating sights and sounds of insurrectionary activities of deprived minorities in the developed nations. Most of these governments are less well equipped than are the countries in the Soviet sphere or China to control what and who comes in and to restrict the dissemination of ideas; but they will erect whatever barriers they can, and thus many Third World countries have lined up with the Soviet coalition in international agencies to oppose the free flow of information across national borders. The government of India, for example, despite its posture of commitment to freedom of speech and press at home, does not take kindly to the prospect of having television broadcasts of the demands of Quebec separatists beamed into home or community receivers in the Punjab.

In the advanced Western democracies, where existing political systems have much greater capacity to absorb domestic dissent without collapsing, there is greater ambivalence among governmental elites concerning the proper response to movements whose express purpose is to undermine the nation-state. On the one hand, the majority of the middle-class population is still loyal to national institutions and symbols and willing to support repressive measures if government leaders claim they are needed to protect national security or even only public order and morals. On the other hand, the growing obsolescence of the nation-state is proclaimed by respected industrial, intellectual, and artistic leaders—most of whom also champion the values of cultural pluralism and local self-determination.

On the one side are loyalists to the traditional nation-state structures and supportive moralities, and on the other side are those who feel the nation-state has become a strait jacket. This axis of polarization could well emerge as the most salient political division in world politics over the coming decades, both within countries and across existing national boundaries.

ENDNOTES

1. Harold R. Isaacs, *Idols of the Tribe: Group Identity and Political Change* (New York: Harper & Row, 1977).

2. See Donald L. Horowitz, *Ethnic Groups in Conflict* (Berkeley: University of California Press, 1985).

3. The mistaken expectations are analyzed by Arend Lijphart, "Political Theories and the Explanation of Ethnic Conflict in the Western World: Falsified Predictions and Plausible Postdictions," in Milton J. Esman, ed., *Ethnic Conflict in the Western World* (Ithaca: Cornell University Press, 1977), pp. 46–78.

4. Another trenchant analysis (anticipating Lijphart's) of the gap between actual ethnic conflict and the earlier theoretical scholarship on nationalism is provided by Walter Connor, "Nation-Building or Nation-Destroying?" *World Politics*, Vol. 24, No. 3 (April 1972), pp. 319–355. The efforts by scholars to catch up with the reality of persisting subnationalism in the industrialized states is reflected in Edward A. Tiryakian and Ronald Rogowski, *New Nationalism of the Developed West: Toward Explanation* (Boston: Allen & Unwin, 1985).

5. On the political implications of perceptions of relative deprivation among homogeneous cultural groups, see Seyom Brown, *The Causes and Prevention of War* (New York: St. Martin's Press, 1987), pp. 30–31. See also Ted Robert Gurr, *Why Men Rebel* (Princeton: Princeton University Press, 1970); and Samuel P. Huntington, "Civil Violence and the Process of Development, "*Adelphi Papers* (London: International Institute for Strategic Studies), No. 83 (December 1971), pp. 1–15.

6. J. C. Beckett, "Northern Ireland," *Journal of Contemporary History*, Vol. 6, No. 1 (1971), pp. 121–134.

7. Jo Thomas, "Anglo-Irish Agreement Pits Both Ends against the Middle," *New York Times*, 24 November 1985.

8. Derek W. Urwin, "Social Cleavages and Political Parties in Belgium: Problems of Institutionalization," *Political Studies*, Vol. 18, No. 3 (September 1970), pp. 320–340.

9. Louis L. Snyder, *Global Mini-Nationalisms: Autonomy or Independence* (Westport, CT: Greenwood Press, 1982), pp. 85–94.

10. Some analysts see the development of other occupational, class, ideological, and regional affiliations in Belgium as becoming more, or at least no less, salient in Belgian politics than the conflict between the Flemish and the Walloons, and forecast that these proliferating cross-cutting associations augur well for the perpetuation of a generally well-functioning nation-state. See, for example, Aristide R. Zolberg, "Splitting the Difference: Federalization without Federalism in Belgium," in Esman, *Ethnic Conflict in the Western World*, pp. 103–142.

11. Stanley Payne, "Catalan and Basque Nationalism," *Journal of Contemporary History*, Vol. 6, No. 1 (1971), pp. 15–51.

12. Snyder, *Global Mini-Nationalism*, pp. 101–110. For reportage on the persistence of Basque terrorism into the middle 1980s see Edward Schumacher, "No End in Sight for Basque Terrorism," *New York Times*, 26 August 1986.

13. Ivo D. Duchacek, "Quebec: A U.S. Neighbor—A Community Unlike Any Other: Dyadic Federalism and Its Confederal Ingredients," a paper for the University Consortium for Research on North America, Conference on Canadian–United States Relations, Fletcher School of Law and Diplomacy, October 1986.

14. Elliot J. Feldman and Lily Gardner Feldman, "Federal Changes and International Policies," a paper for the University Consortium for Research on North America, Conference on Canadian–United States Relations, Fletcher School of Law and Diplomacy, October 1986.

15. H. Gordon Skilling, "Communism and Czechoslovak Traditions," *Journal of International Affairs*, Vol. 20, No. 1 (1966), pp. 118–136; and Snyder, *Global Mini-Nationalisms*, pp. 127–128.

16. Paul Lendvai, "The Possibilities of Social Tensions and Upheavals in Eastern Europe and Their Possible Effects on European Security," *Europe and America in the 1970s: II: Society and Power, Aldephi Papers* (London: Institute for Strategic Studies), No. 71 (November 1970).

17. Bill Keller, "Soviet Ethnic Minorities Take Glasnost into the Streets," *New York Times*, 30 August 1987; "The Ukraine Stirs," *The Economist*, 26 February 1972. See also "Special Issue: Nationalities and Nationalism in the USSR," *Problems of Communism*, Vol. 16, No. 5 (September–October 1967); and Erich Goldhagen, ed., *Ethnic Minorities in the Soviet Union* (New York: Praeger, 1968).

18. Steven Burg, "Elite Conflict in Post-Tito Yugoslavia," *Soviet Studies*, Vol. 38, No. 2 (April 1986), pp. 170–193.

19. See Gunnar P. Nielson, "States and 'Nation-Groups': A Global Taxonomy," in Tiryakian and Rogowski, *New Nationalisms of the Developed West*, pp. 27–56.

20. For the extent of the global expansion of Islam see Geoffrey Barraclough, ed., *The Times Atlas History of the World* (Maplewood: Hammond, 1979), pp. 104–105, 134–135.

21. Ivan Vallier, "The Roman Catholic Church: A Transnational Actor," in Joseph S. Nye and Robert O. Keohane, eds., *Transnational Relations and World Politics* (Cambridge: Harvard University Press, 1972), pp. 479–502.

22. Louis L. Snyder, *Macro-Nationalisms: A History of the Pan-Movements* (Westport, CT: Greenwood Press, 1984), pp. 186–189.

23. The Harris Survey, *Yearbook of Public Opinion 1970* (Louis Harris and Associates, 1971), p. 262.

24. *Ibid.*, pp. 252, 254.

25. "Playing for Time," *Time*, 28 July 1986, pp. 22–23; and "A Cavalry Charge up Capitol Hill," *U. S. News and World Report*, October 1986, pp. 6–7.

26. Daniel Yankelovich Inc., *The Changing Values on Campus: Political and Personal Attitudes of Today's College Students* (New York: Washington Square Press, 1972).

27. See Ronald Inglehart, "The Student Revolution in Europe: Intergenerational Change in Post Industrial Societies," *American Political Science Review*, Vol. 65, No. 4 (December 1971), pp. 991–1017; and Joacim Fest, "The Romantic Counter-Revolution of Our Time: Letter from Germany," *Encounter*, Vol. 36, No. 6 (June 1971), pp. 58–61.

28. Alvin Toffler, *The Third Wave* (New York: Bantam, 1980).

29. Margaret Mead, *Culture and Commitment: A Study of the Generation Gap* (Natural History Press, 1970); quotation from p. xvii.

30. Influential proposals for world government as a means of preventing war and reactions to such proposals are analyzed in Seyom Brown, *The Causes and Prevention of War* (New York: St. Martin's Press, 1987), Chapter 7.

31. National Conference of Catholic Bishops on War and Peace, *The Challenge of Peace: God's Promise and Our Response* (United States Catholic Conference, 1983), Sections 241 and 242.

32. The United Methodist Council of Bishops, *In Defense of Creation: The Nuclear Crisis and a Just Peace* (Nashville: Graded Press, 1986), Foundation Document, p. 37.

33. Rene Dubos and Barbara Ward, *Only One Earth* (New York: Norton, 1972), p. 195.

34. Willy Brandt, Introduction to *North-South: A Program for Survival* (Cambridge, MIT Press, 1980). Report of the Independent Commission on International Development Issues, p. 22.

35. The Brandt Commission 1983, *Common Crisis North-South: Cooperation for World Recovery* (Cambridge: MIT Press, 1983), December 1982 Report of the Independent Commission on International Development Issues.

36. Saul H. Mendlovitz, ed., *On the Creation of a Just World Order: Preferred Worlds*

for the 1990s (New York: The Free Press, 1975).

37. See Robert Cooley Angell, *Peace on the March: Transnational Participation* (New York: Van Nostrand Reinhold, 1969).

38. Bill Keller, "Russia's Restless Youth," *New York Times Magazine*, 26 July 1987, pp. 14 f.; and Philip Taubman, "In Moscow, a New Era?" *New York Times*, 29 July 1987.

PART THREE

The Emergence of New Patterns of World Politics

The interplay of the new forces and old forces analyzed in Parts One and Two point toward the emergence of a complex configuration of world politics—an amalgam of past, present, and still-evolving patterns—appropriately called *polyarchy*.

The global polyarchy grows out of the centrifugal pulls against the cold war coalitions and the transnational and subnational challenges to the nation-state systems. It retains some of the principal alignments and antagonisms of the cold war world, and territorially defined countries claiming to be sovereign nation-states are still among the most powerful political entities. But the polyarchic world features multiple bases of alignment and antagonism, many of them having nothing to do with the US–Soviet rivalry and some of them a reaction against the hegemonic policies of one or both superpowers. Nor is the world in its polyarchic configuration definable simply as a nation-state system; the polyarchy is more accurately viewed as a global system of political groupings and institutions in which the nation-state system is one of the *sub*systems, albeit still the most powerful one.

Chapter 11 outlines the plausible alternatives to the emergence of a polyarchic world and shows why none of these other patterns is as likely to evolve out of the contemporary complex of material and social forces.

Chapter 12 synthesizes from the analysis in Part Two a broad-brushed portrait of the emerging polyarchic world—with its overlapping and cross-cutting webs of association—called Polyarchy I. This largely spontaneous evolution of polyarchy could assume either a dangerous form hardly distinct from a Hobbesian world of war of each against all, or a relatively benign form where the dense interdependencies dissuade most political entities from hostile acts against each other.

Chapter 13 outlines a mature form of polyarchy—called Polyarchy II—that with enlightened statecraft might be constructed out of Polyarchy I. The hallmark of Polyarchy II is the institutionalization of political accountability norms and processes among groups in the global polyarchy that substantially affect each other's lives. The international scaffolding already in existence on which the construction of such a world policy might begin (even before the complete emergence of a potentially unstable Polyarchy I) is assessed. Chapter 13 thus sets a framework for the recommendations in Part Four for building a world polity within which human conflicts can be resolved or managed justly and that can avoid a planet-destroying holocaust.

CHAPTER ELEVEN

Plausible Alternative Futures

Taking into account the social and material forces analyzed in the previous chapters, what are the plausible configurations of world politics in the years ahead? I use the term *plausible* rather than *conceivable* to limit the discussion to those alternatives that could well develop out of the present situation on the basis of normal and expected human behavior. Whereas virtually anything is conceivable, not everything is inherent in the logic of the human situation as we know it.

This chapter will attempt to narrow the field of alternative world futures to those that are theoretically plausible. Chapters 12 and 13 will select from the plausible futures those configurations that appear most imminent and policy relevant, in the sense that contemporary policy options exist for increasing or decreasing the likelihood of their realization.

The basic social and material forces active today impact differently on the surface configurations of international relations than they do on the nation-state system itself. Many of the developments weakening coalition unity, for example, are reviving the autonomous and self-centered policies of the nation-states. At the same time, new challenges to national sovereignty appear to be enlarging the need and opportunities for supranational institution-building, but less along cold war lines than on functional or regional lines. Some of the challenges to established structures are working simultaneously on various levels of world politics and are sometimes mutually reinforcing, but more often in their erosive effects than in their constructive effects.

LOOSE BIPOLARITY

The effects of the new forces (and revived old forces) are most visible at the level of international coalitions.

The relatively neat configuration of the 1950s, a world largely polarized into two camps led by the rival superpowers, has been subject to major erosion: China has defected from the Soviet camp. More than 100 of the world's 165 countries claim to be "nonaligned" along the "East–West" cold war axis. Many nominal members of the cold war coalitions that also happen to be Third World countries are more emotionally at home and indeed proud to be identified as members of the "Southern" coalition. Even the core security communities of the cold war coalition (NATO and the Warsaw Pact) are strained by cross-pressures, as important member countries maintain their own key relationships with countries outside of the coalition which they have no inclination to coordinate through the coalition.

The emergent pattern of international alignment differs markedly from the heyday of the cold war when countries were first of all distinguished by which of the superpower coalitions they belonged to or were aligned with. Rarely would lesser members of either coalition deal bilaterally with members of the opposing camp unless the exchanges were stage-managed by the coalition leader. Even for transactions within the camp, when important political or economic issues were being negotiated, the superpower was usually heavily involved; and bilateral or multilateral dealings among a subset of members were discouraged, unless of course the superpower was one of the parties. There were only a few nonaligned countries—most notably India, Egypt, and Indonesia—that attempted to play the field; but the dominant view among cold war statesmen and analysts was that this international stance was untenable over the long run. Some, such as American Secretary of State John Foster Dulles, branded nonalignment as "immoral."

Today, many of the strongest lines of cooperation continue to be those established during the cold war, such as between the North Atlantic countries and Japan, and within the Soviet-dominated economic bloc called COMECON. But more and more, divergences in world view or social systems are insufficient causes to bar cordial relations; and economic intercourse, multilateral technological projects, and scientific and cultural exchanges are conducted among virtually all possible combinations of countries. Organizations and forums for these purposes are increasingly using functional or geographic rather than ideological criteria for participation. Multilateral groupings established for cooperation in various fields have cross-cutting memberships: For example, some members of a given security group cooperate on regional environmental control with some countries from the adversary security group, and a different subset of each group participates in a space-communications system. This means that rival international coalitions vary in membership according to the issues in dispute.

Accordingly, few policymakers or scholars speak anymore of the present configuration of world politics as "bipolar"; and those that do, use highly qualified formulations such as "loose bipolar" or "militarily bipolar and politically multipolar."[1]

However, loose bipolarity, rather than being viewed as a durable and stable configuration, might just as well be seen as a temporary condition or transition to one of the other alternative futures.

REPOLARIZATION

The polycentric trends in the cold war coalitions could be reversed, with a retightening of alliance bonds, and (as during the first two decades after World War II) a reconcentration of commercial relationships within the coalition and a constriction of East–West trade. If political fraternity were once again imposed by the superpowers as a primary requirement for trade, credit arrangements, investments, and relatively easy convertability of currencies, most Third World countries probably would find it difficult to maintain a nonaligned status.

For the international system again to be truly *bi*polar, China and the Soviet Union would have to renew their alliance against the non-Marxist world, which (for the reasons outlined in Chapter 4) still seems to be a remote possibility.

However, leaving aside China and the few countries that might remain in her orbit, a strong repolarization of international relations around Moscow at one pole and Washington at the other would require at least one of the following developments: (1) The government of either the United States or the Soviet Union would be controlled by a group determined to reimpose a we–they, universalized definition of the Soviet–American rivalry that was both ideologically rigid and geostrategically "zero-sum" (one side's gain is the other side's loss); (2) a series of crises involving peripheral members or associated client states of one of the superpower coalitions on one side, and the rival superpower itself or core members of its coalition on the other side, would demonstrate that weakly aligned countries are at a major disadvantage; or (3) a war or ominous brink-of-war crisis would develop between the superpowers in which their confrontation involved the alerting and movement of their own and allied military forces on virtually all continents.

In the early 1980s, it looked as if the first of these developments might indeed be materializing as the newly elected Reagan administration instituted a set of foreign policies designed to reverse the detente approach of the 1970s. The Reagan grand design was modeled on the militarized containment policies of the Truman and Eisenhower periods.

Resistance to Soviet expansion would once again be the top US international imperative; and friendly countries all around the world would be persuaded to join in a "strategic consensus" premised on the belief that the main threat to their independence came from the Soviets, whose goal, according to President

Reagan, was "the promotion of a world revolution and a one world Socialist or Communist state" and who "reserve unto themselves the right to commit any crime, to lie, to cheat, in order to obtain that...."[2]

The term "free world" came back into vogue in Washington to describe the US-led coalition, and "totalitarian" was the term applied to those aligned with the USSR. The Reagan administration made it known that it intended to play favorites among the countries of every continent: Those that inclined more toward the Kremlin's positions on international issues and toward the Soviet model for structuring domestic society would not be treated as well by the United States as those that resisted Soviet influence.

Military power again would provide the principal means for asserting US influence and containing the Soviets. The leaders in the Kremlin were assumed by the Reaganites to be truly impressed by little in international relations other than who has the military capability and the will to use it. The outcome of civil wars with an East–West dimension (and a large proportion of them were seen this way) would be determined by the military supplies provided to the locals by the superpowers and by the credibility of more direct help from the United States and the Soviet Union to their respective allies and clients. Local balances of military power between US allies and clients on one side and Soviet allies and clients on the other were to be tied into the overall global US–Soviet balance. The Rapid Development Force and other capabilities for projecting US military power into local situations were designed to establish a credible presence that would put the United States in the line of potential Soviet or Soviet-proxy attack, and thereby commit the United States to belligerence in case the Soviets attacked (while not limiting the US main counterattacks to the local arenas chosen by the Soviets).[3]

As it turned out, the revived bipolar system existed more in the minds of Reaganites than in the world of practical international relations. It was totally inconsistent with the strategy of continuing to play upon the Sino-Soviet split. It was grossly at variance with the complex cross-cutting relationships of the Middle East. It risked alienating the United States from many of the more influential countries in Latin America and Africa. And it put the United States at cross-purposes with the international economic policies of the principal NATO allies and Japan, which were increasingly oriented toward developing new opportunities for commerce with the Soviet Union, the East European countries, and China.[4]

Perhaps if the Soviets had responded fully in kind to the cold war revivalism in Washington, thereby confirming the Reagan administration's worst hypotheses, there might have been more of a discernible repolarization of world politics. But the Soviets in the early 1980s were experiencing one of their periodic leadership–succession crises, which effectively stymied a vigorous foreign policy for a few years. The new younger regime headed by Mikhail

Gorbachev, which took over in 1985, appeared to be strongly committed to a greater allocation of resources to domestic development tasks within the Soviet Union and to a restoration of Soviet–American detente (including a further expansion of East–West commerce and arms limitation agreements) to allow more Soviet resources and energies to be devoted to internal problems. Gorbachev's credible posture of international reasonableness and interest in summit-level negotiations with Reagan and other Western leaders simply did not allow the unreconstructed cold warriors in either camp to pursue their global repolarization strategies at this time.

MULTIPOLARITY ON THE BASIS OF REGIONAL COMMUNITIES

Another configuration of international relations that plausibly could grow out of present trends would be comprised of a number of relatively self-contained "communities" of countries, reflecting patterns of material interdependence and/or cultural affinity. Each multicountry community would normally act as a unit when conducting relations with other communities, and these intercommunity relationships would be at least as prominent globally as the relations between nation-states have been in the past. How much nation-to-nation interaction persisted into the new system would be a funtion of the internal structures of the various multicountry communities.

The multicountry communities could exhibit various degrees of internal integration. At the modest end of the scale, community norms and institutions might merely provide for easy interaction within particular regions through the removal of trade barriers and other inhibitions to the free circulation of goods, people, and ideas. In their most substantial manifestation, such communities might be fully elaborated political confederations of states, with central federal institutions performing the major public order and economic allocation functions.

The most natural clustering of countries into communities would seem to be on the basis of their common location in particular regions of the globe. But when it comes to implementing the concept, even geography turns out to be a confusing criterion for community membership. Should the Turks be considered a part of the European Community or the Middle East? Is Mexico primarily North American, Central American, or Latin American? Is Pakistan part of the same region as China, as India, or as Iran? Is Yugoslavia part of Western Europe, Eastern Europe, or another grouping defined as the Mediterranean region?

Up to a point, there may be no necessity to choose to which regional community a particular country belongs. Multiple memberships can of course coexist. But when membership involves commitment to trade freely and accept the investments of one's regional partners and to discriminate against the goods of nonmembers, the threshold separating innocent pluralism from primary obligation has been crossed and may well inhibit the building of particular regional communities.[5]

There are stages in the integration process when a country's identification with one regional grouping at the expense of other relationships raises sharply the issue of which considerations have priority—historical–cultural ties, ideology, military security, or economics. Thus the British government's decision to enter the European Community was fraught with massive implications for both the international and the domestic politics of the United Kingdom. England's inability to avoid being pulled painfully in many directions is a compelling reason why it resists efforts to transform the limited, functionally specific European Community into a full-blown, multipurpose political union, though it can support common action short of federation. France's upper limit of integration into the Community is also rather low, determined in part by a romantic desire to cut a wide swath in global diplomacy, in part by its special relations with the francophone states of Africa, and in part by the hope of making its own deals with Arab oil producers. West Germany's threshold for political integration into Western Europe is probably higher, but not so high as to foreclose its ultimate reunification with East Germany nor to undermine US strategic guarantees. And of course Denmark would not want its membership in the Community to mean a substantial reduction in its ties to Norway, Sweden, and Finland.

The founders of the European Community envisioned a steady increase in integration. Members would progressively extend their Community-wide consensus beyond the narrow sector of economic agreements that brought them together in 1957. In fact, the record reveals as much contrapuntal dissonance as harmony.

The European Community has a directly elected parliament, but it has only the power to recommend. There is a permanent Commission, but it can only implement decisions on which the member governments have agreed. The member governments have not really relinquished their sovereignty, since decisions on matters of importance to any of them require their unanimous approval.

Part of the reason for a failure to move substantially toward the founders' dream of ultimate political unification (the Community is not yet even a full common market in which goods, money, and people can circulate freely, as within a single nation) is the inherent contradiction between an expansion in the Community's membership and a deepening of its consensus.

The enlargement of the Community in 1973 with the accession of the United Kingdom, Ireland, and Denmark set up economic, geopolitical, and cultural tensions between the continental orientation of its six original members and the maritime orientation of its new members. The accession of Greece in 1981 and Spain and Portugal in 1986 has given the poorer, agriculturally oriented "south" more bargaining weight in the Community, which slows down progress toward the integrated free market desired by the advanced industrialized sectors. These various cross-pressures are reflected and intensified in issues and tensions over special treatment to be given former colonies, many of whom have been accorded "associate" memberships, in the Mediterranean, African, Asian, and Caribbean regions.

The European Community probably has evolved as far as it can toward unity, given contemporary political realities. This prognosis might be modified if some exciting new personalities arise to give fresh emotional embodiment to the idea of Europe or if the revival of a severe security threat from the East coupled with an American disengagement makes political unification a practical imperative.

The limited evolution of the European Community provides a backdrop of realism for assessing the prospects of other regional communities evolving, for in Europe the preconditions for unity have been better than elsewhere. The European states have been subjected to a succession of imperialisms in common (Rome, Napoleonic France, Hitler's Germany, the threat of Soviet domination, and the actuality of a hegemonic American presence); they have experienced similar religious conflicts among two strains of Western Christianity and have had to work out a pluralist modus vivendi between them under different national roofs; all have highly mobile elite groups with frequent intermarriage; their economies were industrialized and their polities democratized within roughly the same one-hundred-year period, and they have experienced similar class conflicts, at times organized by transnational political parties; all participated in a common balance-of-power system with highly ritualized rules of diplomatic interaction; and they divested themselves of overseas colonies within the same fifteen-year period. Even so, "the United States of Europe" remains an elusive goal.

What, then, are the prospects for voluntary multicountry communitybuilding in regions where the historical preconditions are less favorable and contemporary cross-pressures more intense?

In Eastern Europe, the Kremlin has squelched all tendencies to define the region as separate from the USSR. Except for the bloc defectors, Yugoslavia and Albania, Rumania is the only country *openly* to reject the supranational implications of the Council for Mutual Economic Assistance (COMECON) as being little more than an arm-lock of the Soviet empire (see Chapter 5). The Rumanians say what the other nations in the area know: Increased regional integration, under present circumstances, can only further subordinate Eastern Europe to the Soviet Union. Nationalism, not multinational community-building, is still the only means for limiting Soviet hegemony in Eastern Europe.

Nor is there any basis for substantially integrating the Northeast Asian region, containing as it does the two rival Oriental superpowers, Japan and China, and a divided Korea. Compared to the earlier cold war period, there has been in recent years a substantial increase in interaction among the countries in the area, a lowering of barriers to economic intercourse, and even some multilateral projects. But there is no reason to expect this interaction to generate pressures for a common market, let alone political integration.

Southeast Asia is resistant to absorption into a community with either of its powerful northern neighbors. The emerging relationship of the smaller Asian nations to China and Japan is analogous to the relationship of the nations of Europe to the Soviet Union and the United States—their natural inclination is to be independent of both giants.

Southeast Asia itself has been looked to as a base for possible regional integration. The area's principal intergovernmental organization, the Association of Southeast Asian Nations (ASEAN), composed of Indonesia, the Philippines, Malaysia, Singapore, and Thailand, is expected to promote active collaboration and mutual assistance among the five countries in economic, social, cultural, technical, scientific, and administrative fields. Though ASEAN is not supposed to be an anticommunist alliance as was its predecessor, the Southeast Asia Treaty Organization (SEATO), none of the communist countries of Southeast Asia (Vietnam, Laos, and Cambodia) are members. And Australia and New Zealand, because of their traditionally close cultural, ethnic, and political associations with Britain and the United States, have been excluded.

However, other than the fact of the ASEAN countries inhabiting the same region of the globe, there is little to bind them to one another. Each member of the Association has overriding political and economic interests outside the region (Indonesia's relations with Japan and Australia are of primary importance; Thailand's relations with the United States and China are more important to its security against Vietnamese aggression than are its relations with the ASEAN partners; and so on). Although there is a basic racial similarity between the peoples of the region, the differences in national culture are large. Indonesia is predominantly Muslim; Thailand is 95 percent Buddhist; and the Philippines are 75 percent Roman Catholic. The only language in which all can communicate with one another is English—but not because of a common colonial experience. Indonesia was a part of the Dutch empire; Singapore and Malaysia were mostly under British control; the Philippines were under Spanish and then US rule; and Thailand has been an independent country for over two centuries.

In the Middle East, many of the Arab countries are not yet ready to welcome

Israel into regional community-building efforts. But what about the Arab countries themselves? Twenty-two Arabic-speaking countries are members of the League of Arab States—an organization set up to coordinate the political, economic, cultural, and military policies of the Arabs toward the non-Arab countries and to mediate disputes among themselves. The primary function of the Arab League, in fact, has been to maintain a common front against Israel. Even in the service of this emotionally unifying purpose, however, Arab League members have not been expected substantially to sacrifice their own sovereignty. Nor has the opposition to Israel proven to be an unambiguous spur to unity. In 1978, Egypt, the most populous and previously most politically prestigious Arab country, was expelled from the organization for conducting its own peace negotiations with Israel in the face of opposition from other League members.

Africa, especially the countries of sub-Sahara Africa (except for the *apartheid* regime of the Republic of South Africa), might seem to be a candidate for regional community-building. The principal vehicle for fostering intra-African cooperation is the Organization of African Unity (OAU), to which most of the countries on the continent belong. Most of the members do share the common heritage of having been colonies of the European powers and of having gained their independence only since World War II. And they share the objectives of ridding the continent of the last remnants of European or white-settler domination (now concentrated in the Republic of South Africa and Namibia) and of opposing attempts by non-African countries to reimpose colonial control or in other ways threaten the sovereignty of the African countries. In addition to providing a forum for the denunciation of neocolonialism and racism, the OAU offers its members dispute resolution services—the assumption being that the inability of the Africans to manage their own conflicts without outside help will give non-African powers a new pretext for imperialistic intervention. However, the member countries are too covetous of their newly won sovereign independence to accept any binding obligation to submit their disputes to OAU adjudication. Moreover, their local rivalries are often very intense; and most of them have been unable to resist offers of military equipment from outside powers to help them in their arms races against their neighbors or to suppress internal dissident groups.

The countries of the Americas are part of a definable geographic region, and the 26-member Organization of American States is supposed to provide the vehicle for coordinating international relations within the hemisphere and forging common approaches to hemispheric problems. (Canada only has "observer" status, and Cuba has been excluded from formal participation since 1962.) In effect, the OAS is the institution through which the countries of *Latin* America can concert their policies in a common front vis-à-vis the United States. But it is also the institution the United States usually relies on in its attempts to obtain hemispheric "legitimacy" for its policies toward and in Latin America—especially in cases where the US government considers it necessary to employ coercive power.

The United States would like to promote hemispheric solidarity as a way of preserving its commercial dominance in the region in the face of growing global competition from the European Community and Japan, and as a means of limiting the Soviet Union's influence in the Third World. But, paradoxically, the main source of solidarity among the Latin Americans is their common resentment of US tendencies to treat the hemisphere as a US sphere of influence.

Yet even their common antipathy toward the "colossus of the North" is not a sufficient bond to override the wide differences among the Latin American countries in regime and ideology (some are military dictatorships, some are capitalist oligarchies, some are representative democracies, some are socialist autocracies). Their mythical solidarity rarely operates on matters of importance to any of them.

Within Latin America, special groups of countries have attempted to coordinate their commercial policies and to reduce barriers to trade among themselves—notably the four-member Central American Common Market (Costa Rica, El Salvador, Guatemala, and Nicaragua) and the five-member Andean Group in South America (Bolivia, Colombia, Ecuador, Peru, and Venezuela). But domestic turmoil and local rivalries currently are too pervasive in these regional subgroups to allow for any substantial progress even toward harmonizing their trading relationships.

The experience since World War II with these various efforts at regional community-building lead to a number of general observations on the factors promoting or inhibiting integration within regions, and on the prospects for any of these combinations influencing the overall pattern of international alignment:

1. Poorer nations within regions are likely to resist regionwide economic integration unless they are given reasonable assurance that: (1) they will be accorded guaranteed access to the other national markets of the region; (2) the goods they will be purchasing within the region will not be overpriced in comparison to what is available to them in the global market; (3) they will not suffer a net loss in export earnings by possible retaliation from extraregional customers; (4) they will be given a better opportunity to develop and diversify their own economies by concentrating their commerce within the region; and (5) intraregional adjustment assistance and other welfare-equalization measures will be available to compensate for dislocations and shortfalls attributable to intraregional disparities. The small likelihood that the richer nations within a region would be willing to provide such assurances, or to bind themselves to

meeting the poorer-country demands, leads to the conclusion that only the loosest forms of integration are politically sustainable among neighboring countries of varied economic power.

2. Some countries within each region, often those most advanced industrially, have major commercial and modernist-sector ties to countries in other regions. Others have strong religious and ethnic ties to neighboring nations outside the region. These extraregional associations can be of equal or greater importance to those countries than their intraregional ties, and in such cases the cross-pressured countries will work against all but the most minimal integration of regions.

3. Regional and ethnic transnational communities within a region sometimes will form into tightly integrated subsystems. This can set the ball of integration rolling by stimulating other groups within the region to integrate, and, where there are good bases for cooperation among these subregional groups, the foundations for confederal institutions will be laid. But if the cultural cleavages are reinforced by economic rivalries within the region, the effects of subregional integration are likely to be just the opposite—tempting militants to escalate specific grievances to generalized intercommunity conflict and producing intraregional polarization, even opposing military alliances, that may in turn attract intervention from powers outside the region.

4. Special economic or political relationships between outside powers and particular countries or groups within a region can stimulate their rivals in the region to establish countervailing special relationships—even military alliances—with other outside benefactors. This process could polarize a region and tie the intraregional polarization dangerously into global rivalries; on the other hand, if the extraregional ties are sufficiently numerous and varied, the region may resist polarization but may be subject to such complex cross-pressuring that it merges into the polyarchic global system (see Chapter 13) and no longer functions as a coherent regional subsystem.

5. Finally, while in theory a multipolar international system based on regional communities should reduce the chances of world war (since conflicts can be managed or quarantined within regions), in practice there is unlikely to be such autonomy of regions in the foreseeable future—especially as the nations of the world become progressively interdependent across all traditional regional lines, and as the "commons" areas that they all use (the oceans, the biospheric environment, and outer space) continue to increase in economic and strategic value. Why should the new regional subsystems (assuming they do emerge) be expected to be content with what they have and to refrain from balance-of-power games against each other any more than did the regional empires of the past?[6]

THE "CLASSICAL" BALANCE OF POWER REINCARNATED

The centrifugal forces pulling apart the cold war coalitions and resisting efforts of recoalescence on a regional basis might appear to be recreating a configuration of international relations akin to the balance-of-power system that prevailed among the European states for a century or so after the Treaty of Westphalia (1648). As described in Chapter 2, one of the hallmarks of this "classical" system was the flexibility with which states formed and reformed alliances in order to preserve their independence and to prevent any imperialistic power from attaining unrivaled dominance. From one perspective, the classical balance of power among sovereign and fully independent countries is the normal and best configuration of international relations, and the polarization of world politics associated with the cold war (or indeed any other axis of ideological polarization) is an aberration. The return of flexible and ad hoc alliances, from this point of view, is a healthy development and should be encouraged.

But is such a reincarnation of the classical system really feasible or desirable?

It should be recalled that the classical balance of power proved to be unsustainable into the nineteenth and twentieth centuries owing to the rise of nationalism and the accompanying democratization of foreign-policy decision making in a number of the most advanced countries. It became progressively more difficult for governments to form alliances with one another or threaten military action on behalf of any causes not intensely felt by the citizenry. Alliances had to be justified on the basis of deeply shared values or vital geopolitical interests and could no longer be easily renounced or reversed. Wars that now required crucial inputs from many sectors of the economy and conscripts from broad segments of the population might no longer be stoppable short of terrible destruction of the societies of the involved countries.

The advent of nuclear weapons and population-hostage deterrent strategies even more radically severs the connections between war, alliances, and diplomacy that were the essence of statecraft in the classical period. Indeed, the fragmentation of the cold war coalitions is due in substantial part to the growing realization that alliance commitments lack credibility to the extent that honoring them would be an act of national suicide.

A revival of the classical system of easy-in, easy-out alliance commitments, even if it were feasible, would hardly be a satisfactory answer to the loss of alliance credibility. If anything, it would carry the worst features of both worlds: the high uncertainty of the classical system with respect to who is really on whose side and with what degree of commitment—a situation conducive to tests of strength, the diplomacy of bluff, and war through miscalculation; and the disjunction between war and rational diplomacy in a world of mass-destruction weapons and passionate nationalisms—a situation in which wars, once started, can easily get out of control and are resistant to termination short of mutual genocide.

Yet a system at least partially analogous to the classical balance-of-power system does seem to be forming out of the residue of the disintegrating cold war coalitions. Most countries are cultivating a diversity of international relationships to avoid overdependence on one set of benefactors or clients; and countries that are laggards in this diversification game find themselves at a disadvantage in diplomatic bargaining encounters with countries that credibly can claim to have "other options." Pakistan shows signs of wanting to emulate the nonalignment posture of her rival, India. Turkey, which has placed most of its diplomatic eggs in the NATO basket, has begun to be envious of Greece's maneuverability and bargaining strength vis-à-vis the United States and the West Europeans. Cuba, jealous of the ability of countries such as Mexico, Colombia, and even little Costa Rica to conduct flexible economic and political diplomacy, is straining at the bit of its dependency on the Soviet Union. Norway, a relatively minor actor in NATO councils, and worried about how much it could really count on its NATO partners in a moment-of-truth confrontation with the Soviets, is increasingly envious of the international diplomatic prestige of neutral Sweden, Sweden's considerable economic activities in Eastern Europe, and even her ability to stand tough against the Soviet Union.

The emergent pattern, however, differs from the classical balance of power in a number of important respects. Countries wanting to enlarge their diplomatic flexibility have adopted, or are moving toward, a posture of durable nonalignment, not the policy of fickle alignments characteristic of the classical period. The prospects for sustained nonalignment as a context for diplomatic flexibility are the product of the diversification of domestic economies and international markets of the contemporary period which, more and more, allow even the smallest countries to shop in the global bazaar for goods, services, and armaments, and even to obtain diplomatic support without locking themselves into dependency on a particular hegemon or bloc of countries.

The great powers and local imperialists are constrained in this emergent nonalignment system by the need to compete among themselves for favorable access and arrangements with the smaller powers, and the realization that crude power plays or other means of inducing subordination will probably alienate those who might otherwise be willing clients.

But precisely because of the difficulty in mobilizing alliances to countervail against a great power (or even a middle-ranking power) that decides to push its weight around, the emergent system lacks the self-equilibrating features of the older classical balance; and this is its principal deficiency as a system for global order and justice. In a period of general global stability—where the globally significant disputes between countries are largely over mundane matters of commerce, and whatever ethnic/nationalistic, religious, or ideological conflicts break out can be confined to local areas—this deficiency in the mobilization of countervailing power is not particularly worrisome. But should one of the great powers, especially a superpower, want to take advantage of this deficiency by engaging in an imperialistic rampage reminiscent of Napoleon or Hitler, the lack of a ready mechanism to put together a concerted response may well tempt the would-be aggressor to engage in fait accompli expansionary moves that its opponents could not reverse without initiating World War III.

Anticipating that in the post-bipolar world the Western countries would be at a disadvantage vis-à-vis an imperialistically inclined Soviet Union, Henry Kissinger, a close student of European "concert" diplomacy of the nineteenth century (see Chapter 2), attempted to commit the Soviet Union, China, and other great powers to a set of norms and consultative procedures to stabilize the emerging system. The essential characteristics and prospects of such a contemporary concert of powers are discussed below.

A NEW CONCERT

Reflecting some of Henry Kissinger's concepts, President Nixon opined at the end of 1971 that "it would be a safer and better world if we have a strong, healthy United States, Europe, Soviet Union, China, Japan; each balancing the other, not playing one against the other, an even balance."[7] This was of course an overly simplified and not entirely accurate rendering of the Nixon–Kissinger effort to bring the Soviet Union and China into the "legitimate" post-cold war international order. In many respects, the effort was successful. The new consultative relationships established in the early 1970s appear to have become a durable feature of contemporary world politics, transcending the on-again, off-again revival of cold war tensions.

But how much of a "concert" is today's system really? Surely it departs substantially from the *ideal* regime of the nineteenth century Concert of Europe (which in practice, as shown in Chapter 2, hardly approached its idealized vision) of regularized meetings of the great powers of the day on the basic norms of the good society—to resolve their conflicts and to agree among themselves prior to any of them taking action that might affect their system of relationships.

Kissinger himself appears to have a more modest view of the depth of the consensus needed to sustain the concert system: A "generally accepted legitimacy" is required. But this "should not be confused with justice." As in the nineteenth century system when it functioned best,

"Legitimacy"... means no more than an international agreement about the nature of workable arrangements and about the permissible aims and methods of foreign policy. It implies the acceptance of the framework of the international order by all the major powers, at least to the extent that no state is so dissatisfied that, like Germany after the Treaty of Versailles, it expresses its dissatisfaction in a revolutionary foreign policy.[8]

This modest view of the essential normative premises of a concert system underlay Kissinger's efforts in the 1970s to commit the Soviet Union to principles of international behavior and consultative obligations that implied abandonment of its global revolutionary aims. Kissinger was under no illusions that General Secretary Brezhnev, merely by signing the 1972 Soviet–American "Declaration of Basic Principles of Relations" (which included the pledge to "always exercise restraint in their mutual relations" and to "negotiate and settle differences by peaceful means...[and] in a spirit of reciprocity, and mutual accommodation and mutal benefit" and the promise to forego "unilateral advantage at the expense of the other, directly or indirectly"), was locking the Soviet Union into an acceptance of the international status quo. As shown in Chapter 6, the Declaration of Basic Principles was the verbal codification of the new "stake in the equilibrium" (Kissinger's formulation) that the Kremlin presumably now had as a result not only of its recognition that the Soviet Union could not survive another world war, but also its decision to participate in the international economy that was still largely run by the capitalist powers.

The new Sino-American relationship initiated in 1972 by Kissinger and Chou En-lai and carried forward by their successors is also part of the new concert. It is reminiscent of the classical balance of power insofar as it is designed to counter Soviet hegemonic aspirations in Asia, and to face the Soviets with the prospect of a two-front war if they become militarily aggressive in either the East or the West. But it is at the same time a concert configuration insofar as it contemplates a durable consultative relationship at the highest levels of the two governments on matters that could affect the vital interests of either in the Asian region.

The concert model has yet another prominent contemporary expression in the annual seven-country economic "summits" among the principal noncommunist industrial countries—the United States, Canada, Britain, France, West Germany, Italy, and Japan—where the effort is to harmonize their often-conflicting economic policies. The seven-country summits are a recognition of the fact that inflation, unemployment, major economic growth, and recession in one part of the advanced industrial world can have major impacts on other parts. Typically, the summit agenda includes not only the international subjects of trade and monetary relations but also matters traditionally regarded as domestic, such as their respective interest-rate policies and their basic fiscal and budgetary strategies. However, the record of accomplishment at the summits is very slight and is reflected in their communiques, which are for the most part abstract and vague general statements designed to obscure their disagreements. In fact, in the actual exchanges that take place at the summits there is as much dissonance as harmony, reflecting the varied and often clashing relationships of the seven with the Soviet Union, China, the oil-producing countries, the developing countries, the newly industrializing countries, and with each other.

Another limited-membership and special-function "concert" has been formed by the principal exporters of nuclear materials and nuclear technology. This so-called London Suppliers Group meets periodically to formulate guidelines for regulating the competition among them in the selling of nuclear wares. Such agreed guidelines are important for restricting the transfer of nuclear materials and processing equipment that could be converted into weapons, for without these mutual pledges of restraint, the nuclear-supplier countries are tempted to win customers by relaxing their controls on weapons-related transactions.

Any attempt to direct the larger system of world order through a particular great-power concert, however, is bound to court the alienation of those who will not be provided a chair. The majority of the excluded are already unhappy with the elitist implications of the affluent "chamber" concerts, as it were, as opposed to meetings *ensemble*, such as the Law of the Sea Conference or other open-membership meetings under the auspices of the United Nations. Yes, there is widespread relief when regular consultations are engaged in between the superpowers, relief that at least they are talking with and not shooting at one another; but this is coupled with suspicion on the part of most other countries that the Big Two are attempting to set up a "condominium" or "duopoly" of power to run the world. Yet if this concert-a-deux is to be enlarged, who should be admitted into the chamber, and on what basis? China, on grounds of population? But then surely India, with a population vastly exceeding the United States or the Soviet Union, should also be admitted—and then, what world-order matters could this quartet handle among themselves in a way that the excluded nations would regard as legitimate? Perhaps the possession of nuclear weapons should be the criterion for a performing chair in the world-order concert—but then countries with a nuclear weapons potential would have a special incentive to produce and deploy them! GNP? But then the principal consultative group becomes a rich country club, and the North–South polarization is worsened. Or if some arbitrary combination of characteristics that, all in all, give a country the capacity to produce wide international effects is the criterion, so that the important energy producers, for example, could be included, then the regional rivals of these countries may feel particularly resentful. (If Venezuela, why not Brazil or Argentina? If Nigeria, why not Zaire? If Indonesia, why not Vietnam and Australia? If Saudi Arabia, why not Egypt? and so on.)[9]

Despite the absence of a universally acceptable basis in logic or "power" for determining concert memberships in the contemporary world of 165 proud nation-states, limited-membership consultative groupings, some relatively permanently institutionalized, have become a common feature of international relations—being a pragmatic diplomatic adaptation to the emergent system wherein each country (whether a superpower or a poor developing country) is enmeshed in a complex web of multiple, functionally specific, often overlapping and cross-cutting relationships.

Those who long for a concert will be disturbed at the cacophony of numerous simultaneous concerts. But the survival of civil society worldwide, no less than domestically, now may well require the capacity to live with the dissonance and a degree of disorder uncongenial to previous generations.

COMMUNITIES BENEATH AND BEYOND THE NATION-STATE

The alternatives thus far assessed are all based on the assumption that the nation-state system remains the dominant political structure of world society. But perhaps this assumption should no longer be taken as self-evident, at least over the long run. A fundamental metamorphosis of the world polity may be in the works—reflecting the social and material forces given special attention in Chapters 8, 9, and 10.

The metamorphosis, if that is what it is, appears to be taking place at three levels of world politics: subnational, transnational, and supranational.

At the subnational level, the inherent contradiction of the nation-state system—the notion that nations and states ought to be congruent—is playing havoc with the survival of the system itself, as the spread of the fever of national self-determination infects virtually every multinational state (which amounts to the large majority of countries). In many countries, energies that ought to be devoted to the complex tasks of societal management of the larger (multi)nation-state are consumed in conflicts between aggrieved subnational communities and defenders of the unity of the larger national polity. In some countries where the national government is ineffective in dealing with the concerns of subnational communities, and especially where such communities are concentrated in particular provinces or localities, provincial or local governments have been asserting themselves, not only as agencies of advocacy for the cultural and human rights of the aggrieved communities, but increasingly as their economic agents in the global marketplace, negotiating trade and investment arrangements with similar subunits of government in other countries.[10]

Regarding the rise of subnationalism as unavoidable and normatively legitimate as a means of maintaining important human rights and cultural values, theorists such as Johan Galtrung have been propounding a model of a future world polity based on much smaller "self-reliant" communities than the average contemporary nation-state. In Galtung's vision, these small polities would be territorially based, but would be criss-crossed and tied together by "a strong web of nonterritorial organizations...putting everybody in community with local neighbors as well as with distant neighbors." There would also have to be "some central authority that can make and enact plans for such matters as world food distribution, world employment, world ecological balance, world water and oxygen budgets and that can administer the riches that belong to all, such as the seabed and the oceans, the bio-atmosphere, the cosmos, [and] subterranean deposits."[11]

As Galtung observes, bonds of community, if given the chance, will naturally transcend territorially defined polities—an increasingly prominent phenomenon in a world where goods, people, and ideas can circulate rapidly and inexpensively around the globe. The easy transnational circulations of goods, people, and ideas has a powerful agency: the multinational corporation. Stimulated by the efforts of advanced commercial enterprise to remove barriers to international transactions, but having also an independent momentum in numerous religious, cultural, ideological, professional, and scientific communities, transnational linkages and co-support groups are becoming as widespread as the domestically oriented interest groups that dominate political life in most countries. More and more, the transnational interests will be forming agencies and institutions to coordinate their demands in various countries and to lobby national legislatures and international organizations.[12] Accordingly, the bargaining or "diplomacy" between these groups is no less the essence of world politics than is the bargaining between the central governments of the nation-states.

In some fields, the frequent and intense transnational interaction among nongovernmental entities have spawned new international arrangements and even new intergovernmental institutions to facilitate and coordinate the bargaining. This has been particularly evident in the fields of international transportation and communications. Maximally, in fields requiring continual global coordination, conflict resolution, and resource allocation among the diverse governmental and nongovernmental actors, the global institutions might themselves begin to take on the characteristics of governments, with legislative, adjudicative, and enforcement powers.[13]

A rapid leap into a post-nation-state, supranational world strains the credulity of most contemporary political scientists and statesmen, but some prominent theorists, regarding such a transformation of world society over the next few decades as the only hope for the survival of the human species, are not put off by the prevailing skepticism. They see many of the forces identified in this book as laying the groundwork for the necessary transformation and believe that it is not too soon to begin to design (or to debate the design of) the constitutional structure of the new supranational world polity and to devise active strategies to hasten the realization of the preferred system.

The most noted contemporary conceptual effort on behalf of transforming the nation-state system into a supranational system has been located in the World Order Models Project of the Institute for World Order, directed by international lawyer Saul H. Mendlovitz. The project has solicited models of world order and justice from around the world; but it is the design for a new world systems developed by the American international lawyer and political activist Richard Falk that has been most vigorously championed by the directors of the project.

Falk's Preferred World Polity, as he calls it, has all the attributes (and then some) of the global constitutional systems put forward by the United World Federalists of a previous generation. It would make laws, adjudicate disputes, and enforce its laws and judicial decisions, in some cases on national and subordinate levels of governments and in some cases directly on nongovernmental organizations and citizens. The decisions of the World Polity would be superordinate over the nation-states and binding upon them.

The central legislative body of the World Polity would be a three-chamber General Assembly with different bases of representation in each chamber and checks-and-balances voting rules to ensure that world laws are based as much as possible on the consent of the governed. The World Polity would have its own armed forces (and a complete monopoly of nuclear and other weapons of mass destruction) to compel adherence to its laws if need be, and if necessary to overwhelm elements who attempt to maintain military forces in violation of the disarmament agreement which it is assumed will precede the establishment of the new system.

Falk recognizes that his design for a new world order will remain only an abstract idea on the bookshelf unless its champions are aligned with influential social and political forces within the existing structures, for those with formal authority in the prevailing state system will have to negotiate the required structural transformations. Shunning violent revolution to put true believers in power, Falk places his hopes in "consciousness raising" of broad segments of the politically active citizenry of all countries as to the perils of maintaining the old order, and the benefits of the envisioned transformation. The new consciousness would then presumably be converted into active interest-group lobbying and electoral politics to make sure that national political elites the world over are committed to the required institutional innovations on the global level.[14]

NONE OF THE ABOVE, ALL OF THE ABOVE

Each of the alternative world futures thus far considered in this chapter has characteristics that are at least partially consistent with the dominant social and material forces of the contemporary period—thus their inclusion among the plausible alternatives—but each also has characteristics that are inconsistent with these forces:

- A repolarization of world politics along cold war lines is consistent with the inability of any of the countries other than the United States or the Soviet Union to protect themselves against aggression from either of these superpowers and with the persistence of fundamental way-of-life antagonisms between Marxists and non-Marxists. But a global repolarization into two camps under the aegis of the superpowers is inconsistent with the inability of the superpowers to provide credible security protection to members of their own camps. The bipolar world is also inconsistent with the unwillingness of most countries to let their ideological inclinations (which in the majority of cases, anyway, have produced hybrid regimes with both capitalist and socialist features) interfere with currently advantageous commercial relationships or with balance-of-power relationships currently needed for protection against local adversaries.

- A multipolar configuration of world politics based primarily on regional clusters of countries is consistent with the common history (often domination by common imperial overlords) experienced by members of some of the regional groupings. A concerting of policies among countries in some regional groupings vis-à-vis countries outside the region is consistent with some of the emergent regional patterns of intense economic interaction. But in many places tight regional coordination, let alone integration, is inconsistent with historic local rivalries that remain more intense than any incentives to cooperate in common regional associations; ideological cleavages often cut across particular regions; in most regions there is highly conflictual competition between neighboring states over commonly used resources; and in some regions countries are determined to pursue international commercial opportunities in the global market more than in their own geographic locale.

- A renaissance of the classical balance of power is consistent with the fragmentation of the cold war coalitions and with the attractiveness of "nonalignment" for many of the countries, particularly in the Third World. But the flexibility of alignments and realignments necessary to restrain aggressive imperialists and to keep the system in equilibrium requires a degree of deference to elite practitioners of diplomacy that is consistent with the nationalistic and populist norms of many of the nation-states. The less powerful states in the system, rather than seeking security through ad hoc alignments, are more inclined to rely on unilateral self-help strategies and military arsenals, including (eventually) their own nuclear weapons, which hardly augurs well for system stability or the avoidance of a planet-destroying nuclear holocaust.

- A new global "concert" of great powers or pattern of limited-member directorates comprising countries that are powerful in certain fields may be consistent with how business is actually conducted in the contemporary world; but it is not compatible with the antihegemonic and international-egalitarian ethos now being asserted by the large majority of countries, who if often excluded from the counsels of decision on matters affecting their welfare are likely to form angry and obstructionist counter-coalitions.

- Finally, the hopes of world-order reformers to transform the nation-state system, or at least to transcend it, are consistent with the growing dissatisfaction with how national governments are attending to the provision of basic amenities and functions of community life (civic peace and the security of persons and property, an orderly market for the exchange of goods and services, social justice, ecological maintenance, and cultural integrity), and the consequent tendency to look to nongovern-tal organizations, subnational levels of government, and international institutions to take up the slack. But the organizations and movements dissatisfied with the performance of their national governments are often at cross-purposes with one another and have yet to produce anything even remotely resembling a consensus on a new world order less reliant on nation-states.

In short, each of these alternative configurations of world politics *could* become dominant in the world of the future. Each exists in embryo, so to speak, in the contemporary world. But each, because of some crucial incompatibilities with some of the important material and social forces, also engenders strong opposition to itself. No one of these configurations alone yet represents an adequate political adaptation by human society to the self-contradictory and ominously self-destructive features of the existing world system.

TOWARD POLYARCHY

If the various forces now at work in world politics, and the patterns of alignment and antagonism to which they give rise, do not presage the ascendancy of any of the world-order visions sketched above, what can we expect the world to look like as we enter the twenty-first century? Assuming no severe world-disrupting developments (such as a war between the superpowers, a severe collapse of the global economy, or a profound destabilization of the planet's ecological systems)—a large assumption, which may prove to be wrong—and assuming none of the contending world-order visions is embraced by a sufficiently charismatic leadership to turn it into the dominant popular cause, the maturation and interaction of the various tendencies with which the existing system is pregnant point to the emergence of a global *polyarchy*.

I avoid the term *anarchy* as a description of either the existing configuration of world politics or the emergent configuration, since *an*archy denotes the *absence* of rule, hierarchy, or law. Clearly, even at the inter-state level, there are now enclaves of order, some rather stable communities (some of which are hierarchically organized), various regional or function-specific regimes of informal or formalized rules of country-to-country behavior (some of which are institutionalized in organizations such as the International Monetary Fund), and even the universalized system of norms of the nation-state system (national sovereignty and mutual nonintervention in domestic affairs) which, while not always respected, continue to constrain the international behavior of most countries. International relations, though it has some anarchic features, is hardly a total Hobbesian "state of nature," a potential war of each against all where every nation's life is nasty, brutish, and short. Nor, obviously, is it a benign self-equilibrating anarchy in which the unilateral pursuit by each country of its own interests produces well-being for all and world peace.

This is not to rule out anarchy of the Hobbesian sort (divine anarchic harmony is surely a fantasy) as a plausible condition of world politics. Rather, it is to observe that the preconditions for global anarchy—the collapse of stable cooperative regimes among countries, and the total erosion of international respect save that which is commanded by brute force—are not present today. These brutish relationships exist between particular sets of countries, yes; but they constitute one facet of a more complex field of conflict and cooperation, hegemonic and subordinate relationships, interdependencies, and integrating and disintegrating communities.

For the present, at least, this complex pattern is assuming the configuration of a *polyarchy*: a situation of many communities, spheres of influence, hegemonic imperiums, interdependencies, trans-state loyalties—some of which overlap, some of which are concentric, some of which are substantially incongruent—that exhibits no clearly dominant axis of alignment and antagonism and has no central steering group or agency.

The structural features and behavioral norms of the emerging polyarchy (which will be elaborated in the next chapter) bear considerable resemblance to the system of "complex interdependence" postulated by Robert Keohane and Joseph Nye[15] and the "new mediaevalism" conceptualized by Hedley Bull.[16]

The polyarchic conception, however, is less inherently benign than the Keohane-Nye model, wherein "Military force is not used by governments toward other governments within the region, or on issues, when [the 'ideal type' of] complex interdependence prevails."[17] The polyarchic system, by contrast, carries no necessary presumption about the use of military force (actors highly inclined to use force exist side by side *in the system* with actors more inclined to use other means of influence), though in some variants of polyarchy (particularly those contemplated in Chapter 13), there would be more constraints against the resort to organized violence than in other variants.

On the other hand, polyarchy as conceived of here is less inherently prone to instability and violence than is Hedley Bull's "new mediaevalism." Bull worries that "the decline of the states system and its transformation into a secular reincarnation of the mediaeval order" will provide even greater opportunity than now exists for "the resort to violence on an international scale by groups other than the state, and the assertion by them of a right to commit such violence."[18] But Bull's nightmare fixes on the most anarchic embodiment of polyarchy—surely, not an implausible development if the decline in the ability of national governments to perform their standard public order functions brings no compensatory taking over of public order functions by other agencies. Yet is this a necessary supposition? Is it not equally plausible that in a polyarchic system new agencies, more congruent with the intense patterns of intergroup interaction, will be accorded rule-making and rule-enforcement authority that will be accepted as legitimate by the affected groups?

As will be argued in the following chapters, which variant of polyarchy becomes the regime globally or in particular regions has not been predetermined by developments up to now, and therefore which of the variants does emerge will depend on the choices and commitments made by politically influential groups in the years ahead.

ENDNOTES

1. The concept of "loose bipolarity" was introduced by Morton A. Kaplan, *System and Process in International Relations* (New York: Wiley, 1957). The "military bipolar and politically multipolar" conceptualization was put forward by Henry Kissinger, "Central Issues in American Foreign Policy," in Kermit Gordon, ed., *Agenda for the Nation* (Washington, DC: The Brookings Institution, 1968), pp. 590–591.

2. Ronald Reagan, news conference of January 29, 1981, *Weekly Compilation of Presidential Documents*, 17(5): 66–67.

3. See Seyom Brown, *The Faces of Power: Constancy and Change in United States Foreign Policy from Truman to Reagan* (New York: Columbia University Press), pp. 567–602, for a more detailed elaboration of the "grand strategy" put forward by the Reagan administration in 1981 and 1982.

4. For the confrontation of Reagan ideological assumptions with the real-world complexities of the 1980s, see *ibid.*, pp. 603–628.

5. Diverse regional paths to world order have been championed by numerous prominent policymakers and scholars, among them Jean Monet, George Ball, Zbigniew Brzezinski, William Bundy, Amitai Etzioni, Karl Deutsch, Julius Nyerere, Raul Prebisch, and J. J. Servan-Schreiber. Much of the enthusiasm for regionalism, which was particularly prevalent in the 1960s, appears in retrospect to have been derived from an infatuation with rather simplistic models of the integration process and from insufficient consideration of the global context of alignments and adversary relations. A skeptical look at this earlier enthusiasm for regionalism is found in Joseph S. Nye, *Peace in Parts: Integration and Conflict in Regional Organization* (Boston: Little, Brown, 1971).

6. A comparison of the war-proneness of multipolar/regional systems and other types of international systems is made in Seyom Brown, *The Causes and Prevention of War* (New York: St. Martin's Press, 1987), Chapter VI.

7. Richard Nixon, interview in *Time*, 3 January 1972, p. 11.

8. Henry A. Kissinger, *World Restored: The Politics of Conservatism in a Revolutionary Age* (New York: Grosset & Dunlap, 1964), p. 1.

9. The analysis of the problematic aspects of the "concert" model borrows from my discussion in *On the Front Burner: Issues in U.S. Foreign Policy* (Boston: Little, Brown, 1984), pp. 179–181. See also Hedley Bull, *The Anarchical Society: A Study of Order in World Politics* (New York: Columbia University Press, 1977), pp. 227–229.

10. Canadians have been particularly inventive in the growing field of international activity by subunits of government. See Elliot Feldman and Lily Gardner Feldman, "The Impact of Federalism on the Organization of Canadian Foreign Policy," *Publius*, Vol. 14, No. 4 (Winter 1984).

11. Johan Galtung, *The True Worlds: A Transnational Perspective* (New York: The Free Press, 1980), pp. 92–94, 344–352.

12. Robert O. Keohane and Joseph S. Nye, Jr., eds., *Transnational Relations and World Politics* (Cambridge: Harvard University Press, 1972).

13. The potential for supranational institution-building to regulate transnational bargaining in the communications and broadcasting fields has been explored in Seyom Brown, Nina Cornell, Larry Fabian, and Edith Brown Weiss, *Regimes for the Ocean, Outer Space, and Weather* (Washington, DC: The Brookings Institution, 1977), pp. 197–203.

14. Richard A. Falk, *A Study of Future Worlds* (New York: The Free Press, 1975). See also Saul H. Mendlovitz, ed., *On the Creation of a Just World Order: Preferred Worlds for the 1990s* (New York: The Free Press, 1975).

15. Robert O. Keohane and Joseph S. Nye, *Power and Interdependence: World Politics in Transition* (Boston: Little, Brown, 1977). The Keohane–Nye book appeared three years after the publication of my *New Forces in World Politics* where, particularly in Chapter 6, "The Emerging System of Multiple Coalitions," virtually all of the features of their "complex interdependence" model were suggested. Both my and the Keohane–Nye paradigms were anticipated in an even earlier groundbreaking piece by Edward L. Morse, "The Transformation of Foreign Policies: Modernization, Interdependence, and Externalization," *World Politics*, Vol. 22, No. 3 (April 1970), pp. 371–392. Morse's ideas are further elaborated in his *Modernization and the Transformation of International Relations* (New York: The Free Press, 1976).

16. Bull, *The Anarchical Society*, pp. 254–256, 285–286, 291–294.

17. Keohane and Nye, *Power and Interdependence*, p. 25.

18. Bull, *The Anarchical Society*, p. 268.

CHAPTER TWELVE

Polyarchy I

The forces now ascendant appear to be leading toward a global society without a dominant structure of cooperation and conflict—a *polyarchy* in which nation-states, subnational groups, and transnational special interests and communities are all vying for the support and loyalty of individuals, and conflicts need to be resolved primarily on the basis of ad hoc bargaining among combinations of these groups that vary from issue to issue. In the polyarchic system, world politics is no longer essentially "international" politics, where who gets what, when, and how is determined on the basis of bargaining and fighting among the nation-states; rather, the international system is now seen as one of the *sub*systems of a larger and more complex field of relationships.

In its emergent form—which I call *Polyarchy I*—the most salient characteristics of the new configuration of world politics seem to be its complexity and unpredictability. However, the complexity and flux exist within some relatively durable structural characteristics and behavior patterns.

THE CROSS-PRESSURED COLD WAR ALIGNMENTS

The antagonisms between Marxists and non-Marxists continue to affect international, transnational, and domestic alignments; and many countries and movements, largely because of relationships established in the bipolar period, retain some form of alliance or client–patron arrangements with one or the other of the two military superpowers. But even though persisting and strong in certain places, the cold war coalitions in their global dimensions are severely cross-pressured by internecine conflicts and competing bases of alignment. Most countries refuse to define themselves as members of either camp; and even formal membership is an unreliable predictor of support for one's cold war brothers and sisters on particular issues.

At least two-thirds of the countries have publicly renounced membership in either of the superpower-led blocs and claim to be "nonaligned" vis-à-vis both the United States and the Soviet Union. Such nonalignment does not preclude cooperation with one or both of the superpowers on specific issues or projects (say, commercial shipping, space communications, or the nonproliferation of nuclear weapons); rather, it induces countries to diversify their dependency relationships and friendships field by field so as not to become camp followers on either side of the superpower rivalry.

In some regions, particularly mainland Southeast Asia and southern Africa, a stronger determinant of local alignments than the differences between Marxists and non-Marxists is the competition for influence between the two largest and most powerful Marxist countries, the Soviet Union and the People's Republic of China. Moreover, the fact that the Kremlin is no longer the Vatican of the Communist Church, as it were, has reinforced "polycentric" trends even within the Soviet Union's core security community in Eastern Europe and has encouraged challenges to the Soviet party's ideological leadership from the Eurocommunist parties of Western Europe.

The Marxist vs. non-Marxist fault line has also been eroded by the mixing of socialist and capitalist approaches to organizing the political economy in most countries on both sides of the ideological divide.

The People's Republic of China, previously the most reluctant of the Marxist–socialist regimes to experiment with capitalist devices, has been experimenting in the 1980s with some rather dramatic departures from Leninist–Maoist principles of state ownership of all the means of production and distribution and of centralized governmental control over most aspects of daily life. How far and fast the Chinese will go in allowing market mechanisms to run their economy and to allow cultural and political pluralism to develop cannot be predicted; but the mere fact that the Chinese leadership considers it necessary and legitimate to explore moving in this direction—admitting that socialism on Marxist–Leninist–Maoist lines may not be the wave of the future—in itself constitutes a sea change with enormous potential for finally shattering the global cold war formations of the post-World War II period.

In the Third World, neither socialism (of the Soviet or Maoist types) nor capitalism of the kind championed by the United States has taken root, and very few Third World leaders show any enthusiasm for cultivating these forms of political economy in their own soil. The reluctance to imitate the giants is not just a function of smaller size and less indigenous resources available in the majority of the developing countries. It is also the result of the recognition on the part of new generations of developing-country economists (less enthralled perhaps than their predecessors with economic theories learned at the University of Chicago, the London School of Economics, or Moscow and Beijing Universities) that the seeds of development will not sprout and flourish in their own countries if they are not bred sufficiently in the local culture. Self-reliance in the realm of ideas has now become a more important stance for nationalistic Third World governments than material self-reliance. And the embarrassing but unavoidable need to compromise one's economic independence in the service of economic growth puts an even greater political premium on the maintenance of ideological nonalignment.

Nor has the theoretical antithesis between socialist and capitalist political economies been borne out in the practical life of most of the industrialized democracies of the West. Virtually all of them allow a great deal of play to the market forces of supply and demand; but at the same time virtually all of them subject the market forces to considerable government regulation and intervention—not only to keep the potentially self-destructive volatility of the free market within bounds, but also in the service of popular egalitarian social-justice values. Although more or less socialistically oriented parties are voted in and out of power in the industrialized western countries, the backlash against market-interventionist policies (such as with the Thatcher government in England, the Reagan administration in the United States, and the Kohl chancellorship in West Germany) does not go so far as to dismantle the welfare state or radically deregulate the economy. The Japanese political economy is unique unto itself, but the intimate and mutually supportive relationship between government and the private industrial sector also defies categorization as either a free market or socialist system.

The experimentation with "market socialism" of some of the countries in the Soviet orbit—most notably in Hungary, but also in East Germany, Czechoslovakia, and Poland—further dissipates even the residual core of ideological polarization in Europe, especially as the economic liberalization is combined with an expansion of East–West commerce.

THE AMORPHOUS THIRD WORLD

In some respects a more salient and durable grouping than the First World (the affluent capitalist West) or the Second World (the socialist East) is the Third World—an amorphous but yet definable and emotionally self-conscious portion of the world polyarchy.

The Third World is a partly locational, partly cultural, partly historical, partly economic, partly racial community. One can belong to this community by virtue of identification (by choice or by consignment) with any one or more of the included populations.

Located mainly in the southern two-thirds of the globe, most of the Third World countries have indigenous cultures and languages that differ markedly from the European cultures and languages that prevailed as far back as the fifth century A. D. from the British Isles to the Ural Mountains and north of the Mediterranean and the Black Seas. The exceptions among the "southern" countries are Australia and New Zealand, whose indigenous populations were smaller than the European, mostly English, settler populations who took them over and stayed to make these lands, in effect, European countries.

Most of these southern populations have the similar historical experience of having been incorporated into the empires of one or another of the major European powers between the fifteenth century and early twentieth century—sometimes changing hands between different European overlords—and having been kept in this colonial condition until being granted independence in the post-World War II period. Almost all of the colonies in Central and South America, however, became independent of Spain and Portugal earlier—during the 1820s. There were significant variations in this colonial experience, to be sure; but a common and deeply searing memory is that of having their indigenous cultures and religions treated as of little value by their imperial European overlords, and often with disrespect.

The physiological distinctiveness (principally skin color) between the southerners and their colonizers, and the fact that the Europeans disparaged the darker skins of the subjugated populations, not infrequently regarding them as inferior races, continues to provide the strongest bond among Third World nations that in other respects—religion, culture, contemporary ideological affinities—may be far apart or even antagonists.

This common experience of racial discrimination is today the most emotionally significant *transnational* bond between many people of relatively darker skins in countries the world over, including between citizens of the "northern" countries (whose ancestors might have been brought north as labor resources) and their southern brothers and sisters.

Finally, these various experiences of Third World peoples that give them a sense of camaraderie against the rest of the world are reinforced by today's global rich–poor gap, with which the North–South divisions are remarkably congruent—not to discount the problems the "Group of 77," the developing country coalition, has in concerting common positions on international economic issues (see Chapter 7).

Those who are skeptical that there really is a Third World can point to problems both in the logic of its definition and in evidence of a lack of consistent community cohesiveness: Either in concept or in practice, does it extend to the countries of North Africa? If so, then why not to the peoples on the northern littoral of the Mediterranean Sea who are racially very similar to the North Africans? Is Turkey in but Greece out? Does it include all of the Muslim countries of the Middle East, including the wealthy oil producers? Is China a Third World country? What about Japan? Are all blacks and Hispanics living in the United States a part of the Third World? What about the indigenous American "Indians"? What about the Asiatic and Muslim people living in the Soviet Union?

The point here, however, is not that the Third World has neatly defined characteristics or acts consistently and coherently in world politics. Rather, it is that the Third World is at least as definable and often as able to concert itself on issues of importance to it as are either of the cold war coalitions. The "South's" internal divisions are no greater than the "West's" or the "East's." The larger groupings are not about to disappear and are each major parts of the global polyarchy, while being themselves each cross-pressured by more particular polyarchic relationships—subcoalitions within the cold war coalitions and within the Third World, plus transcoalition alignments on many issues.

MORE PARTICULAR SPECIAL RELATIONSHIPS

Within and outside of the cold war coalitions, important affinities, alignments, antagonisms, dependency relationships, and institutional arrangements also constitute the stuff of world politics. Some of these have largely to do with military security, some with economics; others are cultural and ideological; some are at cross-purposes; others are mutually reinforcing. All of them are part of the comprehensive system of world politics that sets limits and provides the opportunities for individuals, groups, and states to protect and advance what they value. Effective policymaking and citizenship in the contemporary world cannot avoid taking these special relationships into account, any less than the larger East–West and North–South relationships. Some of the most prominent of the special relationships essential to the workings of the polyarchy are outlined here:

Security Relationships (Other Than the Cold War Coalitions)

1. *US–Soviet.* The two superpowers pose threats to one another independent of their memberships in NATO and the Warsaw Pact. Aware of this, they have incentives to maintain unilateral flexibility to deter, negotiate, and appease one another—especially in the event of extreme crises—outside of their respective alliance systems.
2. *Western Europe-Soviet.*The USSR poses military threats to the West Europeans that, because of the special US–Soviet relationships, are insufficiently countered by NATO responses that would require US participation or approval. The West Europeans, knowing this, have incentives to develop their own capabilities to deter, peacefully bargain with, or fight the Soviet Union.
3. *Western Europe-Arab Middle East.* For most of the West Europeans, the oil they obtain from the Middle Eastern producers is vital to the

functioning of their industrial economies, substantially moreso than Middle Eastern oil is vital to the United States. This, obviously, can put them at cross-purposes with the special relationship the United States maintains with Israel.

4. *US-Japan*. US security officials know that the firm US–Japanese security relationship is necessary to dissuade Japan from a future unilateralist course, which could involve an independent Japanese nuclear force and/or unilateral Japanese policies of appeasing the USSR and/or China or the Arabs. To avoid this, the United States is bound to be specially solicitous of Japan's interests in the commercial field—which sets the stage for intense disagreements within the US policy community as Japan's aggressive international economic policies hurt important US industry groups.

5. *US-China*. The Sino-American relationship has come to be regarded as geostrategically essential to both partners as a counterweight to the rivalry each has with the Soviet Union. (The Soviets now have to contemplate a two-front war if they should become embroiled in a major military confrontation with either.) But this special relationship harms the building of other important US relationships in the area—namely, with China's principal regional antagonists, Vietnam and India—and provides greater opportunities for the Soviets to court China's adversaries.

Economic Relationships

1. *The European Community*. The special relationships among the EC countries experience some conflict with their special relationships with the United States, Canada, and other non-EC members of the Atlantic Community. These tensions are inherent in the different bases and reasons-for-being of the European Community and of NATO and are bound to grow with any further progress toward economic integration in the EC.

2. *The Organization of Economic Cooperation and Development (OECD)*. The so-called community of developed nations—including both the memberships of NATO and the EC plus Japan and the rest of the Scandinavians—not only embodies the tensions between the EC and NATO but goes beyond them. While the OECD is less coherent and less institutionally fleshed-out than the EC or NATO, it may prove to be more viable precisely because it encompasses their divergent interests and is premised on the legitimacy of plural special relationships among its various members.

3. *The Developing-Country Coalition*. Often called the "Group of 77," for the number of countries starting the coalition (which now claims

membership of over one-hundred countries), this group is the subcoalition of the Third World countries having the objective of concerting a common front for reforming the international economic order to make it more "just" (see discussion in Chapter 7), and to maximize the bargaining power of the developing countries vis-à-vis the affluent and industrialized countries. The group itself is highly cross-pressured by conflicts of economic interests between those who produce certain commodities (particularly oil) and those who must import these commodities; between coastal states and landlocked states; and between those who have special associations with particular affluent countries and those who do not. Yet the "Group of 77" periodically overcomes its internal differences and closes ranks to bargain tough on behalf of positions very important to some of its subgroups, particularly in universal membership international forums where one-country/one-vote procedures allow it to pass the resolutions it wants.

4. *The Organization of Petroleum Exporting Countries (OPEC)*. Out of the approximately 30 oil-exporting countries, about a third (most of whom are part of the developing-country coalition) belong to OPEC, the purpose of which is to concert their production and pricing policies to maximize their economic returns rather than to let the price of oil and the amount they produce for export be determined by the market forces of supply and demand. When there is a seller's market for petroleum, as during the early 1970s, such a cartel-like concerting of policy can be a very effective bargaining strategy against the petroleum-consuming industrial countries—so effective that some members may try to convert OPEC into an agency for pressing demands on the world having to do with their particular political concerns (such as the Arab-Israeli conflict). But when supplies of energy become more readily available from non-OPEC sources (as happened during the 1980s), differences between the OPEC countries themselves in petroleum industry structure, overall domestic economic regime, and preferred external customers frustrate the organization's ability to hold members to common bargaining positions even on the price of oil.

5. *Western Europe–Eastern Europe/USSR*. The West Europeans earlier and more intensively than the Americans have attempted to move beyond the economic bifurcation of Europe engendered by the cold war. Accordingly, they feel encumbered by close consultative relations with the United States and Canada on East–West trade. The Europeans, often at the price of consternation in Washington, use their independent capabilities for East–West commerce in unilateral bargaining with the Soviets on political and security issues.

6. *Western Europe–Middle East/Africa*. The West Europeans have high

incentives to develop this larger region as their "co-prosperity sphere," within which they have privileged access, not only to petroleum resources but also to lucrative markets, as compared with the North Americans, Japan, and the Soviets. The non-European powers have high incentives to prevent this. However, the Middle Eastern and African countries exploit these Western European incentives, as well as their former colonial status, to gain themselves special privileges in the European Community.

7. *US-Canada-Latin America*. The United States, partly in reaction to the Europeans' efforts to maintain economic preeminence in the Middle East and Africa, wants to preserve its preeminent economic role in the Western Hemisphere. The West Europeans and Japan are likely to find and attempt to exploit countervailing opportunities (largely resulting from Canadian and Latin American resistance to US economic hegemony) to penetrate this hemispheric market.

Cultural Relationships[2]

1. *Pan-Europa*. Efforts to revive a sense of the wider European civilization transcending the ideological divide have great appeal in Eastern and Western Europe (particularly to intellectuals and artists) and are likely to grow as the countries on both sides try to gain more political and economic autonomy from their respective superpower military protectors.

2. *Pan-Germania*. The never-suppressed desire of the German people to make Germany whole again is paradoxically one of the most important generators of East–West cooperation and East–West tension in Europe— potentially causing a rift between each Germany and its cold war allies, a severe repressive backlash against the East Germans by the Soviets, and a unilateral countermove by the West Germans that the United States would be hard pressed not to support. The high risk that such a sequence would provoke World War III underscores the inherent deep conflict of national interests between each superpower and its German client, and the special compatibility of national interests between the superpowers in the very issue that has been at the heart of the cold war.

3. *Scandinavia*. The strong cultural bonds among Scandinavians limits the extent to which Denmark and Norway can be mobilized into a revival of cold war bipolarism (in NATO) and the extent to which Denmark can support further political integration of the European Community. At the same time, it enhances the bargaining power of Norway and Denmark in the Atlantic Community and that of Finland vis-à-vis the USSR. It also puts neutral Sweden in the advantageous role of holder of the Nordic balance between East and West, which strongly constrains Soviet aggressive moves in the region.

4. *French and British ex-colonial ties.* The sustaining by France and Britain of their relationships with their respective ex-colonies is in large measure dependent upon the ability of the metropolitan powers to preserve cultural–linguistic, shared historical connections, and the idea that the cultural factor is of cardinal importance. They are highly motivated to do so because of the economic privileges each gains in their ex-colonial regions and also because their role as representers of the interests of their former wards in the European Community and OECD forums enhances their own bargaining power vis-à-vis the other advanced industrial countries.

5. *Pan-America.* The United States finds the idea of the hemispheric community a convenient counter to the "old worldism" the Europeans use to sustain their intra-European and ex-colonial special relationships. The American hemisphere as a cultural unit, however, is largely mythological—based on a mystical fusion of the obsolescent geopolitics of the Monroe Doctrine, the self-determination movements against Spain, and the love–hate relationship of Latin Americans and Canadians for the United States. Nevertheless, the Canadians and the Latins cooperate in sustaining the myth for purposes of inducing the United States to treat them equitably rather than on the basis of its superior economic and military power, and to support their interests in international forums. The United States, in addition to its economic motives, sustains the myth to counter Soviet attempts to establish new economic and political footholds in the hemisphere.

6. *The transnational Jewish community.* The durable bonds between Jews in the United States, in other countries, and Israel will continue to assure that the United States maintains its strong special relationship with Israel (thus engendering tensions between Arab countries and the United States as well as US tensions with NATO countries that are reluctant to alienate the Arabs). Strong lobbying of the transnationally well-connected Jewish community also assures that the US government will continue to needle the Soviet government on emigration and other human rights problems of Jews in the USSR—this at some cost to a fully amicable Soviet–American detente.

7. *Pan-Arabia.* Despite their internecine feuds, generated by various ethno-religious factionalisms among them (see discussion of Islam below), the Arabs tend to deploy their legions in protective unity (often with added high-tech weapons provided by the Soviets) when one of their numbers is threatened by either the United States or Israel.

8. *Pan-Africa.* Pan-African unity is more of a myth within Africa (see Chapter 10, pp. 206–207) than is Pan-American unity in the Western Hemisphere. But there is a race-conscious transnational dimension to

Pan-Africanism, centering on the persistence of the *apartheid* regime in South Africa, that has forged connections between US blacks, blacks in Britain and France, and blacks in Africa. This new Pan-Africanism has sustained the black nationalist and Third World identity among American blacks, which functioned in the late 1960s and early 1970s primarily as mobilization ideology to stimulate black agitation on American domestic issues. Now it has a more focused transnational purpose and, through its pressure on the US and other governments on the issue of relations with the South African regime, has become an important force in world politics.[3]

Religious Groups

1. *The Roman Catholics.* About an eighth of the world's population identifies with this branch of Christianity, which is organized hierarchically in a world church under the Pope (the bishop of Rome). In some countries, the Church performs social welfare functions for its members that are not adequately performed by secular authorities; sometimes it serves as a protector (or even source) of political movements regarded as subversive of the established political order (as, for example, in contemporary Poland or Nothern Ireland). Through statements by the Pope and councils of bishops, the Church promulgates rules of moral behavior supposed to be binding on all Catholics no matter where in the world they reside, prudently allowing for national cultural variations. Thus, to the extent that moral and political matters overlap (as they frequently do in totalitarian societies, and as they sometimes do even in highly pluralistic societies—as, for example, with respect to birth control policies or the use of nuclear weapons in war), the fact that loyal Catholics are officials or constituents of any of the active political groups surely can affect the way the world polyarchy functions.

2. *Other Christians.* The other large and globally dispersed Christian denominations, claiming overall some 400 million members, are not as hierarchically organized as the Roman Catholics, and thus their role in the polyarchy is more subject to local variation. Often their diversity and decentralized organization does not allow them to mobilize sufficient constituency pressure to have a substantial effect on public policy within large political units, for it is difficult to formulate a common "Christian" position on most issues. In certain localities, however, non-Catholic Christians will constitute a relatively unified force against perceived efforts by Catholics to dominate public policy and elite social roles; and in other places they will unite with Catholics against perceived efforts of non-Christians to ignore Christian values or discriminate against professed Christians.

3. *Islam*. There are about as many Muslims as there are Roman Catholics (approxiately one-eighth of the world's population), most of whom are concentrated in the crescent-shaped region from Morocco on the West Coast of Africa across to the Middle East and Southwest Asia, down into South Asia, and then Indonesia. Professing to be strict followers of the teachings of the seventh century prophet Muhammad as recorded in the *Koran*, the "nation of Islam" is fractionated into numerous sects. The majority, the Sunni, control most of the Arab countries of the Middle East; the largest minority, the Shi'ah (or Shiites), claiming some 20 million adherents, are in control of Iran and, being also in the majority in Iraq, have been attempting to wrest control of the Iraqi government away from its Sunni leadership. The fundamentalist Shiites are agitators in many Muslim lands for the establishment of theocratic states in the model of the Khomeinist regime in Iran and are thus regarded as a subversive transnational threat by many of the modernist secularized regimes in the Muslim world. The Soviet Union, too, having millions of ethnically Turkish peoples in its southern regions who were once (if not still) Muslim, is apprehensive about the transnationally unifying thrust of the fundamentalist Muslim sects, which in part explains the Kremlin's brutal effort to turn Afghanistan into a Soviet satellite nation. Defense of the community of Islam has also been a rallying cry of militant Palestinians (not all of whom really are religious) in their efforts to garner transnational support for their campaign to establish a state for themselves in territory now controlled by Israel.

4. *Judaism*. The force in world politics of the religious aspects of Judaism is now less than its cultural function of emotionally binding the world's 15 million Jews (wherever they may live) to one another's fate and therefore also to the fate of the state of Israel. (See the discussion above of the transnational Jewish community.)

5. *The "Eastern" religions*. The largest of the religions whose followers are concentrated mainly in Asia (the Hinduism of some 500 million South Asians, mostly in India; the various forms of Buddhism practiced by nearly 300 million people distributed throughout the huge triangular area from Thailand to Japan to Indonesia; the more than 200 million Chinese—some of them still in the People's Republic—who adhere to Confucianism or Taoism; and the 60 million or so Japanese believers in Shinto) do affect the domestic social mores and legal systems of many of the countries of the region. But the co-religionists of these Eastern religions rarely act as a transnational political force, with a common set of demands on their respective national governments; nor, as much as do the Christians, Muslims, and Jews, do they cooperate in any substantial way across national boundaries to protect each other against hostile regimes.

Ecologically Interdependent Communities[4]

There are numerous ecologically interdependent communities that are congruent with international political coalitions or subgroupings within them (for example, the countries bordering the Rhine River—almost all of them members of NATO). The following enumeration, however, is especially selected to illustrate the polyarchic, cross-coalition, and transideological scope of some of the world's major ecological regions in which consciousness of interdependent community obligation has been developing despite political antagonisms.

1. *The Mediterranean littoral.* The health and welfare of peoples bordering the Mediterranean are affected by the condition of the ecology of the sea and its coastal areas. The need to control the damaging effects of overly intensive use of this ecosystem is recognized all around and sometimes generates considerable cooperation between countries that are otherwise hostile.

2. *The Baltic.* The ecological condition of the Baltic Sea also needs cooperative husbanding, and this is manifested in mutually obligatory arrangements and commitments of resources for this purpose among the USSR, Finland, Sweden, Denmark, Norway, West Germany, East Germany, and Poland.

3. *The Danube Basin.* Ecological care of the Danube region involves West Germany, Austria, Czechoslovakia, Hungary, Rumania, Bulgaria, and Yugoslavia in a community relationship transcending their ideological divisions.

4. *The Arctic.* The core community of Arctic users—the Soviet Union, Canada, the United States, Iceland, the United Kingdom, Norway, Sweden, and Denmark—are bound to need to cooperate with one another in elaborating rules and institutions for access and exploitation as technology makes the region more usable.

SPECIAL TRANSNATIONAL ACTORS AND ASSOCIATIONS

Already discussed in greater detail in Chapter 9, but here viewed particularly as important facets of the polyarchic mosaic, are the economic enterprises and professional associations that characteristically traverse and link territorially defined political groupings.

To recapitulate briefly: Many transnational corporations are more powerful than the governments of small or medium-sized countries in their ability to provide or withhold valued material goods and services or jobs through which individuals can earn money to buy goods and services. The power of the largest and most active of the transnational enterprises is often felt even in places where they do not operate corporate subsidiaries, since their impact on the global economy can show up locally in reduced or increased demand, supply, and prices of goods and services and jobs.

More and more, specialized professional and occupational groups also are organized across country and ideological lines. Physical scientists, academics in various fields, health care specialists, athletes—all have relatively permanent worldwide professional associations to represent their interests. For some occupational groups, the interests are bread-and-butter issues, and their transnational associations are designed to operate politically on the organs of social and economic policy of the various countries. (This is particularly the case with some labor unions whose members' jobs are dependent upon the decisions of multinational corporations, and who are attempting to strengthen their own capacity to coordinate pressures and bargain globally for job security, higher pay, improved working conditions, and other amenities.)

Once again, the involved individuals—be they top executives of corporate subisidiaries located abroad, international labor union organizers, officers of one of the international scientific associations, or managers of an international telecommunications consortium—are likely to feel cross-pressured by the competing lines of professional and national identification and accountability to which they are subject. But in their multiple loyalties, these increasingly influential men and women are quintessentially of the generation of the emerging polyarchy.

PEACEFUL AND DANGEROUS VARIANTS OF POLYARCHY I

A world polyarchy in which nation-states, subnational groups, and trans-national special interests and communities are all vying for the support and loyalty of individuals, and in which there are no overarching power structures (highly integrated multicountry alliances, or global or regional supranational institutions for conflict resolution) to discipline overly aggressive actors, could evolve in either benign or malign directions. The record of world politics up to now gives more reason to expect the dangerous variant to be the normal condition of the system; but a peaceful variant could prevail, at least in some locales, if there are enough prudent and capable political leaders around who are committed to making it work.

The Peaceful Variant

In the evolving polyarchy, the most influential political entities ought to be those that are major participants in the widest variety of coalitions and joint or multilateral ventures, since they would have the largest supply of usable political currency—in effect, promissory notes for support on one issue in return for support on another. Conversely, threats to withdraw support would serve as negative sanctions.

Power-maximizing countries or groups would want their own pledges of support universally and highly valued; this support could be in the form of access to natural or industrial resources, the provision of financial assets or credits, technical cooperation, or votes in domestic or international decision-making institutions—the latter often being the principal asset in trade of poorer countries lacking sufficient exchangeable material assets.

As in previous systems, power in the form of promises to apply or withhold military force would still be of decisive importance to countries in conflict over vital security interests. But compared with other forms of power, military force often would have little or even negative utility in bargaining over many of the nonsecurity issues around which coalitions will be forming and reforming in the polyarchy; this is because the threat to apply military power would be seen to carry a high risk of devaluing the other bargaining chips in one's possession—alienating the confronting parties to the extent that they dismantle their cooperative projects and withdraw from coalitions to which the other side belongs. Similar disincentives also ought to work against extreme policies of economic coercion, such as the embargo attempted by the Arab oil producers against Israel's supporters in 1973 or efforts by the United States to strangle the economies of Cuba and other Marxist regimes in the Western Hemisphere.

Pairs of countries with few interlocking associations (as, for example, the countries of Western Europe vis-a-vis the countries of Eastern Europe during the heyday of the cold war, or the alienated relations between most Arab countries and Israel) might still be inclined to rely on coercive strategies for deterring their adversaries from hostile acts. But in the polyarchic system, with its elaborate overlapping of interests and coalitions, the most effective international bargainers ought to be those whose opponents on one issue are still their supporters on other issues. If coercive strategies must be resorted to, the prudent polyarchic statesman would nonetheless attempt to conserve his overall store of influence by proffering, withholding, and withdrawing assets well below levels that will lead to total nation-to-nation or coalition-to-coalition hostility.

Such prudential statesmanship would be rooted in domestic and transnational socioeconomic realities. As important economic segments, technologists, scientists, and other professional elite get drawn more deeply into webs of transnational associations of the polyarchy, many of them would develop vested interests in the maintenance of nonhostile relations with their commercial and professional partners in various nations. They thus would not want to see specific clashes of interest inflated into national or multinational causes célèbres. Some of the transnational groups could be expected to mobilize resources across national jurisdictional lines to pressure domestic parliaments and bureaucracies against such an escalation of conflict.[5]

This vision contemplates a rich international and transnational web of associations for bargaining, registering grievances, and threatening sanctions *before* total nation-to-nation hostility develops. The art of diplomacy in such a system would require an understanding of the structure of this web and its interconnections with public authorities and special interest groups, and a knowledge of how to press upon its sensitive nodes to bring about desired community responses. Since there would be more pressure points, there would be fewer reasons to jump from specific grievance to military threat. Of course, to wield effective power benignly in this transnational bargaining system one would have to be well connected with many of the most influential groups in the polyarchy and to be quite affluent in the assets of value to these groups. But to state this condition is also to state why there are likely to be many groups unwilling to limit their political behavior to the nonviolent rules favored by the groups benefiting most from the peaceful variant of polyarchy.

The Unstable and Dangerous Variant

One prognosis for major trouble in the emerging polyarchy proceeds in part from the rather high likelihood that both the breakup of international security alliances and the challenges to the predominance of the institutions of the nation-state are coming about more quickly and extensively in the US-led coalition than in the Soviet-led coalition. This could provide dangerous temptations for an imperialistically inclined Soviet leadership, and its allies and clients in other countries, to stage aggressive fait-accompli power plays (even involving the use of major military force) under the assumption that the United States and its friends are too disorganized to engage in timely counteraction.[6]

Dangers also inhere in the likelihood that in the United States and Western Europe, where the transnational aspects of the polyarchy are developing most rapidly, and in portions of the Third World that become dependent on the technologies and finances of the affluent industrial world, power would gravitate to elements of society largely unaccountable to the wishes of the less-developed, less-mobile elements. The upper transnational tier would probably comprise corporations and professionals in the high-technology fields, and bargaining among these corporate elites would determine the social order. In some fields, these elites may operate within an institutional setting that gives voice to the wishes of the "stockholders" or immediately affected populations. But with few, if any, multinational public structures to ensure general public-interest accountability, the public at large would lose the political power it has slowly acquired through national parliaments, and those corporate entities able to survive the transnational competition would largely run the show. Moreover, there would be no effective institutional framework for settling disagreements among the corporate sectors, as in national parliaments, with intersectoral bargaining put in the hands of representatives of the general public.

In short, the transnational power structures would lack legitimated authority coextensive with their scope of operation, and if opposed they might need to resort to coercion or else give up some of their power. Widespread discontent among the disadvantaged groups would increase the prospects of active conflict, including physical combat and terrorism, against and among the power elite, and contracts and other intergroup commitments would lack stability. If the rudiments of civil society continued to deteriorate, some families and vulnerable groups might be tempted to rely on communal protective societies for minimal physical and psychological security; some might accept the protection of the powerful corporate groups; others might try to form local leagues of mutual assistance. Polyarchy could turn into anarchy, where raw power is the principal social arbiter.

There is yet another evolution of the polyarchic system, however, that could result from active institution-building to assure greater accountability by elements in the system to one another. It is sufficiently different from either of the two variants discussed in this chapter to merit the name Polyarchy II and to warrant a separate chapter.

ENDNOTES

1. Much of the discussion in this chapter is a distillation and synthesis of the material in Part Two. Accordingly, readers seeking additional examples and sources for many of the generalizations put forward here should consult the more detailed discussion and notes in Chapters 3 through 10.

2. On the role of cultural/linguistic sources of affinity in world politics, see F. C. S. Northrop, *The Taming of Nations: A Study in the Cultural Bases of International Policy* (New York: Macmillan, 1952).

3. On Pan-African sentiment and US relations with South Africa, see David A. Dickson, *United States Foreign Policy Toward Sub-Saharan Africa; Change, Continuity, and Constraint* (New York: University Press of America, 1985), pp. 119–127, 149–154.

4. See the discussion of *Environmental Management* in Chapter 13.

5. Similar speculations are found in Karl Deutsch and J. David Singer, "Multipolar Systems and International Stability," *World Politics*, Vol. 16 (April 1964), pp. 390–406; and Robert Cooley Angell, *Peace on the March: Transnational Participation* (New York: Van Nostrand Reinhold, 1969).

6. How the Western democracies might counteract threats from the Soviet Union in a polyarchic world is discussed in Part Four.

CHAPTER THIRTEEN

Toward Polyarchy II

In the preceding chapter, it was observed that the high unpredictability of political relationships in the unregulated polyarchic system (Polyarchy I) could push world politics in the direction of full-blown anarchy, where any group hoping to survive, let alone protect the range of its interests, would seek to acquire independent capabilities for self-defense. In the contemporary world, this might ultimately mean nuclear weapons, or other means of mass destruction and terror, to deter adversaries from intolerable provocations.

Polyarchy I in its dangerous variant, therefore, could be even more dangerous than a totally unregulated nation-state system. In the nation-state system, at least, the population of the world is divided into definable jurisdictions under the authority of sovereign national governments, each responsible for what the people in its jurisdiction do internationally. Deterrent threats directed at such sovereign national governments have a reasonable chance of working.[1] In Polyarchy I, however, the inability of national governments to be in fact sovereign within their jurisdictions, and the existence of many subnational and transnational groups who are accountable only unto themselves, portends a chaotically insecure world—a world in which even weapons of mass destruction might be obtained by groups who aren't squeamish about using terror to achieve their ends and who are too internationally dispersed to be targets of deterrent or retaliatory strategies.

The fate of us all—indeed, the survival of the human species—thus may depend on assuring that the dangerous variant of Polyarchy I does not become the dominant configuration in world politics.

One way to avoid the dangerous variant of Polyarchy I might be to repress or reverse all polyarchic tendencies in the existing system. But if this study is essentially correct in its analysis of how the interplay of old and new forces over the centuries has profoundly shaped the emergence of the contemporary world polity, then efforts to avoid the general condition of polyarchy will be likely to fail, for they will cut too deeply across the grain of the evolved, and still-evolving, modern social fabric.

Another way to avoid the dangerous variant of Polyarchy I is for groups or countries in their strategic interaction and bargaining with one another to rely principally on offerings or withholdings of positive assets rather than on threats of harm and pain. But this leaves too much to the chance that such policies of "enlightened self-restraint" will seem the most strategically efficacious to the important actors on a case-by-case basis. Again, the history of world politics gives little ground for confidence that situations will not emerge that will sorely tempt some of the implicated actors to put the immediate gains to be obtained by treating others badly ahead of the value of durable peace. Often, all it takes is one aggressively brutal actor to transform an otherwise benign system into a system dominated by coercive threats and counterthreats.

The challenge for the would-be enlightened statesmen of the polyarchy is to build durable incentives for the maintenance of positive bargaining and cooperation into the very structure of the system.

This brings us back to perhaps the most crucial theoretical question in the field of international relations, the question that some of the brightest young scholars in the field have returned to in recent years, namely, *under what circumstances will self-interested actors in a world polity lacking a central mechanism for law-making and law-enforcement establish and maintain international regimes of positive coordination and collaboration?*[22] Not surprisingly, the new scholarship has rediscovered that such cooperative international regimes are most likely to be established and adhered to when the anticipated costs to the relevant actors (as perceived by them) of unilateral business-as-usual policies clearly will be greater than the costs (again as perceived by them) of establishing and maintaining cooperative regimes and adhering to their behavioral norms.

With the help of game theory, public goods theory, and analogies with the behavior of profit-maximizing firms in free markets, some of the international regime analysts have found how the unconstrained pursuit of self-interest by states (and/or other actors) in an anarchic (or polyarchic) world will often lead to unnecessarily negative or unsatisfactory outcomes for each of them. But they also have found that learning can and does take place—on the basis of repeatedly experiencing negative outcomes from the egoistic pursuit of maximalist goals, and through obtaining information on rivals' value preferences and strategies—which can and sometimes does result in the negotiation of commitments to settle for suboptimal outcomes, and sometimes in institutions to assure mutual compliance with such commitments.[3]

In short, the polyarchic world—in which significant actors are motivated by self-interest—is not at all inconsistent with relationships of mutual accountability, some of them highly institutionalized. But not all of the essential accountability relationships are likely to grow "naturally" out of the harsh soil of polyarchy. Many of them will have to be *constructed*.

POLITICAL ACCOUNTABILITY AS A GLOBAL NORM

I use the term *Polyarchy II* to describe a constructed configuration of the overall world polity, building on many of the social and material forces present in Polyarchy I. As envisioned, the world would be still polyarchic with respect to group memberships and loyalties but would also be highly pervaded by international and transnational webs of political accountability, many of them global in scope. Political accountability would be the central "norm" of the system in both a sociological and ethical sense—as both descriptor and desideratum. In Polyarchy II, the major actors would normally be constrained by accountability processes and principles; and most of the world's peoples would regard this basic regime as legitimate and morally superior to the available alternatives.

The normative core of the political accountability regime would be the principle that *those whose actions substantially affect the way other people live are answerable to those whom they affect, and normally should act only with the consent of the affected.* Procedurally, this means that the substantially affected populations (or their representatives, as approved by them) would be participants in the decision processes that authorize those actions. Put negatively, internationally significant actions—whether by national governments or subnational governments, nongovernmental groups, transnational organizations, or regional or international institutions—are illegitimate to the extent that those opposing such actions have not been given a fair opportunity to influence the relevant decisions.

This desideratum, of course, begs many important questions: How are the accountability-assuring decision-making processes to be organized, and how will nonstate actors be represented in them? And particularly for the nonstate actors, what groups of people deserve to have representatives seated at the principal tables of decision? On what basis are the various groups to choose their representatives? (Should democratic principles of selecting representatives be insisted upon, or should each population group be permitted its own system of selection?) Which populations are indeed likely to be "substantially affected" and therefore legitimate consent groups in more permanently organized decision-making institutions in particular fields?

Most of the answers to these complex questions cannot be derived directly from the core accountability principle, nor from other standard principles of political or legal philosophy. The answers, as for analogous questions in complex domestic political systems, will have to be worked out through the political bargaining processes among the groups that set up and participate in the regime. But significantly, and in contrast with its predecessor regimes in world politics, the fact that the constitutive principle of Polyarchy II is mutual accountability rather than sovereignty can be expected to have considerable impact on the debates over the legitimacy of alternative decision processes and on the institutions that evolve.

At least one basic institution-building norm, however, is implied already in the accountability principle and ought generally, and in specific fields, to constrain the organizational evolution of Polyarchy II: *Activities and projects with highly interdependent effects should be brought under common institutional roofs*. Such high intersectoral interdependence is particularly evident, for example, in the overlapping fields of industrial development and ecological protection. Relatively specialized bodies could still perform certain functions, but they should be accountable to general policy directives and guidelines set by umbrella institutions. Where interdependent effects are direct and substantial, the specialized interests might be made more accountable to one another and to general public interests by the device of subjecting the budgets of the more specialized agencies to review and final approval by the more general supervisory bodies.

Clearly, a world polity in which political accountability was the core legitimizing principle would feature—given the thickening and intertwining of horizontal interdependence (place to place) and vertical interdependence (sector to sector) in contemporary society—a dense web of multifunctional/multilateral institutions, some regionally concentrated, but many organized on a global scale. Whether, when, and how such a world polity might evolve further into some kind of "world state" cannot be anticipated from our current vantage point. That question could well become a matter of significant political debate *after* the emergence of Polyarchy II.

The urgent normative and practical issues in the current world polity have to do with how to manage the emergent polyarchy so as to assure the healthy survival of the human species. The analysis in these pages has suggested that this means exploring ways of building Polyarchy II.

SOME PRELIMINARY SCAFFOLDING

Fortunately, Polyarchy II does not have to be constructed on totally unprepared ground. There are numerous accountability relationships (some of them rather elaborately institutionalized) already in place, which enlightened statesmen since the early nineteenth century have felt it necessary to construct to moderate and stabilize the workings of the balance of power in the nation-state system. (See Chapter 2.)

Existing accountability relationships on which and between which new accountability connections can be built and institutionalized are most evident in the fields of international commerce, environmental management, and international transportation and communications. In each of these fields there are often obvious "positive sum" cooperative alternatives to the absolute losses to be suffered by all parties if they persist in unregulated unilateral behavior. Some preliminary scaffolding also exists in the security field, where mutual-gain accountability relationships among mistrustful adversaries are very difficult to institutionalize, but where the incentives are high owing to the realization that the consequences of unconstrained power-plays, arms races, and war can be disastrous.[4]

Trade and Monetary Regimes

In the commercial fields, important mutual accountability structures that can be built upon are already in place, in the form of the General Agreement on Tariffs and Trade (GATT) and the International Monetary Fund (IMF). The accountability obligations countries have undertaken in the GATT and IMF do not represent any kind of altruistically motivated responsibility; rather, the abandonment of pure unilateralism, the acceptance of general rules, and the obligation to participate in multilateral consultative and decision processes is the product of the widespread belief that the catastrophic worldwide depression of the 1930s (which in many ways helped bring on World War II) was the consequence of the preexisting international anarchy in trade and monetary relations, and that without a substantial regime of mutual accountability such a catastrophe or worse could again occur.

But these two pillars of the post-World War II accountability regime have been severely shaken and eroded by many of the polyarchic forces of the period—the centrifugal pulls against cold war unity, the decline of US hegemony, the rise of the social-welfare state, the interpenetration of national economies by transnational enterprises and financial networks, and the reactive growth of national protectionism—to the point where, without new supportive institution-building, their capacity to prevent the recrudescence of dangerous unilateralism is doubtful.

The GATT regime.   The mutual accountability norm is the essence of the GATT, reflected in its rules of reciprocity and nondiscrimination and embodied in its multilateral negotiations and dispute-resolution procedures for removing barriers to free trade across national borders. *Reciprocity* means that measures adopted by countries to affect their trade, whether bilateral or multilateral, are to be internationally coordinated so that they are "mutually advantageous." The *nondiscrimination* rule, as stipulated in the General Agreement of 1947, requires that "any advantage, favor, privilege or immunity granted by any contracting party to any product originating or destined for any other country shall be accorded immediately and unconditionally to the like product originating in or destined for the territories of all other contracting parties." (The

GATT allows some exceptions to this most-favored-nation rule of equal treatment when trade barriers are removed among partners in a customs union or free trade association and when special preferences are given to purchases from the developing countries.)[5]

The impact of the polyarchic trends on the GATT regime is registered in (1) the increasing unilateral resort to nontariff barriers by countries to protect their weak economic sectors from foreign import competition; (2) the rise of discriminatory trading arrangements among particular groups of countries; (3) the reluctance of most of the Third World countries to join the GATT; and (4) the decay of the GATT procedures of dispute settlement.[6]

The Tokyo Round of GATT trade negotiations, concluded in 1979, concentrated on nontariff barriers but was by and large a weak adaptation to the threats to the regime, rather than a concerted reaffirmation of its basic free trade principles.[7] Yet even in their accommodation to the new protectionism, the governments represented at the Tokyo Round—by the very fact of their meeting and jointly legitimating various realistic exceptions to free trade and endorsing procedures to assure that the implementation of these exceptions would be reciprocal—did preserve and reassert their obligation to be multilaterally accountable.

The IMF system.   The formalized accountability of the governments of nation-states to one another in their official international trade policies is only one dimension of the problem of achieving accountability between societies for what they do to each other economically. The ability of a society to pay for what it needs to purchase to sustain its values is highly dependent upon the money at its disposal and its exchange value in the international market. As shown in Chapter 9, not only countries, but private banks and investors in control of huge sums of money, by moving their money around or changing its exchange value, can make or break virtually overnight the financial condition of the less powerful; they also risk paralyzing the commercial markets on which the powerful themselves depend for their own prosperity. Aware of this, and not wanting a repeat of the irresponsible monetary practices that exacerbated the Great Depression, the economic statesmen who designed the post-World War II monetary regime provided for a degree of mutual accountability heretofore regarded as inconsistent with national sovereignty.

The forty-four countries meeting at Bretton Woods, New Hampshire, in 1944, in establishing the International Monetary Fund (IMF) and the International Bank for Reconstruction and Development (IBRD, or World Bank), in effect set up a central bank for the international system and agreed to be bound by mutually agreed-upon rules for controlling the international exchange value of their respective currencies.

Some of the rules fashioned at Bretton Woods have not survived—most consequentially, the original agreement for a system of fixed exchange rates—leading to the oft-heard observation that the Bretton Woods system has been scuttled. As put by one observer, "Exchange rates of major currencies are no longer pegged; they float. Currency reserves are no longer convertible into gold; they are inconvertible. And the main source of balance-of-payments financing is no longer the IMF but private banking institutions."[8]

But the basic world monetary institutions of the system, while flimsy and battered, are intact, and their functions are being continually elaborated. Their very precariousness has been a stimulus to urgent attempts to buttress them against the forces that threaten to totally collapse the system; namely, the largely unmonitored movement of vast sums of money across national borders by nongovernmental commercial institutions (multinational banks and multinational corporations); the adoption of unilateral "monetarist" policies by national governments (manipulations of the supply of money, interest-rate management, governmental borrowing) to control inflation and recession; and competitive alterations in the exchange value of national currencies (and associated speculative surges in the international money markets) to counteract balance-of-trade and balance-of-payments deficits.[9]

Efforts to preserve international accountability in the monetary field have included: multilateral agreements to constrain market-determined exchange rates within stipulated ranges; commitments to refrain from unilateral (meaning prior to consultation with other members of the IMF) currency devaluations and related mercantilist policies; expansion of the Special Drawing Rights (SDRs) the IMF can issue for balance-of-payments support; at least a symbolic assumption of collective responsibility at the prime-ministerial level of the Big Seven monetary powers—the United States, the United Kingdom, France, West Germany, Japan, Italy, and Canada—through the institution of annual seven-nation "summits" devoted largely to their common economic problems; the more regular use of the IMF consultative machinery at the level of financial ministries or directors of national central banks by various subgroups of members (The Group of Ten, The Group of Twenty, etc.); and in general expanding the opportunities for developing-country participation in IMF deliberations, particularly on the subjects of balance-of-payments support and international debt.

The accountability process in the present internatioanl monetary system, however, remains more consultative than collaborative (despite frequent bursts of high-blown rhetoric about monetary cooperation), and more ad hoc than would seem to be required to institutionalize efficient, let alone equitable, public-interest control over the money markets of the world.

From the vantage point of the latter 1980s, having experimented for some fifteen years with a much looser international monetary regime than contemplated in the original Bretton Woods agreement, experienced public officials and corporate executives seem more ready to grant the truth of Richard Cooper's judgment (offered in 1972) that

> the model regime which we implicitly use at present—autonomous and purposeful nation-states in harmonious and unrestricted economic intercourse, through the competitive market place...governed by occasional treaties and conventions to assure good conduct and to iron out modest problems of overlapping jurisdiction, leaving virtually all economic decisions to national governments—is simply not viable in the long run.[10]

Cooper's judgment has now become the conventional elite wisdom and is echoed in the words of the 1985 edition of a widely used and respected college text on international political economy: "If interdependence is to be managed, it will require new forms of international authority that assume responsibility once thought to be the prerogative of national government."[11]

Prescriptions for building on the framework of the IMF and GATT institutions, even with the support of the emerging elite consensus that major new acts of construction are necessary, will not be easy to implement. It is still electorally risky in the industrial democracies for political leaders in locally or nationally oriented constituencies to endorse such supranational institutions as are needed to share in the performance of functions still primarily under the authority of the nation-state—namely, economic stabilization, taxation to provide public goods and services, regulatory policies concerning business and unions, and redistributional policies. Moreover, the countries professing adherence to Marxist concepts of political economy and the countries of the Third World, despite their growing demands to participate in international decisions affecting the world economy, lack even the beginnings of an elite consensus in support of allowing their own countries to be bound by decisions of supranational institutions. Ways of cultivating the needed receptivity are discussed in Part Four.

International Obligations and Institutions for Promoting Economic Development

Some preliminary scaffolding also exists on which more substantial structures of political accountability could be built between the affluent and economically disadvantaged elements of world society.

But the rudiments of such "North–South" political accountability are found largely outside of the GATT/IMF/World Bank institutions which, while important as agencies for resource transfers to the developing countries, are run ("noblesse oblige") by the affluent industrialized societies of North America, Western Europe, and Japan. The charters and voting rules of this triumvirate of international economic institutions assure that in any of their important deliberations the affluent will make the decisions. There have been some membership enlargements and procedural modifications in each of the three principal organizations and various of their specialized committees to provide more opportunity for the developing countries to register their concerns and propose policies—to take the demands of the disadvantaged "into account," as it were—but not to the extent that the affluent countries' controlling decision powers would be diminished.

The evolution of more than token political accountability by the minority of affluent countries to the disadvantaged majority has been anticipated in two types of institutions: (1) the universal (or near universal) membership bodies of the United Nations and its regional and specialized functional offshoots where each country has one vote, or where other voting and bargaining procedures are designed to facilitate real influence on decisions by the affected as well as by those who possess the material resources; and (2) the bargaining arrangements established between special sets of materially interdependent countries and/or economic sectors in which the affluent have come to realize that their own well-being requires the uncoerced cooperation of the disadvantaged.

UNCTAD. The prototype of the universal-membership North–South accountability arrangement is the United Nations Conference on Trade and Development (UNCTAD). Convened in 1964, after the Third World countries achieved numerical control of the UN General Assembly—the authorizing body—UNCTAD, subsequently institutionalized as a regular UN organization with its own secretariat, became the principal forum through which the developing-country coalition confronted the industrialized countries with demands for a new international economic order responsive to the needs of the developing countries as they themselves defined them. (See Chapter 7 for a discussion of the substance of these demands and the industrialized-country responses.) Had the most ambitious hope of the founders of UNCTAD been realized—namely, that it would become the legitimating body for all policies that substantially affected the economic well-being of the developing countries—a true North–South political accountability system might have emerged. But precisely because this political implication was inherent in its structure, the affluent countries (with a few exceptions such as Sweden, The Netherlands, and Canada) downgraded UNCTAD's status by having relatively low-level functionaries represent them at its meetings and generally dismissed its resolutions as expressions of Third World opinion and not the products of genuine North–South bargaining.

To compensate for the affluent-country downgrading of UNCTAD and UNCTAD-sponsored resolutions that are endorsed by the General Assembly and other universal membership bodies, the developing-country coalition and influential nongovernmental supporters of greater North–South accountability (most notably the Brandt Commission) have been calling for global economic "summits" at the heads-of-government level, involving at least the principal northern and southern countries. These summit meetings hopefully would spawn and give legitimacy to a series of global negotiations on the substance of the developing-country demands for a new international economic order. One such summit was hosted by the President of Mexico in Cancun in 1981 and was attended by most of the heads of government of the major industrial countries including an initially reluctant President Reagan—who finally agreed to attend at the strong urging of Canadian Prime Minister Pierre Elliot Trudeau. Surprisingly, the American president (perhaps influenced by the global media spotlight on this high-level extravaganza) joined his counterparts in accepting the idea of global negotiations on the demands of the poor countries but, along with Prime Minister Margaret Thatcher of Britain and Chancellor Helmut Schmidt of West Germany, refused to become part of the consensus that such negotiations should be under the aegis of UN bodies, where each country has one vote. These three Western leaders made it clear that as far as they were concerned, no substantive international decisions by General Assembly-type forums could overrule the policies of the IMF, the World Bank, or the GATT.[12] The final Cancun communique reflected this standing North–South impasse. The idea of global North–South summits and negotiations was revived in the Brandt Commission's 1983 report *Common Crisis* but as yet has not resulted in the reconvening of such a forum.[13]

The Law of the Sea.   The closest approximation to Third World visions of a universal accountability system in which each country would have equal voting weight on international economic matters affecting all countries was the decade-long UN Conference on the Law of the Sea. As put by Stephen Krasner,

> The ability of developing countries to secure an international treaty that embodied their preferred principals and norms was facilitated by a decision-making structure that proved equal, formal access for all states, and which gave many Third World States entree to the private, specialized negotiating groups where the text was actually formulated. Such an arrangement would have been unthinkable in the nineteenth century, when the major maritime nations set and enforced rules for the ocean.[14]

The resulting Convention on the Law of the Sea, signed in 1982 by more than one-hundred countries, in some of its provisions perpetuates this "democratization" of the international political regime, which is one of the main reasons that the government of the United States, under the Reagan administration, refused to sign the Convention.

Especially objectionable to the Reagan administration, but for many of the Third World countries the symbolic centerpiece of the new ocean regime, was the International Sea-Bed Authority established to manage the exploitation of mineral nodules on the floor of the deep ocean. The Law of the Sea treaty holds these resources, being beyond national jurisdiction, to be "the common heritage of mankind" and therefore must be managed by and for the benefit of the community of nations as a whole—which according to the distributive justice norms of the Third World coalition means for the particular benefit of the most economically needy countries.

The International Sea-Bed Authority itself (acting through its "Enterprise"), along with public agencies of the member governments and private corporations, is given authority to exploit the resources of the deep seabed. If a corporation or agency other than the international Enterprise finds an appropriate mining site, the site must be divided in two parts, from which the Enterprise decides which half it will exploit and which will be left to the private corporation or agency to exploit. The International Sea-Bed Authority will also receive a percentage of the profits gained by all exploiters for redistribution to the poor countries on an equitable basis as determined by the Authority.[15]

All countries party to the Law of the Sea treaty are members of the International Sea-Bed Authority and have one vote in its Assembly, "the supreme organ." The Assembly selects the thirty-six member Council whose responsibility it is to make the more specific decisions about seabed exploitation subject to the approval of the Assembly. The treaty stipulates that the seats in the Council shall be allocated as follows: (1) four seats to countries that are large consumers of metals, one of which must be from Eastern Europe; (2) four seats to countries that are major investors in nodule exploitation, including again one from Eastern Europe; (3) four seats to land-based producers of the metals likely to be mined from the deep seabed, two of which must be developing countries; (4) six seats to developing countries with "special interests" (such as being landlocked or having large populations); and (5) eighteen seats to countries from the world's various geographic regions. All in all, the voting rules in the Council and Assembly assure that the major industrialized countries, even if acting in concert, could not determine the Sea-Bed Authority's policies, nor would they have sufficient numbers be able to legally block many types of substantive decisions.

How the International Sea-Bed Authority will actually function, however, remains in considerable doubt, given the refusal of the United States and some of its allies to subscribe to the treaty and their announced determination to work out rules among themselves for exploiting lucrative sites.

The Lomé Convention. Accountability relationships betwen particular sets of economically interdependent Northern and Southern countries is typified by the negotiations between the countries of the European Community and sixty-three countries in Africa, the Caribbean, and the Pacific—mostly former colonies of the EC countries—to accord these developing countries special marketing privileges in the European Common Market and to provide them with special financial help. Under the basic terms agreed to at Lomé in 1975 (and amended in 1979), all manufactured goods and 96 percent of the agricultural goods produced by this subset of developing countries can enter the European Common Market tariff-free and quota-free. No formal tariff-elimination reciprocity is required of the developing countries toward imports from the EC countries (the EC countries grant that their former colonial wards may need to protect their infant industries during the process of development), but preferential treatment to the EC is accorded in many ways, from the facilitation of investments and the location of corporate subsidiaries to the processing of import license requests. In addition, the Lomé Convention obligates the EC countries to provide export stabilization support to the developing-country members under negotiated formulas specifying levels of transfer payments to be made to countries whose export earnings fall below a certain percentage of their gross national product.[16]

Commodity price-stabilization agreements.   The industrial and developing countries have gone part of the way demanded by the "Group of 77" in negotiating minimum price levels at which the consumer countries will agree to purchase the designated primary product and support the maintenance of "buffer stocks" if its price on the international market falls below that level. Such commodity agreements, with provision for implementing processes, have been agreed to for coffee, tin, rubber, olives, sugar, wheat, and cocoa. The developing countries have been unsuccessful in obtaining "indexing" agreements, however, that would mandate a rise in the prices of primary commodities proportionate to price increases in the industrial sector. (See Chapter 7 for a fuller discussion of this North–South issue.)

In 1980, a three-year negotiation under UNCTAD auspices succeeded in representative industrial and developing countries' signing The Articles of Agreement for a Common Fund to finance the purchasing of buffer stocks across primary various commodity fields, but as of 1987 the Common Fund Agreement had failed to gain sufficient ratifications to enter into force.[17]

Arms Control

Even between the two military superpowers—who in Polyarchy I remain political adversaries and whose military arsenals still are designed primarily to deter or fight against each other—some mutual accountability arrangements have been instituted with respect to the size and contents of their military arsenals and the testing and deployment of particular kinds of weapons. Moreover, they have collaborated in fashioning in the Nuclear Nonproliferation Treaty (NPT) what is potentially the embryo of a more fully developed security system for a Polyarchy II world.

The SALT regime. The Strategic Arms Limitation Talks (SALT) of the 1970s and the agreements they produced—the 1972 Treaty on the Limitation of Anti-Ballistic Missile Systems, the 1972 Interim Agreement on the Limitation of Strategic Offensive Arms, and the unratified Strategic Arms Limitation Treaty of 1979—were specific expressions of the shared recognition by the United States and the Soviet Union that a nuclear war between them would be suicidal for both of them, but there were many weapons in their respective arsenals (existing and prospective) that might well make such an insane war more likely. In agreeing to observe specified quantitative and qualitative limits in particular categories of strategic weapons, and in setting up a Standing Consultative Commission staffed by technical experts from each side to develop procedures for compliance and to hear complaints of noncompliance, the two governments established the principle that they are answerable to each other for much of what they do in the strategic weapons field.

Forbearance regimes for the "Commons." The superpowers also are party to a number of multilateral agreements to keep weapons or particular types of weapons out of Antarctica, the international areas of the seabed, and outer space and celestial bodies, and to subject their activities in these commons areas to a certain amount of multilateral or adversarial inspection to verify compliance:

- Under the Antarctica Treaty, all military deployments and activities, including weapons tests, are banned from the frozen continent; and all of the contracting parties have access to all areas of the continent to carry out inspections to verify compliance with these prohibitions. Argentina, Australia, New Zealand, the United Kingdom, and the United States have all exercised the right of inspection (including substantial inspection of Soviet facilities).[18] The treaty also provides that any disputes arising out of the countries' access to or use of Antarctica that cannot be resolved by direct talks, mediation, arbitration, or other peaceful means are to be referred to the International Court of Justice.

- The Treaty on Principles Governing the Activities of States in the Exploration and Use of Outer Space, Including the Moon and Other Celestial Bodies, signed in 1967, affirms that these areas are not subject to national appropriation by claim or sovereignty, occupation, or any other means; and it commits the parties not to place in orbit around the Earth, install on the moon or any other celestial body, or otherwise station in outer space nuclear or any other weapons of mass destruction. The treaty also prohibits the use of the moon and other celestial bodies for establishing military bases, installations, or fortifications; testing weapons of any kind; or conducting military maneuvers. And on the moon and other celestial bodies all stations, installations, equipment, and space vehicles are to be open to inspection (with prior notice) to all parties to the treaty.[19]

- The Treaty on the Prohibition of the Emplacement of Nuclear Weapons and Other Weapons of Mass Destruction on the Seabed and the Ocean Floor and the Subsoil Thereof, signed in 1971, provides that parties to the treaty shall have the right to verify compliance with the treaty's prohibitions through observing all activities of other states on the seabed and ocean floor provided the observation does not interfere with such activities. If states are unable to resolve one another's doubts about such activities, the treaty suggests (but does not mandate) that the matter should be referred to the UN Security Council.[20]

Confidence-building measures. The 32 European signatories, plus the Soviet Union, the United States, and Canada, agreed in 1975 under the auspices of the Conference on Security and Cooperation in Europe (the Helsinki Accords) to provide advance notification of substantial military maneuvers and to exchange observers of such maneuvers. The Helsinki measures were elaborated and expanded in the 1986 Stockholm agreement.[21] Some notifications of troop movements have been provided, and there have been a few instances when observers from the adversary camp have been present at maneuvers.

Starting with the 1963 Soviet–American agreement, after the Cuban missile crisis, to establish the "Hotline" direct communications link between the White House and the Kremlin, there have been a series of rather fruitful negotiations between the two superpowers on means to avoid accidents or miscalculation that might result in nuclear war. These negotiations have produced:

- The 1971 Accidental Measures Agreement, which requires each side to notify the other in advance of missile launches beyond its territory and to immediately inform one another of any incident (such as the possible accidental or unauthorized detonation of nuclear weapons) that could cause the outbreak of nuclear war.
- The 1971 agreement upgrading the Hotline with two space-satellite communications circuits.
- The 1972 Incidents at Sea Agreement, firming up navigational rules and notification procedures for preventing collisions at sea and actions that might endanger their ships or aircraft.
- The 1985 agreement (with Japan as a third principal party) improving safety measures on air routes in the North Pacific.

There also has been continuing dialogue between the Soviet–American technical groups attached to their various bilateral arms negotiations forums on means of improving timely information exchanges on missile launches, military exercises, and other potentially threatening moves.[22] President Reagan and General Secretary Gorbachev in their 1985 summit called for the establishment of jointly staffed "nuclear risk-reduction centers" to be located in Washington and Moscow, which would be in continuous communication with each other.[23] In 1987 US and Soviet negotiators agreed to set up these centers, but not yet with joint staffing.

The NPT regime. In the peace and security field, the most ambitious step taken toward a Polyarchy II world (since the cold war and then the recent ascendancy of polyarchic forces precluded turning the United Nations into a genuine collective security system) has been the Nuclear Nonproliferation Treaty (NPT) of 1968. With respect to the structure of world politics, the NPT is of potentially greater significance than the bilateral agreements between the United States and the Soviet Union for limiting strategic weapons, which can only codify and reinforce the military dimensions of the superpower standoff. The NPT is a renewal of an attempt (started in 1946 and dropped with the failure of the Baruch Plan) to adapt the world political system to meet the threat of nuclear weapons.

The NPT is an extraordinary bargain between, on the one side, three of the five countries possessing nuclear weapons and, on the other side, some 124 of the 160 countries that do not have nuclear weapons. It provides that the "have not" countries will forego acquiring nuclear weapons in return for receiving substantial assistance from the nuclear "have" countries in developing their own peaceful nuclear energy programs. The signatory countries with nuclear weapons are obligated by Article I of the treaty not to transfer nuclear weapons or materials that could be converted into nuclear weapons to any nonnuclear weapon country. The signatories without nuclear weapons are obligated by Article II not to accept any such transfers nor any other assistance in the manufacture of nuclear weapons.

Article III is the centerpiece of the NPT. It obligates each nonweapon signatory to negotiate a specially tailored "safeguards" agreement with the International Atomic Energy Agency (IAEA) to assure, primarily through inspection by the IAEA, that there is no diversion of nuclear energy or materials from peaceful uses to nuclear weapons or other explosive devices. The nuclear supplier countries also are obligated by Article III to subject their transferred nuclear material and equipment to IAEA safeguards.

The nuclear "have" signatories are obligated by Articles IV and V to "the fullest possible exchange of equipment, materials and scientific information for the peaceful uses of nuclear energy...with due consideration for the needs of the developing areas of the world." And in Article VI the nuclear powers further promise to pursue negotiations leading toward the cessation of the nuclear arms race and eventually general and complete disarmament.[24]

But the NPT, like the other components of the scaffolding from which a Polyarchy II system might be built, is in need of substantial strengthening if it is not to come tumbling down under the stress of material and social forces now battering it. More and more countries are acquiring a nuclear industrial base capable of producing weapons-grade material. At least five nonsignatory countries suspected of ambition to join the ranks of nuclear-armed countries (Israel, South Africa, India, Pakistan, Argentina, and perhaps Brazil) are operating unsafeguarded facilities (not subject to IAEA inspection) that can produce weapons-grade material. Some countries, even though parties to the NPT, appear to be highly motivated to acquire nuclear weapons (Iraq, for example, whose large French-supplied research reactor was destroyed by Israeli bombers in 1981; and Libya, which, although lacking the required industrial/ technological infrastructure to produce effective nuclear weapons, is known to have been shopping in the world market for either ready-made weapons or ready-made weapons-production facilities, including technical teams to operate them).[25]

To avert a runaway expansion in numbers of nuclear-weapons countries by the early twenty-first century, the central accountability mechanism—the IAEA or some functional equivalent—will need, at a minimum, to be accorded enhanced rights of inspection of all nuclear facilities. Optimally, suppliers of nuclear weapons materials and power-plant components would agree to funnel all such transfers through the IAEA and would empower that institution to tie all peaceful-use transfers to a recipient's faithful adherence to the letter and spirit of the NPT. But the prospects for any strengthening of the NPT regime, let alone a major enhancement of IAEA powers, appear to be slim unless (as the have-not countries have been insisting at periodic NPT review conferences) the nuclear superpowers demonstrate, through their own substantial nuclear disarmament, that they no longer believe nuclear weapons are a useful means of protecting or advancing national interests. (See the discussion in Chapter 14 on preventing nuclear holocaust for suggestions on how this objective might be pursued.)

Transportation and Communication Regimes

The need to establish "rules of the road" to handle the increasingly congested traffic on the oceans, in the air, and on broadcasting frequencies has led to an abandonment of completely open access, free-use regimes for the international routes and media of transportation and communication. The proliferation of uses and users has also necessitated a certain amount of international intrusion into domestic regimes for regulating transportation and communication where domestic activities can affect foreign users' equitable and safe access to commonly used areas or resources. International institutions designed to minimize unnecessary clashes and confrontation and even to allocate scarce (or preferred) resources in these fields are nothing new, but an expansion of their functions and enforcement powers, and in some cases a reform of their decision processes, is required to meet the accountability requirements of a Polyarchy II world.

The International Maritime Organization (IMO) is the world's organization of ocean shippers—governments, corporations, and cartels—through which the shippers agree on common criteria for licensing carriers and setting rates and on common standards of maritime safety, navigational efficiency, and the control of marine pollution from ships. Accountability to coastal interests, particularly those suffering from ship-caused pollution, has been provided to some extent in recent years by institutional and rule-making modifications to provide the coastal interests more of a voice in IMO deliberations.[26]

The International Civil Aviation Organization (ICAO) is the international instrumentality through which governments establish uniform standards and practices to assure safety (including security from hijacking), to set limitations to control noise, and to provide for the well-being and convenience of passengers. A member unable to implement established ICAO standards and procedures is obligated to notify the Organization, which then disseminates this information to all members.[27] It was under the aegis of ICAO that a detailed multinational experts' investigation was conducted of the circumstances resulting in the Soviets shooting down in 1983 of a Korean Airlines passenger airplane; and it was this ICAO investigation that led to the issuance by ICAO of improved guidelines for signaling and communications from aircraft to aircraft and between aircraft and ground control so as to avoid such fatal mistakes.[28]

Worldwide regulation of the use of the principal natural resources used in electronic communications—the electromagnetic frequency spectrum and, with the increasing role of space-satellites, the geostationary orbit—is the responsibility of the 100-year-old International Telecommunication Union (ITU). Over the years, this organization has developed a complex array of institutional and standard setting arrangements making for a fairly high degree of international accountability in the use of these resources. The ITU is a prototypical Polyarchy II institution, for it involves not only governments but also other entities. Private operating agencies in the communications field and scientific and industrial organizations play an important role in the ad hoc working or study groups of ITU consultative committees and, because of the complex and technical nature of modern telecommunications, tend to exercise major influence on the recommendations of the consultative committees and on the formal decisions of ITU regulatory boards.

The periodic World Administrative Radio Conference (WARC) of the ITU, because of its role in assigning frequencies and slots in the preferred orbit for communications satellites, has become the arena of intense bargaining between the advanced space powers and countries who hope someday to have their own satellites deployed in space. At the 1985 WARC, the more than one-hundred countries represented agreed to the principle of "equitable" access to the geostationary orbit and also to a procedure that would allow countries not now possessing satellites to reserve positions on that orbit in advance. It was also agreed that the WARC scheduled for 1988 would make such specific orbital-slot allocations.[29]

Environmental Management

The need for political accountability norms and institutions among major actors in the global polyarchy—whether they be national governments, private corporations, or multilateral agencies—is nowhere more evident than in the "environmental" field, where interlinked ecologies whose continued integrity is essential for healthy human existence traverse virtually all of the political–legal jurisdictions that human communities have constructed. As shown in Chapter 10, recent and contemporary innovations in science and technology have not only exacerbated the problem (by providing humans with the wherewithal to produce large perturbations in the natural environment), but they have also provided the tools for gaining information and understanding of the complicated ecological interdependencies that sustain human life on this planet.

Limited progress has been made since the late 1960s, in response to the growing awareness of transnational ecological interdependencies, to ensure that those responsible for each other's living environment *in fact* are responsible *in law*. Most of the countries of the world and many nongovernmental organizations attended the 1972 UN Conference on the Human Environment. A consciousness-raising event, rather than a negotiating forum, the Stockholm conference hatched no treaties, but it did produce ringing declarations affirming mutual accountability across national lines (qualified by Third World insistence on the right of sovereign countries to develop their own domestic resources) and led to the creation of a permanent world environment agency.

The new global agency, the United Nations Environmental Program (UNEP), with a 58-member Governing Council and a Secretariat lodged at Nairobi, Kenya, is mandated by the UN General Assembly to study, monitor, and report on threats to the international environment of broad international significance, and to facilitate international cooperation in all matters affecting the human environment. To these ends, the UNEP was accorded some authority to initiate its own environmental programs and to finance and review those of other specialized UN agencies such as the Food and Agriculture Organization, the World Health Organization, the International Maritime Organization, and the International Atomic Energy Agency.[30] However, precisely because the objectives of the UNEP overlap, and in some respects clash (as, for example, concerning the use of fertilizers and pesticides) with the programs of these other specialized agencies, the hoped-for interagency cooperation has fallen far short of the goals of the founders of the UNEP, and the UN General Assembly has not provided the UNEP with sufficient financial resources or specific coordinating authority to implement its mandate adequately.[31]

Despite the resistance of established institutions to according environmental interests greater political and legal clout, constituencies dependent upon the sustained health of particular ecologies have been translating their growing awareness into lobbying pressure on national governments and multilateral agencies. These pressures are sure to grow in the decades ahead and to provide a sociopolitical base for constructing Polyarchy II institutions more congruent with the patterns of ecological interdependence. Meanwhile, some concerned constituencies already have moved their national governments to negotiate numerous environmental accountability arrangements with other countries, such as:

- the 1973 International Convention for the Prevention of Pollution from Ships (with 1978 amendments)
- the 1974 Paris Convention for the Prevention of Marine Pollution from Land-Based Sources
- the 1979 Economic Commission for Europe Treaty on Long-Range Transboundary Air Pollution
- the 1979 Convention for the Conservation of Migratory Species
- the 1980 Protocol for the Protection of the Mediterranean Sea Against Pollution from Land-Based Sources
- the 1981 Convention for the Protection of the South-East Pacific Region Against Pollution
- the 1981 Convention for the Protection of the West and Central African Region Against Pollution
- the 1983 Convention for the Protection of the Greater Caribbean Region Against Pollution
- the 1985 and 1987 Conventions for the Protection of the Ozone Layer[32]

Most of the progress in institutionalizing environmental accountability has been by groups of countries in a particular region using a common water resource, such as the various international fisheries commissions (e.g., the International Pacific Salmon Fisheries Commission and the Mixed Commission for Black Sea Fisheries);[33] the International Commission for the Protection of the Rhine Against Pollution (whose monitoring capabilities were strengthened considerably after a November 1986 fire in a Swiss chemical plant spewed 30 tons of toxic substances into the Rhine); the Danube Commission; the River Niger Commission; the Joint Canadian–American Boundary Commission; and the Mediterranean Action Plan. Some of the agreements have been generated entirely by the local states, but many have been stimulated and sponsored by the UNEP's program for controlling regional pollution.[34]

The Mediterranean Action Plan (called the Med Plan) has become the model for such UNEP-sponsored regional accountability agreements. All the littoral states, except Albania, have been involved in the negotiations and are signatories to a set of interlocking conventions to monitor and abate land-source and sea-source pollution and to coordinate research and planning to deal with these problems. They all also contribute administrative and budgetary support, supplemented by funds from the UNEP itself, to a modest secretariat staffed with personnel from the member countries.[35]

The Med Plan—which in less than a decade's operation has reversed the standard prognosis by environmentalists that the Mediterranean's death was imminent (see discussion in Chapter 9 on marine and river ecosystems)—is a striking example of how creative statesmanship can turn the complexities of Polyarchy I into a Polyarchy II accountability system: The Med Plan's co-operating membership comprises sets of states that are ordinarily politically antagonistic toward each other (Israel and the Arabs, Egypt and Libya, Turkey and Greece, Algeria and Morocco), and others that normally favor very different approaches to the role of environmental considerations in economic development (France and Italy as industrialized members of the European Community vs. Algeria as a leading "Group of 77" militant). Sensitive to these antagonisms, the UNEP Secretariat injected itself into the negotiating process to divert, modulate, and buffer them—using financial side-payments and promises of special technical assistance to some parties; cultivating consensus among the scientists from the various countries who would then act as a lobby on their governments; and inducing certain countries (Israel, in particular) to assume a low profile in the negotiations so as to avoid contaminating the growing incentives to cooperate in the environmental field with highly sensitive but extraneous political issues.

It is not the intention here to make too much of the amount of international collaboration, let alone institution-building, that has been attained in the environmental/ecological field. Even in the fisheries commissions, in which the ecological interdependencies are also near-term economic welfare issues for the involved populations and there is a shared recognition that everyone will lose if unregulated competition leads to resource depletions below sustainable yields, efforts to institutionalize authoritative rule-making and rule-enforcement procedures congruent with the natural and economic interdependencies still run aground on the hard shores of traditional considerations of national sovereignty. The rising ecological consciousness still has not changed a basic conclusion in the 1972 *Report on Regulatory Fishery Bodies* by the Food and Agriculture Organization: "Regulatory fishery bodies do not possess supranational powers as the conservation measures they formulate and adopt are not directly binding on individual fishermen without legislative action being taken to this effect by member countries. In fact, these measures are seldom binding on member countries themselves."[36]

In short, the environmental conditions for human health and well-being in many parts of the world continue to deteriorate and to threaten the entire human community owing to the lack of sufficient progress toward a Polyarchy II polity that would be be responsive to the world's crucial ecological interdependencies. The Med Plan is an exception; but in its very exceptionalism are clues to how the traditional obstacles to mutual accountability may be overcome.

The opportunities for statecraft and action by laypersons to give the political evolution of the human community further pushes in the direction of the needed Polyarchy II processes and institutions are outlined in Part Four.

ENDNOTES

1. Confidence that sovereign national governments even when (or particularly when) armed with nuclear weapons will act responsibly and rationally, and therefore will be deterred from military adventures against each other, underlies the arguments of Kenneth Waltz that the proliferation of nuclear weapons to many countries might not be so bad after all. See his "What Will the Spread of Nuclear Weapons Do to the World?" in John Kerry King, ed., *The International Political Effects of the Spread of Nuclear Weapons* (Washington: GPO, 1979), pp. 165–196.

2. The most representative source of the thinking of the "international regime" theorists and analysts is Stephen D. Krasner, ed., *International Regimes* (Ithaca: Cornell University Press, 1983). See also Kenneth Oye, ed., *Cooperation under Anarchy* (Princeton: Princeton University Press, 1986).

3. See especially Arthur A. Stein, "Coordination and Collaboration: Regimes in an Anarchic World," in Krasner, *ibid.*, 115–140; and Robert O. Keohane, "The Demand for International Regimes," also in Krasner, *ibid.*, pp. 141–171.

4. Robert Jervis, "Security Regimes," *ibid.*, pp. 173–194, provides an illuminating comparative analysis of the differences and similarities affecting regime formation in the security field and other fields of international interaction.

5. Kenneth W. Dam, *The GATT: Law and International Economic Organization* (Chicago: University of Chicago Press, 1970), pp. 391–392.

6. Charles Lipson, "The Transformation of Trade: The Sources and Effects of Regime Change," in Krasner, ed., *International Regimes*, pp. 233–271.

7. An excellent assessment of the implications of the Tokyo Round for the norms of the GATT regime is provided in Jock A. Finlayson and Mark W. Zacher, "The GATT and the Regulation of Trade Barriers: Regime Dynamics and Functions," in Krasner, *ibid.*, pp. 273–314.

8. Benjamin J. Cohen, "Balance of Payments Financing: The Evolution of a Regime," in Krasner, *ibid.*, p. 315.

9. On the forces undermining the Bretton Woods and post-Bretton Woods monetary

regime, see Joan Edleman Spero, *The Politics of International Economic Relations* (New York: St. Martin's Press, 1985), pp. 35–86.

10. Richard N. Cooper, "Economic Interdependence and Foreign Policy in the Seventies," *World Politics*, Vol. 24, No. 2 (January 1972), pp. 159–181; quotations from p. 175.

11. Spero, *The Politics of International Economic Relations*, p. 85.

12. On President Reagan's reluctant participation at the Cancun Conference and his attitude toward such North–South negotiations, see Seyom Brown, *The Faces of Power: Constancy and Change in United States Foreign Policy from Truman to Reagan* (New York: Columbia University Press, 1983), pp. 595–600.

13. The Brandt Commission, *Common Crisis North-South: Cooperation for World Recovery* (Cambridge: MIT Press, 1983).

14. Stephen Krasner, *Structural Conflict: The Third World against Global Liberalism* (Berkeley: University of California Press, 1985), p. 232.

15. United Nations Conference on the Law of the Sea, *Law of the Sea: Official Text with Annexes and Index* (New York: United Nations, 1983).

16. Harold K. Jacobson, *Networks of Interdependence: International Organizations and the Global Political System* (New York: Knopf, 1984), p. 225.

17. For a brief description of commodity agreements and the Common Fund, see Jacobson, *ibid.*, pp. 258–259, 267–268.

18. United States Arms Control and Disarmament Agency, *Arms Control and Disarmament Agreements* (New Brunswick: Transaction Books, 1984), pp. 20–21.

19. Arms Control and Disarmament Agency, *ibid.*, pp. 51–55.

20. Arms Control and Disarmament Agency, *ibid.*, pp. 102–105.

21. Gerhard Mally, "The CDE and European Security in the 1980s," *Department of State Bulletin*, Vol. 84, No. 2082 (January 1984), pp. 49–51; "Key Sections of Document at Stockholm Meeting on Security," *New York Times*, 22 September 1986.

22. William Langer Ury and Richard Smoke, *Beyond the Hotline: Controlling a Nuclear Crisis* (Cambridge: Harvard University Law School, 1984).

23. "Nuclear Risk Reduction System," Report of the Nunn/Warner Group on Nuclear Risk Reduction, *Congressional Record*, Vol. 130, No. 8 (1 February 1984).

24. Nuclear Non-Proliferation Treaty, full text in Arms Control and Disarmament Agency, *Arms Control and Disarmament Agreements*, pp. 91–95.

25. Congressional Research Service, *Nuclear Proliferation Factbook* (Washington: GPO, 1985); and Leonard S. Spector, *Nuclear Proliferation Today* (New York: Vintage, 1984).

26. Seyom Brown, Nina W. Cornell, Larry L. Fabian, and Edith Brown Weiss, *Regimes for the Ocean, Outer Space, and Weather* (Washington, DC: The Brookings Institution, 1977), pp. 47–49.

27. Jacobson, *Networks of Interdependence*, p. 240.

28. Alexander Dallin, *Black Box: KAL 007 and the Superpowers* (Berkeley: University of California Press, 1985).

29. Thomas W. Netter, "Third World Seeks Its Place in Space," *New York Times*, 15 September 1985.

30. Maurice Strong, "One Year after Stockholm: An Ecological Approach to Management," *Foreign Affairs*, Vol. 51, No. 4 (July 1973), pp. 690–707.

31. On the lack of effectiveness of the UNEP within the United Nations system, see William Ophuls, *Ecology and the Politics of Scarcity: Prologue to a Political Theory of the Steady State* (San Francisco: W. H. Freeman, 1977), pp. 216–219.

32. My source for the list of international environmental conventions is Peter M. Haas, "Progress in International Environmental Protection," a paper prepared for delivery at the 1985 Annual Meeting of the American Political Science Association, New Orleans.

33. On the role and organization of international fisheries commissions, see Brown et al., *Regimes for the Ocean, Outer Space, and Weather*, pp. 58–62.

34. Lyton Keith Caldwell, *International Environmental Policy* (Durham: Duke University Press, 1984).

35. My information on the Med Plan is drawn from the excellent analysis in Peter M. Haas's paper, "Progress in International Environmental Protection."

36. United Nations, Food and Agriculture Organizations, Department of Fisheries, *Report on Regulatory Fishery Bodies* (Rome: FAO, 1972).

PART FOUR

Practical Applications

The analysis in the previous chapters pointed to the conclusion that informed and deliberate acts of statecraft are required to assure that world politics does not degenerate into a condition of brutal anarchy in the decades ahead. The final two chapters explore the implications of that conclusion, and the analysis on which it is based, for contemporary global statecraft and US foreign policy.

Chapter 14 outlines the immediate and long-term policy imperatives for avoiding nuclear holocaust, the prevention of environmental disturbances to the planet's biosphere that could jeopardize healthy human existence, and the eradication of the world's enclaves of terrible starvation and disease. It argues that these objectives can be pursued today through a range of practical policy initiatives that do not require, as a precondition, a radical transformation of the world polity. But the chapter also presents a vision of a future world polity addressed to the underlying causes of the threats that now need immediate attention. The larger challenge of global statecraft is to deal with the urgent imperatives in ways that are conducive to the evolution of the better world polity.

Chapter 15 translates the prescriptions for global statecraft into guidance for American foreign policy. It argues that the United States is fully capable, because of its basic societal values and its geopolitical situation, of responding constructively to challenges posed by the trends analyzed in this book. But the new directions called for—the encouragement of international depolarization, the pursuit of global accountability, the support of transnationalism, and the demilitarization of diplomacy—would require considerable departure from recent emphases in US foreign policy.

CHAPTER FOURTEEN

Implications for Contemporary Statecraft

A situation in which survival itself is at stake ought to discipline the organism, compelling it to slough off or postpone secondary wants and indulgences—at least those reducing the chances of survival—and to adopt a strategy, a prioritized agenda of behavior, for overcoming the most dangerous threats. This is the situation today of the human species; and those who would be its leaders, who deserve to be regarded as world statesmen or stateswomen, must therefore comprehend the nature of the impending threats to the survival of humankind and be able to translate this understanding into a realistic set of imperatives for counteracting them. Some of the required policies must deal with immediately looming threats and will have to be instituted on an urgent basis. Longer-term policies are also essential, however, to deal with the underlying sources of the threats to species survival and well-being, to lessen their frequency and force. But neither the immediate nor longer-term policies will prove effective unless they are consistent with the contemporary interplay of new forces and old forces described in the previous chapters.

PURSUING IMMEDIATE SURVIVAL IMPERATIVES WHILE REFORMING THE WORLD POLITY

The analysis in the previous chapters showed that the most ominous threats to the survival and well-being of the human species can be traced to the basic failure of political creativity to keep pace with scientific and technological creativity. Unfortunately, many of the basic reforms needed to overcome this political lag will take decades to mature, and meanwhile the planet Earth itself or large regions of the globe could be made uninhabitable; short of this, tens of millions could be killed by avoidable wars, starvation, and disease. Countermeasures against the more immediate of these threats need to be devised and instituted now, even though some of the urgent countermeasures may deal mainly with symptoms of mankind's political deficiencies and not yet sufficiently with basic causes. But the basic causes, as will be shown below, can be worked on simultaneously with efforts to counteract the symptoms.

The highest priority tasks of contemporary statecraft—both immediate and long-range—are the prevention of nuclear holocaust; the prevention of disruptions of the Earth's biospheric balance; and the elimination of enclaves of starvation and disease.

The Prevention of Nuclear Holocaust[1]

It is unnecessary to argue the objective of preventing nuclear holocaust. All serious studies of the effects of nuclear war—whether conducted by the defense establishments of the United States and the Soviet Union or by independent scientists—show that a war between the United States and the Soviet Union in which both exploded only a fraction (say anywhere from one-tenth to one-half) of their strategic nuclear weapons on each other would be an irretrievable and unredeemable disaster.[2]

Even those like US Secretary of Defense Caspar Weinberger who in the early 1980s talked of "prevailing" in a "protracted nuclear war" have since conceded that "in a nuclear war with the Soviet Union there would be no winner."[3] Astronomer Carl Sagan and many of his scientific colleagues who have studied the phenomenon of "nuclear winter" go even farther, claiming: "There is a real danger of the extinction of humanity. A threshold exists at which...[a] climatic catastrophe could be triggered....A major first strike may be an act of national suicide, even if no retaliation occurs."[4] There has been controversy in the scientific community over Sagan's "nuclear winter" nightmare; but the controversy is not so much over whether such a climatic catastrophe would result from a superpower nuclear war as it is over just how many megatons would have to be detonated to actually trigger the global environmental disturbances.[5]

There is, of course, substantial disagreement (between social scientists as well as between statesmen) over *how to prevent* this most terrible event the human species would ever experience and probably would not be able to survive.

Ronald Reagan holds that his Strategic Defense Initiative (SDI), by providing a shield against strategic attack, will make nuclear war obsolete. Proponents of reliance on Mutual Assured Destruction (MAD) capabilities for deterring superpower war contend exactly the opposite; namely, that military programs for protecting population centers and industry from destruction in a strategic nuclear war will undermine the inhibitions against starting such a war in the first place. Others emphasize the importance of renouncing any first use of nuclear weapons and of redressing conventional force imbalances in theaters of

potential US–Soviet confrontation. Still others insist on a substantial dismantling of nuclear arsenals as an urgent necessity. And there are those, found
among the "hawks" as well as the "doves," who regard the arms race and
military balance mainly as symptoms of underlying political conflicts and see
the only hope of preventing nuclear holocaust in measures to deal with the
political sources of Soviet–American tensions.

The first imperatives of a statecraft that would prevent nuclear holocaust,
therefore, are to choose between the various prescriptions that are in direct
contradiction to each other and to establish priorities among the policies
chosen.

Reducing nuclear first-strike incentives.   That there should be no advantage to a nuclear first strike has been a premise of the SALT and START
negotiations to limit strategic nuclear weapons. Proponents of the SDI also
claim that the program's contemplated multilayered defense against nulcear
attack would be the best way to discourage an enemy first strike. Other analysts,
this author among them, see an offensive "counterforce" attack potential in the
SDI, particularly in its space-based components.

If the imperative of precluding any nuclear first-strike advantage is to be
conscientiously pursued, there will need to be some major modifications of the
existing nuclear arsenals on both sides, and some weapons planned for future
deployment, including space-based weapons, may need to be prohibited. The
most provocative weapons are those that could be effective in hobbling the
enemy's military capability if they were used at the outset of military hostilities
and that are also highly vulnerable to destruction by the enemy if not used at
the outset.

The multiple-warhead land-based ICBMs now deployed by each side have
these dangerous use-them-or-lose-them characteristics. Their accuracy and
destructive power pose a threat to the other side's ICBMs, while their
vulnerability to destruction prior to launch (plus the damage they can inflict if
launched) make them high-priority and time-urgent targets for enemy ICBMs.
An arms control agreement to phase such weapons out of the inventories of
both sides would be highly desirable, and it would be sufficiently verifiable even
with national, nonintrusive means of inspection. But neither side need wait for
a negotiated agreement before starting to phase these provocative weapons out
of its inventory, for a unilateral move of this kind would enhance the security of
the side that undertook it, particularly if the unilateral reduction of the ICBMs
were accompanied by a susbstitution of less vulnerable strategic weapons, such
as those carried by submarines or new single-warhead and mobile land-based
ICBMs.

Some of the antiballistic missiles contemplated in the American SDI (and
Soviet counterpart programs), even though ostensibly "defensive," could also

tempt strategic first strikes or preemptive blows. Potentially the most dangerous are the laser or other high-energy beam weapons being developed for
deployment on spacecraft with the mission of destroying enemy ICBMs in their
"boost phase" (that is, immediately after launch), before the multiple warheads
on the ICBMs have separated from their launch vehicles. The speed and
accuracy of the boost-phase interceptors and their deployment in orbiting
spacecraft would give them the wherewithal to be used also in a surprise or
preemptive first strike against enemy weapons that had not yet been fired.
Thus whether or not the side deploying such space-based interceptors originally
intended to use them in a first strike, and whether or not they would be
effective in destroying already-launched ICBMs, the space-weapons themselves
would become prime targets at the outset of a strategic conflict and consequently
there would be great pressures to use them preemptively.

Another high-priority and crucial item on the arms control agenda should be
the vulnerability to destruction of the command and control systems for the
strategic nuclear forces. Since command and control must be intact for effective
retaliation to take place (and therefore for deterrent threats to be credible),
their vulnerability leads each side to adopt dangerous and highly provocative
arrangements to launch the prime strategic forces at the enemy before enemy
weapons land on one's territory—which means, in effect, to launch thousands
of strategic nuclear weapons simply on the basis of warning that the enemy
attack is coming. Again, much of what needs to be done to reduce the
vulnerability of command and control, and the resulting temptations to attack
preemptively, can be accomplished unilaterally, through dispersal and protection of the highest national command centers and their subordinate commands.
However, in some fields agreement between the superpowers would be
important. For example, communications used in strategic command and
control are highly dependent upon space communications satellites, and
therefore, whatever the fate of SDI programs, a mutual ban on antisatellite
weapons should be pursued.[6]

Eliminating reliance on nuclear escalation in Europe. NATO's reliance
on threat to turn any major East–West war in Europe into nuclear war appears
to have "worked" up to now—in the sense of deterring the Soviets from
exploiting the presumed conventional superiority of the Warsaw Pact. But the
basic changes in the strategic situation since the 1950s, when NATO adopted
this strategy, and the maturing of polyarchic tendencies in both of the cold war
coalitions (see Chapters 3–5), have reduced the credibility and appropriateness
of the nuclear escalation threat to such an extent that continuing to rely on it
may induce the very temptations and miscalculations in Central Europe that
could bring on World War III.

The profound inhibitions on the United States becoming involved in a strategic exchange of blows with the Soviet Union could very well paralyze any effective NATO response to a major Soviet provocation in Europe, given that such a NATO response implies a heavy US participation in nuclear attacks against Warsaw Pact forces. The general awareness of these inhibitions could sorely tempt the Kremlin in some future East–West confrontation to stage a rapid fait accompli with conventional forces—say, the takeover of West Berlin—confident that at the "moment of truth" NATO would shrink from initiating nuclear war.

Worse yet, what has happened so many times in human history might happen again: Those taken advantage of by the coldly calculating aggressor might yet act "irrationally" to defend themselves—in the case at hand, the NATO countries implement their doctrine of nuclear escalation and bring on the mutually suicidal holocaust. Such apocalyptic scenarios become all the more plausible as the erosion of unity in both alliances allows individual member states more leeway to move on their own in ways that could catalyze a more general confrontation, a growing danger in the evolving attraction/repulsion relationship between the two Germanies.

An integrated strategy for the prevention of nuclear holocaust, therefore, would seem to require that the reduction or elimination of superpower nuclear missile deployments in the center of Europe (as contemplated in the interme-diate nuclear force negotiations underway in 1987) be accompanied by the rectification of the imbalance in conventional military power between NATO and the Warsaw Pact. The latter purpose could be accomplished either by nonsymmetrical mutual reductions to essentially equalize the nonnuclear military capabilities each alliance deploys in Central Europe or, failing this, by an upgrading of NATO's nonnuclear deployments.

The force-reduction route to an equalization of the conventional balance in Central Europe has been the province of the Mutual and Balanced Force Reduction (MBFR) negotiations between NATO and the Warsaw Pact. At the MBFR conference table, the Soviets in recent years—contrary to their earlier insistence that the conventional force balance in Europe was already roughly equal—have indicated a willingness to agree to a symmetrical reductions down to common numerical ceilings. But the translation of this important agreement in principle into a detailed schedule of mutual reductions has been held up by an East–West disagreement over how many troops the Warsaw Pact currently has deployed in Central Europe.

A persisting impasse in the MBFR negotiations might appear to leave the United States and its allies with little choice, if they are to reduce their reliance on nuclear weapons, other than to substantially increase their nonnuclear military forces in the European theater.

The linkage between reducing the reliance on nuclear threats and increasing the West's nonnuclear fighting capabilities is explicit in the widely debated

1982 proposal by former US Secretary of Defense Robert McNamara and his colleagues that NATO adopt a policy of no first use of nuclear weapons: A nuclear no-first-use policy, say the authors, "would draw new attention to the importance of maintaining and improving the...conventional forces in Europe...[which are] better instruments for stability in crisis as well as for maintenance of the nuclear firebreak so vital to us all."[7] Not surprisingly, the no-first-use proposal has received very little support among West European military planners. "What matters most," runs a typical counterargument, "is to concentrate not only on the prevention of nuclear war, but on how to prevent *any* war, conventional war as well....A renunciation of the first use of nuclear weapons...would liberate the Soviet Union from the decisive nuclear risk—and thereby from the constraint that has kept the Soviet Union, up to now, from using military force, even for limited purposes, against Western Europe."[8]

But if the standard West European opposition to the renunciation of the first use of nuclear weapons—namely, that this would disastrously undermine the deterrence of conventional war—continues to be reflected in NATO strategy, then, clearly, the United States and its allies will want to preserve whatever military advantages they might hope to gain by striking first with their nuclear weapons in the event of war with the Soviet Union. And the Soviets, accordingly, must be expected to design their nuclear forces to preempt the NATO nuclear attack by striking first themselves. Is there no escape, then, from these destabilizing preparations?

Reducing reliance on military deterrence in general. NATO's seemingly insoluble predicament suggests that it may be time to consider more radical alternatives, such as that proposed by Gene Sharp in his ground-breaking study *Making Europe Unconquerable: The Potential of Civilian-Based Deterrence and Defence*.[9] Sharp argues that neither NATO's current nuclear-reliant strategy of deterrence nor the conventional-force alternatives of McNamara and his colleagues meet the two essential criteria of effective deterrence and defense: "It is...necessary that the consequences of the failure of any deterrence system not be catastrophic [to the deterrer]. Remedial means capable of defending the attacked society must be ready for operation." It is now widely recognized that a nuclear war for the control of Europe would leave no Europe worth controlling. But, as Sharp points out, authoritative NATO studies also show that, given modern "conventional" weaponry, a nonnuclear war for control of Europe could produce significantly more destruction than did the Second World War.[10] The only sensible and credible alternative, contends Sharp, is to base deterrence and defense on "civilian forms of struggle" pioneered by Mahatma Gandhi and his disciples—active resistance that eschews physical violence but nonetheless imposes unacceptable costs on the attackers:

Many kinds of political noncooperation, strikes, economic boycotts, symbolic protests, civil disobedience, social boycotts, and more extreme methods of disruption and intervention are among the weapons of this policy....In addition, the civilian defenders aim to subvert the loyalty of the aggressor's troops and functionaries, to make them unreliable in carrying out orders and repression, and even to induce them to mutiny.

If the would-be aggressor can be convincingly shown by his potential victims that they are determined to resist and are prepared to make their society "politically indigestible and ungovernable" if he attempts to take them over, then deterrence has a good chance of working.[11] Sharp admits that this type of deterrence cannot be guaranteed to work, but goes on to argue that

> Unlike failure of nuclear deterrence, the failure of civilian-based defence preparations to deter invasion of Western Europe does not bring the likelihood of annihilation....
> Not only does human life continue and hope for victory remain, but at this point the struggle enters a new active stage with a direct confrontation of forces. The defense struggle itself begins.[12]

Sharp is well aware that such a reorientation of deterrence and defense policies would require a massive education and training program of leaders and the general populace. He contends, however, that such "transarmament," as he calls the process, could be phased in by stages as a society develops the will and capability for effective nonviolent resistance, and that reliance on the existing forms of nuclear and conventional deterrence and defense meanwhile could be partly retained and phased out in stages so as not to create a power vacuum that would tempt an aggressor.

Preventing the spread of nuclear weapons. Just as a significant reduction of the prospects for nuclear holocaust escalating out of East–West confrontation in Europe may require some radical change in prevailing security regimes, so the prospect that a nuclear World War III may be catalyzed by nuclear actors other than the two superpowers compels considerably more than the business-as-usual approach to the looming new generation of nuclear proliferation problems.

It is now nearly twenty years since the negotiation of the Treaty on the Non-proliferation of Nuclear Weapons (NPT), and still over a third of the world's countries have neither signed nor ratified the treaty. By the end of the century, most of these countries will have the technical capability to develop nuclear weapons. Many already have the capability, and a few—Israel, South Africa, India—might already have nuclear weapons secretly stored away but, in order not to provoke regional rivals into quickly acquiring their own, choose not to reveal them.[13] When any one of these countries crosses the threshold between being simply nuclear-capable and actually deploying nuclear weapons, contagion is likely to set in. Once the process of proliferation openly resumes (having apparently stopped at least for the time being with five nuclear-armed powers: the United States, the USSR, Britain, France, and China), it would be unrealistic to assume that Japan would be willing to maintain its nonnuclear status. Nor would other states aspiring to be major powers—Brazil, Argentina, Indonesia, Vietnam, Nigeria—deny themselves what is becoming an ordinary attribute of military prowess.

Some military strategists and academic theorists discount the consequences of the spread of nuclear weapons, predicting that the threat of nuclear devastation which inhibits the United States and the Soviet Union from going to war against each other will produce similar inhibitions on the part of other countries acquiring nuclear weapons. War-prone adversaries such as India and Pakistan, or Israel and her Arab neighbors, presumably will be injected with a healthy fear of the consequences of war once they acquire the means to swiftly obliterate each other. The superpowers, too, presumably will be deterred from attempting to engage in "nuclear blackmail" against small nuclear countries with whom they are in confrontation, thus reducing one of the principal sources of dangerous miscalculation between the superpowers.[14]

The flaw in the sanguine appraisals of the consequences of nuclear prolifera-tion—and it could be a fatal flaw, not only for the countries involved, but for the world—is that they fail to take into account the high likelihood that the nouveau-nuclear countries' newly acquired nuclear arsenals are likely to comprise (or to appear to comprise) vulnerable use-them-or-lose-them weap-ons. In an intense crisis, there are high incentives to fire such weapons preemptively to hobble the enemy's weapons before they destroy one's own. Moreover, the argument that spreading such weapons around will reduce the chances of nuclear blackmail and miscalculation overlooks the great asymmetry between superpower nuclear arsenals and those of countries with fledgling nuclear capabilities, and the very real possibility that a superpower in a hostile relationship with a country beginning to deploy nuclear weapons will be highly tempted to remove its small enemy's new arsenal with a "surgical strike" before it is fully deployed.

Fortunately, there is still widespread support, even on the part of countries with techncial and economic capabilities for developing their own substantial nuclear arsenals, for the NPT regime of strict restraints on the utilization and international transfer of weapons-grade nuclear materials and nuclear energy equipment that could be used to produce nuclear weapons.

Unfortunately, however, the technical controls and safeguards capable of being applied internationally will not prevent countries who are determined to have them from acquiring nuclear weapons. Means need to be found for counteracting the political and strategic incentives for countries to obtain independent nuclear arsenals, and this requires coming to grips with the profoundly insecure status of the nonnuclear countries: the insecurity produced by the realization that to the extent countries now possessing nuclear weapons, especially the superpowers, are unconditionally deterred from attacking each other with nuclear weapons, the existing nuclear-armed countries may feel that they can get away with nuclear threats against nonnuclear countries (even allies of a rival nuclear-armed power), without incurring credible threats of nuclear retaliation.

The standard prescription for the predicament of the nonnuclear countries is to attempt to shore up alliance commitments and other security guarantees provided them by their nuclear-armed friends. But the alliances and security guarantees have become flimsy precisely because it has become too scary for either superpower to deliberately initiate nuclear war against the other for any reason except to preempt an attack against oneself that appears inevitable. The standard rhetoric, deployments, or alliance-reconsolidation measures simply fail to deal with this situation; moreover, they go against the grain of the long-term trend toward polyarchy outlined in the previous chapters.

Solving the nuclear proliferation problem through attempts to firm up alliance security guarantees is, as it were, quixotic tilting at windmills. Indeed, the effort to restore credibility to extended nuclear deterrent umbrellas only exacerbates the predicament it is supposed to deal with, since it gives new emphasis to the reliance on the nuclear weapons in the present international system and to the nakedness of those who are not protected by them.

A nonproliferation regime with any real prospect for avoiding the otherwise inevitable spread of nuclear weapons would need to deemphasize the political and military value for the countries that already possess them. Thus, in the periodic review conferences among signatories of the NPT, the nonnuclear members of the NPT regime have been angrily demanding that the superpowers take more seriously their pledge in Article VI of the Treaty to pursue negotiations leading to their own nuclear disarmament. The message is unmistakable: The majority are unwilling to put up with second-class status much longer, including subjecting themselves to international inspection to ensure they are not producing weapons—unless the superpowers themselves reduce reliance on nuclear weapons.

Reducing and controlling the superpower rivalry.   Efforts to defang the nuclear superpowers, so to speak, are an important part of an integrated strategy for preventing nuclear holocaust; but the nuclear arms, while dangerous in and of themselves, are also symptoms of the fundamental geopolitical rivalry between the United States and the Soviet Union. To the extent that this rivalry is perceived on both sides as likely to draw them into military confrontation, neither will totally disarm itself of its most lethal weapons; each will suspect the other of maintaining, and therefore itself will maintain—either openly or clandestinely—at least a residual "assured destruction" force, if for no other reason than to deter the other from an attempt to achieve dominance in particular confrontations (or even globally) through a sudden display of military superiority. A durable strategy for avoiding nuclear holocaust, accordingly, must include policies for reducing and controlling the geostrategic, ideological, and psychological factors in the superpower rivalry that could draw them into lethal confrontations.

Fortunately, there need be no clash of *vital* interests between the superpowers. Neither must wrest territory away from the other to secure its own national integrity or material well-being. Each does, to be sure, have a high interest in commercial and military access to other areas of the globe, but there is nothing inherently incompatible with either one's security or material well-being in the other's maintaining such access. If the Soviet Union attempted to gain *preclusive* access or control over the energy resources of the Middle East, the United States might feel vitally threatened. But there is no reason why the USSR should need such preclusive access in order to supplement its own energy resources. Nor are the boundaries of the United States and the Soviet Union overlapped by national or ethnic groups that one or the other feels compelled to "liberate" and incorporate into its own territory.

It would be naive, however, to assume that either the United States or the Soviet Union would be content to restrict its international activities only to those absolutely essential for securing its own territorial integrity and independence from the other, under the premise that the other was also acting from purely defensive motives.[15]

The Soviet regime, even as its Marxist–Leninist ideology wanes, carries the geopolitical legacy of the Russian empire. This legacy alone impels all occupants of the Kremlin to give high value to the preservation of a belt of satellite countries on the western borders of the USSR, to the protection of its eastern and southern frontiers against Asian and Muslim encroachments, and to the maintenance of permanent access to the oceans of the world. In securing even these "legitimate" Russian imperial interests, the Soviets will be unable to avoid impinging on the rival geopolitical interests of the United States.

For its part, the United States has inherited from England the role of organizing the oceanic powers to prevent the domination of the Eurasian landmass, and in particular its strategic "rimland," by a hegemonic continental power. (See Chapter 2.) Since the Truman Doctrine (1947), this has been a cardinal objective of US foreign policy—justified by the teachings of classical Anglo-American geopolitical theorists that an imperial "heartland" power, if allowed to gain control of the rimland, would be in a position to dominate the world. In the contemporary period, the principal Western industrial countries and Japan have become highly dependent for their economic well-being upon overseas access to one another and to countries that once were part of their imperial domains, especially the energy producers; and these main lines of communication and transport either traverse the Eurasian rimland or pass close by its coasts and require servicing stations on the rimland.

However much the leaders of the United States and the other leading capitalist powers insist that their maintenance of allies and client states all along the vast Eurasian periphery of the USSR implies no aggressive intent toward the Soviets, the Kremlin—combining historical memories of Russian territorial vulnerabilities with Marxist–Leninist theories of capitalist encirclement—cannot help but see much of the US presence on the rimland as hostile. Accordingly, it remains a central and long-term aim of Soviet policy to dislodge from Eurasia any US military bases—actual or potential—that could be used against the USSR and to break up any anti-Soviet alliances between the United States and countries on the Eurasian landmass or nearby islands. Understandably, if there were ever to be a Third World War, the Soviets would want to be in a position to maximally disrupt the oceanic powers' lines of supply and communication in and around the rimland without having to divert the lion's share of Soviet naval capabilities to this task.

Moreover, modern technologies, allowing the superpowers to project power to, but also to be attacked from, intercontinental distances, has led to an expansive definition of the "rimland." The geopolitically significant regions that strategists in Washington and Moscow consider imperative to keep out of the other's sphere of control now include the Mediterranean and Indian Ocean littorals of Africa. If we add to this the oil-rich and mineral-rich countries of Sub-Saharan Africa, which many geopoliticians are inclined to do, then very few countries beyond America would not be important to the security of *both* superpowers and therefore potential foci of confrontation.

From a strict military calculus, the Americas should not be an arena of dangerous superpower confrontation. There is no vital security need for the Soviets to maintain bases or allies in the Western Hemisphere. Soviet activities and support of allies in Latin America clearly are the product of ideology and prestige considerations rather than military necessity. And even as the Soviets have seized opportunities to establish allies in the Caribbean and Central America, the ability of the United States to protect itself (as demonstrated as far back as the Cuban missile crisis) has not been thereby substantially diminished. The revolution in military technologies has made it more difficult for countries to protect themselves against strategic forces halfway around the world or in the deep oceans than against hostile enemy outposts close to their borders. But psychologically, any Soviet outposts in the Western Hemisphere, particularly military bases and deployments, engender American feelings of vulnerability and of being encircled by hostile neighbors, so that even relatively minor Soviet encroachments, which for opportunistic reasons the Soviets will be tempted to pursue, can produce a combative American response.

The United States and the Soviet Union thus can be drawn into confrontation for reasons beyond their clashing national security objectives. The reasons of state for both superpowers include world-order grand designs that are not simply instruments of or rationalizations for material self-interest.

While it is doubtful that the General Secretary of the Communist Party of the Soviet Union looks at himself in the mirror every morning and asks "What can I do for the world revolution?" or that the American president loses much sleep over the inability of people in other countries to enjoy the blessings of free enterprise and American-style political democracy, there is considerable preoccupation in the Kremlin and the White House with crises generated by their respective commitments to causes each side regards as historically progressive or noble.

The recognition that the geopolitical and ideological sources of the US–Soviet rivalry are laid rather deep, however, need not discourage efforts to modify the relationship in the service of the imperative of preventing confrontations that could lead to superpower war and nuclear holocaust. Despite the uncertain prospects for success, there are opportunities for the United States and the Soviet Union to reduce the likelihood of their being drawn into wars against one another, particularly in presumably "up for grabs" areas of the Third World, even those of prime geopolitical importance:

1. Consistent with the polyarchic trends described in previous chapters, both superpowers could convey to the other in word and deed that their objective was not to deny the other influence in these areas but only to retain one's own access and opportunity to compete for influence. Accordingly, they could institute a series of military disengagement/neutralization arrangements (either explicit or tacit) in which as a minimum neither would establish military bases in these areas, and as a maximum both also would refrain from sponsoring the military buildup of client states and political movements in these areas.

2. The superpower military disengagement would be reinforced by the encouragement of genuine nonalignment of countries in the relevant regions. The various countries would, of course, maintain flexibility to support, on grounds of their own interests, particular policies pursued by either the United States or the Soviet Union and to seek the support of either or both superpowers for their own projects and policies. But Washington and Moscow would refrain from pressuring these countries to become across-the-board and permanent allies; they would not be rhetorically castigated or threatened with material sanctions to prevent their benign cooperation with the rival superpower.

3. The policy of international depolarization would be complemented by superpower tolerance for ideologically divergent domestic regimes, par-

ticularly among the nonaligned, but even in countries still nominally within their own camp. There would be no insistence by the US government, for example, that countries wishing to qualify for economic assistance renounce Marxist principles of political–economic organization and not be headed by Marxists or by coalitions including Marxists; nor would the United States actively sponsor anti-Marxist opposition groups within countries governed by Marxist or neo-Marxist regimes. The Soviets, for their part, would allow their East European neighbors more leeway to experiment with market economies and pluralistic polities.

Both superpowers, in short, would respect the determination of indigenous peoples to resist outside domination and would rely principally on the strength of this basic cultural force to contain the other's imperial temptations. Moreover, in a depolarized world where most countries maintained cooperative relationships with both the United States and the Soviet Union while remaining politically independent of each and nonalignment had become the basis of the legitimate world order, neither superpower would need to be so compulsive about protecting the position of its ideological brothers and sisters wherever they might be threatened. Both superpowers (or either one, which in some cases would be sufficient to avoid an unnecessary confrontation) would be provided with acceptable justification for refusing to become militarily involved in conflicts whose outcome, one way or another, would not really threaten its vital security interests.

Although we can state the conditions for a moderation of the Soviet–American global rivalry and the avoidance of situations leading to the kind of high-stakes confrontations that could lead to war, it would be illusory to expect that in fact we will succeed in avoiding all such war-prone superpower conflicts in the years ahead. Some confrontations over clashing interests must be expected, and in such situations the burden of arresting escalation toward nuclear holocaust will need to be assumed by diplomats and crisis managers.

The fact that the United States and the Soviet Union have not become embroiled in war with each other should not lead to complacency that the diplomatic arts have been well learned on both sides. There have been some narrow escapes—in a number of Soviet–American confrontations over Berlin, in the Cuban missile crisis, in the Middle East, in the Indochina conflict—where the superpowers themselves came perilously close to blows. And there are grounds for worry that the wrong lessons may have been learned from these cases by the crisis managers on both sides.

The Americans may be tempted to draw the conclusion that an unyielding stance and willingness to initiate military hostilities works, that faced with "steel," as former President Nixon put it, the Soviets will prudently back off positions they have staked out for themselves. But the Soviets may well infer from their past international encounters (in Eastern Europe where they fended off Western intervention, and in the Cuban missile crisis where they had to yield) that the prevailing balance of military power does, as the traditional "realists" claim, determine the political outcome.

These contrary inferences from past confrontations are cause for special concern, given many of the developments pointed to in the previous chapters—in particular the condition of essential strategic parity, the constriction of the scope of interests each country must defend to defend itself, and the blurring of alliance commitments. Because of these trends, more than at any time in the history of the US–Soviet relationship, conditions are now ripe for terrible games of "chicken," in which both sides commit themselves to incompatible secondary (or even tertiary) objectives so visibly that neither can back down without great humiliation. The danger is that each becomes all the more determined to demonstrate an irrevocable commitment to persist toward its objective, in the hope that the certainty of a head-on collision will convince the *other* side to swerve out of the way first.

What is needed is a reorientation of diplomacy, a retooling of diplomats, and a reeducation of the populace to deemphasize the military chips in international bargaining, which have become the stock in trade of cold war diplomacy, and to positively exploit the new economic and institutional chips becoming available as depolarization proceeds and webs of international accountability are woven (see Chapter 13). Such a diplomacy does not have to await the full realization of cold war depolarization strategies outlined above but can positively exploit the diverse lines of interdependence, affinity, and antagonisms already present and developing.

In a polyarchic world of diversifying relationships, there are far more opportunities, and more incentives, to bargain with carrots rather than with sticks. Because adversaries on one issue may be partners on others, prudence dictates that diplomats refrain, even while dealing with adversaries, from tactics that may engender hostility of long duration. Countries such as the United States and the Soviet Union, which have the assets needed to establish cooperative relationships around the globe, have plenty of cards to play without having to resort to military coercion should the bargaining get tough.

Finally, the superpowers should not consider it to be a denigration of their status and prestige to avoid escalation to war, or to terminate some future war between them, by accepting the conflict resolution services of third parties whether these be formal institutions such as the International Court of Justice or the conflict resolution panels of various specialized international agencies, or mediation by particular statesmen who are neutral on the issues in dispute. Anticipating this, it is vitally important that the superpowers act to enhance the prestige of such international conflict resolution institutions and processes, utilizing them regularly for relatively minor disputes (such as conflicts over coastal zone jurisdictions in the Bering Straits), prior to a desperate need to rely on them in an intense crisis.

The Prevention of Biospheric Disruptions

A new statecraft also has now become imperative to deal with the risks to the continued healthy survival of life on Earth posed by disturbances to the planet's essential ecological balances of climate, air, water, and soil. As pointed out in Chapter 9, human society need not engage in thermonuclear war to validate religious prophecies of the end of the world. The remarkable biospheric envelope that has sustained living organisms on this unique planet could also be placed in jeopardy inadvertently by a variety of everyday human activities that are entirely constructive in intent but that are producing highly destructive side effects on the natural environment.

To be sure, there is considerable debate among scientists over how sensitive the biospheric balance really is to various man-made disturbances—the effects of chlorofluorocarbons, for example, on the capacity of the ozone layer to screen out cancer-producing sunrays (see pages 182–183), or the alterations in global climate that may be produced by fossil-fuel burning, deforestation, and various industrial processes (see pages 183–184). But the fact that in virtually every country a significant segment of the reputable scientific community forecasts biospheric catastrophe if particular activities of humans are not substantially abated in the near future ought to be a sufficient basis for instituting global controls on these activities as soon as possible.[16]

Despite the scientific debates and uncertainties, therefore, an ecologically responsible statecraft would as a minimum press for universal conventions that would obligate countries to:

1. *Prohibit industrial projects and the use of machines, goods, and processes that produce chlorofluorocarbons and other substances that can thin out the planet's ozone layer.*
2. *Prohibit new industrial and agricultural projects (including large-scale deforestation) that would substantially increase the carbon dioxide content of the atmosphere.* (A maximalist policy would also decisively cut back on existing sources of carbon dioxide.)
3. *Provide economically disadvantaged peoples with compensatory techno-logical and financial assistance for alternative ecologically sound projects in cases where the essential prohibitions would retard the economic development programs of the disadvantaged.*

Collaterally, the following international coordination processes need to be instituted and/or expanded:[17]

- *Internationalization of capabilities for gathering and assessing information on threats to essential biospheric balances.* Human society requires more independent, politically neutral, analyses of the sources of the potential life-threatening disturbances. Although it is neither desirable nor possible to "denationalize" all the relevant information, the interests of every nation are served to the extent that there are multiple sources of information on the environmental threats, that the information is maximally disseminated among the scientists of all countries, and that assessments of immediate and potential threats are subject to "certification" by international scientific panels. Less developed countries without adequate monitoring capabilities of their own are in particular need of reliable, and politically neutral, international scientific assessments, especially when such assessments have policy implications with economic consequences (as, for example, the need to restrict the use of certain agricultural pesticides or to arrest new industrialization programs).

- *Expansion of international consultative processes on potential threats to the biosphere—aimed at clarifying conflicting interests and exposing the range of choices available to the international community.* The principal responsibility for assuring meaningful consultation falls on the countries with advanced scientific and technological capabilities. By and large, the well-endowed countries have been deficient in bringing their actions under international purview, and they have admitted only grudgingly and minimally that they should be held accountable to those who might be affected by their actions. This reluctance to establish the percent of accountability is politically understandable in the short run but nonetheless imprudent. Enlightened statesmanship must be based on the realization that over the long run the biospheric management problems will require an expansion of community decision authority and a widening international membership in these communities. In the meantime, there are opportunities to expand consultation without running great political risks among regional or functionally defined nuclei of particular countries, corporations, and other interest groups, as for example those who share in the intensive use of a common river basin, air-shed, or fishing ground.

- *A major campaign of worldwide public education in the nature of the biospheric threats and the kinds of international accountability regimes that may be required to adequately counter them.* This policy arena heretofore has been the province of narrow specialists, and pressures for legislative action and administrative decisions have emanated almost entirely from special industries or special-interest consumer groups. But the general public, if it is to be supportive of the broadened international accountability called for—which inevitably will require some diminution in *national* "sovereignty"—needs to know more about the impact of new and planned technologies on transnational ecologies and needs a better political education in the international management alternatives. Presidents, cabinet ministers, and aspirants to high political office need to bring these matters into the arena of prominent public discourse and debate—to give them a popular "sex appeal," so to speak, equal to the standard high-visibility issues of war and peace, human rights, and tariffs and trade.

The Elimination of Enclaves of Starvation and Disease

Every two seconds these days a child dies *unnecessarily* of starvation or disease—most of the horrible tragedies occurring in the poverty belts of Africa and Asia. These childhood deaths, plus the unnatural deaths each year of millions of adults in the destitute regions, are avoidable in both an individual and global sense: Timely availability of food or medical assistance could well save their lives. And the required food and medical assistance could be provided—if *political* obstacles were removed—out of existing world supplies, without risk to better situated elements of the world's population.

The total value of goods and services produced worldwide each year exceeds $13 trillion; and the per capita income in the affluent industrialized countries is running well over $10,000. The fact that approximately one-fifth of the Earth's 5 billion beings has a below-subsistence income of less than $600 a year (in some countries such as Ethiopia and Bangladesh, the average is less than $150 a year, or 40 cents a day) must be attributable to a failure of political inventiveness and will, for if only one-tenth of what the world produces each year (the amount now spent on military forces) were divided equally among the bottom fifth of the world's poor, every human being could have an income well above the subsistence threshold.

Moreover, the myth that the eradication of premature death by starvation and disease is self-defeating, in that the result will be a dramatic increase in the world's population-to-food ratio, has been exploded by serious demographic and sociological scholarship. Rather, the threat of overpopulation, as the Brandt Commission pointed out in its 1983 report, has its source in poverty itself:

> Indeed...unless broadly based development reaches and changes the lives of ordinary people, rapid population growth will continue. Only as education spreads, as health programmes keep existing children alive, as families have secure incomes which do not depend on increasing their numbers, will incentives for large families disappear and population growth be kept within manageable grounds. Yet it is precisely such development which is threatened in the current crisis.[18]

Clearly, the causes and potential amelioration of intolerable poverty in a world of general abundance lie less in the iron laws of economics than in the steel fences of politics.

The political barriers to the eradication of the enclaves of starvation and disease, as shown in Chapter 7, operate at both ends of the affluence–poverty spectrum—inhibiting potential donors from providing help and preventing the timely distribution by receiving agencies in the poor countries of the help that is contributed.

In the affluent countries, resistance to legislating adequate levels of foreign aid is sustained on the popular level by demagogic appeals to the middle and working classes that resources transferred abroad to attack poverty will either come out of their hides in the form of higher income taxes or will be subtracted from resources otherwise available for domestic economic development. Resistance is sustained at the level of policymaking elites by the traditional "realist" assumptions: (1) that hardly any of the needy countries are geopolitically significant and (2) that, anyway, such marginal economic development as may be induced in the aid-receiving countries, rather than producing political stability, will more often than not stimulate popular receptivity to radical movements, as citizen expectations rise faster than living standards can be improved.

In truth, substantial resources for foreign economic development programs could rather easily be skimmed off the top of the high-consumption economies in the industrial world, in the form of nearly invisible surcharges on international travel and luxury purchases.[19] Furthermore, there are good "realist" (nonaltruistic) economic, if not geostrategic, reasons for the advanced industrial countries to help the poor countries develop economically. Private lending institutions have huge outstanding loans to developing countries, and many multinational corporations have substantial investments in manufacturing subsidiaries in the Third World. Widespread economic collapse and bankruptcy in the Third World will be recycled back into the industrialized world in the form of higher interest rates, tighter credit, and reduced demand. Labor unions and elected politicians who purport to speak for them have been slower than the international corporate sector to learn that the well-being of their constituents is threatened less by the export of jobs to lower wage-rate countries than the import and export of recession to and from the Third World. In the "global city," no less in New York, London, and Rome, a severe depression in the populous lower class can endanger the well-being of the city as a whole.

Beginning in 1985, the affluent minority of the world's population received a new shock of recognition, with reports of the international spread of the killer disease AIDS, that the global mobility provided them by the twentieth century's technological revolution made them more profoundly interdependent than ever with the world's poor and disease-ridden peoples. Reflecting statistics that AIDS was becoming a disaster of pandemic proportions, the head of the World Health Organization, in a November 1986 announcement of an emergency global effort to combat the disease, stressed the fact that the "industrialized and developing countries are in the same boat."[20]

Fortunately, even apart from the AIDS scare, there are indications of the growth of public concern in the affluent countries for the fate of the world's destitute peoples that might be turned into support for more enlightened official policies. The remarkable success of the 1985 effort by popular entertainers and artists (highlighted by the specially composed rock song "We Are the World") to raise money to aid the starving population of the East African Sahel took many prematurely cynical politicians by surprise. The 1985 phenomenon should not be dismissed as a one-time catharsis. Private voluntary organizations such as Oxfam, Save the Children, Medecins sans Frontiers, the International Red Cross, CARE, and various religious institutions have been tapping into the growing popular concern. These private efforts, in addition to raising impressive contributions, have been gaining useful experience in avoiding the bureaucratic red-tape and other obstacles (especially in the recipient countries) that frustrate attempts by donor governments and United Nations agencies to deliver funds and supplies to the people most in need. This experience can be made available to public agencies as they mount serious international poverty-alleviation and disease-fighting programs.

There are also experienced financial and economic development experts ready to translate into specific and workable policies what has been stated here in the form of broad imperatives. The second report of the Brandt Commission (authored by eminant financial statesmen) is rich is such practicable measures, including:

- substantial increases in International Monetary Fund (IMF) quotas and increases in IMF Special Drawing Rights for developing countries
- enlargement and improvement of the IMF Compensatory Financing Facility
- improvement in IMF terms and conditions for poorer borrowers
- augmented borrowing authority for the World Bank, with increased soft loans and aid for the low-income countries
- a major increase in Official (government-to-government) Development Assistance to the poorest countries
- greater national and international support for the work of voluntary agencies[21]

As put by Commission chairman Willy Brandt,

Today, responsible women and men, and the younger generation above all, realize in their daily lives that their own condition is no longer isolated: their jobs, their food, their energy—even the solvency of their local bank—depend upon and influence the development of people, communities, and countries at the other end of the world.[22]

BUILDING THE FUTURE WORLD POLITY

Most of the imperatives of statecraft just discussed assume the continuance of the basic structure of the nation-state system and its norms of national sovereignty and noninterference by countries in each other's domestic affairs. But in the previous chapters it was shown that the inherited structure and norms of the nation-state system are increasingly incongruent with the polyarchic reality of contemporary world politics: The territorial configurations of existing countries often do not match the most intensive patterns of human interaction and ecological interdependence; many nations do not have states of their own; few states adequately represent the nations within them; and national governments, lacking sufficient reach in authority and physical control over what enters and leaves their jurisdictions and even over what happens to their more stationary material and human resources, are losing the capacity to perform the essential functions of governance (maintaining minimal public peace and security, facilitating orderly commerce, husbanding essential ecologies, providing social justice, and preserving the integrity of ethnic and religious communities).

In Chapter 12, I argued that if world society continued to drift on these rising polyarchic currents the prospects were bleak for the maintenance of civic peace and justice around the world, and even for the survival of the human species itself. If this argument is essentially correct, then many of the imperatives of statecraft outlined above are little more than urgent holding actions—"fingers in the dike," as it were—woefully inadequate to stave off the floodtide of worldwide anarchy that will hasten the degradation of the planet's life-support systems, and sooner or later, produce the dreaded nuclear holocaust.

In Chapter 13, however, I postulated an alternative evolution of the world polity, not inconsistent with the rising polyarchic currents, but one that would direct and harness the polyarchic forces in the service of a system of global order and justice congruent with the complex reality of the highly pluralistic yet increasingly interdependent human society. This configuration of the world polity, called Polyarchy II to emphasize its continuity with prevailing trends, will not evolve automatically out of the existing system. Its emergence, rather, requires deliberate acts of constructive statecraft, enformed by a vision of the behavioral norms, political processes, and institutions of governance that are to be the essential features of the new world polity.

The "vision" need not be a blueprint, however. It is best conceived of as a set of desiderata to guide contemporarty statecraft—to provide a normative framework over and above the more immediate self-interest considerations of countries, transnational and subnational movements, corporate and other private groups—that will allow political leaders, their constituents, and independent analysts to evaluate contending policies for consistency with the vision. There is no requirement for altruism on the part of the relevant actors, only that they act consistently with their enlightened self-interests.

The Constituitive Principle of Accountability

In contrast to the nation-state system, in which the constituitive principle is the sovereignty of each country, the constituitive principle of the new world polity would be accountability. This principle is central to the constitutional and legal systems prevailing *within* most democratically organized nation-states and many nonstate communities. At its core is the premise that those whose behavior substantially affects the well-being of others are accountable to the affected. Projected on to the world polity, the accountability principle takes cognizance of and is meant to correct the effective political disenfranchisement of millions, in some cases billions of people, including the citizens of purportedly democratic polities, that is the consequence of the new technologically based capabilities of governments or powerful private actors to jeopardize the lives, material well-being, and ways of life of the people in both neighboring and remote jurisdictions.

At a minimum, the principle would require that potentially victimized populations at least be consulted by those whose actions might cause them major harm. At a maximum, the substantially affected would be provided a veto over actions they did not like. The international procedural and structural embodiments of such accountability obligations are potentially far-reaching, highly controversial, and will be extraordinarily difficult to negotiate in some fields, especially where the affected populations demand not merely a fair opportunity to express their view but also seats and voting power at the principal tables of decision.

As indicated in Chapter 13, some progress along these lines already has been made in some fields among particular sets of interdependent actors (notably international finance, transportation and communication, and the environment). The vision does not contemplate unified or simultaneous progress in implementing the accountability principle in all fields or in all parts of the world, and surely not for the foreseeable future anything approaching a centralized world state. Rather, the realistic goal is a complex, often intersecting web of accountability institutions—some organized around particular sectors of economic activity, some involving only minimal consultative obligations, some involving heavy multifunctional and cross-sector accountability among countries with a tradition of cooperation.

Major debates in the emerging world polity would no doubt center on how to implement the accountability principle—in contrast to the existing world polity where the major debates and confrontations are over who has violated whose sovereignty. Indeed, such a change in concern and definition of self-interest is precisely the purpose of asking that the new statecraft embrace accountability as its prime procedural desideratum.

Opportunities for Cosmopolitan Leadership

Liberated from the overriding preoccupation with national sovereignty, political leaders in the emerging world polity would have more leeway, consistent with, and encouraged by, the accountability principle, to respond to other values and needs of human society—many of which cannot be adequately tended to without a more open and wider conception of community than that which has prevailed for more than three centuries in the modern state system.

Ethnic and religious groups transcending nation-state jurisdictions could more persuasively demand that their own national governments act to advance the human rights of their brothers and sisters in foreign jurisdictions. Economically disadvantaged populations within poor countries could more "legitimately" invoke distributive justice norms within the larger world community to bring pressure on the affluent to tend to the needs of the poor. And those with an appreciation of the risks human technological applications pose to crucial ecological balances could more effectively represent the wider communities that are threatened, and indeed humankind as a whole.[23]

The emergence of a denser network of institutions transcending national jurisdictions with authority to resolve disputes and allocate resources in various fields—including human rights, the global economy, and the natural environment—and the opportunities for transnational constituencies to bring pressures on these institutions would put a new premium on political leadership skills for effectively functioning in these arenas. Leaders with a cosmopolitan orientation, who can speak to and debate knowledgeably about the "world interest," would be sought by constituencies eager to defend their interests in the new world polity, just as in a previous era leadership gravitated to those whose horizons extended beyond their towns and villages and who could make cogent connections between the parochial interests of their immediate constituents and the more inclusive interests of the national polities then emerging.

ENDNOTES

1. The main ideas in this section received a preliminary airing in Seyom Brown, "Toward an Integrated Strategy for the Prevention of Nuclear Holocaust," a paper prepared for the panel on Perspectives on Preventing Nuclear War at the International Studies Association annual convention, March 27, 1986, Anaheim, California. See also Chapter 10 of Seyom Brown, *The Causes and Prevention of War* (New York: St. Martin's Press, 1987).

2. See National Research Council, *The Effects on the Atmosphere of a Major Nuclear Exchange* (Washington, DC: National Academy Press, 1985); and Paul Ehrlich, Carl Sagan, Donald Kennedy, and Walter Orr Roberts, *The Cold and the Dark: The World after Nuclear War* (New York: Norton, 1984).

3. Caspar W. Weinberger, *Annual Report to the Congress Fiscal Year 1987* (Washington, DC: Department of Defense, 5 February 1986), p. 36.

4. Carl Sagan, "Nuclear Winter and Climatic Catastrophe: Some Policy Implications," *Foreign Affairs*, Vol. 3, No. 62 (Winter 1983/84), pp. 1283–1300.

5. For a skeptical view of the thesis that severe climate changes would be produced by nuclear war, see Starley L. Thompson and Stephen H. Schneider, "Nuclear Winter Reappraised," *Foreign Affairs*, Vol. 64, No. 5 (Summer 1986), pp. 981–1005. Sagan's reply is in the correspondence section of *Foreign Affairs*, Vol. 65, No. 1 (Fall 1986), pp. 163–168.

6. For measures to secure survivable command and control systems, see Bruce C. Blair, *Strategic Command and Control: Redefining the Nuclear Threat* (Washington, DC: The Brookings Institution, 1985).

7. McGeorge Bundy, George F. Kennan, Robert S. McNamara, and Gerard Smith, "Nuclear Weapons and the Atlantic Alliance," *Foreign Affairs*, Vol. 60, No. 6 (Summer 1982), pp. 1157–1170.

8. Karl Kaiser, Georg Leber, Alois Mertes, and Franz-Josef Schulze, "Nuclear Weapons and the Preservation of Peace," *Foreign Affairs*, Vol. 60, No. 5 (Summer 1982), pp. 1157–1170.

9. Gene Sharp, *Making Europe Unconquerable: The Potential of Civilian-Based Deterrence and Defence* (Cambridge: Ballinger, 1985).

10. *Ibid.*, pp. 17–29.

11. *Ibid.*, p. 50.

12. *Ibid.*, pp. 108–109.

13. Leonard S. Spector, *Nuclear Proliferation Today* (New York: Vintage, 1984).

14. For arguments on the potential positive effects for world peace of the spread of nuclear weapons see Kenneth Waltz, "What Will the Spread of Nuclear Weapons Do to the World?" in John Kerry King, ed., *International Political Effects of the Spread of Nuclear Weapons* (Washington, DC: GPO, 1979).

15. The exposition in this section of the geopolitical and ideological factors that could stimulate Soviet–American military confrontations draws heavily on ideas developed in Seyom Brown "Confronting the Soviet Union: Why, Where, and How?" a paper delivered at the Eighth Annual National Security Affairs Conference (July 13–15, 1981) of the National Defense University, published by the National Defense University Press in 1981 in *The 1980s: Decade of Confrontation?* See also Seyom Brown, "Power and Prudence in Dealing with the USSR," in Richard Melanson, ed., *Neither Cold War nor Detente? Soviet-American Relations in the 1980s* (Charlottesville: University Press of Virginia, 1982), pp. 215–236.

16. A rich analysis of the range of policy options available to countries and international agencies for countering the global environmental threats is provided by James E. Harf and B. Thomas Trout, *The Politics of Global Resources: Energy, Environment, Population, and Food* (Durham: Duke University Press, 1986).

17. The recommendations for international coordination on global ecological matters are adapted from a study I directed for the Brookings Institution: Seyom Brown, Nina W. Cornell, Larry L. Fabian, and Edith Brown Weiss, *Regimes for the Ocean, Outer Space, and Weather* (Washington, DC: The Brookings Institution, 1977), especially pages 239–249.

18. The Brandt Commission, *Common Crisis North-South: Cooperation for World Recovery* (Cambridge: MIT Press, 1983), p. 79.

19. Independent Commission for International Economic Cooperation, *North-South: A Program for Survival* (Cambridge: MIT Press, 1980), pp. 244–245.

20. Lawrence K. Altman, "Global Program Aims to Combat AIDS 'Disaster,'" *New York Times*, 21 November 1986.

21. The Brandt Commission, *Common Crisis*, pp. 152–154.

22. Willy Brandt, "Introduction," *ibid.*, p. 9.

23. For a philosophically sophisticated disquisition on how a cosmopolitan concept of the world polity can affect the substance of international statecraft (and theories of international relations and world politics), see Charles R. Beitz, *Political Theory and International Relations* (Princeton: Princeton University Press, 1979). See also Ernst B. Haas, "Words Can Hurt You; or Who Said What to Whom about Regimes," in Stephen D. Krasner, *International Regimes* (Ithaca: Cornell University Press, 1983), pp. 23–59.

CHAPTER FIFTEEN

Guidelines for a New US Foreign Policy

The implications for statecraft drawn in Chapter 14 will achieve practical effect only as they are applied to and implemented by powerful actors in the existing system. This is not a book on US foreign policy; but since I am a citizen of the United States, and on occasion a policy consultant to this country's foreign affairs agencies, it is appropriate that I attempt to translate the implications, at least in a preliminary way, into guidance for US foreign policy.[1]

Fortunately, the policy imperatives I have outlined above need not be inconsistent with the deepest values of American society, nor with a world order conducive to the continuation of the American democratic experiment, nor with vital geopolitical objectives such as the containment of Soviet expansion. Indeed, I would argue that both as world order goals and as here-and-now guidance for US foreign policy they are likely to better serve the security and material needs of the American people and to better express the ethos of this country's multicultural experiment in democratic pluralism than have most of the foreign policies pursued by the United States since World War II.

The new US foreign policy to be derived from the analysis in the body of this book can be organized around four themes: depolarization, expansion of international accountability, legitimation of transnationalism, and demilitarization.

DEPOLARIZATION

Most countries, if given a choice, prefer to be nonaligned between the rival ideological blocs organized by the United States and the Soviet Union. They prefer to have a diversity of dependence relationships rather than to be dependent on one superpower for their security and economic well-being. American policymakers should look positively on this change from the early decades of the cold war. A pluralistic world order, after all, is more congenial to US interests and to the traditions of US diplomacy than it is to the interests and diplomacy of the Soviet Union even under Gorbachev.

A US policy that positively exploits the centrifugal forces—in a phrase, that encourages international "depolarization"—would be at cross-purposes with the two-camps approach to international relations still propagated by the Kremlin to sustain its control over East European governments and to curry favor with Marxist movements around the world. But it would require that the anti-Marxist, antisocialist ideological bent manifested by US foreign policy, particularly during the first two decades following World War II, and then again in the 1980s, be dropped.[2]

In its passive form, the depolarization strategy rules out intervention in other countries aimed at deciding political contests between leftists and rightists. In its active form, it seeks opportunities to identify the United States with the widest array of "progressive" forces possible in order to drive a wedge between the Soviet-oriented left and the more broadly based democratic and populist left.

Although most Third World governments strike a posture of nonalignment between the superpowers, and although many are professedly Marxist, almost all of them are more attracted to economic and technological intercourse with the United States than with the Soviet Union. Even Third World countries currently aligned with the Soviet Union, such as Angola, Mozambique, Cuba, Nicaragua, and even Vietnam, are not entirely happy with their role as Soviet clients. They envy the relative freedom of international maneuver enjoyed by countries such as India, Algeria, Nigeria, Tanzania, and Mexico and have expressed interest in improving relations with the United States. It would not take much encouragement, perhaps only practical opportunity for commerce and technology transfers negotiated without fanfare and without explicit anti-Soviet posturing, to induce such client states to emulate Egypt's move to genuine nonalignment in 1973–1975.

The new policy also would attempt to forge links with popular antigovernment movements in countries currently ruled by repressive regimes unresponsive to demands for greater political and economic democracy—even when the antigovernment movements are led by Marxists or quasi-Marxists.

Recent US policy in southern Africa provides exemplary cases validating the need and realism of a US strategy of depolarization. A model for the new policy is the US–British cooperation in 1979 with the Marxist leader, Robert Mugabe, of the Patriotic Front for the Liberation of Zimbabwe, which involved heavy Anglo-American pressure on the white minority Rhodesian government of Ian Smith to peacefully transfer power to the revolutionary black leadership. By so doing, the United States salvaged for itself in southern Africa a position of influence with the ascending political forces. A not inconsiderable side benefit was the parallel diminution of Soviet influence.[3] A model of how *not* to act has been US policy in Angola, both during the anticolonial revolution against the Portuguese and toward the postcolonial Marxist government after 1976: In a knee-jerk reaction against Soviet and Cuban aid to the anticolonial faction led by Agostino Neto, the United States backed the factions that lost out in the contest to supplant the Portuguese regime. Beginning in 1981, the Reagan administration, in concert with the white minority government in the Republic of South Africa, has expanded US assistance to insurgents against the Angolan government—thereby compelling the regime in Luanda to become even more dependent on Moscow, despite the many indications, among them congenial arrangements Luanda has worked out with Gulf Oil to continue operations in the country, that the "People's Republic of Angola" really does not want to become totally absorbed within the Soviet camp.

Even in Eastern Europe, where the Soviet Union has been least tolerant of inclinations toward nonalignment, there are new opportunities to stimulate existing centrifugal tendencies—for example, Hungary's experiments with market incentives and Rumania's relatively independent foreign policy, and Poland's revived nationalism—simply by responding favorably to Gorbachev's encouragement of expanded East–West contacts. Let the Kremlin wrestle with the implications for its sphere of control. The Soviet Union, not the United States, should bear the opprobrium of restricting the restoration of a pan-European political economy across the East–West divide.

EXPANSION OF INTERNATIONAL ACCOUNTABILITY

The twentieth century revolutions in communications, transportation, and industrial processes, as well as the desire of countries and other political entities to diversify their dependence relationships, has multiplied the trade and financial ties that link nation to nation. It also has created a need for innovative statesmanship, which the United States is particularly well-equipped to provide if it abandons much of the unilateralist, we-are-accountable-to-nobody philosophy that has prevailed in Washington in recent years.

The new statesmanship should be made to rest on the principle of international accountability (as elaborated in Chapter 14), which holds that those whose behavior substantially affects the well-being of others should be held accountable to them. This principle acknowledges that the crisis of the contemporary political order stems precisely from the failure of the primary jurisdictions of governance—the nation-states—to coincide with patterns of interdependence. Thus, it appropriately expands the concept of the consent of the governed to the consent of the affected.

A first order of business under a US foreign policy supportive of international accountability would be to reverse the Reagan administration's refusal to sign the Law of the Sea treaty of 1982. The Law of the Sea treaty not only holds the signatory governments and the private firms they charter accountable to one another and to agreed-upon norms for how the ocean commons are used; it also establishes the principle of mutual accountability for activities within offshore "economic zones" and even within territorial seas and straits traditionally under exclusive national jurisdiction. Most countries have agreed to subject themselves to the rules and dispute-resolution processes of the treaty, even those provisions that govern actions within their national jurisdictions—fishing, waste disposal, and the imposition of special navigation procedures—that can degrade ocean resources or significantly interfere with the normal oceanic activities of other countries. The Reagan administration, in contrast, offered adherence only to those treaty provisions with which it wholly agreed, meaning most of the treaty apart from the deep-sea mining regime (which Reagan labeled "international socialism"). But if such selective adherence were to be emulated by other countries, the regime of international accountability would be destroyed, along with provisions for which the United States fought long and hard, such as unimpeded transit through straits and internationally standardized navigation rules for coastal waters.

New accountability arrangements also are needed to help the United States and other countries deal constructively with one of the most significant trends in the global economy: the movement of industrial manufacturing plants from the developed North to the diversifying economies of the South. Protectionist measures designed to prevent this shift ultimately are very costly, for investment capital, like water, naturally flows toward lower areas until the costs of production are equalized. Rather, the industrial countries are better advised to cooperate with one another in managing the transition into postindustrialism—that is, allowing many "hardware" and finished-goods industries to relocate in the Third World while concentrating advanced-country growth in the new "software" and knowledge industries. Adapting to this historic transition without mutually damaging competition between West Europeans, Japanese, and Americans may well require internationally coordinated timetables for conversion to postindustrialism, including, perhaps, international adjustment funds to help finance the retraining of workers, and drawing rights on the funds available to countries bearing temporary hardships in production and employment.[4]

Simultaneously, a parallel dialogue needs to be renewed with the Group of 77 coalition on how a more equitable international economic order may be created, one that will be more responsive to the extreme vulnerabilities of the poorest developing countries to the cruelly indifferent forces of the global economy. Not all of the recommendations of the Brandt commission, such as taxes on international commerce and transportation to raise revenue for the poor countries, need to be accepted. But the United States should take the lead in responding to the Commission's call for new approaches "to overcome the shortcomings of the present system of development assistance and at the same time [to] strengthen...universal collective burden sharing."[5]

Nor is it necessary to endorse, unrevised, the standard package of developing country demands for the shape of the new international economic order. These demands have included indexing commodity prices to the price of industrial goods, preferential access to the markets of industrialized countries, loan-repayment extensions and interest forgiveness, special claims on the reserve assets of the International Monetary Fund, and increased developing-country representation in international economic institutions. But these demands, if not acceptable outright, can be viewed as points of departure for initiation of more constructive negotiations between the advantaged and disadvantaged countries.

LEGITIMATION OF TRANSNATIONALISM

Policies of depolarization and international accountability, while they would help the United States and other countries adapt to the emerging patterns of world politics, can do so only partially. Because these adaptations apply mainly to official state-to-state relationships, they alone cannot establish congruence between political and legal structures and the human relationships such structures are designed to reflect and regulate. They are a necessary but inadequate response to the increasing assertiveness of groups and organizations across state bounds, a phenomenon whose implications for traditional international relations are too profound to be ignored.

The most prominent and most commented-on of the nonstate organizations—the multinational corporation—is still regarded as somewhat of a freak by traditional statists on the right and the left. The only way politicians have found to respond to the weaker elements of the economy who fear displacement by the transnational giants has been to impose protectionist shackles on the movement of capital, plant, and marketing operations across state lines. But the protectionist devices cannot be expected to control this remarkably flexible human invention which, like the electronic revolution and the rapid circulation of information and assets around the globe, is here to stay.

A more constructive approach to the multinational corporation would attempt not to confine the scope of its operations to existing jurisdictions of national polities, but to develop transnational associations to regulate and check those operations. Transnational labor and public interest groups should be formed and encouraged to pressure the corporations, if necessary through transnationally organized strikes and boycotts, to equalize their wage rates and employee benefits, to pursue environmentally responsible policies in all countries, and to compensate regions that suffer economic dislocations because of a corporation's activities. Eventually, transnational or supranational labor laws and other legal controls will need to be formed to bring order, predictabili-ty, and fairness to this arena. But countervailing transnational power will need to be organized first, and this almost certainly will require tolerance, if not encouragement, on the part of the United States and other powerful industrial countries.

New transnational political institutions are also needed to handle the refusal of ethnic and religious groups in one country to countenance the persecution of their brothers and sisters in others. President Jimmy Carter's statement that "No member of the United Nations can claim that mistreatment of its citizens is solely its own business" and his administration's serious, but not very successful, effort to make human rights a centerpiece of US foreign policy were but one attempt to respond to this phenomenon.[6]

But the determination and growing capacity of the aggrieved groups themselves to organize transnational organizations and movements—some-times terroristic ones—to transform themselves from mere objects of diploma-cy into major actors on the world stage (as have the Shiite Muslims of the Middle East), to topple governments, and to undermine the actions of established international organizations may require more controversial policies. The United States, for example, may need to reconsider its standing refusal to allow the Palestine Liberation Organization or its successor to participate as a negotiating party in its own right in international efforts to settle the Arab–Israeli conflict over the governance of the West Bank and the Gaza Strip. To bargain with the PLO or other such transnational groups does not constitute an approval of their tactics or demands. It does recognize their power to negate in practice what states may agree to in law. Finding ways to induce such movements to participate constructively in international forums and negoti-ating arenas, and to forestall their desperate resort to violence to prosecute their demands, is among the most important challenges to statesmanship and the maintenance of world civic order.

Any legal-political order if it is to endure must reflect the distribution of power. In the contemporary world, this means taking into account, even legitimating, powerful nonstate actors. The only alternative is to try to smash them, a strategy inconsistent with the fourth and final element of a new US foreign policy adaptive to emerging world realities.

DEMILITARIZATION

The survival of the human species itself depends on the ability of the superpowers to avoid becoming embroiled in a major war against each other, and this, as was shown in Chapters 12 and 14, makes it imperative to work toward a general reduction of the role of force in world politics.

Most efforts to reduce the role of force in world politics since World War II have concentrated on controlling the production and deployments of armaments, particularly nuclear weapons and other means of mass destruction. Most official arms control proposals have been formulated by specialists in national security policy and military hardware and have reflected these narrow frames of reference. Only for a brief period, during the SALT negotiations of the early 1970s, were US arms control efforts part of a larger effort to demilitarize relations between the superpowers. With detente since discredited, arms controllers have tried to steer arms negotiations that promise success away from those seemingly intractable issues on which the interests of the United States and the Soviet Union diverge and which may jeopardize progress in this crucial field.

Paradoxically, the peace movement itself has become "militarized." It has concentrated its efforts against particular weapons programs, such as the Strategic Defense Initiative, the MX, cruise missiles, and Pershing IIs; has engaged in often highly technical and esoteric debates on the precise nature of the military balance; and sometimes has forgotten that armaments are symptoms, not only exacerbators, of political disputes and power contests between nations. To be sure, military imbalances may well affect the frequency and intensity of international conflicts, and if rectified may help prevent escalation to war; but efforts to achieve and maintain a military balance rarely help resolve the disputes that cause confrontations, and therefore provide no real assurance that war will not occur.

The force stabilization and mutual arms reduction measures that have become the stock in trade of the arms control community are enormously useful to the extent that they prohibit first-strike and other destabilizing weapons and strategies that may encourage a preemptive launch. But these stabilizing measures, and the attention and talent devoted to them, do not lead in any direct way to a reduced reliance on military power or to substantially reduced military arsenals. Indeed, proposals to limit certain destabilizing weapons, such as the MX, often are accompanied by proposals to augment the arsenal with safer and more efficient weapons, the single-warhead Midgetman, for example. And serious US proposals to reduce reliance on nuclear weapons, whether through substantial nuclear disarmament or prohibitions on the first use of nuclears, usually carry the corollary of an expansion of NATO's conventional forces.

The sad truth is that to alter the principal military balances—up *or* down, within the limits of what is politically plausible at this time—is likely to have no significant effect by itself on the likelihood of war or peace. If world politics is to be demilitarized substantially, there must also be bold initiatives taken outside the military arena.[7] The prospects for such initiatives need not be as bleak as generally assumed if the emerging world realities described in these pages are seized upon and put to the service of this task.

Nonmilitary forms of power, particularly economic and technological inter-dependencies and diverse international transnational associations, must be enhanced and expanded if military force is to become a less important means of influence than it has been. Progress along these lines need not await a reduction in the world's deployed military forces. In fact, the expansion of nonmilitary forms of power could well facilitate arms reductions as the political utility of military power is eclipsed by other tools of statecraft.

Conditions are now present for such a demilitarized statecraft to be advanced by the United States. The principal ingredients of such an American peace strategy can be fashioned out of the other planks of the new US foreign policy described above.

First, the United States in undertaking a strategy of depolarization responsive to the polyarchic disintegration of the bipolar world could help reduce the utility of militarized diplomacy. The disintegration of bipolarity ought to make it more efficacious for the United States to rely on diplomatic carrots rather than sticks. Because our adversaries on one issue may well be our partners on others, prudence dictates that we refrain, even when dealing with adversaries, from coercive tactics that may engender hostility of long duration. Moreover, the emergence of the polyarchic world system, with its multiple and cross-cutting relationships, allows a country such as the United States, which has the assets needed to establish cooperative relationships around the globe, plenty of cards to play without having to resort to military coercion should the bargaining get tough.

Second, the enhancement of processes and institutions to strengthen interna-tional accountability should increase the number of peaceful diplomatic options available to the disadvantaged and dissatisfied who want to press their demands. With greater hope of equitable redress through the system, political leaders, especially in the Third World, should have less reason to provoke lethal international confrontations to assuage their humiliated national egos and to compel more powerful countries to heed their demands. More accountable international institutions also would allow the Soviet Union fewer opportunities to construct a worldwide "antiimperialist" coalition of the alienated, one symptom of which has been the increase in Soviet arms transfer to Third World clients in recent years.

Third, the objective of demilitarization would be aided by according greater international status to nonstate movements and organizations. If they have been provided with access to mechanisms for peaceful change, repressed elements may become less ready to resort to terrorism and violent revolution. At present, civil conflicts provoked by aggrieved parties often invite the foreign-assisted buildup of military forces, which in turn appear threatening to neighboring countries, who then feel compelled to strengthen their own military forces. If either is drawn into this process, as is not unusual, the rival superpower is likely to attribute motives of aggrandizement to the intervening superpower and therefore feel the need to counterintervene. The legitimation of nonstate actors is hardly a panacea for pervasive civil violence in a turbulent world, but the provision of this additional safety valve, if combined with strategies of depolarization and international accountability, could well help stabilize some of the dangerously volatile relationships in the emerging polyarchy. Otherwise, as in Europe before World War I, a local conflict may spark a general conflagration.

Finally, while pursuing such adaptive strategies at the level of basic world politics, the United States should be better situated than it has been in recent decades to forbear from the threat or application of force even when our principal adversaries do not. This strategy of forbearance should not be confused with spineless fear or simple squeamishness in the face of violent conflict. It is designed to reflect that the actual or threatened use of military force, whether by the Soviet Union or by the United States, particularly against weaker third parties, is a profound admission of impotence likely to alienate more people than it wins over, both within the zone of immediate confrontation and worldwide. Under this policy, the United States would not give up its ability to apply force, if it chooses, in the event the Kremlin is not deterred by the costs it will bear from an unopposed use force. But US decision makers and the US public would be prepared as well for situations in which the United States might choose quite consciously to stand aloof as the Soviet Union creates its own quagmires. Moreover, it would dispense with the mindless tendency to regard each Soviet "success" as a setback for the United States.

The worst of times, as Dickens observed, can also be the best. Just so, skilled statesmen and stateswomen, aware that occasionally things may get worse before they can get better, will seek to exploit crises in the old order to shape a new and more durable order. It is the argument of this book that human society in general and the United States in particular are now passing through one of those periods of peril and opportunity. The recent revival of an ideologically strident and militarized US foreign policy, from this perspective, is seen to be the quixotic flailing about of an outdated approach to world affairs.

The collapse of the old order need portend neither anarchy nor Armageddon, provided the forces generating the collapse are adequately understood; for then it will be realized that many of them can be channeled to the task of building a more civilized and just world polity.

ENDNOTES

1. This chapter incorporates some of the exposition in Seyom Brown, "New Forces Revisited: Lessons of a Turbulent Decade," *World Policy Journal*, Winter 1984, pp. 397–418.

2. For the fluctuating emphasis given to anti-Marxism and antisocialism by various US policymakers since World War II, see Seyom Brown, *The Faces of Power: Constancy and Change in United States Foreign Policy from Truman to Reagan* (New York: Columbia University Press, 1983).

3. *Ibid.*, pp. 479–481.

4. See Robert B. Reich, "Beyond Free Trade," *Foreign Affairs*, Vol. 61, No. 4 (Spring 1983), pp. 773–804.

5. Independent Commission on International Development Issues (Cambridge: MIT Press, 1980). See also the Brandt Commission 1983, *Common Crisis North-South: Cooperation for World Recovery* (Cambridge: MIT Press, 1983).

6. Jimmy Carter, Address before the United Nations General Assembly, March 17, 1977.

7. For an extended treatment of the interplay of arms races and nonmilitary factors on incidence and role of war in international relations, see Seyom Brown, *The Causes and Prevention of War* (New York: St. Martin's Press, 1987).

Index